MODERN MOBILITY ALOFT

In the series *Urban Life, Landscape, and Policy*, edited by David Stradling, Larry Bennett, and Davarian Baldwin. Founding editor, Zane L. Miller.

ALSO IN THIS SERIES:

Mark Shiel, ed., *Architectures of Revolt: The Cinematic City circa 1968*

Maureen Donaghy, *Democratizing Urban Development: Community Organizations for Housing across the United States and Brazil*

Maureen A. Flanagan, *Constructing the Patriarchal City: Gender and the Built Environments of London, Dublin, Toronto, and Chicago, 1870s into the 1940s*

Harold L. Platt, *Sinking Chicago: Climate Change and the Remaking of a Flood-Prone Environment*

Pamela Wilcox, Francis T. Cullen, and Ben Feldmeyer, *Communities and Crime: An Enduring American Challenge*

J. Mark Souther, *Believing in Cleveland: Managing Decline in "The Best Location in the Nation"*

Nathanael Lauster, *The Death and Life of the Single-Family House: Lessons from Vancouver on Building a Livable City*

Aaron Cowan, *A Nice Place to Visit: Tourism and Urban Revitalization in the Postwar Rustbelt*

Carolyn Gallaher, *The Politics of Staying Put: Condo Conversion and Tenant Right-to-Buy in Washington, DC*

Evrick Brown and Timothy Shortell, eds., *Walking in Cities: Quotidian Mobility as Urban Theory, Method, and Practice*

Michael T. Maly and Heather Dalmage, *Vanishing Eden: White Construction of Memory, Meaning, and Identity in a Racially Changing City*

Harold L. Platt, *Building the Urban Environment: Visions of the Organic City in the United States, Europe, and Latin America*

Kristin M. Szylvian, *The Mutual Housing Experiment: New Deal Communities for the Urban Middle Class*

Kathryn Wilson, *Ethnic Renewal in Philadelphia's Chinatown: Space, Place, and Struggle*

Robert Gioielli, *Environmental Activism and the Urban Crisis: Baltimore, St. Louis, Chicago*

Robert B. Fairbanks, *The War on Slums in the Southwest: Public Housing and Slum Clearance in Texas, Arizona, and New Mexico, 1936–1965*

Carlton Wade Basmajian, *Atlanta Unbound: Enabling Sprawl through Policy and Planning*

Scott Larson, *"Building Like Moses with Jacobs in Mind": Contemporary Planning in New York City*

Gary Rivlin, *Fire on the Prairie: Harold Washington, Chicago Politics, and the Roots of the Obama Presidency*

William Issel, *Church and State in the City: Catholics and Politics in Twentieth-Century San Francisco*

Jerome Hodos, *Second Cities: Globalization and Local Politics in Manchester and Philadelphia*

Julia L. Foulkes, *To the City: Urban Photographs of the New Deal*

William Issel, *For Both Cross and Flag: Catholic Action, Anti-Catholicism, and National Security Politics in World War II San Francisco*

Lisa Hoffman, *Patriotic Professionalism in Urban China: Fostering Talent*

John D. Fairfield, *The Public and Its Possibilities: Triumphs and Tragedies in the American City*

Andrew Hurley, *Beyond Preservation: Using Public History to Revitalize Inner Cities*

MODERN MOBILITY ALOFT

Elevated Highways, Architecture, and Urban Change in Pre-Interstate America

AMY D. FINSTEIN

TEMPLE UNIVERSITY PRESS *Philadelphia | Rome | Tokyo*

TEMPLE UNIVERSITY PRESS
Philadelphia, Pennsylvania 19122
tupress.temple.edu

Published 2020

Library of Congress Cataloging-in-Publication Data

Names: Finstein, Amy D., 1976– author.
Title: Modern mobility aloft : elevated highways, architecture, and urban change in pre-interstate America / Amy D. Finstein.
Other titles: Urban life, landscape, and policy.
Description: Philadelphia : Temple University Press, 2020. | Series: Urban life, landscape, and policy | Includes bibliographical references and index. |
Identifiers: LCCN 2019052141 (print) | LCCN 2019052142 (ebook) | ISBN 9781439919194 (pdf) | ISBN 9781439919170 (cloth) | ISBN 9781439919187 (paperback)
Subjects: LCSH: Elevated highways—United States—History. | Elevated highways—United States—Design and construction. | City planning—United States.
Classification: LCC HE355.3.E94 (ebook) | LCC HE355.3.E94 F56 2020 (print) | DDC 711/ .73—dc23
LC record available at https://lccn.loc.gov/2019052141

♾ The paper used in this publication meets the requirements of the American National Standard for Information Sciences—Permanence of Paper for Printed Library Materials, ANSI Z39.48-1992

Printed in the United States of America

9 8 7 6 5 4 3 2 1

To my parents

Lois and Arthur Finstein

who started me on my journey

and

my husband

Chuck Schneider

who is my copilot

CONTENTS

ACKNOWLEDGMENTS

THE SEED FOR THIS BOOK was planted in the late 1990s when I worked in downtown Boston during the construction and disruption of the "Big Dig." As I watched workers wrestle to liberate the city from an elevated highway not even a half-century old, I wondered about the origins of the audacious idea to construct an aboveground road through the city. Once in graduate school, I was fortunate to have a team of mentors and advisors who supported my scholarly exploration of the history of this landscape and others like it. This book is the culmination of those efforts. Thanks first and foremost to Richard Guy Wilson for his guidance, scholarly acumen, and unwavering enthusiasm. His scholarship and mentorship have indelibly shaped the way I see and evaluate the world, and I am grateful for his wisdom, support, and wit. Daphne Spain built my scholarly background in urban history, helped steer my dissertation, and has remained a steadfast advisor and friend ever since. Immense gratitude also to Louis Nelson, Olivier Zunz, Dell Upton, and John Maciuika, whose teaching, scholarship, and feedback deeply impacted this project.

This book benefited from discussions with and advice from many other scholars and experts in their fields. Robert Fogelson and Clay McShane provided not only key precedents in their scholarship but also valuable mentoring and introductions. I also am thankful for the counsel and expertise of John Reps, Raymond Mohl, Mark Rose, Eric Avila, Owen Gutfreund, David Blanke, Mary Dierickx, and Skip Smallridge, who shared feedback and ideas at conferences and individually. I am lucky to count as mentors and friends an amazing group of scholars who offered guidance and encouragement throughout, including Daniel Abramson, Lisa Krissoff Boehm, Martha McNamara, Alice Friedman, Kristina Wilson, David Karmon, Amanda Luyster, Stephen Whitfield, Alan Avery-Peck, and Christine

Cipriani. Thanks also to Hope Dinsmore for her expert Chicago photography. I also am indebted to the late Zane Miller for his early excitement and feedback about the project and for the initial introduction to Temple University Press.

Due to the relatively recent date of Boston's Central Artery, I benefited from the opportunity to consult individuals and firms directly involved with its design, construction, and demolition. I am grateful to Cranston Rogers, Bruce Campbell, John Cusack, Lenny Barbieri, and Fred Salvucci for talking with me about their involvement in the different phases of the project, and thanks to Fred Yalouris at Mass Highway for facilitating front-row access to Big Dig demolition and construction sites. Thanks to the Knight/Turek family, Kevin Buckley at Knight, Bagge & Anderson, and Emile J. Hamwey at Fay, Spofford & Thorndike (now Stantec) for sharing their files and archives with me.

The hunt for project documentation engaged a wide array of collections, with help from amazing librarians and archivists. Thanks to the Municipal Reference Department at the Chicago Public Library, the Ryerson and Burnham Libraries at the Art Institute of Chicago, Katie Levi and the Research Center at the Chicago History Museum, and Joan Pomaranc at A.I.A. Chicago. New York assistance came from Kenneth Cobb, Leonora Gidlund, and Michael Lorenzini at the New York City Municipal Archives; Christine Bruzzese at New York's City Hall Library; Julie Tozer and Janet Parks at Columbia University's Avery Art and Architecture Library; Vincenzo Rutigliano at the New York Public Library; Michael Caratzas at the City of New York Landmarks Preservation Commission; and Lauren Robinson at the Museum of the City of New York. Boston-based thanks to Lisa Tuite at the former Boston Globe Library, Kristen Swett at the City of Boston Archives, Mary Daniels at the Frances Loeb Library at the Harvard Graduate School of Design, and Jennifer Fauxsmith and Caitlin Jones at the Massachusetts State Archives. Thanks also to the librarians and interlibrary loan staff at the University of Virginia, Massachusetts College of Art and Design, and College of the Holy Cross, who gathered countless other books and articles.

Special thanks to the team at Temple University Press who enthusiastically and expertly guided the book through the publishing process. Thank you to my editor, Aaron Javsicas; series editor David Stradling; and the entire design and production team at TUP. Gratitude also to two anonymous reviewers who provided thoughtful and pointed feedback on the manuscript.

For financial support over this project's evolution, I thank the Department of Architectural History at the University of Virginia, the Center for Work and Service at Wellesley College, and the Committee on Faculty Scholarship at College of the Holy Cross.

My friends have consulted, listened, and cheered as this project grew. Love and thanks to Bijal Parikh, Astrid Liverman, and Susan Wolpe for being my steadfast core. For far-ranging acts of friendship, including lodging, editing, feedback, and general love and support, I thank Av and Janet Posner, Nancy and Larry Greengrass, Pauline and Ron Milnarik, Elizabeth Milnarik, and Larry Wolpe.

Parts of a project like this are supported most heavily by one's family, and I am lucky to have a family willing to contribute edits, child care, and enthusiasm—sometimes simultaneously. For their love and support I thank my brothers, Joshua and David, and their entourages; and my in-laws, Albert Schneider and the late Edna-mae Schneider. My parents, Lois and Arthur Finstein, inadvertently sparked my love of architecture and have served as my cheerleaders, coconspirators, and editors for all of the adventures that have followed. I thank them for their love and zest for learning that infuses everything they do. My children, Zachary and Sela, have provided equal parts enthusiasm, motivation, and comic relief, and I love and thank them for all three. My husband, Chuck Schneider, deserves the most applause for his ongoing roles of sounding board, editor, and partner in all things. His endless love, support, and good humor sustain me every day.

MODERN MOBILITY ALOFT

INTRODUCTION

> The whole trouble comes from the old idea that the street should be laid out on the natural ground level. There is nothing to justify this way of thinking; in fact, if we begin with the opposite theory that sidewalks and roadway [*sic*] should be built at a height sufficient to allow space beneath them for all public service installations, the difficulties will entirely disappear. (1911)
>
> —EUGENE HÉNARD, "The Cities of the Future"

> In order to provide for changes of use, the elastic street has been suggested. Thus far the elasticity has been horizontal. There is no reason, however, to preclude vertical elasticity for a further segregation of street use in existing congested districts. Steps in this direction have already been taken in the construction of rapid transit lines upon elevated structures and in subways, thus removing one of the principal elements of street traffic. In a few instances, double level vehicle streets have been constructed. (1920)
>
> —ERNEST P. GOODRICH, "The Urban Auto Problem"

IN THE LATE 1990S AND EARLY 2000S, pedestrians in Boston's financial and waterfront districts found their pathways interrupted or changed on an almost daily basis. Throngs of residents and workers navigated temporary sidewalks flanked by plywood enclosures and crossed streets interrupted by metal plates protecting open wounds in the ground. Peeks through chain-link fencing and around construction barriers yielded views of a still-functioning elevated highway straddling more than a mile of construction and excavation sites. This scenario magnified the typical noise of an urban landscape, with the sounds of local and highway traffic competing for dominance with excavators, trucks, and jackhammers. As time went on, this scene changed, with wounds closed, paths rerouted, traffic from the elevated highway redirected into new tunneled highways, and the highway's blighting metal structure removed. The city gradually transformed, all because of the need to remedy the impact of an elevated highway built barely fifty years earlier.

These events unfolded thanks to Boston's famous "Big Dig," the massive public works project that replaced the city's overcrowded elevated highway with a new subterranean version topped by public parks, all while keeping the old highway functioning during the construction process. The genesis of this book resulted from observing and questioning Boston's evolving landscape. Surely no one set out to create a problem for future generations by lacing an elevated highway through the city. What were the original intentions for this elevated highway, and how did its ultimate impacts differ from those envisioned by its creators? As I researched the answers to these questions, I found that Boston was actually one of several American cities that used the construction of elevated highways as bold assertions of economic, architectural, and transportation modernity in an era when it was not common to do so. Designed jointly by engineers, urban planners, architects, and municipal leaders, these skyward roads provided a solution to the particular challenges of adapting existing cities to fit changing patterns of urban growth and transportation. Their constructed nature necessarily defined the terms of their impact and reception. Soaring aboveground over sections of busy cities, elevated highways physically affected more people than just those who drove on them. They stood as tangible proclamations of the importance of automobility in the American city. Because of this, their design features and architectural impacts narrated a complex interweaving of early twentieth-century social, architectural, transportation, and urban design challenges.

The highways in this study occupy a specific time frame between the heyday of the railroad in the mid- to late nineteenth century and the advent of mass automobility in the mid-twentieth century. They serve as physical manifestations of the evolution from one transportation model to another. Their geographic and temporal locations testify to this connection, as they often evolved on the literal paths of defunct elevated railroad lines or addressed deficiencies in existing rail, street, or water transport networks. At the same time, the highways' relationships to larger urban improvement efforts and trends in architectural style recount a parallel evolution in architecture and urban design. Designers projected elevated highways as the most cutting-edge solutions to urban traffic congestion, but their architectural iterations of these projects varied widely. This evinces the malleability of the notion of modern architecture and modern urbanism in the early twentieth century and positions elevated highways as visual evidence of this evolving dialogue.

Early twentieth-century American cities provided the backdrops for these developments. Their dense cores, largely creations of the nineteenth century, offered modest masonry and wood buildings at a scale geared toward pedestrians, horses and carriages, and early mass transit options like the omnibus, the trolley, and the railroad. As the automobile gained in popularity, its technologically empowered materials, shapes, and speeds contrasted sharply with this physical fabric. Moreover, the automobile challenged the communal attitude of previous transit options and tested the capacity of urban thoroughfares. Automobiles compounded congestion on urban streets, where a cacophony of different types of users and vehicles already jockeyed for space. The automobile's spatial requirements—both on and off the streets—proved problematic. Cars required significant infrastructural support in the form of filling stations, repair shops, and parking spaces. The dense nature of existing cities limited the possibilities for easily constructing such amenities. As such, the popularization of the automobile immediately highlighted a disparity between emerging technological possibilities and existing physical landscapes.

Faced with this discrepancy, metropolitan leaders, architects, and urban planners began to imagine how they might recast cities to accommodate and match the modernity of the new technological age. Responses to this question varied widely. City Beautiful advocates offered visions of highly coordinated urban utility and beauty that relied on the machine age to create geometrically aligned streets, public plazas, and classically referenced architecture. Engineers and urban planners used quantitative evidence about current traffic, housing, transit, and business conditions to provide policy suggestions and long-term plans for redirecting urban growth. Avant-garde architects and design publications forecast entirely new urban landscapes that exploited skyscraper forms and embraced automobile-based transportation. But despite their divergent approaches, the resulting dialogue collectively reflected a new scale of urban planning and a broadening definition of modern American architecture. And most importantly for this study, all stakeholders included elevated highways and vertical traffic separations as central features of their futuristic visions.

This book positions three elevated highways in distinctly different urban settings—Chicago, New York, and Boston—with divergent stylistic approaches as evidence of a clear typology of urban elevated highways that united previous conceptions of urban design and transportation with contemporary definitions of modern architecture and automobility. The term "elevated highway," as used here, reflects the constructed nature of the subject roads and their designers' awareness of, and intentions for, impacting neighboring urban fabric. In Chicago, the subject road's elevated nature was not immediately evident, as the project actually raised the surrounding area's ground plane to match the top level of the new multitiered roadway. In New York and Boston, the subject roads showcased more obvious elevated superstructures built atop existing ground planes. While these are notable distinctions, the use of the term "elevated highway" seeks both to conjure immediate imagery for the reader and to assert designers' shared visions for physically and architecturally constructing the urban landscape to make way for modern transportation. In Chicago, Wacker Drive (proposed 1909; built 1924–1926) redefined the Chicago River waterfront with a Beaux Arts multilevel roadway that simultaneously eliminated the city's clogged and unsightly produce market, streamlined intermodal transportation, eased Loop congestion, and stimulated new development along the river (figs. I.1–I.2). The Art Deco forms of New York City's West Side Elevated Highway (officially the Miller Highway; proposed 1924; built 1929–1937) brought high-speed automotive access to the Hudson River's working waterfront after decades of stalled debates about improving freight and passenger transportation along this corridor (figs. I.3–I.4). Finally, Boston's Central Artery (officially the John F. Fitzgerald Expressway; proposed 1930; built 1951–1959) provided a functional and visual retort to Boston's waning status as a modern economic center by lacing the raw, engineered trusses of a combined

Figure I.1 Wacker Drive, soon after completion, 1926. (Chicago Plan Commission, *Souvenir of Wacker Drive* [Chicago: Plan Commission, 1926], 15. Courtesy Herlihy Mid-Continent Construction Co.)

Figure I.2 Riverside promenade, Wacker Drive, 1926. (Chicago Plan Commission, *Souvenir of Wacker Drive* [Chicago: Plan Commission, 1926], back cover. Courtesy Herlihy Mid-Continent Construction Co.)

regional highway and local bypass road through its urban core (figs. I.5–I.6). In all three instances, the physicality of the highways synthesized larger dialogues about economic vitality, civic beautification, transportation efficiency, and architectural modernity.

Chicago's iteration of this conundrum derived from its industrial roots, burgeoning downtown, and strong fear of civic inferiority. The city's key geographic location on the banks of Lake Michigan and along the Chicago River had long established its importance as an industrial and trading center, and the expansion of the railroad in the nineteenth century had confirmed this role. The city's downtown core, ringed by the elevated railroad, was slightly south of the river and lacked a clear relationship to this, the city's defining geographic feature. Moreover, the areas directly bounding the river reflected the shabbier side of old Chicago commerce, most notably the chaotic and congested South Water Street produce market. Fearing the growth limitations of these conditions and wary of keeping pace with older East Coast cities, Daniel H. Burnham and Edward H. Bennett envisioned systematically recasting Chicago's organizational, functional, and architectural systems to produce a coordinated image of civic grandeur. Their ideal plan of 1909, the so-called *Plan of Chicago*, positioned a triple-decked, Beaux Arts roadway skirting the southeastern shore of the Chicago River as a critical piece of the city's organizational and aesthetic renovation. The elevated nature of this new road was to be invisible from the south, as the elevation of surrounding streets would rise to meet the road's upper deck. Views from the river's northern shore, however, would reveal the functional complexity of the new thoroughfare. Its multiple constructed levels were designed to simultaneously ease access to and along the riverfront, separate local from long-distance vehicles, and replace the visual and experiential chaos of the existing riverfront with an architecturally unified civic space. Though it would take almost twenty years for this design to be realized as Wacker Drive, its approach represented all that was modern about contemporary urban design, traffic planning, and architecture.

In contrast to Wacker Drive's origins within Chicago's comprehensive city plan, New York's West Side Elevated Highway evolved as a specific revision to a well-established landscape. Manhattan's Hudson River waterfront had long been an important railroad corridor and shipping venue with a dense infrastructure of piers and railroad yards. However, the monopoly of the New York Central and Hudson Railroad complicated operations along the waterfront, necessitating convoluted transfers between water, rail, and street vehicles. The on-grade path of the railroad not only provided visual and auditory disruptions to city streets but also posed real dangers to the vehicles and pedestrians sharing them. Moreover, waterfront shipping interests found it ever more difficult to get their goods to and through the city as increasing automobile usage compounded Manhattan street congestion. All of these conditions compelled mounting discussion of west side transportation improvements between the 1890s and the early 1920s. While the New York Central and Hudson Railroad and the City of New York repeatedly failed to reach

Figure I.3 West Side Elevated Highway, New York City, looking north. (Borough President of Manhattan, and Triborough Bridge and Tunnel Authority, *Miller Highway West Side Elevated Improvement.* [New York: n.p., February 4, 1957], 5. Courtesy NYC Municipal Archives.)

Figure I.4 West Side Elevated Highway, looking north at Gansvoort Street, 1974. (Library of Congress, Prints and Photographs Division, Historic American Engineering Record, Reproduction number HAER NY, 31-NEYO,88-1. https://www.loc.gov [accessed December 5, 2019]).

agreement on a solution, their debates birthed the idea for an elevated highway along the west side. Manhattan borough president Julius Miller adopted this idea and successfully lobbied for its realization in the early 1920s. The result was an Art Deco-ornamented elevated expressway running down the middle of existing waterfront streets between Canal Street and Seventy-Second Street. It simultaneously bypassed local north-south congestion, provided regional north-south access, and proclaimed a new streamlined visual identity for the waterfront.

Boston shared the congestion and economic concerns faced by Chicago and New York yet struggled with an entirely different landscape as its design canvas. Limited by its amoeba-shaped peninsula and narrow connection to the mainland, Boston's city plan had developed organically in response to the natural features of its landmass. This made for dense development and irregular street patterns, neither of which proved particularly hospitable to new modes of transportation. Railroads struggled with this issue in the nineteenth century, as the two main stations—at the northern and southern poles of the city—lacked street or rail connections between them. Improvement plans sponsored by the railroads and the city each envisioned new rail or street connections between the two, but nothing came of these ideas. As automobiles further complicated urban movement, the notion of more direct north-south access reemerged as the centerpiece of a comprehensive thoroughfare plan for the city. Statistician-turned-traffic-planner Robert H. Whitten envisioned an elevated express road threaded through a new corridor in the city's urban fabric. Like the West Side Elevated Highway, it would function both as a means to bypass local street congestion and a high-speed artery for through traffic. This idea

Figure I.5 Central Artery weaving through downtown Boston, looking west, 1962. (TC4.03 1186x Box 1 Boston Central Artery September 18, 1962. Massachusetts State Archives.)

Figure I.6 Completed section of Central Artery, near Haverhill Street, November 2, 1954. (TC4.07 1277x Box 5 Photo no. 179 November 2, 1954. Massachusetts State Archives.)

languished on paper for nearly twenty years as the Depression and World War II redirected attention and funds. In the postwar era, leaders returned to this scheme as critical to the city's resurgence in the wake of waning economic fortunes. When finally realized as the Central Artery in the 1950s, and despite a modified path, the road closely resembled the functional and aesthetic model cast by Whitten decades earlier. It followed an inland route bordering the central business district and offered high-speed automotive access within and through downtown Boston. Its steel superstructure, sporting horizontal banding and prominent rivets, rendered a dramatically modern, new presence in the city's landscape.

Together, the Central Artery, West Side Elevated Highway, and Wacker Drive illustrate the far-reaching implications of the automobile on transportation, urban form, and architecture during the first half of the twentieth century. Their evolutions detail the marked contrasts between existing urban environments and the mechanized forms, hastening speeds, and related freedoms of the new automobile age. Boston, New York, and Chicago faced similar problems in the early twentieth century, despite different geographic landscapes and local histories. Their responses to these conditions embraced similar visions of automotive, architectural, and urban modernity even as the nuances of each project varied. It is the physicality of the completed highways that sets them apart from on-grade highways, civic beautification efforts, or individual buildings. These roads impacted cities in multiple realms, affecting those driving on them as well as those moving around and near them at ground level. Their underpinnings, sometimes plain steel trusses and other times articulated with stylized embellishments, edified the arrival of the automobile in the modern urban landscape.

The focus on these three cities is informed by three circumstances. First, well-established cities like Chicago, New York, and Boston faced a different set of challenges in incorporating automobiles into their landscapes than did younger cities, where less density and more available land afforded greater malleability of the urban landscape. Design ideas like vertical traffic separations and elevated highways had particular appeal to cities where density and expansion opportunities already seemed limited. Because of this, the construction of elevated highways had particularly dramatic ramifications.

Second, the continuity of circumstances in these three locations provides a framework for evaluating and understanding the proliferation of elevated highways in other American cities in the pre-Interstate era (before 1956). As automobiles became more popular, smaller or less dense cities faced many of the same challenges as their larger counterparts, and countless cities considered or planned elevated-highway solutions, including Detroit, St. Paul, St. Louis, and Philadelphia.[1] Comparable built examples include the Pulaski Skyway in New Jersey (1930–1932), the Gowanus Parkway in Queens (1941), Buffalo's Skyway (1953), and Seattle's Alaskan Way Viaduct (1953).

Third, the relevance of the Chicago, New York, and Boston examples is heightened by subsequent additions to, and reevaluation and revision of, each example.

Chicago extended Wacker Drive, first on its western end in the 1940s and then east to Lake Michigan in the 1970s. The ideological underpinnings and aesthetic treatment of these sections proved far different from those of Burnham and Bennett's original roadway. In 2002, Chicago completed a $200 million reconstruction, restoration, and cleaning program for the original east-west portion of Wacker Drive. Then, between 2009 and 2016, the city improved Wacker Drive's public appeal by adding new walkways, benches, public art, and shops and restaurants to create the so-called "Chicago Riverwalk." Additional similar improvements east of Michigan Avenue are still ongoing. These projects have reframed Wacker Drive's significance to focus on its multitiered streetscape and civic engagement instead of its singular efficiency as an automotive thoroughfare.[2]

In New York, after a section of the West Side Elevated Highway collapsed in 1973, the city demolished much of the elevated roadway, citing its deteriorated condition as a liability both for drivers and the city. Ensuing controversy about how to reconstruct the western waterfront and a new iteration of the highway dominated public discourse for much of the rest of the century. It finally culminated in the construction of an on-grade highway along the waterfront, with elevated portions remaining only at the road's northernmost reach. The new West Side Highway was completed in 2001.[3]

In Boston, revisions to the Central Artery and its new corridor of parks reached completion in 2007. Soon after the highway's original dedication in 1959, traffic volumes on the road far surpassed its projected capacity. This new traffic problem, paired with increasingly popular antielevated highway sentiments from laypeople and planning officials alike, encouraged local disdain for the road. The purported solution to these concerns was the Central Artery/Tunnel Project (the "Big Dig"), outlined earlier. Built between 1991 and 2007, it removed the auditory and physical disruption wrought by its predecessor.

Together, these recent revisions underscore the connection between our contemporary landscape and the historical pattern of urban elevated highways. Instead of staid projects with limited lifespans, these highways significantly affected subsequent development patterns in each city and ultimately have posed major challenges to contemporary designers. They are also distinctly different from the elevated highways built after 1956 using federal Interstate funding, a cadre whose government sponsorship dictated and homogenized their forms.[4] Understanding the sequence of these design iterations helps to explain America's current urban landscapes.

The Roadmap

This study addresses urban elevated highways as a specific subset of American architectural and urban history, rather than solely as engineering projects or as incidental components of larger civic improvement histories. It demonstrates their synthesis and reflection of larger architectural and cultural issues and invites architectural history to figure prominently in evaluating the design significance and impact of these early automotive constructs.

In *The Machine in the Garden*, Leo Marx established nineteenth-century industrialization as the glaring challenge to America's pastoral ideal. Marx contended that "progress," as a persuasive and pervasive ideal in nineteenth-century America, eventually overran the equally powerful infatuation with the country's natural landscape. He positioned the railroad's intrusion onto the American frontier as the quintessential harbinger of the condition of modernity as it directly impacted the public's view and use of the American landscape.[5] This book builds on Marx's pivotal model by positioning the rise of the automobile and its representation of machined progress as the twentieth-century equivalent of his paradigm. It maintains that elevated expressways pierced the ideological and aesthetic character of American cities, imposing a new image of modern transportation, architecture, and urban life. The chapters that follow will chart this path.

Part I, "The Problem of Congestion," establishes the national context of existing urban conditions, modern architecture, and growing automobility in the late nineteenth and early twentieth centuries, and chronicles the resulting myriad ideas for controlling urban growth and urban traffic across the country, including Chicago, New York, and Boston. Part II, "Elevated Expectations," traces the design processes for Wacker Drive, the West Side Elevated Highway, and the Central Artery. Within the context of the three cities' widely divergent landscapes, planning processes, and design vocabularies, these chapters reveal the cities' parallel problems, shared hopes for revitalization, and common selection of elevated highways as redemptive solutions. Part III, "Bridges and Divides," presents the implementation of the three main subject roads and their immediate aftermaths, and then traces the afterlives of all three highways, first through the replication of their typology via the federal Interstate program and then through the specific lifespans of, and subsequent changes to, each example.

In the twenty-first century, our planet finds itself on the brink of environmental disaster, thanks in no small part to America's dependence on and exploitation of automotive transportation. Since architecture and urban design record and edify social change, our current built environment reveals well-intentioned design concepts that have been exponentially expanded and replicated to their detriment. The history and development of urban elevated highways provides one medium for tracing this pattern. Early elevated highways marked the start of a massive shift in American city-building, one that began to adapt the urban environment to suit the automobile. Constructed roads uniquely offered both engineering utility and architectural presence, making them harbingers of both transportation trends and architectural fashion. As such, the elevated highways discussed in the following pages are important on two levels: as historical artifacts with complex and as-yet-unaddressed design histories, and as references for subsequent development approaches that have largely determined our contemporary American landscape.

I

THE PROBLEM OF CONGESTION

1

A RECIPE FOR DYSTOPIA

Technology, Speed, and Privatization in the Nineteenth-Century City

> Visiting a number of American cities after a lapse of eleven or twelve years, one is struck by the enormous increase in the difficulty of moving about in the towns. So many motor cars are now in use that the value and time-saving capacity of each car has been greatly reduced. Particularly is this the case in the larger towns, where the difficulty and delay in getting about have certainly increased to a very considerable extent, owing to the stoppages at the very numerous cross-streets which result from the American system of planning, and owing to the difficulty of finding a place to park the car anywhere near the spot that is being visited. (1923)
>
> —Raymond Unwin, "America Revisited"

BETWEEN THE MID-NINETEENTH CENTURY and the Great Depression, America's oldest cities struggled to reconcile a growing mismatch between overburdened public transit systems, architecturally complex but increasingly dense business districts, and crippling automobile congestion. These circumstances manifested the impact of three innovations that had radically and successively altered the basis for urban life and urban form. First was the railroad, itself a tremendous achievement in engineering, which empowered corresponding new levels of movement for both goods and people. It enabled travel at two degrees: one at the national level, moving large amounts of goods over long distances; and the other at the local level, where steam railroads, street trolleys, and subways allowed people to move fluidly to and within metropolitan regions. Second was the evolution of the skyscraper, which marked a new direction in the conception of individual works of architecture and, to a larger degree, the structure and functioning of cities as symbiotic organisms. The development of tall buildings showcased not only new building technologies and styles but also new modes of commercial entrepreneurship. As iconic corporate buildings outpaced the height and stylistic fashion of religious and governmental monuments, city centers increasingly edified private enterprise.[1] Such autonomy became more important for individual people as well. Though individualism and independence always underwrote the most basic tenets of American identity, nothing bolstered this sentiment more comprehensively than the third example: the popularization of the automobile. The advent of automobility introduced new possibilities for autonomous personal transportation, and in so doing, radically upset the primacy of public transportation in American cities. Personal automobility altered the popular conception of the city and its streets as a collective enterprise and instead posited an infinite number of "personalized landscapes" that responded to each individual's needs. The combined ramifications of these three innovations radically changed the economic, social, and physical structure of American cities.

This chapter examines the railroad, the skyscraper, and the automobile through the fixed thematic lenses of technology, speed, and privatization to showcase the shared circumstances and interrelated impacts of these innovations on urban centers. Urban planners, architects, and municipal leaders responded to economic and physical woes by reevaluating the literal structure of their cities. Their studies yielded proposals for utopian invention and local reorganization, both of which fueled enthusiasm for the insertion of elevated highways into existing urban settings.

The Railroad City

The technological evolution of the urban railroad during the nineteenth century responded to emergent community needs and also stimulated incessant demand for subsequent improvements. The horse railway, which gained popularity in the 1850s, established a benchmark for this pattern. In New York City, the horse railways served a three- to four-mile radius around the city—the distance that a horse could reliably cover in an hour's time. With smooth tracks and a specific right-of-way, the horse railway improved on its predecessor, the horse-drawn omnibus, whose lack of clear path made it subject to inconsistent and congested urban street conditions. While these improvements secured the horse railway's dominance in most American cities through the 1870s, the range and reliability of the horse railway could not keep pace with population growth and demand, compelling transit leaders to explore new options by the 1880s.[2]

Resulting proposals included a wide range of technologically imaginative schemes for motive power and route. Some advocated applying the steam power of the continental railroads to the urban setting, though most regarded it as too dangerous and expensive for the density of cities. San Francisco inventor Andrew Halladie perfected the first cable-powered street railway in 1873, where stationary engines powered overhead cables that would move large cars through the streets at constant speeds. This model worked particularly well for traversing the hills of Halladie's hometown, but was not feasible in cities like Boston where narrow curving streets rendered a cable system impractical. The electric streetcar provided the most viable improvement, where off-site steam engines generated electricity that overhead wires carried and transferred to the electric motors of individual cars via rooftop poles. This system proved more flexible than the cable system, for which intersections had posed particular problems, and eliminated worry about mobile steam engines exploding in crowded urban streets. By 1902, electric streetcars constituted 94 percent of street railway mileage nationwide.[3]

The public's insatiable desire for ever-faster transportation stood at the heart of this technological evolution. Speed mattered in two realms: the rate at which one could move from one place to another; and a related element, the time it took to do so. Although electric streetcars certainly outpaced horse railways in terms of pace, capacity, and reach, their shared rights-of-way on public streets meant that they had to compete for space with horses, carriages, pedestrians, and omnibuses, ultimately slowing the streetcars and resulting in sometimes gruesome accidents between horse-drawn and mechanical vehicles.[4] Such incidents not only disrupted individual travel but also eroded the public's perceptions of streetcar efficiency and safety. Even as streetcars literally moved faster than their horse-drawn predecessors, their progress was repeatedly and notoriously slowed by the very vitality of the urban core.

For many, the solution to such congestion lay in giving trains dedicated paths either aboveground or underground.[5] Elevated railways provided especially expedient and cost-effective solutions. New York inventor John Stevens dreamed of an elevated railroad as early as 1832, followed by proposals in the 1840s by John Randel, Jr., the surveyor for New York's 1811 Commissioners' Plan. Randel's plan answered calls for both safe power and utmost efficiency. He proposed a train running along both sides of Broadway powered by an endless belt connected to stationary engines. Instead of slowing to pick up passengers, the train would be fed by smaller "tender" vehicles that would accelerate to match the train's speed, lock to the train to exchange passengers, and then disengage to return to their stations. The stations were to be fed by elevators that would take passengers from street to platform level. Such creative solutions notwithstanding, New York's Common Council rejected this scheme in 1848 citing fear that the elevated line's physical presence and accompanying noise would adversely affect the land values of abutting properties. Only twenty years later, however, New York boasted the nation's first elevated railroad—an experimental cable-powered line along Greenwich Street. The drawbacks of elevated lines had not changed during the intervening years, but faced with increasingly dire traffic conditions, officials approved elevated lines as expedient solutions to urban congestion woes.[6]

New York implemented elevated railroads first and set a model that Brooklyn, Chicago, and Boston followed. Following the experimental line of 1868, elevated railroad construction boomed in Manhattan, particularly in the late 1870s and 1880s. Elevated railroads generally utilized the same steam or electric power as other railroad applications, but their dedicated paths above public streets freed them from the congestion that thwarted other modes of urban transit.[7] When New York inaugurated the Metropolitan Elevated Railway along Sixth Avenue in June 1878, newspaper headlines excitedly recounted the expanded capacity, speed, and business opportunities afforded by the new line, and within a few weeks, boasted about significant increases in business activity along the elevated railroad's path.[8]

Elevated lines arrived in Chicago twenty-five years after those in New York but penetrated the Windy City's core in a deeper and more lasting way than anywhere else. The elevated superstructures encircled and distinguished Chicago's downtown business district, which became known as the Loop, and facilitated easy connections to rail lines serving other parts of the metropolitan area. This new downtown accessibility raised local transit to a level of importance that matched Chicago's prominence as a railroad hub for national passenger and freight transport. Such ease of movement to and around the Loop cemented the elevated railroad's economic centrality, spawning even greater development around its fringes.[9]

Not only was the pace and economic impact of elevated railroad travel exciting, but the experience of moving through the city at the second-story level brought a fascinating new dimension to urban transit. Opening-day accounts of the Chicago elevated railroad included reports of surprising scenes, with shades accidentally left open to reveal the minutiae of daily life and workers distracted by the spectacle of trains flying by second-floor windows.[10] In New York, one well-known guidebook to the city celebrated the experiential qualities of the city's new elevated, exclaiming: "New-Yorkers are borne along, swiftly and comfortably, high up above the streets, in view of the wonderful changing panorama of the Empire City, and in a fresh and wholesome atmosphere. A ride on the London Metropolitan Railway is a depressing necessity; but a flight along the New-York elevated rails is a refreshment."[11] This notwithstanding, such ebullient accounts of elevated rail travel separated the riding experience from the more mundane reality of living or working near the path of elevated trains. This latter condition, dominated by noise, darkness, and filth, ultimately came to define the historical legacy of elevated railroads.

While the elevated lines initially reduced street-level chaos, decreased travel times, and added a sublime quality to urban transit, they also introduced a new host of problems. First and foremost, they impacted adjoining properties along their routes. Though widely advocated as a boost to neighboring property values, proximity to an elevated railroad more often threatened demolition of individual buildings, or if not, included heavy shadows from its complex metal underpinnings, great noise, and smoke and hot embers from the airbound trains.[12] One worried New Yorker, upon hearing of plans to build elevated railroads in Chicago, wrote an editorial to *The Chicago Tribune* to warn against this "intolerable nuisance" whose drawbacks far outweighed its promised benefits.[13] For countless others along elevated routes in Boston, New York, Brooklyn, and Chicago, elevated railroads wreaked havoc on the vitality of streets, the prosperity of adjoining businesses, and the tranquility of neighboring homes. After Chicago proceeded with construction of the new Metropolitan Elevated Railway (despite the preceding author's plea), *The Chicago Tribune* reported that "it looks as though a cyclone had swept through, completely ridding a strip forty feet wide of every building that stood in its path."[14] Ironically, elevated highways would follow a similar pattern in the early twentieth century—both in their structural pattern and in their negative impact. Even though elevated railroads were quickly villainized for their environmental costs, the next generation of planners seemed to think that elevated highways would sidestep the same fate.

Elevated railroads also failed to satisfy the needs of growing urban populations with expanding settlement patterns and insatiable desires for ever-hastening movement. In New York, citizens lamented the overcrowding, discomfort, and inefficiency of elevated rail travel.[15] Limited by street patterns, frequent stops, and engines that did not achieve and maintain adequate speed, elevated railroads left New Yorkers feeling unsatisfied. Citizens increasingly lobbied for a subway system. Though costly to build, a subterranean system would create a dedicated path for rapid transit, thereby unclogging existing streets. Fueled by such concerns, Manhattan celebrated the opening of its subway in October 1904. Seven years earlier, however, smaller and more provincial Boston had inaugurated the nation's first subway running underneath Tremont Street parallel to the Boston Common.[16]

Boston's topography and slower growth meant that its transportation infrastructure had evolved differently even as it responded to challenges similar to those in New York and Chicago. Boston's physical footprint was quite small, focused on a peninsula joined to the mainland by a skinny strip of land. Its colonial heritage and hilly landscape had created an organic, tangled street pattern. These factors had three significant effects on Boston's development. First, the city's peninsula form limited its potential for outward growth, concentrating businesses in one dense downtown area. Second, this density meant that even as the city's population grew more slowly than New York's, its business center was just as congested—if not more so. Third, the irregular street pattern and topography thwarted the widespread insertion of elevated railway lines, leaving streetcars as the main means of public transit until the late 1890s. The streetcars competed with omnibuses and pedestrians for room on already narrow, twisting roads. The combined impact of these conditions rendered the speed of movement in and around the downtown core as miserably slow, and city officials recognized the need for major intervention. Their solution was the inversion of the elevated railway—the subway.[17]

The creation of Boston's subway reflected technological innovation, the desire for hastening speed, and the increasingly privatized nature of American society. As elsewhere, these first two factors fueled one another—with one mode of transportation raising expectations for faster movement, thereby creating more demand, more congestion, and eventually the need for different mechanical solutions to meet the new level of public patronage. Electrification provided the critical technical achievement that empowered the construction of the subway in Boston. Until Boston's foray into subterranean transit, American cities generally had shunned subways, questioning their safety, noxious environments for riders, and exorbitant costs. Reason suggested that the risk and expense of subway tunneling was not worthwhile when above-ground solutions already were available and cost far less.[18]

Boston's particular situation reduced the relevance of such objections. First, the city's repeated rejection of elevated railroads became a foil against which subways grew more appealing. Boston's narrow, winding streets had rendered the construction of elevated tracks virtually impossible in the downtown core. Even when there might have been room, citizens expressed concern about the devastating impact of train derailments and the danger of hot embers falling from above. In addition, the rights-of-way required for elevated railroads would have disrupted the city's urban fabric, the consequences of which already had become clear in New York. The hallowed ground of the Boston Common became particularly controversial in this context, as elevated railroad advocates had proposed elevated lines bordering or running through the park. Railroad promoters saw the Common as a free right-of-way, but citizens felt passionate about the history and integrity of the Common, and rallied to defeat repeated elevated railroad proposals. Defense of the park ultimately made a subway quite an appealing alternative, as it could run silently under the Common's Tremont Street border, maintaining the park, requiring little disruption of adjoining property, subtracting the risk of elevated train derailments, and finally bringing rapid transit close to the central business district.

Second, electrification of Boston streetcars in the 1880s had demonstrated the potential for silent, nonexplosive, and smoke-free urban transit—advantages that specifically answered the drawbacks of steam power. Putting this motive power in an enclosed tunnel would be far less dangerous and disruptive than its steam predecessor. Finally, a subway in Boston could be built at a much shallower depth than that in London by using surface excavations instead of deep subterranean tunneling. This was possible because the proposed route primarily followed existing streets instead of claiming private buildings. So while street surfaces would be disturbed for the project, concerns about ventilation, illness, and depth were largely assuaged. With such specific answers to global and local precedents, a subway seemed increasingly realistic for Boston.[19]

The city of Boston initiated, planned, and financed the construction of the new subway, an approach that was different from most previous urban transit projects in the city. Private rail companies had created Boston's entire street railway system, with multiple companies operating separate competing lines. The city oversaw the administration of this system, granting franchise rights, establishing rights-of-way, and imposing regulations on the individual companies. This meant that Boston benefited from greatly improved transportation options with minimal administrative or economic expenditures.

However, by the 1880s and 1890s, the private lines—now largely absorbed into the privately held West End Street Railway—were failing to meet the city's transportation needs.[20] The governor and the mayor intervened by establishing a Rapid Transit Commission to study all aspects of Boston transportation. The commission's recommendations included the consolidation of steam railroad terminals, the creation of an elevated railroad reaching to and encircling the central business district, and the extension of this railroad underneath the Boston Common to connect to other parts of the city. The Massachusetts legislature ultimately approved the core of this proposal in 1894, and Boston voters followed with a narrow endorsement in a special city election. While debate over the elevated railroad persisted for many more years, the subway project—with particular support from Mayor Nathan Matthews, who underscored its importance by invoking an obscure law that authorized him to construct such a channel under Tremont Street—broke ground on March 28, 1895. Financed by the city through forty-year bonds, the subway was completed in less than four years and at almost $1 million less than its $5 million budget.[21]

When the first section of the subway opened on September 1, 1897, the press hailed it as an engineering and transportation milestone. *Scientific American* featured in-depth profiles of the project both during construction and after completion, detailing the ills of Boston's previous street congestion, the technical features of the new subway, and its achievements in easing urban movement.[22] Of course the biggest benefit of the new subway was its speed. On the day of the subway's official launch, the front page of *The Boston Globe* proclaimed, "NOW FOR SPEED," and featured five renderings of station interiors, subway entrances, and local landmarks along the new transit line.[23] The new subway drew patrons so efficiently that the surface streets in its immediate vicinity were suddenly passable.[24] With this achievement, Boston, a city with frequently conservative tastes regarding architecture and development, had embraced new technology to create a model urban transportation system that sped personal movement and unclogged surface streets—two achievements that many larger cities would try to emulate in the following years.

On a national scale, the growth of public transit systems in the late nineteenth century reflected the growing impact of private interests and privatization. In Boston, Henry M. Whitney, the founder of Boston's West End Street Railway, gradually bought up interests in the city's five other streetcar companies to create a monopoly over local transit. While state regulators were weary of the monopoly, the appeal of coordinated rail service to assuage downtown congestion swayed public and legislative opinion in Whitney's favor. He streamlined operations, coordinated train schedules, and unified fares across all of his routes. But Whitney also had his own prosperity in mind, as his new rail lines frequently connected to speculative land that he owned and planned to develop. Once Whitney left Boston to pursue other ventures in 1893, the West End Company's assertiveness in expanding the rail system declined.[25] This eventually compelled the city to initiate the comprehensive planning that would result in municipal construction of the subway. Eventually the West End Street Railway leased and operated the new subway for the city, but its role in expanding the metropolitan transit network clearly waxed and waned with its owner's personal interest.[26]

The other way that railroads reflected increasing privatization was their empowerment of private home ownership. As demonstrated by Whitney's situation, railroad companies often had interests beyond ticket fares in encouraging ridership between cities and new suburban developments. Such entrepreneurship reinforced a growing social distinction between cities and their surrounding suburbs. Huge waves of immigration and increasing industrialization changed the social and literal landscape of American cities in the nineteenth century, with eager immigrants providing a willing pool of workers for growing factories and crowded housing and health concerns evolving from the new density of people. Such conditions heightened existing concerns about urban sanitation, congestion, pollution, and health, and when paired with the new mobility of public transit, encouraged middle- and upper-class urbanites to seek refuge in ex-urban areas.[27] Social activists, architects, and medical authorities fueled this trend by positioning the bucolic landscape of "the country" as the foil to the ailing nineteenth-century city. Suburban home ownership, therefore, offered the best of both worlds: a private, clean home away from the city, but connected to the boon of urban commerce via public transit. It was a balance made possible only by the evolution of the railroad.[28]

The Skyscraper City

The skyscraper brought even more complexity to late nineteenth- and early twentieth-century urban centers. The growth and maturation of the American economy provided the pivotal impetus for a new type of urban business building. The evolution of skyscrapers from modest, wall-bearing structures to high-style, steel skeletal icons reflects a series of responses to the same three categories of stimuli applied earlier to the railroad.

The interests of private companies underwrote three critical aspects of skyscraper development. First was the increasing separation of paperwork and bookkeeping from the production-oriented facets of business. As companies in the manufacturing, warehousing, or shipping sectors expanded, record-keeping became more essential and required additional personnel to generate, process, and file requisite paperwork. The explosive growth of international communications and commerce during the middle of the nineteenth century compounded the situation. This new scope of business demanded a supporting network of lawyers, bankers, insurers, brokerage firms, newspapers, trade journals, and telegraph companies—all of whom needed flexible office spaces close to their business associates. Such conditions inflated the market for urban office space, sending rents soaring and compelling property owners to maximize development on their lots. Thus, the growth of private businesses and their resultant pressure on private property holders created a prime opportunity for architectural innovation. The tall building—first distinguished solely by height, program, and capacity, and then increasingly by innovative structure, technology, and aesthetics—offered a unique response to these conditions.[29]

In addition to satisfying the crying need for office space, tall buildings offered their owners iconic advertising cachet. Many companies sponsored tall new buildings that bore their company monikers—implying a link between newfound architectural prominence and the success of their businesses. Tall buildings became visual symbols of their sponsoring businesses, participating in a game of aesthetic and literal one-upmanship in city skylines. In addition, signature skyscrapers typically offered far more office space than the building's owner needed, leaving space available to lease for lucrative and predictable rental income.[30]

While lacking the corporate sponsorship, speculative skyscrapers were driven by this same capitalist energy. Private developers recognized the demand for prime office space and built skyscrapers to meet these needs and maximize related profits.[31] This created a pattern where corporate owners and private developers competed to maintain the dominance of their buildings. The story of one New York City block exemplifies this dynamic. The Singer Company established its New York headquarters on Broadway in 1896 and constructed modest additions in 1898 and 1899. In 1906, Singer embarked on a grand building campaign to unify the existing buildings and to add a forty-seven-story signature tower, which opened in 1908. Only two years later, however, a forty-three-story speculative office tower began to rise on a lot directly next door. When completed, the speculative City Investing Building challenged the Singer Building in stature and revenue. Not only did the tower soar higher, offer more flexible floor plans, and feature fancier amenities than the Singer Building, it also consequently threatened the profitability of the sewing magnate's rental spaces. While the prestige of the Singer Building kept it rented, market forces drove its evolution and subsequent challenge by the neighboring structure.[32] With this in mind, private enterprise emerged as both the executor and beneficiary of commercial architecture in the late nineteenth century.

Economic forces created the demand for skyscrapers, but technological advances facilitated their evolution. Some technologies empowered the literal height of tall buildings, as improvements in iron and steel framing, wind bracing, fireproofing, and foundations allowed buildings to reach progressively loftier heights. Others, like electricity, heating, cooling and ventilation, elevators, and telegraphs/telephones eased the implications of human activity within these towers. The combination and application of these systems in tall buildings supported the interest in economy that fueled skyscraper construction and ultimately birthed a new architectural form.

Most building technologies evolved separately from tall buildings, deriving instead from the work of engineers, scientists, and inventors. However, the increasing demand for office space and the inadequacy of existing building systems in efficiently providing it stimulated the integration of the two. The evolution of metal structural systems illustrates this well. Early experimentation with wrought and cast iron happened abroad, where they had been used as small structural pieces for centuries. By the middle of the nineteenth century, American engineers and architects also had begun to use iron for specialized pieces of their buildings, but when the Englishman Henry Bessemer mastered the inexpensive refining of steel in 1855 (emulated in the United States around the same time), metal structural members evolved from unusual features to integral building components. Steel offered greater tensile strength and flexibility, a higher melting point, and now easier manufacture than its predecessors. By the 1870s and 1880s, steel components increasingly called into question the efficiency and cost of traditional wall-bearing masonry for the construction of tall buildings.[33]

Two iconic Chicago skyscrapers demonstrate the polarities of this technological evolution. Chicago's Monadnock Building (Burnham and Root, 1884–1891) simultaneously embraced some new building technologies while resisting others (fig. 1.1). Much of this duality derived from the client's request for a sixteen-story structure built of traditional wall-bearing masonry. This demand meant that even as the architects utilized steel skeletal construction in other contemporary commissions, they used cast iron and wrought iron only for the Monadnock Building's internal frame and its window spandrels. In order to carry the load of the sixteen-stories of masonry above, the walls at the base of the building had to be six feet thick. Such girth ate significantly into the useable space on the ground floor, contradicting the inherent efficiency expected in a tall office building. Moreover, supporting the immense weight of the building on Chicago's soft soils posed a challenge to traditional foundation methods. Root, trained as both an architect and engineer, conceived of a new foundation approach of a reinforced-concrete raft that would sit atop wood pilings driven into the ground. This raft distributed the weight of the building equally, allowing it to settle evenly and to liberate basement space that in other structures had been filled with huge masonry footings. This approach, derived to compensate for the Monadnock's conservative structure, proved an innovative technique that quickly became the norm for skyscraper construction.[34]

Burnham and Root's Reliance Building (1889–1895), a contemporary of the Monadnock Building, exemplifies the programmatic and artistic opportunities afforded by steel skeletal construction (fig. 1.2). Though it rises the same sixteen stories as the Monadnock Building, the Reliance Building's absence of large masonry piers enables it to offer significantly more usable (and rentable) space on each floor. The Reliance's most noteworthy achievement is the symbiotic relationship between its skeletal frame and its exterior form. With the exterior walls relieved of any load-bearing responsibility, large expanses of glass flow around the building's undulating bay windows, bordered above and below with terra-cotta panels that visually syncopate its stacked levels. This exterior delights in the lightness and openness empowered by its materials in the same way that Root's design at the Monadnock Building reveled in the density and weight of its masonry walls. For this reason, critics hailed the Reliance Building as a turning point for modern commercial architecture—one that derived visual cues from the mastery of new structural methods.

In addition to the achievement of its structural system, the Reliance Building offered cutting-edge building technologies, including ventilation, heating and cooling, electricity, plumbing, and filtered water, all of which facilitated human activity within the confines of a tall building. Each of these systems represented individual achievements in engineering progress, and responded to both the technical and health-oriented challenges of modern life.[35] Another cadre of technologies,

Figure 1.1 Monadnock Building, Chicago. Burnham and Root, 1884–1891. (Chicago History Museum, ICHi-051002; Kaufmann & Fabry Co., photographer.)

Figure 1.2 Reliance Building, Chicago. Burnham and Root, 1889–1895. (Author photograph.)

including elevators, telegraphs, telephones, and typewriters, introduced great conveniences to daily business. It was no coincidence that the Reliance Building's four elevators offered state-of-the-art engineering, safety, and artistry, as the building's owner was elevator magnate William E. Hale. Hale and his firm, the Hale Elevator Company, had contributed to the invention and refinement of the hydraulic elevator, and his company dominated the elevator market in Chicago.[36] Elevators eased individual stair-climbing burdens and hastened the general pace of life within skyscrapers. Paired with steel skeletal construction, elevators delivered tall buildings from an era of masonry determinism to one where the sky became the joint destination of buildings and their users.

The elevator implicitly highlights the importance of speed—in movement, communications, and business—that increasingly dominated urban life at the end of the nineteenth century. In facilitating quick and easy movement within tall buildings, elevators encouraged swift communications and exchanges between businesses in the same locale. If visiting another building, patrons could easily move to and from a given office, making efficient use of their time. Other technological milestones like the telegraph, telephone, and typewriter had similar impacts. Such instruments contributed to the already changing pace of business and became essential tools for the corporate offices that occupied new skyscrapers.[37]

Finally, the very density of skyscraper-strewn business districts affected the pace of business and urban life. Separate from the disembodied communication afforded by the telephone, the proximity of businesses to one another offered great conveniences to workers and clients. Businesses could hold meetings with other parties and provide services to neighboring companies much more easily than in sparsely settled areas. Railroad terminals and mercantile ports were generally close to downtown areas, which streamlined the shipping and receiving of goods from afar. The compound effect of these benefits raised expectations for the pace and convenience of urban business, setting the stage for even more growth in the coming decades.

By the early 1900s, then, the American skyscraper had evolved through a critical series of technological, economic, and spatial transformations such that the possibilities for its spatial efficiency and architectural expression seemed infinite. Architects tested a broad range of stylistic models to capture the zeitgeist of the new century, yielding skyscrapers sheathed in garb ranging from Gothic to classical. This visual variety notwithstanding, historical models increasingly seemed ill-suited to the technical advancement of modern engineering and the pace of modern commerce. Design dialogues increasingly focused on developing an architectural language specific to the skyscraper form, and the 1920s and 1930s yielded many distinct answers to this challenge. This discourse extended to question the structure and aesthetics of urban environments themselves—something that ultimately cast elevated highways as critical components in redefining the organization, efficiency, and appearance of modern cities.

The Automotive City

In 1897, *Scientific American* lauded the motor car as the most attention-grabbing engineering accomplishment of the year.[38] Though still in its technological infancy, the automobile promised liberation from the geographical, temporal, and communal strictures of nineteenth-century urban movement. As automotive technology and its supporting infrastructure matured in the following years, its promise seemed limitless. However, the growth of automotive culture ultimately provoked a host of new challenges for American cities, including greater traffic congestion, demand for parking areas, pollution, magnified class distinctions, and waning interest in public transit. These effects peaked in the 1920s, evinced by architects and city planners who increasingly sought to systematize the relationship between urban form and personal automobiles. As with the railroad and the skyscraper, the same thematic lenses of technology, speed, and privatization illuminate the evolution of these effects. Even more than the other two examples, it is a synthesis of these three factors that birthed America's automobile culture.

The societal changes wrought by the railroad and the skyscraper laid seeds that made the automobile irresistible to the American populace. As seen in the progression from horse-railways to streetcars, streetcars to elevated railroads, and then elevated railroads to subways, railroad technology could hardly keep pace with the demand for more efficient urban transit. In each of these stages, the iterations of rail transit promised patrons successively greater ranges of movement, speed, and convenience. By the late nineteenth century, daily commuters to increasingly teeming business districts were overwhelming all of these transit options. Throngs of commuters now competed for room on city streets with omnibuses, trolleys, streetcars, horses, other pedestrians, and bicycles. This street congestion literally prevented street railways from adhering to established schedules or maintaining efficient speeds. Elevated railway and subway capacities became significantly overburdened, making rides uncomfortable and unwieldy, and the construction of new elevated and subway lines could not keep pace with demand for access to further-removed parts of metropolitan areas.[39] Such conditions reduced the appeal of mass transit but left riders with few alternatives.

In the face of this congestion, the improvement and mastery of automobile technology could not have been better timed. The "invention" of the internal combustion automobile was less a singular moment of ingenuity than a well-timed convergence of many individual innovations. European and American inventors had experimented with a variety of power sources and carriage designs for self-propelled vehicles beginning in the late eighteenth century. France and England boasted early steam-powered vehicles—with the French government sponsoring development of a steam truck to carry cannons in the late 1770s and an English engineer successfully pioneering a steam carriage in 1801. American inventors nearly matched this pace, with Maryland inventor Oliver Evans patenting a steam vehicle in 1787. These examples were the first of nearly a century of experimentation with steam-powered vehicles on both sides of the Atlantic.[40]

Though not ultimately adopted on a wide scale, steam vehicles provided the backbone of engineering technology that underwrote internal-combustion automobiles. Steam automobiles were fairly well developed by the mid-nineteenth century, but their predisposition toward boiler explosions limited the public's acceptance of them on public streets. Many felt that steam technology better suited the railroad where the rails' smooth surface and the tracks' relative isolation limited the likelihood and potential dangers of boiler disasters. Even as these objections limited their widespread adoption, subsequent iterations of steam vehicles produced a wide array of other automotive components. Steering apparatuses, axles, gearshifts, lightweight differential joints, steel frames, and pneumatic tires each refined the maneuverability, reliability, and safety of these early vehicles. By the 1870s and 1880s, steam automobiles had evolved enough to be technically feasible, but public opinion and regulation still stifled their progress. Fire-pumpers, farm threshers, and steam rollers showcased the most mainstream applications of steam technology. Once European inventors began to experiment with internal combustion engines in the 1860s and 1870s, they applied their new motive force to the basic structural components of steam vehicles.[41]

Three other groups of technological innovations joined steam vehicles in spawning modern automobility. The first was the mastery of the internal combustion engine. France pioneered the first internal combustion engine in 1860 as a portable power source for industrial plants. German engineers refined the French invention over the next two decades, showcasing their product for the first time in America at the 1876 Centennial Exposition in Philadelphia. By 1885, German engineer Gottleib Daimler had mastered a lighter and more powerful version of the engine and tested it in four motor vehicles in the following four years. Another German engineer, Carl Benz, applied the internal combustion engine to a tricycle in 1885, with successive improvements that culminated in the first commercially available gasoline automobile in 1887. Development progressed quickly from this point. European manufacturers led the industry in both innovation and sales, though American companies clamored to compete as well. Steam-vehicle manufacturers experimented with gasoline motors, and bicycle firms transitioned some of their operations toward the manufacture of automobiles. By 1900, both the U.S. and Europe had verifiable automobile industries—evinced by the United States' inclusion of statistics for this market sector in its 1899 census. Over the next two decades, America surpassed Europe in both the manufacture and consumption of automobiles, setting the stage for America's intense relationship with personal automobiles.[42]

The second family of technical achievement encompassed road construction. Neither Europe nor America had an infrastructure of well-paved roads to support heavier dependence on personal vehicles. Although English engineers had advanced techniques for building harder, smoother road surfaces in the early nineteenth century, these efforts had been outpaced by the relative convenience of running steam locomotives on fixed rail systems. As late as the 1890s, half of the mileage of streets in American cities remained unpaved. Since abutting property owners were often responsible for paving, the materials, quality, and extent of paving varied widely, and primarily satisfied the traction needs of horses. At this same time, the mass production of inexpensive bicycles stimulated new interest in road improvements. Bicycles offered low-cost, nimble, and autonomous transportation, qualities that offered exciting potential for a broad socioeconomic audience. Since bicycles demanded smoother riding surfaces than their equine counterparts, bicycle manufacturers and organizations lobbied for new roads. These efforts stimulated not only an increase in the construction of asphalt road surfaces but also the creation of government organizations dedicated to improving the nation's roads. Largely thanks to efforts headed by bicycle magnate Albert A. Pope, in 1893 the Department of Agriculture established the Office of Road Inquiry—what would become the Bureau of Public Roads. The Office of Road Inquiry collected factual data on the country's road system, providing statistical evidence of the poor road conditions lamented by many. It argued that better roads would reduce wear on both equine- and motor-powered vehicles, allowing more efficient transport of large loads and reduced expenses for individuals and the public. Automotive enthusiasts joined the lobby, positioning the hazard of driving an automobile on inadequate pavement as even more worrisome than that for bicycles. The combined pressure stimulated the first legislative proposal for a national highway policy in 1902. Though no such policy materialized until 1916, earlier in the century individual states did begin to establish their own highway departments and started to upgrade their roads.[43]

With improving vehicles and a growing road network, efficient and economical manufacture of automobiles provided the third technological ingredient for mass automobility in America. The scarcity, cost, and fragility of early automobiles had limited their accessibility to the American public. Not only were they expensive to purchase but also their finicky operation, frequent breakdowns, and specialized maintenance requirements compelled owners to employ dedicated chauffeurs to drive and maintain their vehicles. Only the wealthiest classes could afford such expenses. All of this changed in the early twentieth century as manufacturers showcased automobiles with improved reliability, easier operation, and lower prices. The new dependability derived from mastery of both technical and design elements. For example, steering wheels began to replace boat-like steering tillers, carburetors and accelerator pedals gave greater control of vehicle speed, smaller-diameter pneumatic tires and spring suspensions provided smoother riding experiences, and enclosed vehicles with acetylene headlamps enabled nighttime and all-weather driving. Such improvements broadened the appeal and feasibility of operation for average citizens.[44]

The standardization and systematization of automobile manufacturing dropped automobile prices to a level that also was within reach of a much wider populace.

Beginning in 1903, the Cadillac Motor Car Company pioneered consecutive refinements in the machining of automobile parts. Its strict tolerances for accuracy in machining resulted in better vehicle performance and also in greater interchangeability of parts between models. Around the same time, the Buick Motor Company made strides in building large volumes of moderately priced vehicles. Buick purchased, relocated, and streamlined operations of manufacturers of critical automobile components, thereby centralizing manufacturing efforts at two large plants in Jackson and Flint, Michigan. The company also established a network of wholesale and retail distributors, which extended its products' reach into many regions of the country. By 1908, Buick had the largest automobile plant in the world, with unmatched volume and value of its products.[45]

While Cadillac, Buick, and others significantly refined individual manufacturing techniques, the Ford Motor Company synthesized and extended these principles to create a scale of production and economy that far surpassed those of its competitors. A persistent inventor, Henry Ford built experimental vehicles as early as 1896 and established his own company in 1903. From the outset Ford sought to develop cars that were financially accessible to America's middle class. The Ford Motor Company offered three different models during its earliest years, but quickly honed its energies to concentrate on only the Model T by 1909. This singular focus required the mastery of only one design and its supporting parts, and empowered further simplification of the production process. Ford adopted the moving assembly line from Buick, borrowed the interchangeability of parts from Cadillac, and then improved on both. Wherever possible, machine power replaced human labor. Motorized conveyors moved vehicles along assembly lines at a steady pace. Similar devices transported individual components from the warehouses to the assembly lines in the exact order in which they would be required. Specialized sub-assembly lines concentrated on building dashboards, front axles, and car bodies, and a glass plant produced continuous plate glass on site. The compound effect of these innovations raised Ford's rate of production and lowered the price of its automobiles. By the eve of World War I, Ford's technically empowered approach to manufacturing had secured nearly half of the national market for new cars.[46]

The growth of automobility relied on more than the simple technological achievement, efficient production, or low cost of motor vehicles. All of these milestones were fueled by the public's appetite for greater speeds of movement. Compared to the horse, the automobile's most immediate predecessor for non-rail transportation, the motor car offered greater reliability, efficiency, and speed. Where horses were subject to illness, fatigue, and varying strength and disposition, automobiles provided a mechanical alternative free of such restrictions. Its speeds paralleled those of the railroad but without the limited route of railroad tracks. And of course in a commercial world where time and money were increasingly linked, automobiles were seen as a way to maximize both. The *New York Times* reflected: "The motor influence, in short, has changed conditions of life in every phase—we move faster, get our mail and freight more quickly, buy and sell products more surely, and we even scorn the handicaps that once were put upon our business or pleasure travel by storm or snowdrift."[47]

As with the railroad, however, automotive speed had complicated ramifications. For some, the simple attainment of ever-faster speeds constituted reason for great celebration. In the late nineteenth and early twentieth centuries, automobile races were frequent sporting events in both Europe and America, where competitors showcased the improving reliability and pace of contemporary vehicles. Some manufacturers used their competitive successes as fodder for advertising campaigns, offering consumers the opportunity to buy the same model vehicle that had set the latest speed records. Speed became not only an object for celebration but also one that could be purchased and personalized. Of course the competition for ever greater speeds meant that records did not stand for long.[48] Automotive speeds, related publicity, and American consumerism could hardly keep pace with one another.

Early automobile enthusiasts envisioned that the speed and flexibility of the automobile would solve urban street congestion. This optimism derived in part from the successful precedent of the streetcar, which had demonstrated how technology could improve urban travel (its limitations notwithstanding). The unlimited route and speed of the automobile created the opportunity for even greater impact. In addition, motor cars occupied less space than horses and carriages and did not litter the streets with excrement or dead animals. The combined impact of these features stood to liberate large amounts of street space—increasing vehicular capacity and rate of movement by extension. This positioned automobiles favorably in the minds of many.[49] As automobile use grew, however, these favorable predictions gave way to grave reports about the dangers of automotive speed in urban areas. Not unlike streetcars before them, automobiles posed a great risk to urban pedestrians. The quantity of automobiles, their irregular routes, relatively inexperienced operators, and (initially) unregulated speeds only magnified safety concerns. Speed became a contentious issue for both auto enthusiasts and urban street goers. Each group expected safety and felt entitled to freedom of movement, but the opposing constituency limited the possibility of both. Because of this conflict, regulation of automobile speed became a hotly debated, erratically enforced, and seemingly unsolvable urban woe. Many planners and municipal leaders envisioned separating distinct types of urban traffic from one another, thereby improving public safety while maintaining the freedom of automotive speed. Such options became frequent components of the urban improvement and utopian plans of the 1920s and 1930s—plans that manifested themselves in elevated urban highways in the following years.

Finally, the privatized nature of automobile transportation compounded the appeal of its technological and speed milestones. As established earlier, all of the variants of nineteenth-century urban transportation—including omnibuses, trolleys, streetcars, elevated railroads, and subways—operated on a community scale. But with crowding, mechanical failures, and schedule and route limitations, these models generated much public frustration as well. In contrast, the automobile offered an apparatus and radius of personal movement that no longer depended on community infrastructure for its reach. The inherent freedom in this model appealed to America's individualistic culture. Three distinct examples demonstrate the breadth of this impact.

First, from their inception, motor cars symbolized social status and personal autonomy. In the earliest years, this was because only the wealthy could afford to own and operate automobiles. Newspaper coverage reinforced this social distinction, lavishing great attention on the prestigious road races and exclusive automobile clubs frequented by affluent car owners. Attempts to travel new routes and distances via automobile also received heavy coverage. Such events were far removed from the strictures of mass transit faced by most Americans and emphasized the individualistic potential of automobility. As automobile prices began to fall, this status became increasingly accessible to the middle class.[50] The automobile, then, manifested the antithesis of mass transportation: the personalization of when, where, and how people could move.

Second, the flexibility of the automobile generated new definitions of daily activities, leisure travel, and residential settlement that supported personal independence. Whereas daily tasks like shopping, doctor appointments, and visits with friends and family might have been limited previously by the timetable, route, or proximity of mass transit, the family automobile provided schedule-free movement along a self-determined path. Similar flexibility applied to leisure travel, which encompassed short drives during evenings or weekends, or longer journeys to distant locales. For the average American, the automobile empowered the very possibility of pleasure travel and the flexibility of its time and destination. A full onslaught of newspaper articles and advertisements underscored this connection. Automobiles were shown cruising off into the vast countryside, climbing steep inclines, and wandering through bucolic settings. Such implications of adventure and conquest encapsulated multiple layers of America's national identity—a connection to the landscape, a self-determined destiny, and a belief in technological progress.[51]

These three elements also fueled the automobile's stimulation of suburban escapism. As discussed in relation to the railroad, Victorian cities aroused great public concern regarding sanitation, pollution, overcrowding, and congestion. Street railways stimulated one response to these conditions, facilitating new development of and access to suburban growth on the outskirts of central business districts. In the years between the two World Wars, automobiles reenergized this type of suburban growth. In the same way that the automobile freed individuals from mass transit, the single-family suburban house liberated families from the crowding of urban neighborhoods and supplanted them with personal autonomy, low density, privacy, and fresh air. One 1919 advertisement for a neighborhood of bungalows near Los Angeles boasted, "Every city convenience but **no city taxes**. A convenient distance from downtown by 5-cent car line or by fine boulevards. Full bearing walnut trees in yard."[52] This seemed like the apex of a privatized American existence, and in the 1920s, soaring automobile registrations and exponential suburban growth demonstrated the extent of its appeal.[53] Suburban growth also had important implications for urban areas, which still housed more than half of the nation's population. The new culture of commuting brought a daily flood of additional vehicles to downtowns, where they complicated existing traffic woes and demanded huge amounts of parking space. This fueled municipal attention to traffic regulation, parking management, and urban design in the 1920s and 1930s. Suburbanization, as a manifestation of individualism, privatization, and automobility, decidedly altered the public urban realm.

Finally, the spread of automobile culture precipitated a change in the public perception of streets, shifting their role from privately maintained resources for the public good, to publicly constructed arteries serving private automotive interests. In the nineteenth century, urban streets served a variety of functional and social purposes. They physically connected places to one another and provided the basic armature of urban form. Streets also provided the backbone for social interaction by hosting markets, playful children, and daily commiseration amongst neighbors and friends.[54] Municipalities often left street maintenance and paving to property owners, reflecting the sentiment that those who benefited most from streets should finance them. This resulted in unpredictable street conditions, including uneven grading, irregular paving, and frequent obstructions by local garbage and sewerage. The emerging trends of street railway construction, residential decentralization, commercial privatization, and public health concerns all highlighted these poor conditions. In the interest of maintaining economic stability and quieting public unrest, city governments increasingly took responsibility for street grading, paving, maintenance, and sanitation. This transition marked a new perception of streets as public amenities essential to community movement, health, and economic stability.[55]

The automobile further complicated this dynamic. Personal automobiles privatized travel but used public streets as their rights-of-way. This created a new type of relationship between municipal infrastructure and individuals, as car owners depended not on transit companies but on passable roads as hosts for their urban movement. This separated individual interests from those of the community in an unprecedented way. New conflicts—between automobiles and mass transit, and between conceptions of streets as vibrant urban links and those of streets as dedicated automotive thoroughfares—would fuel critical debates about urban development throughout the twentieth century.

Trains, Skyscrapers, and Automobiles, Oh My!

From the vantage point of the early 1920s, by which time automobiles had become commonplace, there was persuasive quantitative and qualitative evidence about the compound impact of the railroad, the skyscraper, and the automobile on America's physical and cultural landscapes. Electric street railway mileage, indicative of one late nineteenth-century urban transit norm, had peaked in 1917 and begun to recede.[56] More permissive building codes and surging economic prominence compelled ever-higher numbers and heights of skyscrapers. New York's agglomeration of tall buildings far surpassed those of any other American city, with Chicago following second. Smaller cities saw proportionally similar development of tall buildings, although local building-height restrictions hindered skyscraper construction in some cities.[57]

In Boston, conservative building codes reflected practical concerns about fire hazards, economic worries about overbuilding, and abstract ideas about the preservation and purity of local landmarks. The city enacted its first height restriction following the Great Fire of 1872, which had devastated sixty-five acres of the downtown core. To make structures as low and accessible as possible in the event of another fire, the city limited downtown building heights. Successive restrictions tried to limit overdevelopment in the face of lackluster returns from some of the city's first tall buildings. A final category of restrictions sought to combat tall buildings in the name of safeguarding the city's remaining historic fabric. Buildings along the edges of parks and parkways were capped at seventy feet; and beginning in 1899, structures in and around the Massachusetts State House needed to remain below seventy feet to maintain the prominence of its golden dome in the skyline.[58] Various incarnations of these height restrictions persisted in Boston until 1928, which meant that new building heights, styles, and commercial economies, like those developing more rapidly in New York and Chicago, did not reach Boston until the eve of the Great Depression, or more meaningfully, until after World War II.

As skyscrapers began to change the architectural topography of American cities, population shifts and increasing automobile usage further complicated urban conditions. Between 1910 and 1920, the percentage of Americans living in urban areas swelled from 45.7 to 51.2 percent—marking the first time in the country's history that the majority of the population inhabited cities.[59] Growing urban populations coincided with the aforementioned waning presence of street railways and rising automobile usage. Between 1900 and 1925, automobile registrations soared from eight thousand vehicles nationally to nearly 17.5 million vehicles.[60] Cities housed a great number of these vehicles—not only because of the wealth concentrated in urban areas but also because cities initially offered wider and better-paved streets than rural areas.[61] This surging automobile presence compounded changes already underway due to urban population growth and skyscraper construction.

Together, these factors undermined existing standards of safety, efficiency, and urban decorum. Nineteenth-century streets had already been crowded by pedestrians, horses and carriages, peddlers, streetcars, and elevated railways. The new density of skyscraper-strewn business districts intensified this mix as floods of workers daily commuted to and from their offices. As this workforce, among others, introduced more automobiles to urban streets, street congestion quickly grew frenetic,

Figure 1.3 "Dance of Death" cartoon. *American City* 35, no. 3 (September 1926): 317. (*American City*/Wright's Media.)

with automobiles increasingly hitting one another or hitting pedestrians. Chicago alone suffered 212 automobile fatalities in 1915, and 328 in 1919. Philadelphia, which saw only ninety-one automobile deaths in 1915, lost 226 people to the same cause in 1918.[62] By 1925, the annual national tally of automobile-related deaths had reached 21,900.[63] Local newspapers and trade journals loudly lamented such fatalities, with one calling "death by motor car" a "national menace."[64] Newspaper cartoons reflected similar angst, exemplified by a 1926 illustration from *The American City* (fig. 1.3) featuring an angel of death and an automobile looming over a city street, having already crushed three people, flanked by throngs of fleeing pedestrians.[65] Such images reinforced the perception of the automobile as a major urban aggressor and understandably bred fear and frustration from street goers and civic leaders alike.

Aside from safety concerns, the most urgent issue generated by urban automobile use was staggering traffic congestion (fig. 1.4). Automobiles had effectively been too successful, as their burgeoning popularity flooded cities with a type and amount of vehicles that its streets were not designed to hold. This meant that after having completed huge public-transit initiatives to combat urban transportation woes at the turn of the century, Chicago, New York, and Boston (among others) faced similarly frustrating congestion of a new kind only twenty years later. The *New York Times* called traffic congestion New York's "foremost problem" in 1923, comparing it to a cobra slowly strangling its victim.[66] A 1929 Boston headline labeled its city as the place "Where Traffic Crawls."[67] And a Chicago automobile manufacturer "declared war" on traffic in Chicago's Loop in 1926, offering $25,000 toward the construction of a double-level intersection at the crossing of two of Chicago's busiest streets.[68]

Traffic jams themselves, though problematic, were not the true target of these complaints. Rather, these objections reflected the social and economic costs of traffic congestion. Clogged streets translated into late employees, delayed deliv-

Figure 1.4 "A Creeping Sickness" cartoon. *American City* 40, no. 4 (April 1929): 116. (*American City*/Wright's Media.)

eries, and missed meetings, all of which bred greater levels of stress, lost revenue, and faltering local economies. Automotive traffic became not just a logistical problem but also a serious threat to the vitality of individual cities.[69] Beginning early in the twentieth century but climaxing in the 1920s and 1930s, metropolitan leaders, economists, traffic engineers, sociologists, novelists, planners, architects, and artists cultivated a rich dialogue about the problems of, and potential solutions to, modern urban conditions. Many experts felt that there was no way to escape the growing pressure on urban infrastructure without radical changes to American life and city form. Their proposals—regulatory, fantastic, or otherwise—responded to the widespread impact of urban automobile use, and fueled municipally sponsored schemes for urban change that mirrored the aesthetic, structural, and sensory modernity of the automotive age.

2

ROAD-COLORED GLASSES

Dreaming and Engineering Urban Futures

> What is going to become of this civilization, mad over machines and overrun with them? It has been suggested that subways be dug under the cities to take the motors off the street, that they be parked by the thousands in great caverns underground. A counter proposal is offered that tunnels be thrust beneath crossings, so that the wayfaring man may reach the other side in safety. The idea of going down under has its attractions, but also its disadvantages. Holes in the ground cost money. Taxes are heavy; digging is expensive. An attempt to dig our way completely through this problem could result in nothing less than the confiscation of all property above ground to pay the bill. (1923)
>
> —Uncle Dudley, "Get Off the Earth"

THE URBAN ELEVATED HIGHWAYS of the 1920s and 1930s developed in response to a complex dialogue among designers, engineers, social scientists, and municipal leaders about how to reconcile automotive freedom with existing urban landscapes. The congestion, increasing fatalities, and general chaos of early twentieth-century cities alarmed all of these professionals and, as a result, spawned proposals for urban change that ranged from the practical to the eccentric. Four major categories summarize their far-reaching suggestions for urban change: regulatory responses to traffic, parking, and business; engineering solutions showcasing new technologies; large-scale engineering studies and beautification plans; and dreams of architectural and social utopias to recast contemporary urbanism. Although many of the suggestions never reached fruition, elements from each category served as benchmarks for subsequent improvement efforts. Urban elevated highways drew from all four of these subsets. Touted as the life-blood of many ideal plans, elevated highways separated types of traffic and allowed uninterrupted, high-speed automotive travel; they mimicked the increasing density and verticality of modern urban centers in their constructed nature; and they provided physical evidence of their sponsoring cities' progressive attitudes toward engineering, automobiles, urban mobility, and architecture. As Chicago, New York and Boston tried to address their specific transportation challenges, and despite their distinctly different landscapes, elevated highways became central pieces of each city's redevelopment efforts. This chapter deconstructs this commonality, first exploring the range of regulatory and engineering responses to early automobile congestion, then detailing the comprehensive schemes for urban change offered by architects and planners, and ultimately revealing elevated highway construction as an idealistic synthesis of and response to these ideals.

Stop Lights and Stop-Gap Measures

Regulatory interference provided the first level of attack on urban congestion. Most early regulations took aim at modifying the speed and patterns of urban movement. New York City experienced some of the earliest efforts in this regard as local socialite William Phelps Eno authored the first comprehensive set of traffic rules in 1903. An amateur planner who ultimately established an international traffic consulting business, Eno outlined basic traffic principles that endure to the present day. His guidelines mandated that slower vehicles stay to the right, with faster ones passing at left; forbade parking within ten feet of street corners; demanded that hand signals be used before stopping or turning; gave streetcars the right-of-way over individual carriages or automobiles; and favored one-way rotaries to sort and funnel traffic through major intersections. Local officials added to Eno's framework, restricting left turns along portions of Fifth Avenue, discouraging on-street parking, establishing a minimum driving age of sixteen, requiring headlights for nighttime driving, and setting a speed limit of twelve miles per hour in the downtown area. Other cities followed suit with similar laws and also experimented with basic licensing and registration protocols.[1] These early efforts responded to the cacophony of vehicle types and inconsistent operating techniques that made urban streets so dangerous for pedestrians and vehicular passengers alike. As automobile usage exponentially grew in the first two decades of the twentieth century, municipal leaders formalized, strengthened, and supplemented such policies.

Police patrols and traffic-control signals provided two other facets of early regulation. Philadelphia created the nation's first specialized traffic squad in 1904, and in 1907 New York City established its traffic bureau. By 1911, similar institutions had appeared in Baltimore, Chicago, Cleveland, Detroit, and St. Louis. Such squads enforced local traffic rules and directed vehicles at complicated intersections. However, their responsibilities grew far more complex following the Ford Motor Company's 1908 introduction of the Model T, after which time automobile usage skyrocketed nationwide. This swell overwhelmed police patrols, who could not effectively regulate the huge volumes of traffic even when multiple officers staffed critical intersections. Moreover, these traffic patrols often usurped at least one third of a given city's police force, making it both an inefficient and expensive use of manpower.[2]

Various forms of mechanized traffic-control systems followed. Toledo, Ohio, experimented with semaphore signals beginning in 1908, which used flags mounted on posts to order travelers to stop, go, or yield. New York tried placing police in mid-intersection towers to direct traffic in 1915. Though these systems, which were derivatives of railroad practices, spread to many other cities, semaphores proved too hard to see and towers too much of a street obstruction to succeed in the long term. Traffic-control lights and stop signs proved more viable solutions. In 1914, Cleveland installed the first red and green traffic-control light—another descendent of railroad signal protocols. Police stationed on the side of the intersection manually controlled the overhead light, which regulated traffic in two opposing directions while other officers controlled cross streets. Significant refinements followed, including the addition of a yellow caution signal, the development of four-direction lights, visibility improvements, and system automation. Chicago and New York both sported manually controlled traffic lights by 1918; Boston joined the trend in 1925.[3]

Stop signs were the other major innovation in traffic-management tools at this time. A Detroit police officer pioneered the octagonal, easy-to-recognize sign in 1914, and it quickly became a popular solution for intersections that were not busy enough to warrant on-site police supervision. Automotive booster organizations and city governments saw stop signs as a great improvement, positioning them as economical approaches to traffic mediation and improved road safety. Chicago installed the new signs along high-speed parkways in 1916, and most major cities had followed suit for heavy traffic routes to metropolitan suburbs by 1920.[4]

A variety of driving, parking, delivery, and operational restrictions offered other means for easing urban vehicular movement. One-way streets were a particularly popular solution. Philadelphia adopted one-way streets in 1908, and Boston followed the next year. The narrow, winding streets in these cities were especially inhospitable to the ever-growing throng of vehicles, and single-direction traffic flow simplified movement considerably. Cities with more regular street plans also found one-way streets helpful: New York implemented its first directional restrictions in 1915, Washington, DC, had one-way streets by 1917, and Chicago experimented with them in the early 1920s.[5] While the implementation of one-way streets did cause some initial confusion and complaints among drivers, directional restrictions made a big difference in smoothing urban traffic flow.

While driving protocols, traffic signals, and one-way streets all affected urban drivers, they only impacted how motorists behaved—not their right to access a given area. Parking regulations, however, did question the premise of accessibility. As automobile usage grew in the 1910s and 1920s, so too did the impact of parked cars on downtown streets. The onslaught of daily vehicles exceeded the capacity of on-street parking, compelling many drivers to resort to double or triple parking. As motorists repeatedly circled city blocks in search of parking spaces, they only compounded local congestion. The tangle of parked cars reduced overall street capacities, thereby slowing streetcars, obstructing views of oncoming traffic, hindering emergency access to burning buildings, and arguably affecting the financial health of local businesses. Hoping to organize and streamline this chaos, many traffic engineers and municipal leaders saw parking regulations as a promising solution.[6]

Parking regulations fell into two categories, parking bans and parking limits, both of which were heavily contested. Parking bans involved the complete prohibition of parking on downtown streets, usually during the morning and evening rush hours. Chicago imposed a rush-hour ban in 1917, Los Angeles did so in 1919, Boston in 1924, and Philadelphia instituted a short-lived ban in January 1927. In all of these cases, ban advocates (who often included traffic engineers and local rail executives) felt that the specific timeframe of the restrictions would preserve access to downtown businesses while also smoothing movement during peak travel times. In most cases, however, such bans were fleeting. Local business and automobile clubs rallied against the restrictions, arguing that even as the bans may have alleviated some immediate congestion, they discouraged customers from patronizing downtown businesses, driving them instead to competitors on the urban fringe. The threat of economic stagnation was enough to compel most city leaders to quickly reverse the bans, often replacing them with selective bans on key streets instead of entire business districts.[7]

Parking limits offered a more flexible, if not also problematic, solution. Parking limits restricted the length of an automobile's stay in a given downtown area, thereby aiming to move traffic in and out of central business districts more steadily. Local business owners ardently supported parking limits, positioning them as the only way to combat congestion without discouraging motorists from doing business downtown at all. Parking limits, however, had three significant drawbacks. First, rather than actually removing traffic from city streets, these restrictions tended to stimulate greater movement within their bounds by compelling motorists to find new spots for their vehicles after the expiration of their parking spaces' allotted times. Second, it was logistically and financially difficult to enforce the posted parking limits. Police forces did not have the manpower to properly monitor downtown parking areas; and when citations were issued, local court systems frequently downplayed their importance relative to more serious criminal matters. Third, even with parking limits there still were not enough parking spaces to accommodate demand. The promise of on-street parking—albeit time limited—maintained the appeal of driving downtown and therefore had little impact on reducing street traffic in the long term. Even as most municipalities did implement various parking limits, few drivers respected the limits enough to adhere to them; and those who followed the rules only redoubled traffic jams as they searched for coveted downtown spaces.[8]

Dedicated automobile storage facilities—parking lots and parking garages—offered another answer to the parking dilemma. At the 1925 International City and Regional Planning Conference, Pittsburgh planner Morris Knowles proclaimed parking garages as a long-term solution to traffic congestion and parking chaos, and other planners, city leaders, and especially motorists, shared this perspective. Throughout the late 1920s and mid-1930s, as parking bans and parking limits decreased the amount of on-street parking, cities, retailers, and specific parking companies steadily added off-street parking options. Landowners transformed empty urban parcels into small parking lots, providing quick answers to public demand and profitable utilization of otherwise inactive land. Municipal governments appended parking to public improvement projects, lining unused green spaces and riverfronts with parking facilities.[9] New York motorists even targeted Central Park as a resource for parking remediation, unsuccessfully proposing to replace the park's pond with a thirty-thousand-car parking lot and accompanying garage. Individual retailers also contributed by providing parking facilities either integral to their buildings or at existing garages nearby. When Boston department store Jordan Marsh announced plans to build a dedicated eight-story parking garage for its patrons in 1924, it claimed to be the first-known venture of this kind. As the Great Depression provoked increased building vacancies, some property owners chose to demolish and replace their existing structures with parking facilities, thereby hoping to maintain some level of profitability.[10] Together, these parking initiatives demonstrate a critical shift in traffic-management efforts in the 1920s and 1930s, moving from regulating and/or discouraging urban automobile use to providing a physical infrastructure that accommodated and (arguably) encouraged it, which had far-reaching implications for successive decades.

A last set of regulatory efforts targeted congestion by altering the patterns of daily business activities. Highway engineering professor John S. Crandell argued that twenty-four-hour operation of certain industries would inherently reduce urban congestion during daytime hours, and proposed all-night operation for trucks servicing wholesale, municipal, or building materials needs. Following the lead of continuously operating freight trains and trucks, he reasoned that these classes of vehicles—which he saw as both major contributors to and victims of daily street congestion—would benefit most from a similar schedule. Crandell's plan outlined nighttime garbage collection, express package pick-ups, freight station and dock operation, and movement to and from construction sites. By removing these slow and bulky members of the urban mélange, Crandell theorized that business and passenger traffic would have far more room on city streets.[11]

Crandell was not alone in his focus on truck traffic and freight deliveries, as many cities debated similar solutions in the late 1920s. New York retailer R. H. Macy & Co. proposed one such scheme in 1926, suggesting that all mercantile shipping and receiving departments operate at night, thereby removing large amounts of daytime traffic from city streets. Another theoretical solution proposed creating freight distribution centers along urban fringes, which would remove freight traffic from critical business districts and allow more efficient local delivery of goods. Infrastructure-oriented proposals included using subway lines to distribute mail to outlying areas and creating dedicated elevated highways for freight trucking.[12] Though some localities did experiment with variations of these ideas, the onset of the Great Depression delayed or derailed widespread implementation of such plans for some time. However, the variety and intensity of debate about such proposals testifies to the extreme ramifications of automotive congestion shared by countless American cities. Urban congestion was not just about inconvenience—it impacted the economic, social, and physical vitality of large geographic areas.

The Engineered City

Engineering and infrastructure improvements constituted another category of responses to urban congestion.[13] With the counsel of traffic engineers, commercial lobbyists, and automotive clubs, municipal leaders considered proposals for paving improvements, street widening, new roads, traffic separations, pedestrian bridges, elevated sidewalks, elevated streets, and fantastic schemes empowered by futuristic technologies. Rather than offering comprehensive visions for urban reinvention, such designs provided targeted reactions to specific issues and locations.

Street paving and widening were some of the earliest and easiest interventions. Greater amounts of traffic and ever-heavier vehicles damaged existing streets, compelling public works departments to refine paving surfaces and techniques. Engineers had geared previous street surfaces of asphalt and brick toward comfortable traction for horses, but by the 1920s horse usage was on the decline and these soft and inconsistent surfaces were rendering streets undrivable, thus adding to automotive congestion. This caused many cities to begin paving with concrete, which provided a more rigid and consistent surface for automobiles.[14]

Most other municipal efforts centered on widening existing streets. A presentation at the 1916 National Conference on City Planning in Cleveland outlined the benefits of street widening as an expedient and effective solution to traffic relief.[15] The relative ease and low cost of street widening made it a popular solution nationwide. New York widened Twenty-Third Street in 1910, narrowed the sidewalks along Fifth Avenue to provide two new lanes for traffic in 1912, and completed successive widening projects through the 1920s.[16] Boston's narrow and sinewy streets made street widening more complex and controversial since implementation often required the seizure of private property along targeted routes. While Boston proposed to widen major thoroughfares as early as 1900, city leaders spent most of the 1910s and 1920s debating these schemes, only later to implement a select few.[17] Overwhelming costs, public outcry, and disagreement among government and business groups similarly delayed completion of paving and street widening projects in Chicago until the 1920s. Even once such projects were complete, their impacts usually were less triumphant than anticipated. Drivers understandably favored the new streets—but did so to a fault. The streets quickly attracted more traffic than they could handle, causing even more congestion. So, after investing millions of dollars, displacing citizens and businesses, and robbing streets of pedestrian amenities, cities found themselves revisiting the same—if not worsening—congestion dilemmas.[18]

Another family of engineering ideas focused on sorting and distributing different types of traffic via grade separations, pedestrian bridges, and elevated sidewalks. Engineers proposed solutions that emulated rapid transit protocols, including overpasses and underpasses to maintain the flow of through traffic at critical

Figure 2.1 Loew Bridge over Broadway, New York City. Ritch and Griffiths, 1866–1867. (Courtesy New York City Municipal Archives.)

intersections, bypasses around central business districts to remove long-distance traffic from local streets, laws privileging automobiles on certain streets, regulations about the time and tenure of commercial deliveries, and segregation of traffic by travel speed. These approaches became increasingly common between 1900 and the late 1920s, resulting in some measurable impacts nationwide.[19]

The most imaginative schemes for sorting street traffic related to the separation of pedestrians from vehicular users. An 1866 pedestrian bridge across Broadway in New York showcases a particularly early project in this vein, predating the automobile itself. A local hat merchant initiated the bridge project, arguing that Broadway was already so clogged that pedestrians could not cross the street to access his shop. He successfully petitioned the Common Council to take responsibility for facilitating such access, and they constructed the footbridge, known as the Loew Bridge (Ritch & Griffiths), from 1866 to 1867 (fig. 2.1). Some found the cast iron bridge to be quite an asset in navigating Broadway, while others—notably including a competing hat merchant whose property abutted the bridge—complained about the shadows cast by the structure and claimed that it attracted loiterers. Complainants argued that the bridge was too high, and that its form was not ornate enough to dominate a major thoroughfare. These grievances had such a strong impact that the city dismantled the bridge in 1869.[20]

The Loew Bridge controversy highlights two key issues that repeatedly affected transportation improvement projects: the balance between public and private interests, and the physical impact of a project on the urban realm. On the first issue, boosters touted the bridge as a great convenience to multiple constituencies, simultaneously removing pedestrian traffic from local streets, facilitating more flexible urban movement, and improving access to private businesses on both sides of Broadway. However, proximity to the bridge strongly colored individual reactions. As it encroached on local sidewalks and cast shadows on adjoining businesses, the Loew Bridge provoked resentment from its closest neighbors. Subsequent public transportation projects, including new roads, elevated railroads, subways, and elevated highways, generated similar reactions.

Regarding the second issue, the physical presence of the bridge seemed an incongruous intrusion onto the familiar urban landscape. Unlike surface roadways, a footbridge had spatial and aesthetic implications relative to the scale and tenor of surrounding architecture. The height of the Loew Bridge and the exposed nature of its cast iron form flew in the face of more restrained and historicized architectural conventions—its classically referenced ornamentation notwithstanding. One observer, following the bridge's demolition, wondered why the bridge could not have more successfully met the city's needs: "There ought to be ingenuity enough in this City, one would think, to devise a light convenient structure which would accomplish this object [providing a safe means of crossing Broadway] without being in the way of anybody or very seriously offending anybody's taste by its hideousness."[21] This balance between utility, beauty, and context was a much sought after, though little agreed upon, characteristic of subsequent public works projects. The complexity of existing cities and the seeming simplicity of adding new planes of movement maintained the appeal of elevated solutions, and proposals for multi-level transportation systems flourished in the late nineteenth and early twentieth centuries.

Proposals for multi-level transportation depended on two key assumptions about its relationship to street congestion. First, advocates reasoned that special elevated or subterranean conveyances would necessarily move more quickly than their street-level predecessors since they would not need to compete with other users for space. Second, the removal of some traffic from the street surface would effectively "widen" roads, thereby increasing their capacity and reducing congestion.[22] This reasoning empowered the construction of subways and elevated railways—the most mainstream implementation of such ideas in the nineteenth century. By the early twentieth century, however, a broad assortment of leaders began to apply similar reasoning to street surfaces and sidewalks. Their resulting proposals ranged from subterranean footpaths to networks of dirigible stations, with most slated to occupy air rights in between.

Three distinct time frames define the evolution of multilevel designs for urban transportation. The first is the era preceding the 1908 introduction of the Model T, when railroads, horses, carts, and pedestrians still dominated urban streets. Proposals from this period echoed the basic principles of elevated railroad and subway design, using stacked horizontal planes to bolster the speed and capacity of urban movement. As early as 1903, New York City mayor Seth Low casually

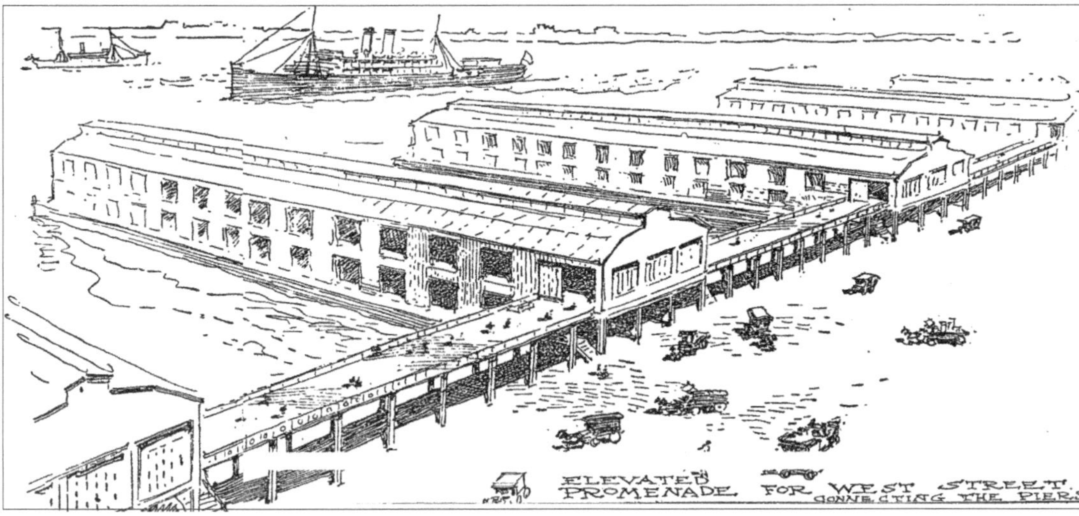

Figure 2.2 Charles Lamb's suggestion for an elevated pedestrian promenade along Hudson River shore, 1908. ("For Beauty and Utility in New York." *New York Times*, November 29, 1908, SM3.)

quipped that four-storied streets would soon be the only solution to the city's traffic congestion. *Scientific American* expanded on Low's comments, outlining a scheme that would have extended elevated railroad platforms to the edges of surrounding buildings, thereby providing enough room for a road and pedestrian walkway on each side of the tracks.[23] New York railroad tycoons Cornelius Vanderbilt and Stuyvesant Fish backed a 1904 proposal for a moving pedestrian platform atop New York's Williamsburg Bridge that was to have glided silently and continuously on rubber tires, allowing passengers to enter and exit with ease.[24] In 1907, *Scientific American* showcased another plan that outlined three distinct levels of movement for New York, with an upper street surface dedicated to streetcars, pedestrians, and "light vehicles" atop a lower level for more cumbersome and delay-prone freight traffic, which could directly access the basements of neighboring structures. A subway could run underneath this double-deck scenario, providing three parallel levels of movement.[25]

As Ford's Model T added an increasing number of automobiles to urban streets, transportation plans increasingly included automobiles in their schemes, though did not specifically cater to them. Rather, architects around the globe envisioned further iterations of stacked levels of movement. New York architect Charles R. Lamb proposed "hanging" elevated sidewalks along the second story of Manhattan skyscrapers, creating a floating grid of pedestrian walkways free of competition with horses, carriages, and automobiles. Lamb also proposed an elevated promenade along the piers of Manhattan's western shore, a scheme that would have relieved pedestrians of dodging local truck traffic and offered unique views of the water (fig. 2.2).[26] The eventual construction of the West Side Highway echoed elements of this design.

French architect Eugene Hénard forecast elevated streets as the critical backbone

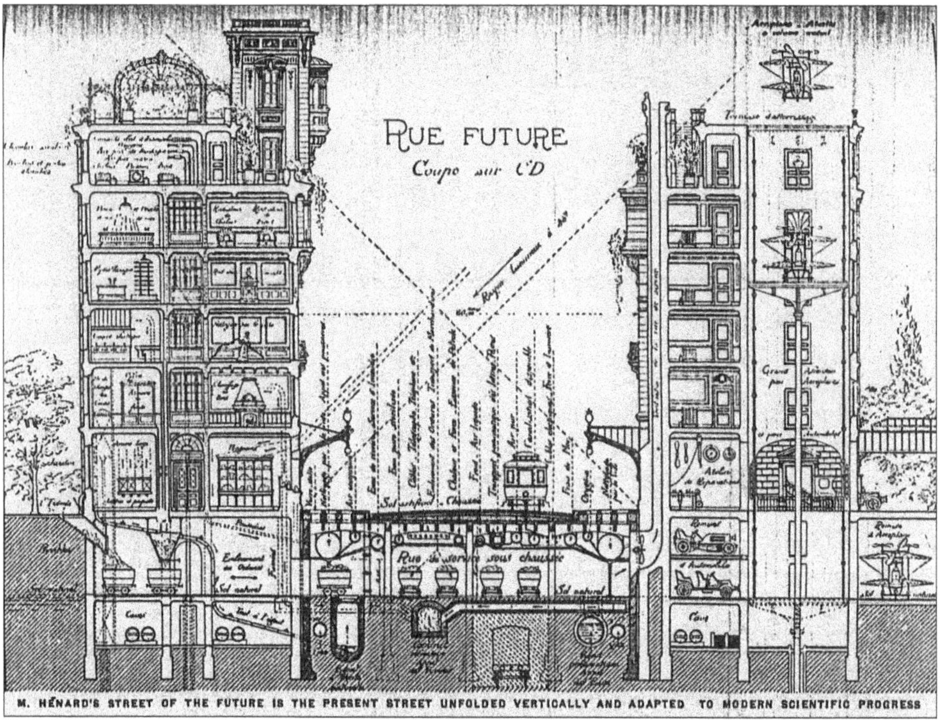

Figure 2.3 French architect Eugene Hénard's sectional view of a futuristic street, 1911. (Hénard, Eugene. "The Cities of the Future." *American City* [January 1911]: 29. *American City*/Wright's Media.)

of his multilayered proposal for urban movement (fig. 2.3). Hénard argued against the inefficiency of repeatedly disrupting street surfaces to install subterranean pipes and cables. He proposed constructing streets at a higher elevation, thereby creating a basement level for easy installation and servicing of infrastructure components. His system also featured dedicated tunnels for railroad-based freight shipping and long-distance transportation, moving sidewalks, and air travel facilitated by rooftop landing places for "airships." Hénard's plan was more ambiguous about the role of automobiles specifically, showing them stored within the lower levels of buildings, but not clearly assigned a place for movement within his sectional street diagrams. This probably reflects the early date of Hénard's design, where the full impact of the automobile was not yet clear. While Hénard's scheme was better suited to the construction of new cities than the modification of existing ones—a caveat that he himself recognized—his separation and systematization of urban functions became an important model for subsequent designers and engineers.[27]

Many other proposed urban interventions echoed Hénard's interest in underground passages and flying machines. In 1911, New York City considered installing a subterranean pedestrian path beneath three blocks of Forty-Second Street to relieve intense pedestrian congestion. A Boston reporter covering the New York developments suggested that such a scheme would be well-suited for his city as well.[28] Naval inventor John P. Holland encouraged air travel as the most promising response to urban congestion. Holland proclaimed that his 1908 invention of a "personal airship" would soon be within financial and operational reach of everyday citizens and would displace existing reliance on trains and subways.[29] Larger "aerocars" and zeppelins were the favored ideas for long-distance air travel, and by the early 1920s a series of inventors were trying to establish long-distance transportation companies that would operate aerocars, hydroplanes, or dirigibles. Advocates argued that air travel provided more flexibility than existing methods of ground transportation and required less infrastructure. One scheme even positioned air travel as appropriate for local urban transit, envisioning passenger dirigibles that would pick up and discharge passengers from aerial stations accessed by speed elevators.[30] Instead of negotiating or regulating street traffic, these designs opted for movement in entirely new dimensions.

By the 1920s, automobile usage had swelled to such staggering levels that designers tried to manage it more specifically. New York City was a frequent subject, as it faced what many felt to be the worst traffic problems in the country. One 1923 scheme proposed building a 100-foot-wide sunken boulevard down the center of Manhattan, providing an uninterrupted eight-lane roadway. Reserved for automobiles and free of intersections with crosstown traffic, this boulevard was to accommodate eighteen thousand vehicles per hour—six times the capacity of Fifth Avenue at the time. *Scientific American*, in its profile of the project, specifically touted this scheme's "universal applicability," implying that it could be implemented successfully in many other locations.[31]

New York City engineer Arthur S. Tuttle, who subsequently contributed to the planning and construction of the West Side Highway, focused on arcaded sidewalks as an efficient means of increasing street capacity. Tuttle proposed threading sidewalks through the ground level of commercial buildings, allowing the buildings' structural supports to syncopate the streetscape and provide protection from inclement weather. This would liberate the former sidewalk space for increased road capacity (fig. 2.4).[32] While the concept of arcaded sidewalks

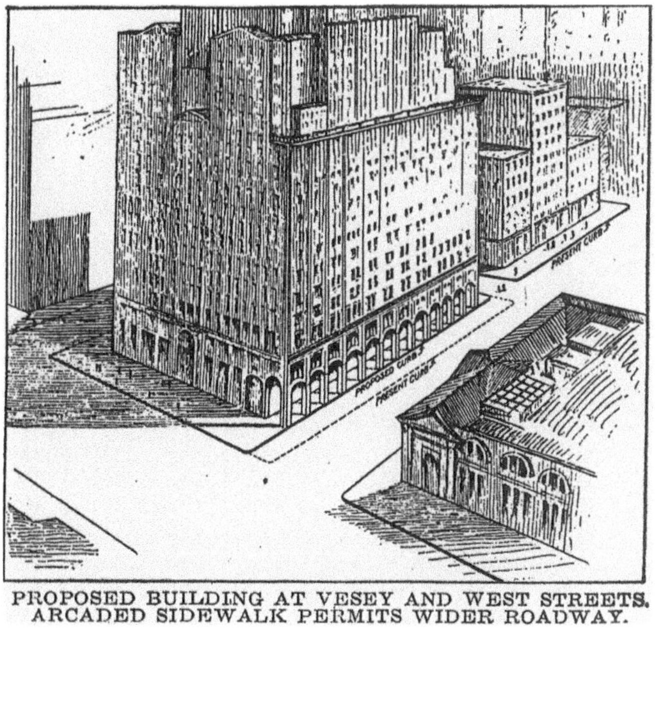

PROPOSED BUILDING AT VESEY AND WEST STREETS.
ARCADED SIDEWALK PERMITS WIDER ROADWAY.

Figure 2.4 Proposal by Arthur A. Tuttle for arcaded sidewalks as a way to gain additional street space, 1924. (© Hanley Wood. "Traffic and City Streets." *Public Works* 55, no. 2 [February 1924]: 45. Courtesy *Public Works*/Hanley Wood.)

Figure 2.5 Multi-tiered vision for Manhattan traffic offered by New York City Transition Commission, 1924. ("Super-Streets and Subways: Tentative Details of a Traffic Plan Recommended for New York City." *Scientific American* 131 no. 3 [September 1924]: cover. Reproduced with permission. Copyright © 1924 Scientific American, a division of Nature America, Inc. All rights reserved.)

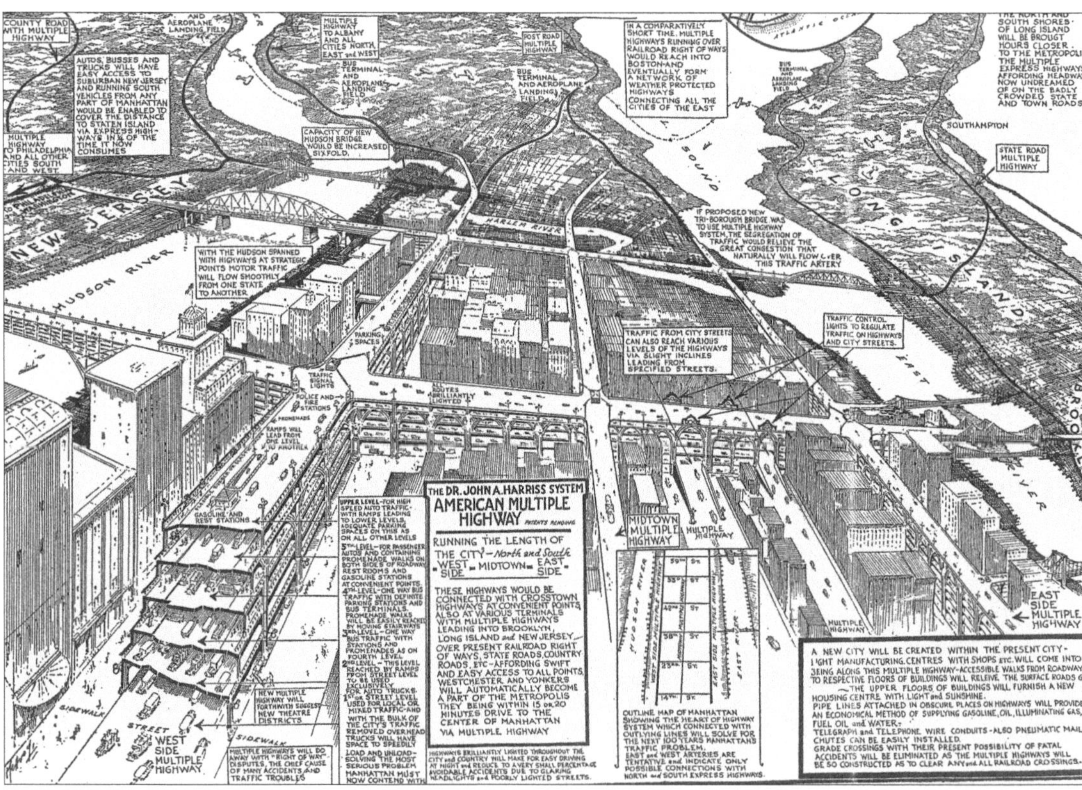

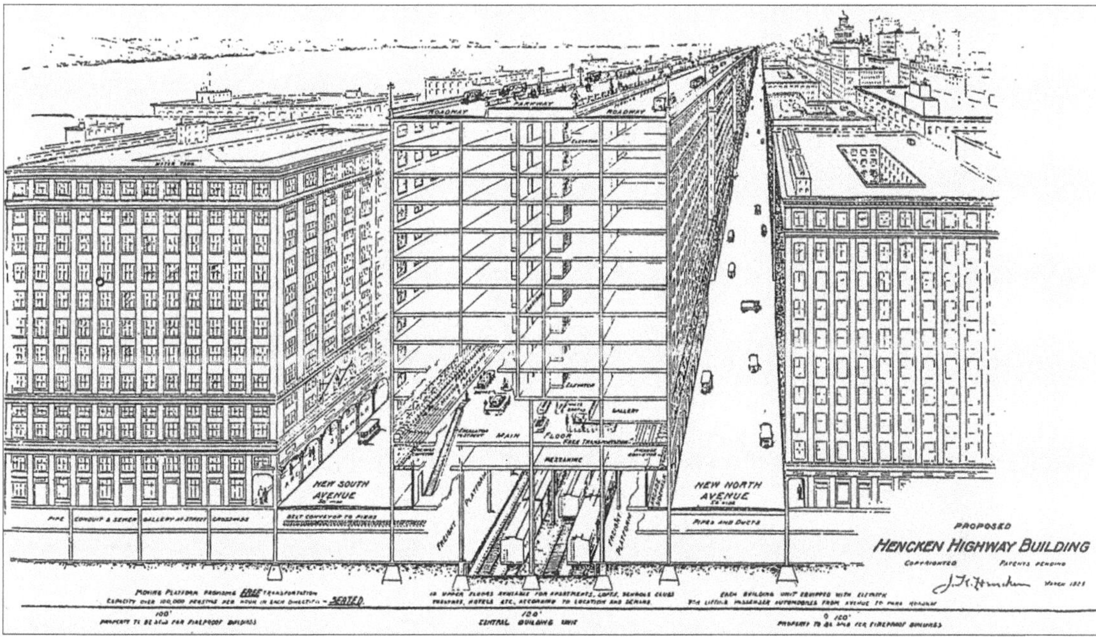

Figure 2.7 Engineer John K. Hencken's plan for moving pedestrian platforms and automotive highways atop twelve-story Manhattan buildings, 1927. ("And How About This? Henckenway." *American City* 36, no. 6 [June 1927]: 802. *American City*/Wright's Media.)

dates back centuries, the proposed intersection of private commercial property with the public's interest in sidewalks and traffic relief contradicted conventional separations between private real estate and public works. This made the implementation of Tuttle's scheme at one of Manhattan's premier Art Deco skyscrapers, the Barclay-Vesey Building (McKenzie, Voorhees, and Gmelin Architects, 1923–27), all the more noteworthy.

Many other plans of the late 1920s echoed calls for filtering traffic through variants of grade separations, multideck streets, and elevated sidewalks (figs. 2.5–2.7). One scheme proposed installing pedestrian bridges across all automotive roadways in large cities to eliminate competing interests on local streets.[33] New York fielded countless proposals for multideck streets (reaching as high as six decks tall in one case), streets atop elevated railroads, and routing streets through buildings for more direct connections. Chicago planners called for raised sidewalks and traffic grade separations, particularly within the congested Loop (fig. 2.8).[34] Though distinguished by design nuances, such plans reflected a common enthusiasm for the multitiered possibilities afforded by modern construction, and a vision of using multideck urban streets to activate multiple levels of adjoining buildings. Without integration into more comprehensive visions for urban growth,

Figure 2.6 (facing page, bottom) Dr. John A. Harriss's proposal for six-level streets crisscrossing Manhattan, 1927. ("And This? Dr. John A. Harriss Proposes Six-Deck Streets." *American City* 36, no. 6 [June 1927]: 804. *American City*/Wright's Media.)

Figure 2.8 Edward Bennett's conception of raised sidewalks for Chicago, 1926. ("Raised Sidewalks and Traffic Separation Urged for Chicago." *American City* 35, no. 3 [September 1926]: 335. *American City*/Wright's Media.)

however, such schemes were logistically and financially difficult to implement. It was not until major traffic studies and planning efforts endorsed and integrated proposals for engineering-empowered traffic relief that any of these multilayered streetscapes flirted with reality.

The Practical, Beautiful, Planned City

In the 1910s and 1920s, as city leaders grew more aware of the large scope of urban problems and the piecemeal nature of previously proposed solutions, they turned to increasingly specialized experts for advice on street, infrastructure, transit, sanitation, and traffic conditions and improvements. However, competing interests quickly complicated this process. Private organizations often spearheaded their own planning studies, and individual personalities colored the direction and reception of reports and recommendations. As a result, four trends define the evolution of this urban planning dialogue. First, two distinct types of planning reports emerged: focused studies of individual problems, and comprehensive city plans. The all-inclusive plans usually followed the specialized reports and subsequently incorporated their data and recommendations. Second, embarking on such planning efforts acted as a proclamation of civic pride and the desire to match or exceed the efforts of other cities. One city's documents often specifically cited the accomplishments of competing locations as evidence of the necessity and modernity of their own efforts. Third, the complexity of these efforts spawned the institutionalization of planning nationwide with the creation of local planning boards and professional planning organizations. Finally, as cities hired the same planning professionals, certain design approaches saw widespread replication across the country. The sum total of these developments specifically influenced the popularity of elevated highways as traffic studies, street plans, master plans, and vying local authorities all positioned multilevel streets as critical to their agendas.

In the context of specialized studies, a variety of public agencies, community organizations, and concerned individuals developed focused reports on a wide array of issues. Experts studied Chicago's tenements in 1901, its mass transit network in 1902, its parks, paving surfaces, and railway network in 1904, and its harbor facilities in 1909.[35] New York and Boston saw similar investigations.[36] The resulting reports provided focused strategies for tackling specific issues, with technical information geared toward professional and municipal audiences. They reflected the contemporary popularity of the City Practical movement, a function-focused relative of the City Beautiful movement, which sought to quantify and fix the ills of modern urban systems. Without integration into more comprehensive plans, however, these individual reports had limited, if not sometimes contradictory, impacts.

In contrast, large-scale city plans sought to unite, coordinate, and systematically implement changes to multiple layers of urban form. Local arts organizations or newly formed government committees typically initiated such comprehensive planning since most municipalities did not yet have formal planning authorities. This unique dialogue between private interests and local governments reflected the growing appeal of City Beautiful thinking, which was primarily an urban political movement that encouraged the synthesis of urban utility, functionalism, and beauty.[37] Social reformers, architects, and politicians had come to recognize the interwoven nature of physical, social, economic, and aesthetic problems and rallied behind urban planning and civic-minded architecture as tools to impact all of these conditions.

In Chicago, private interests—commercial, mercantile, and artistic—cultivated the city's famed 1909 city plan. Soon after the close of the renowned World's Columbian Exposition of 1893, Fair Director of Works Daniel Burnham, upon reflecting on the clarity and architectural unity that made the fairgrounds so powerful, casually developed a scheme for eight miles of the Chicago lakefront from the Chicago River to Jackson Park. Burnham shared this classically inspired plan with friends in 1896, but then shelved the idea for almost a decade until momentum for a comprehensive city plan compelled him to revisit it. Two private civic advocacy groups, the Merchants Club and the Commercial Club, had flirted with sponsoring a major city plan in the early years of the century, but nothing materialized until three elite businessmen from the Merchants Club took personal interest in accelerating these efforts. In 1906, at the urging of insurance executive Charles Dyer Norton, railroad magnate Frederic A. Delano, and local merchant Charles H. Wacker, the Merchants Club established a committee to evaluate the city's condition and to provide suggestions for how it might be improved. The committee wanted Burnham to lead their effort, but as a member of the Commercial Club he felt bound to support that organization's similar endeavors. This conflict was resolved when the two clubs merged in 1907 and Burnham began to work in earnest. Norton, Delano, and Wacker became the core of the committee aiding Burnham and Bennett's design work, with Norton as chairman, Delano as vice-chairman, and Wacker as secretary. After three years of work, the Commercial Club presented the completed *Plan of Chicago* to the city in 1909, and the city formally adopted it the following year.[38] Thus, the roots of what would become America's most famous city plan began not with municipal government but with businessmen who sought to improve their city—with the obvious goal of improving their private businesses by extension.

Boston experienced a similarly homegrown, though more short-lived, planning initiative between 1909 and 1912 called Boston-1915. Local department-store magnate Edward A. Filene headed a group of select Boston leaders, including future Supreme Court Justice Louis D. Brandeis, in initiating a comprehensive planning effort. Filene's group felt that the city's economic, social, political, and physical problems needed to be addressed as a whole, and sought to establish a targeted vision for Boston five years in the future. "Boston-1915" invited sixteen hundred agencies to send representatives to the effort and then divided these delegates into specialized subcommittees for each of the four areas.[39] They wanted to publish a full city plan by 1912 that would synthesize the specialized sub-reports, offering literal direction on how improvements should proceed and visual imagery of Boston's future. The Boston-1915 movement took particular inspiration from the recent planning accomplishments in Chicago, going so far as to invite Daniel Burnham to speak at their exposition's opening ceremonies—an offer he declined.[40] Instead, the 1909 inaugural celebration featured, among others, Jane Addams of Chicago's Hull House, who applauded Boston's efforts at self-reflection and encouraged a careful balance between social reform and physical beautification. During the exposition's one-month term visitors enjoyed exhibits on Boston's previous accomplishments, those of other cities, new achievements in flight and transportation, and expert guest lectures on topics including public water consumption, sanitation, schools, labor conditions, women's suffrage, and urban congestion.[41] The exposition reflected the purest ideals of the City Beautiful movement, believing in the power of methodical analysis and planning to generate greater social and idealistic cohesion within the community and civic beauty and grandeur in its constructed fabric.

As in Chicago, these private efforts ultimately provoked responses from local officials. In the spring of 1911, the Massachusetts legislature authorized Governor Eugene N. Foss to appoint a temporary committee to investigate the need for a metropolitan plan. Foss selected Filene, architect Randolph Coolidge Jr., and landscape architect and planner John Nolen to tackle this charge. Their report, submitted to the legislature in January 1912, recommended the creation of a permanent metropolitan planning commission for the city of Boston and thirty-seven surrounding cities and towns. The proposed regional commission would have the authority to review and postpone plans pending evaluation of their relationship to larger metropolitan planning goals. However, this type of authority unnerved legislators from suburban communities, who felt that their autonomy would be threatened by such an arrangement. Thus, when the bill for the metropolitan planning commission came up for a vote in April 1912, the legislature failed to pass it, effectively ending the Boston-1915 movement.[42] Mayor Fitzgerald ultimately did create a city planning board in 1914, which guided a series of neighborhood assessments, plans, and studies of individual urban issues throughout the 1910s and 1920s. In the late 1920s, the city planning board initiated the comprehensive transportation plan that formally proposed an elevated north-south express highway as a critical road improvement—what would become the Central Artery.

In contrast to Chicago and Boston, New York's comprehensive planning efforts originated from within the city's municipal government, though ultimately also incorporated private efforts. In 1903, Mayor Seth Low established the New York City Improvement Commission, though its background reveals it as the concomitant creation of municipal leadership, private lobbyists, and media pressure. Low was an active member of New York's Municipal Art Society, a civic advocacy group established in 1893 to promote excellence in architecture and urban planning. The Municipal Art Society had independently studied many aspects of the city's physical conditions and had successfully initiated a dialogue about urban progress among the city's other private societies for merchants, trade, manufacturing, sculpture, painting, and architecture. Upon his election, Low sought to install a similar model of collaboration and forethought in the city's government. Low's agenda coincided with national acclaim for Washington, DC's McMillan Commission and its efforts to beautify the nation's capital, and also with local newspaper editorials urging similar urban improvement efforts in New York.[43] Low authorized the commission in December 1903, and the group rushed first to prepare a preliminary report for 1904, and then submitted a final report in 1907. These documents outlined what the commission saw as the city's most pressing needs, including upgrades to shipping piers, the creation of parks along the upper northwest corner of Manhattan, streamlining of traffic on Fifth Avenue, planning of public buildings, and, notably, debate about an elevated street along the Hudson River waterfront.[44] Despite these lofty intentions, however, few of the commission's recommendations saw realization. Cost was the main reason for their failure, though the density of the existing landscape and the challenges of implementing such large-scale change also hampered their success. This notwithstanding, the 1904 and 1907 reports established benchmarks to which successive planning efforts would continually refer.[45]

In addition to the real planning issues recorded in all three cities, sentiments of economic competition and municipal boosterism significantly fueled improvement initiatives. In Chicago, the *Plan of Chicago*'s sponsorship by the Merchants and Commercial Clubs inherently reflected the interdependence of the city's physical form and its economic prowess, and the text repeatedly reinforced this by likening Chicago's commerce-driven growth to city planning benchmarks including ancient Egypt, Napoleon's remaking of Paris, and the McMillan Commission's contemporary plan for Washington, DC.[46] The Chicago Plan Commission, a municipal committee organized to review and recommend implementation of specific *Plan of Chicago* projects, encouraged such comparisons in its systematic campaign to promote the plan and cultivate public enthusiasm for its success. Chairman Charles H. Wacker and public relations expert Walter D. Moody organized publications, lectures, exhibitions, slide presentations, and even school curricula that exposed multiple age groups and levels of society to the plan's agenda. These efforts combated early public perceptions of Burnham's scheme as impractical and overly idealistic, and instead stressed the useful improvements and conveniences that comprehensive planning would bring to the city.[47] Wacker, Moody, and Plan Commission Office Manager Eugene Taylor delivered nearly five hundred public lectures about the *Plan of Chicago* between 1909 and 1919, with roughly thirty-five lectures annually through the 1920s.[48] These presentations, paired with the Chicago school system's adoption of Walter Moody's textbook, *Wacker's Manual of the Plan of Chicago*, ensured that Chicago's public was thoroughly and repeatedly exposed to the salvation promised by comprehensive urban planning.[49]

Boston's planning efforts reveal similar positioning regarding municipal vitality and competition. In 1906, a report by the Boston Society of Architects' Committee on Municipal Improvement recorded many of Boston's accomplishments but also outlined specific areas for enhancement that it qualified through comparisons to other cities' planning efforts. Using examples as diverse as Budapest, Rio de Janeiro, London, St. Louis, Cleveland, and New York, the report positioned Boston as out of step with contemporary developments.[50] The committee used such comparisons to lobby for the appointment of a government commission to more thoroughly address their areas of inquiry—something that materialized in 1907 with the creation of a collaborative city-state commission called the Joint Board on Metropolitan Improvements.[51]

In the following years, Boston leaders took increasing interest in other cities' improvement efforts. The Boston-1915 movement reflected this sentiment, as did Boston mayor Andrew J. Peters's 1920 request to the Boston City Planning Board to assemble a report on large municipal improvements being made by other cities. The board's 1921 response cataloged the programmatic, geographic, and financial statistics for more than a dozen major cities and included brief synopses of happenings in even more locations. The board used these findings to advocate for a comprehensive city plan for Boston. Mayor James M. Curley responded by appropriating funds to hire an outside expert to guide the development of a comprehensive plan, and in 1922 the city of Boston retained Nelson P. Lewis, chief engineer of the Board of Estimate and Apportionment of New York City, as its consultant.[52] Hiring Lewis, who was instrumental in the development of New York's planning and zoning policies during these years, showcased Boston's efforts to match the level of achievement modeled elsewhere and foreshadowed the spread of specific planning ideologies across many diverse locations.

In Lewis's hometown of New York City, city planning pursuits reflected municipal pride more than concerned competition. New York leaders were not as insecure about their city's commercial, mercantile, or artistic future as their counterparts in Chicago and Boston. Instead of taking inventory of accomplishments in other locations, New York's documents tended to use the city's recent achievements as fuel for future progress. This was true of a 1914 report by the newly established Committee on the City Plan, founded to coordinate improvement efforts being conducted by distinct municipal departments. Its status report carefully recounted previous comprehensive planning efforts, outlined the individual projects completed thus far, and positioned both as object lessons for further growth, effectively using the city's own evolution as evidence of the preexisting ingenuity and strength necessary for future successes.[53]

A major byproduct of infrastructure and economic-oriented planning discussions was the institutionalization of new local planning authorities and the creation of professional planning organizations. New Haven and Hartford, Connecticut, established the nation's earliest city planning agencies in 1907, with similar offices following in Chicago in 1909 and Boston in 1914.[54] Though their scope of responsibility and enforcement varied, such municipal sanction was a pivotal turning point for most cities, leading to more coordinated planning and design efforts for long-term change. The profession of city planning saw similar formalization at this time, including the 1909 founding of the National Conference on City Planning, an annual meeting that cultivated a dialogue among the myriad of professionals working on planning issues. Harvard University offered the first course in city planning at an American university in the same year. New planning periodicals also began to appear, including *The Survey* (1909), *American City* (1909), and *National Municipal Review* (1912).[55] Further professional credence came with the founding of the American City Planning Institute (ACPI; later the American Institute of Planners) in 1917. Comparable professional organizations for architects and landscape architects dated to the nineteenth century, and while the National Conference on City Planning had provided an annual event for exchanging ideas, it did not provide the year-round connectivity afforded by a professional association. The ACPI filled this void. Its fifty-two charter members reflected the diversity of vocations working in city planning, including landscape architects, engineers, attorneys, architects, realtors, publishers, economists, tax specialists, educators, public officials, housing reformers, and writers. Key figures among these founding members included Nelson P. Lewis (an engineer), Edward Bassett (an attorney), Robert Whitten (a statistician), and Edward H. Bennett (an architect), each of whom would play pivotal roles in the subsequent design of elevated highways for New York, Boston, and Chicago. Harvard University provided the profession with further authority as an academic discipline when it established a School of City Planning in 1929. These events contributed to a steady nationwide increase in city planning initiatives in the 1910s and 1920s, culminating in countless official city plans by the late 1920s.[56]

The final layer of this mounting urban planning dialogue derived from the specific consultants who propagated certain approaches to architecture and urban design. In each of the cities profiled here, key personalities from one location repeatedly consulted for others, thereby replicating planning approaches or even specific design ideas in multiple locations. Civil engineer Nelson P. Lewis (1856–1924), served the city of New York as chief engineer of the Board of Estimate and Apportionment between 1902 and 1920. During this time he also served as an advisory member of the New York City Improvement Commission when it authored its 1904 and 1907 municipal improvement reports, served on the New York Heights of Building Commission that initiated the city's 1916 zoning ordinance, and authored his own book on modern city planning. In his book, and in his other official reports for the city, Lewis repeatedly advocated for the centrality of engineering in city planning, positioning the municipal engineer as the "first man on the ground," with the unique responsibility of laying the groundwork for rational city building and coordinating the collaborative efforts of architects, landscape architects, and the like.[57] Relative to the automobile's impact on urban conditions, Lewis maintained that careful planning and street improvements could ease traffic congestion without discouraging automobile use. His desire for efficiency of movement and minimal disruption to the urban fabric led to his support for an elevated highway along Manhattan's western waterfront, a sentiment he presented to the National Highway Traffic Association in 1920. After Lewis left New York's employ, he served as director of physical surveys for the Russell Sage Foundation's *Regional Plan of New York and its Environs*, and from 1922 until his death in 1924, advised Boston and its City Planning Board on the development of zoning laws and a city plan.[58]

Two other New York-based consultants advised Boston leaders in the 1920s and 1930s, again promoting the overlap of key ideas and organizations. The first was Edward M. Bassett (1892–1948), a lawyer and former U.S. congressman (1902–1905) who was an integral member of city planning and zoning commissions in Brooklyn and Manhattan during the 1910s and 1920s, including chairman of the New York Heights of Building Commission, and with Lewis, a founding member of the American City Planning Institute. Thanks to his legal background, Bassett favored methodical urban growth through city and state regulation. This skill brought him to Boston in 1923, when he briefly advised the City Planning Board on legislation limiting local building heights. Bassett visited cities in every state as an external expert and advisor, and later authored multiple books on city planning.[59]

In the 1910s Bassett worked closely with the consultant who would play the most pivotal role in highway planning for Boston in the following decade, Robert H. Whitten (1873–1936). With a background in law and statistics, Whitten began as the secretary to the City Planning and Zoning Commission of New York in 1914, and quickly gained experience and notoriety. He worked as a planning consultant for the city of Cleveland from 1918 to 1921, culminating in the publication of a comprehensive guide for street development, *The Cleveland Thorofare Plan* (1921). Whitten authored similar plans for Atlanta (1922) and Providence (1926) before the Boston City Planning Board hired him as their advisor in 1927. In professional presentations, journal articles, and consulting reports, Whitten presented street traffic as the largest threat to civic vitality because of its reverberating effects on the pace, efficiency, and ultimate success of local economies. While aware of the daunting financial implications of large-scale street modifications, Whitten positioned such modernizing efforts as integral to the longevity of any city. His 1930 report for Boston, the *Report on a Thoroughfare Plan for Boston*, proposed a two-level express street as just such a fundamental improvement. This road was to run along a north-south axis, connecting main gateways to the city and bypassing centers of congestion. To support this concept, Whitten touted the achievements of similar express roads, notably sending pictures of New York's recently completed West Side Elevated Highway to the Boston City Planning Board.[60] Even as Whitten's proposal lingered in Boston for more than twenty years before its realization as the Central Artery, successive publications and presentations of this ideal elevated urban expressway gained great exposure for Whitten and his consulting practice. He became heavily involved with preparation of the Russell Sage Foundation's *Regional Plan of New York and Its Environs*, working with Edward Bassett and Thomas Adams to author two sections on neighborhood planning and the development of unbuilt areas.[61] Through this progression, Boston became both a beneficiary of and further inspiration for Whitten's growth as a planning professional and his propagation of highway-focused planning ideals.

In the realm of traffic analysis, Miller McClintock (1894–1960) provided a similarly recurrent source of advice for American cities. A former English teacher, McClintock launched a new career studying municipal government and urban traffic, and received a Ph.D. from Harvard in 1924. Soon thereafter he established the Bureau for Street Traffic Research—initially founded at UCLA but subsequently transferred to Harvard in 1925. McClintock brought a focused academic and scientific approach to traffic analysis that was especially appealing to municipal leaders seeking authoritative advice for their congestion woes. He authored traffic reports for Los Angeles (1924), Chicago (1926 and 1932), San Francisco (1927, 1931, and 1937), Providence (1928), Boston (1928), Washington, DC (1930), and Kansas City (1930) in quick succession, while also authoring countless articles in both professional journals and mainstream newspapers. McClintock offered a decidedly pro-automobile approach and felt that their fluid movement could be accomplished with new traffic regulations, better parking, the separation of pedestrian and automotive traffic, and the staggering of retail and commercial business hours. His 1928 report for Boston focused on these types of regulatory measures for traffic relief. But later, McClintock favored elevated highways as critical components of traffic management in other cities. His 1932 suggestions for Chicago included major elevated highways stretching west, northwest, and southwest from the Loop; and his proposals for San Francisco included twenty-six miles of elevated roads leading to and around its downtown core. McClintock saw elevated highways as economic necessities, minimizing disruption to the existing urban fabric while providing uninterrupted passage for huge volumes of traffic. Through his prolific consulting practice, McClintock brought this ideology to many diverse locations, reinforcing enthusiasm for elevated roads as complimentary components to regulatory traffic management approaches.[62]

If McClintock demonstrates the growth and transmission of traffic planning ideas, then Daniel Burnham represents a similar pattern for architecture and urban planning. Trained through a series of apprenticeships, Burnham (1846–1912) gained critical acclaim for the succession of Chicago skyscrapers that he designed with his partner John Welborn Root in the last quarter of the nineteenth century. His appointment as director of works for the 1893 World's Columbian Exposition in Chicago infused his career with new energy and national prominence. His leadership for the exposition demonstrated the functional and aesthetic rigor that comprehensive planning could bring to the creation of an entire city—albeit a temporary one—and marked a critical moment in American architectural history. The completed fairgrounds stressed clear, axial organization of spaces, monumentality, and classically based architectural unity, and fueled mounting enthusiasm for City Beautiful planning nationwide. Its organizational clarity, efficient infrastructure, and visual cohesion established Burnham's repute as a desirable expert on city planning.

Between the closing of the fair and his death in 1912, Burnham authored a number of city plans himself and advised many other communities on general planning efforts. Part of this prominence derived from his service as president of the American Institute of Architects from 1893 to 1894, in which capacity he lobbied for improving the quality of federal architecture. This national perspective made him a logical choice to head Michigan senator James McMillan's Senate Park Commission, which formed in 1901 to outline a plan for the national capital's future. This role not only reinforced Burnham's national reputation but also codified the American public's awareness of urban planning. Following the completed *Senate Park Commission Plan of 1902*, Burnham authored plans for Cleveland (1903), San Francisco (1905), and the capital of the Philippines, Manila (1905), which, though executed in fragments at best, stimulated Burnham's hometown of Chicago to revisit previous interest in a comprehensive city plan. The scope and publicity surrounding Burnham's 1909 *Plan of Chicago* only intensified his appeal to other communities. Cities including Oakland, Fort Worth, Atlantic City, St. Louis, Minneapolis, Detroit, Montreal, Nashville, Newark, Brooklyn, and Tampa requested his services between 1905 and 1912, though his failing health compelled him to decline all of these invitations. Burnham typically paired his refusals with pointed advice on a city's primary issues, and often recommended a colleague to fulfill the desired planning role—most typically his collaborator, Edward H. Bennett.[63]

Burnham's planning legacy was to reposition a city's commercial successes as inherently linked to efficient structure and transportation, principles that he used to underwrite the classical forms of his plans. Taking cues from European precedents and especially Baron Georges-Eugène Haussmann's redesign of Paris, Burnham's grand axial boulevards were as much about direct routes between key locations as they were about procession and architectural grandeur. This can be seen in what would become Wacker Drive, initially called the South Water Street Improvement in the *Plan of Chicago*. This two-level road was to separate commercial and local traffic, reducing intersections, facilitating easier freight deliveries, and speeding movement for both constituencies. Its Beaux Arts architectural treatment cloaked its inherently efficiency-oriented nature, becoming the road's primary legacy.

Following Burnham's death, Edward H. Bennett (1875–1954) continued to champion implementation of the *Plan of Chicago* (including Wacker Drive) and related planning ideologies. In fact, there is some evidence that Bennett contributed the major details of the Chicago plan, expanding significantly on the general guidelines given to him by his supervisor. Bennett joined Burnham's firm in 1903 as a fresh graduate of the École des Beaux-Arts and soon became Burnham's on-site manager (and collaborator) for the research and writing of San Francisco's comprehensive plan. Between 1906 and 1910, Bennett worked full time on developing the Chicago plan, coordinating the work of many different consultants and authoring much of the plan's technical analysis. Bennett became the Chicago plan's most lasting advocate, serving as city planning consultant to the Chicago Plan Commission until 1930, and in that role, supervising the plan's implementation—including the construction of Wacker Drive. Bennett established his own firm in 1910 and in that capacity authored comprehensive plans for Detroit, Minneapolis, Brooklyn, Denver, Buffalo, Portland, St. Paul, and Ottawa in the following years. Bennett also contributed to the Russell Sage Foundation's *Regional Plan of New York and Its Environs*, to which Edward Bassett, Robert Whitten, and Nelson Lewis, among a long list of other notable architects and planners, also contributed. The broad scope of Bennett's planning practice thereby made him an important vehicle for the dissemination and exchange of ideas regarding comprehensive planning and architectural style.[64]

As traffic congestion grew worse in the 1910s and 1920s, Bennett became an increasingly vocal advocate for limited access roadways, elevated highways, and other innovative traffic management proposals. In a presentation to the Fifth National Conference on City Planning in 1913, Bennett explained: "The most important consideration of the city plan, and one to which everything practically leads in the end, is the street system."[65] Bennett's advocacy for street improvements in Chicago included a multifaceted campaign for the South Water Street Improvement, including the preparation of traffic analyses and projections, evaluation of the road's impact on neighboring land values, cost estimates, and its architectural treatment.[66] In the late 1920s and 1930s, Bennett also urged Chicago to add raised sidewalks, covered arcades, and elevated roads to separate distinct types of traffic, maximize urban space, and minimize disruption to the existing city.[67] These activities reveal the nuances of Bennett's approach, using his Beaux Arts background to evaluate the organization and flow of a given city in a way that was distinct from the classical architectural treatment that he separately favored.

Bennett, Burnham, Whitten, Bassett, and Lewis represent some of the key personalities involved in debating and directing American city planning and architecture in the early twentieth century. Their diverse backgrounds in engineering, statistics, law, traffic management, and architecture reflect the complexity of urban planning as a discipline, calling on all of these subjects to forecast and accommodate an unknown future. Despite these distinct perspectives, traffic improvements—and, specifically, elevated roadways—factored heavily in accommodating common goals for modern transportation, urban efficiency, and civic beauty. As such practitioners lectured and worked in different areas, they introduced new constituencies to their ideas and created an urban planning trend that, separate from architectural style, favored constructed roadways as thoroughly modern and efficient solutions to pressing urban woes.

Urbane Urban Dreams

As planners and municipal leaders analyzed existing urban conditions and envisioned targeted solutions, literary and architectural circles grappled with the same issues from theoretical utopian perspectives. The resulting utopian projections became important social stimuli, reinforcing disillusionment with contemporary conditions and encouraging visions of a distinctly different future. In contrast to nineteenth-century utopias derived from social and religious principles, utopias of the late nineteenth and early twentieth centuries clung to technology as the major vehicle of social salvation and architectural innovation. As the popular and professional presses exposed the American public to such ideas, enthusiasm grew for actual urban improvement plans modeled on similarly idealistic foundations. This phenomenon played an important role in cultivating interest in elevated roadway schemes. Seen as technologically avant-garde and architecturally daring, elevated highways figured prominently in this body of utopian theory and inspired civic leaders and local architects to implement similar imagery.

Two categories of utopian projections are key to this study: utopian literature, including novels, stories, and illustrations in the popular press; and utopian architecture and urban planning schemes, disseminated through professional journals and mainstream media alike. Novelists dominated utopian literature before 1900. The contrast between deteriorating urban conditions and technological advancement in the late nineteenth century prompted writers to envision ideal futures where this disparity had been resolved. Well-known examples of such science-fiction novels include Frenchman Jules Verne's *Journey to the Center of the Earth* (1864), *Twenty Thousand Leagues under the Sea* (1870), and *Around the World in Eighty Days* (1873), in which Verne excitedly forecast the adventure and discovery that new and emerging types of travel might bring to the world. Edward Bellamy, in *Looking Backward, 1887–2000* (1888), focused on the social improvements that the future might hold, including a socialist government, equal distribution of wealth and goods, reduced working hours, and early retirement. In the twenty years following the publication of *Looking Backward*, nearly two hundred separate utopian (or dystopian) works appeared in America alone, evincing the country's appetite for widespread change—or at least the dream of it.[68]

Between 1900 and 1920, professional illustrators showcased utopian ideas in popular magazines. *Scribner's*, *Atlantic Monthly*, and *Harper's* frequently featured futuristic short stories, often accompanied by illustrations of urban futures full of dizzying skyscrapers, multilevel tramways, and personal airships. The emergence of popular science magazines in the early twentieth century reinforced this forward-looking enthusiasm. Intent on making science accessible to young readers, inventor and author Hugo Gernsback founded *Modern Electrics* magazine in 1908, which subsequently became *Science and Invention* in 1920. While certainly "light" reading, such magazines provided an important psychological outlet for readers, allowing them to project how contemporary changes in society might provide new opportunities and lifestyles in the future.[69]

The imagery in these publications forecast future cities as extrapolations of present capitalist growth patterns. Aerial views typically highlighted dense assemblages of soaring skyscrapers, some topped by landing platforms for air vehicles and others interwoven between multilevel highways.[70] Moses King's atlases of current and projected scenes in New York City, issued annually as *King's Views of New York* between 1896 and 1915, laced streets with multiple levels of elevated railways, connected ever-taller skyscrapers with spindly pedestrian bridges, and filled the sky with blimps and airships (fig. 2.9). Such scenes outwardly appeared as quite different from current conditions, but these features were already available, albeit at smaller scales, in contemporary American cities. King's imagined New York merely expanded existing development trends, thereby increasing the amount and density of urban construction, but not altering its fundamental principles.[71] According to the popular press at the time, the future of American cities was simultaneously different, exciting, and more of the same.

The architectural community, in contrast, developed utopian city plans based on new rationales for ordering space, people, and transportation. Though the heyday of such all-encompassing proposals was the 1920s and 1930s, isolated examples appeared in the first two decades of the twentieth century. Architect and patent

Figure 2.9 1909 cover of *King's Views of New York*. (*King's Views of New York 1896–1915 & Brooklyn 1905*. Compiled by Moses King. Reprint, New York: Arno Press, 1980, 1909 edition, 1.)

Figure 2.10 (facing page), Architect Edgar Chambless's conception for "Roadtown," 1910. ("New Idea of Building Homes." *Washington Post*, April 13, 1913: MS1.)

ROADTOWN, AS PLANNED BY WESTERN ARCHITECT, LOOKS LIKE SKYSCRAPER LAID ON ITS SIDE.

inventor Edgar Chambless (1870–1936) developed a proposal for a new type of linear city in 1910 that he called "Roadtown" (fig. 2.10). In a book of the same name, Chambless proposed to synchronize production, transportation, and consumption by turning the modern skyscraper on its side. This megastructure-like form would accommodate noiseless trains at the basement level, with apartment houses and commercial spaces above, topped in turn by an outdoor boulevard for casual recreation. Chambless envisioned using concrete construction methods from Thomas Edison that would afford efficient, fireproof structures, while lacing infrastructure for pipes and wiring throughout to provide for easy expansion and technological upgrades in the long term. Chambless argued that Roadtowns could be built cheaply and efficiently in America's undeveloped countryside, beginning where existing cities' transit systems ended, thereby linking new communities to established cities and giving residents the benefits of nature without sacrificing the commercial and social advantages of a dense community. Complete with a community-oriented social structure including cooperative kitchens, childcare, and stores, Chambless's model could expand infinitely across the country, saving people from the social disorder that he saw as cultivated by unplanned urban growth.[72]

The most well-known utopian plans of the 1920s came from modern architect Le Corbusier (1887–1965). A staunch believer in the power of organization to rehabilitate urban form, Le Corbusier dreamed of replacing the confusion of nineteenth-century cities with equally dense but rigorously organized new urban patterns. He explored these ideas in successive designs including the ideal "Ville Contemporaine" (1922) and "Ville Radieuse" (1935) plans, the "Ville Voisin" plan for Paris (1924), and published his theories of urban design in 1929 as *Urbanisme* (later translated as *The City of To-Morrow and its Planning*). Predicated on a clear social order with centralized authority to implement change, the "Ville Contemporaine" (Contemporary City for Three Million) scheme used zoning, skyscrapers, and streamlined transportation to systematize urban functions, increase urban density, and provide greater interaction with nature. A gridiron plan of four-hundred-yard blocks provided the framework for the ideal city, which then could be subdivided or combined to accommodate different spatial needs. A transportation terminal stood at the very center, flanked by the twenty-four soaring skyscrapers of the main business district. These skyscrapers sat within smaller parks that offered elevated pedestrian malls to house the city's leisure functions, including restaurants, theaters, and art galleries. Blocks of modernist housing for the business class formed a concentric ring around the business district, completing the rectangular hub of the city. Parks and nature reserves were to encircle the business district, providing refreshing foils to the man-made regularity of the rest of the city. Le Corbusier positioned industrial functions and warehouses on the urban fringes, and envisioned smaller satellite communities for the working class. This system unapologetically applied zoning principles to both land and people, imposing a rigorous organizational hierarchy that he thought would bring salvation to modern society. Le Corbusier reasoned that inhabitants of all social classes would feel fulfilled and content in an environment designed to maximize efficiency and anticipate worldly and social needs.[73]

The lifeblood of Le Corbusier's ideal city was its transportation system. An early automobile enthusiast, Le Corbusier paid special attention to streamlining automotive travel. He categorized urban traffic according to its purpose and speed and envisioned three distinct levels of specialized roads to accommodate each typology. The lowest level was to correspond to that of typical basements, inconspicuously accommodating heavy delivery traffic below the main street. Ground-level roads would accommodate local traffic carrying light goods, providing predictable connections to all areas of the city. Elevated arterial bridges between 120 and 180 yards wide were to compose the top level, running north-south and east-west across the city. Their crossing was marked by a great transportation terminal, which connected this automotive infrastructure to other modes of travel. The roof of the terminal was to accommodate aircrafts, while its lower levels welcomed railroad traffic from three levels of subterranean railroads, again distinguished by speed and destination (local or long distance) to maximize efficiency. Thus, the transportation terminal was the literal and functional center of Le Corbusier's utopian city. Not only did the terminal and its corresponding network of roads and rails provide the city's armature, but it also sorted and channeled the city's residents and workers into their specialized zones. The elevated highways were the only major visual signs of this system—fibrous tissue connecting the city's distinct parts. Cast as broad, uncluttered swaths in Le Corbusier's drawings, the elevated highways reached out infinitely to the surrounding landscape and confidently defined the city's four quarters. The simplicity of their forms and authority of their linear routes romanticized the ease of urban automotive travel. The persuasiveness of this imagery made it a recurring source of inspiration for subsequent urban improvement efforts—often with less glamorous results.[74]

American architect Hugh Ferriss shared Le Corbusier's conviction that modern transportation and modern architecture could affect widespread urban change. An almost exact contemporary of Le Corbusier, Ferriss (1889–1962) took particular inspiration from New York's 1916 zoning ordinance, creating ideal cities based on distinct building zones, setback skyscrapers, and an awareness of contemporary building and real estate practices. Beginning in 1922, Ferriss and architect Harvey Wiley Corbett collaborated on a theoretical study of how best to maximize space and profits for commercial skyscrapers designed according to the new regulations. In a series of resulting newspaper articles, Ferriss argued that since the new regulations forced architects to work within a common proportional system, the resulting buildings would showcase volumetric unity amidst architectural freedom. Ferriss crafted dramatic black-and-white illustrations to support this claim, projecting a city of regularly spaced setback skyscrapers stretching infinitely to the horizon, dwarfing pedestrians and interrupted only by the grid of streets. The contrast between these images and the reality of contemporary New York canonized the architectural modernity of the setback skyscraper form.[75]

Ferriss used subsequent drawings, public exhibitions, and a book to bring variants of these ideas to a broad audience. He and Corbett organized the 1925 Titan City exhibition, an endeavor sponsored by and displayed at the Wanamaker department store, which forecast New York's imagined evolution a century in the future. Visitors experienced huge monochromatic murals by Ferriss and miniature models lining the hallways, all of which supported an urban ideal of high-density, rigorously organized, and technologically empowered cities.[76] Ferriss's own book,

Metropolis of Tomorrow (1929), went even further in lamenting existing American cities as products of unconscious design and transformed what were typically piecemeal infrastructure solutions into the bases for a complete urban system. He outlined "a city of the imagination" of regularly dispersed skyscrapers united by proportionally smaller buildings, rooftop greenery, and a system of multilevel streets (fig. 2.11). Broad spaces between skyscrapers would eliminate the troubling pattern of congestion and deep shadows prevalent in existing building patterns, bringing light, air, and panoramic vistas to those in the towers. Like Le Corbusier, Ferriss used geometry, zoning, and gardens to organize his ideal city, creating distinct areas for business, art, and science grouped around a central park and linked by a network of roads. Building heights would be limited to six stories except at the intersection of the major roads, where towers of up to one-hundred stories would pair amenities like shops, restaurants, banks, and post offices with office space. Ferriss laced a multitiered transportation system through and underneath these buildings, offering aerial pedestrian walkways above ground-level local roads, subterranean express roads, and a subway system. The power of Ferriss's utopia lay in its systemic integration of these components as a complete urban system, removing the disadvantages of piecemeal implementation.[77]

Ferriss's work was closely related to that of his New York colleagues Harvey Wiley Corbett and Raymond Hood. Following his collaborative study with Ferriss, Corbett (1873–1954) became a vocal advocate for the potential of zoning laws and building codes to gradually improve urban conditions, publishing articles in periodicals including *Architectural Forum*, *American City*, *Literary Digest*, and the *New York Times* throughout the 1920s. Corbett's articles often borrowed Ferriss's drawings as illustrations and echoed Ferriss's enthusiasm for skyscrapers and multilevel streets as empowered by these new laws. Corbett's frequent and energetic writings established him as an authority on these matters, and he contributed this expertise to studies on traffic separations for the *Regional Plan of New York and Its Environs*.

While Ferriss's work remained primarily theoretical, Corbett completed designs for skyscrapers in many different cities, helping to codify this new commercial form as the defining urban architecture of the age. His most famous commission was Rockefeller Center, a collaborative project begun in 1927 by his firm and two others, including that of Raymond Hood. The project required comprehensive planning for six square blocks of urban real estate, a rare opportunity in which the designers synthesized modern skyscraper forms, modern transportation, and previous City Beautiful calls for grand civic spaces. The completed design included not only towers of commercial office space but also common open spaces filled with pedestrian walkways, gardens, and restaurants, and used subterranean passageways to connect them to one another. The towers sported Ferriss's and Corbett's favored setback forms, articulated with Art Deco ornamentation that reveled in the shapes and materials of the modern age. Rockefeller Center provided

Figure 2.11 Bird's-eye view of Hugh Ferriss's "City of the Imagination," 1929. (Ferriss, Hugh. *The Metropolis of Tomorrow.* New York: Princeton Architectural Press, 1986: 108.)

a full-scale model of what the future of American cities could be in the hands of Corbett, Hood, and their contemporaries, and encouraged the successive flurry of Art Deco skyscrapers that emerged in New York in the early 1930s.[78]

Raymond Hood's involvement with Rockefeller Center crowned a frenzied decade during which time he had risen from obscurity to become one of the preeminent skyscraper architects in the country. This shift came when Hood (1881–1934) collaborated with a classmate from the École des Beaux Arts, John Mead Howells (1868–1959), on the winning entry for the 1922 Chicago Tribune Tower Competition. Hood and Howells's new skyscraper design was historicist in inspiration but codified the symbolic power of an iconic skyscraper form. Following this commission they embarked on a quick succession of designs for New York skyscrapers, each further removed from eclectic sources and more focused on the power of singular tower geometries. Between 1924 and 1927, Hood developed a plan for recasting New York's zoning codes to further combat the city's physical congestion. Titled "City of Towers," Hood's scheme outlined an inversely proportional relationship between a building's street frontage and its height, rewarding smaller ground-level footprints with higher height allowances. He envisioned that a skyscraper's unused land could be transformed into wider streets, thereby helping to allay traffic congestion. Since this scheme did not require the wholesale destruction of existing cities, Hood hoped that graduate replacement of individual buildings would yield a landscape of skyscrapers spaced widely within expansive parks. Part of this scheme clearly recalled Le Corbusier's Ville Contemporaine, while the proportional relationship between street frontage and building height presaged zoning laws that New York would implement thirty years later in 1961.[79]

Hood authored a series of subsequent utopian plans in the late 1920s that played with variations of skyscrapers connected by megastructure-like bridges, or megastructure buildings containing industry, retail, amusement, and housing. These forecasts borrowed heavily from other designers (most notably Le Corbusier) and failed to constitute as clear an agenda for the future of urban America as those of his colleagues.[80] However, Hood's value lies in articulating the trajectory of urban utopian thought in the late 1920s and early 1930s. Hood was at the epicenter of New York's skyscraper boom and a friend and collaborator of other notable utopian designers. His designs for real buildings and his dreams of new urban forms emerged from a larger professional dialogue about the future of modern urban America.

While Hood, Corbett, Ferriss, and Le Corbusier sought new types of urban forms, Frank Lloyd Wright disliked the centralized authority and urban trend of contemporary America. Wright (1867–1959) saw the organism of the city itself as flawed and instead proposed a utopian vision of radical decentralization that prized individual autonomy and communion with nature. He argued that the modern forms of telephone communication and automobile transportation negated the previous limitations of geographic distance, making cities obsolete. This provided, according to Wright, the opportunity to develop a pattern of infinitely expandable rural settlement with an economy based on small farms, small factories, and community exchange. Wright first articulated these utopian theories in a series of lectures at Princeton University in 1930, then published them in book form as *The Disappearing City* (1932) and subsequently rebranded and republicized his ideas as "Broadacre City" in the mid-1930s.[81]

Broadacre City derived from Wright's steadfast faith in three things: nature, the family unit, and the automobile. Wright's scheme provided a perpetually repeatable pattern of rural development in which each individual owned and cultivated a piece of land. Wright echoed sentiments first articulated by Thomas Jefferson, maintaining that land ownership confirmed one's individuality in a true democracy because it removed the modern strictures of competition and capitalism that he saw as damaging. Families would cultivate small farms on each tract of land, yielding both their own food and a commodity to be traded with others. He cast factories and businesses in supporting roles to this basic family unit and maintained that people could work part-time in disciplines of their choosing. He argued that the flexibility of this model would remove the drudgery of work associated with typical economic systems and would provide the currency for a huge roadside market where people could socialize and trade yields from their farms. Wright punctuated each community with a solitary tower for local government—a lone urban form centering an otherwise low-slung, ex-urban landscape.[82]

The automobile facilitated Wright's entire system, providing a somewhat ironic mechanized foil to Broadacre City's dominant focus on nature and family. Wright viewed the automobile as a tool that empowered individualism and this new social order. In contrast to typical cities where pedestrian walkability determined the boundaries of community, an automobile-based society condensed miles of travel to mere minutes in time. He therefore scaled Broadacre City to the distances easily travelled by a car moving at sixty miles per hour. A network of on-grade superhighways provided the infrastructure for this, extending across and between individual communities. Wright endowed the highways themselves with little aesthetic presence: their rectilinear geometry regulated the landscape, but their scale was dwarfed by the even more overpowering expanse of the surrounding countryside. At the residential scale, automobiles manifested themselves in the number of garages appended to Wright's otherwise modest house designs. This was to be the singular external sign of social status in Broadacre City—an almost satirical footnote to Wright's otherwise ennobled scheme of social harmony.[83] Broadacre City expressed new technology and modern transportation in different ways than the utopias of Wright's contemporaries but was no less reliant on the potential of these advances.

Variations of utopian schemes that wrestled with technology's impact on America's future also dominated the world's fairs of the 1930s. Chicago's 1933 Century of Progress International Exposition, overseen by committee members including Raymond Hood, Harvey Wiley Corbett, and Edward H. Bennett, united the themes of science and business in its exhibitions. Chicago architect George Frederick Keck offered new housing prototypes of glass and steel that showcased a machined aesthetic and efficient construction and maintenance. Maverick architect and inventor Buckminster Fuller contributed his radical automobile design for the Dymaxion Car; and automobile companies including Ford, General Motors, and Chrysler presented automobile-inspired architecture and novel approaches to automobile manufacturing and refueling. These exhibits offered glimpses into promising futures where the drudgery of contemporary transportation, housing, and employment had been remedied by modern technology.[84]

At the 1939 New York World's Fair, industrial designer Norman Bel Geddes (1893–1958) synthesized these independent elements in a comprehensive projection of how science and the automobile would change (and save) the entire American landscape by 1960. His "Futurama" exhibit for General Motors showed a country networked together by a vast system of superhighways. These roads would allow travel at speeds up to 150 miles per hour and would connect to subsidiary feeder roads for local traffic. For the urban centers, Bel Geddes conjured his utopian contemporaries' enthusiasm for skyscrapers, elevated pedestrian walkways, and multilevel automotive highways. These ideas were presented to fairgoers via huge models that visitors saw from the safe perch of moving conveyors. The end of the ride deposited visitors into a full-scale model of Bel Geddes's streamlined future, punctuating his utopian dream with apparent reality.[85] As a major public event, the fair exposed a huge audience to the dialogue about architecture, urbanism, automobiles, and the future that previously had thrived only in professional circles. It crowned nearly three decades of mounting debate within the avant-garde design community and resolutely invited the American public to join the discussion.

In 1903, when *Scientific American* predicted that "four-storied streets" could be a realistic solution to New York City's traffic congestion, automobile usage was still in its infancy.[86] While more than twenty years passed before actual construction of an elevated highway in Manhattan, the intervening years saw city leaders, engineers, novelists, architects, and inventors nationwide spill much additional ink in proposing and revisiting various schemes for urban traffic relief. New regulations quelled early traffic disorganization, and engineering schemes tried to address individual bottlenecks with only mild success. Municipal improvement plans sought to broaden this discussion by implementing new agendas for street organization, urban aesthetics, and civic welfare. The literary and architectural communities tackled the dilemma from a similarly all-inclusive perspective, dreaming about how technology could save and reinvent urban life. Elevated highways figured prominently in all of these approaches. By separating distinct types of traffic from one another, these lofty roads would provide the organizational rigor desired by traffic engineers and municipal leaders alike. City Beautiful advocates lauded the efficiency of this model and integrated it into plans for widespread urban redevelopment and beautification. For novelists and architects, elevated roads synthesized the potential of architecture and transportation in the modern technological age. They provided the connective tissue to link skyscrapers, automobiles, airplanes, and superhighways in the urban realm, and in so doing acquired great practical and visual import. This multidimensional dialogue established the potency of elevated highways as transportation, infrastructure, and architectural models, priming the American population for their widespread implementation in the following years.

II

ELEVATED EXPECTATIONS

INTRODUCTION

> The reformed South Water street would no longer be a food market but a handsome shopping and wholesale street. One side of it—the side bordering on the river—would be taken away entirely and the whole street, from Michigan avenue to Market street, would be double decked. (1919)
>
> —"City Plan—South Water Street Improvement"

> The highway will be twenty feet above street level, affording ample clearance for surface traffic. The structure itself will be of steel, but will be covered with cement as a protection. The general design will, it is said, be simple but graceful. (1926)
>
> —"New York to Build Elevated Highway"

> Up in the sky will go some of our Boston traffic within the next two or three years. And there'll be no jay walkers to bother the drivers there. . . . The design will be what architects call "functional." That, in effect, means streamlined with no unnecessary doodads. (1950)
>
> —K. S. Bartlett, "Some Problems to Be Overcome before Boston's Traffic Goes 'Up in the Sky' on Aerial Highway"

Newspaper coverage of impending elevated highways in Chicago, New York, and Boston offered similar predictions for the transformative impact and physical presence that such new roads would bring to their cities. With wildly different topographies, economies, political leaders, and architectural advisors, such shared conclusions initially appear unlikely. But while their specific conditions varied, these cities each acquired elevated highways for remarkably similar reasons. Six shared elements illustrate this commonality. First, in all three cases elevated highways derived from transportation improvement proposals that had lingered for decades. Congestion in and around the future highway corridors had been growing since before the automobile age, and while earlier schemes catered to nonmotorized vehicles, they were easily updated to meet the new automotive era. Second, the targeted congestion in all three cities involved waterfront areas—in Chicago, a riverfront, and for New York and Boston, coastal harbors. These ports had wrought each city's commercial successes, but increasing quantities of goods and ill-suited shipping and transfer facilities had overburdened them. Thus, waterfront congestion was more than inconvenient for street-goers; it affected the commercial and mercantile health of each city. This explains the third shared characteristic, the conflation of freight and shipping interests with transportation improvement efforts. Initial calls for improved piers, waterfront streets, and freight transfer stations evolved into appeals for high-speed transportation connections to and from each city's waterfront. These discussions eventually extended to elevated highways.

The fourth common factor involved the legacy and limitations of railroad transportation. The evolution of railroad routes and technology had fueled local commerce and established public expectations for ease of movement. However, the privatized nature of the railroad industry, paired with deficient proximities to key port facilities, created problems in all three cities. Efforts to remedy these situations were arduous and slow, and as automotive technology gained ground, many advocated for creating infrastructure to support private automotive transportation instead. With the precedent of the elevated railroad, elevated streets seemed an exciting and modern way to bring this new network to and through dense urban areas.

The fifth commonality among the three cities was that elevated highways simultaneously (and somewhat contradictorily) drew on the unpopular precedent of the elevated railway while embracing futuristic notions of speed, independence, and multilevel transportation. Moreover, experts promised that elevated roads would spur reinvestment and redevelopment in dilapidated urban areas. Celebrated planning and architecture advisors synthesized these elements in master plans with seductive renderings for each city, and then relied on lesser-known local engineers and designers to finesse project details.

Finally, in all three cases, advocacy for and against elevated highways revealed special interests among civic organizations and distinct levels of government. Business interests typically favored elevated highway proposals because of their promised boon to local economies. Only when businesses were to be directly disrupted did they loudly object to project plans. Arts advocacy organizations in New York and Boston followed a similar pattern, rallying against the aesthetic intrusion of elevated structures; but when faced with their assured construction, they switched to lobbying for beautification and mediation efforts instead. In Chicago, arts and commercial organizations played a unique role since they jointly sponsored the urban beautification plan that included the multilevel street. They brought this proposal to the local government, who subsequently worked with them to implement it. In contrast, municipal leaders in New York and Boston initiated and championed their elevated highway proposals, but had to reconcile the accompanying financial and spatial implications with private interests and other levels of government. In New York this meant rectifying the highway's relationship to the Grand Central Railroad and to nearby improvements in Riverside Park. In Boston this involved negotiating between neighborhood groups and state government, each of whom had conflicting goals for the new expressway.

The following three chapters examine the design processes for Wacker Drive, the West Side Elevated Highway, and the Central Artery with these shared factors in mind. They honor the projects' distinct evolutions by addressing them individually but link them through the above thematic commonalities. In sum, this section maintains that while the existing conditions, planning processes, and design details varied widely, the three cities' road projects developed from parallel problems, shared hopes for urban revitalization, and a common belief in elevated highways as visible, efficient, and modern responses to these conditions.

3

BEAUX ARTS CHICAGO

> The Chicago River . . . has become a dumping spot and a cesspool; bridges of every possible style and condition span it at irregular intervals and at all angles . . . (1909)
>
> —Burnham and Bennett, *Plan of Chicago*

CHICAGO'S WACKER DRIVE is unique among this study's three subject roads in that the highway's design was part of a comprehensive city plan for urban beautification, not a piecemeal solution to pressing traffic congestion. That is not to undervalue Chicago's traffic problems in the early twentieth century, which were indeed significant. But the 1909 *Plan of Chicago*, which predated widespread automobility, took an all-encompassing approach to empowering all types of movement through the city while also beautifying the urban environment. Adoption and implementation of what would become Wacker Drive was therefore another step in an orchestrated progression of urban improvements. Due to its critical riverside location, double-tiered elevation, displacement of existing buildings and tenants, and ultimate automotive constituency, Wacker Drive assumed great visual and social import as an arbiter of modern urban planning approaches.

Wacker Drive's eventual site along the southern banks of the Chicago River represented all that was essential to the city's growth and success (fig. 3.1). A small frontier settlement in the early nineteenth century, the city had grown into a major mercantile and industrial hub. This metamorphosis was because of Chicago's key location on the shores of Lake Michigan and straddling the Chicago River, making it a natural midcontinental center of transportation, commerce, and communication. By midcentury, connections to Atlantic- and Pacific-bound railroads had cemented the city's importance and it could boast ten railroad trunk lines, three thousand miles of railroad track, fifty-eight passenger rail stations, and thirty-eight freight rail stations.[1] Chicago had become the gateway for goods and people destined for all parts of the continent.

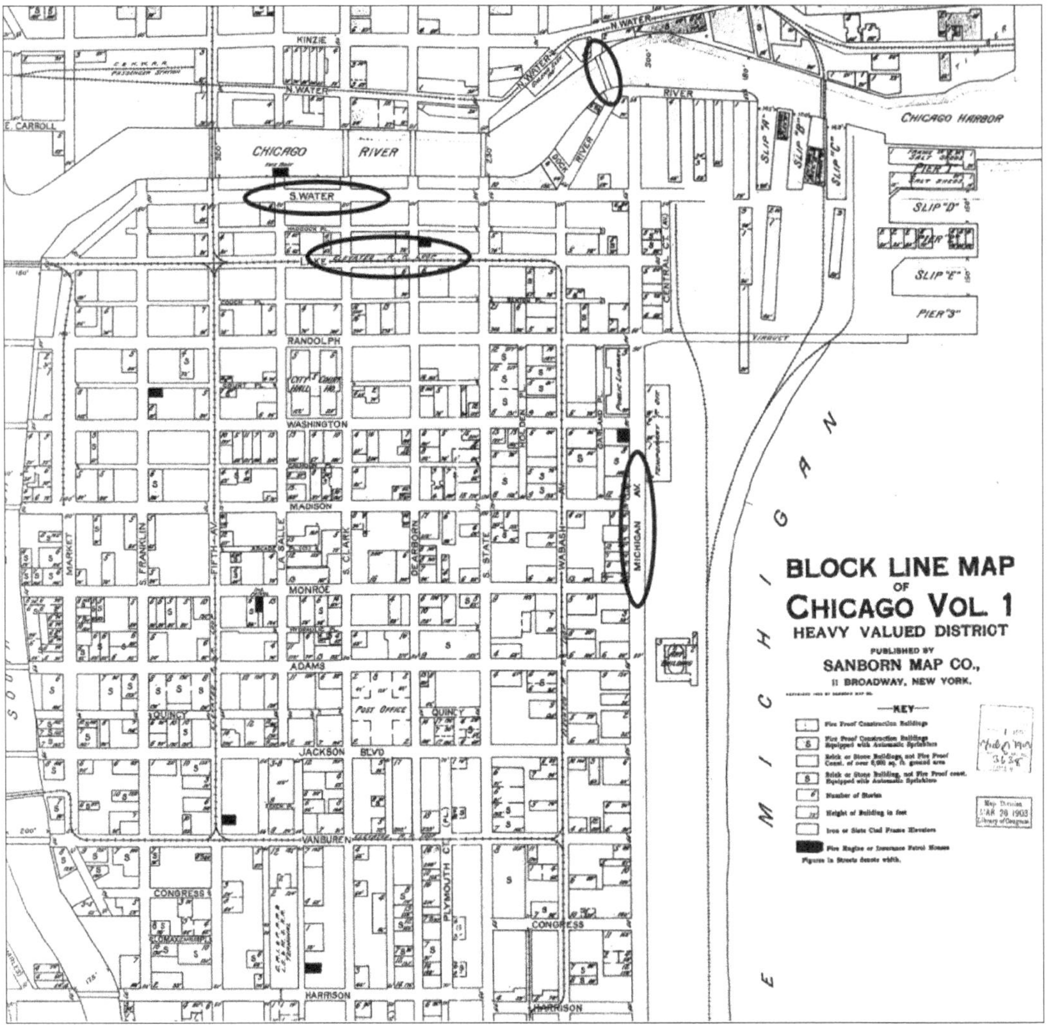

Figure 3.1 Map of Chicago's central business district, 1906. Markings added to indicate (clockwise from top right): Rush Street Bridge, Michigan Avenue, elevated "Loop" railroad, and South Water Street. (Sanborn Map Company, Insurance Maps, Chicago, Illinois. [Sanborn Map Company, 1906], Sheet 0C. Digital Sanborn Maps, http://sanborn.umi.com [accessed June 14, 2019.])

While so much of Chicago's national success stemmed from its railroad and freight infrastructure, local conditions depended heavily on the city's wholesale market on South Water Street—the epicenter of the city's food chain (fig. 3.2). Capitalizing on the street's proximity to nearby docks and shipping areas, South Water Street had long served as the city's wholesale market for fresh produce and poultry. Run-down warehouses and industrial buildings lined both sides of the street, and trucks and wagons daily flooded its confines to showcase their goods beneath awnings hung from the adjacent structures. In 1910 the *Chicago Daily Tribune* estimated that twenty thousand vehicles populated the district daily, transferring goods from area freight yards and delivering crops from beyond the city limits. Piles of vegetables, fruits, butter, poultry, and eggs lined the sidewalks and storefronts, with merchants and customers teeming throughout.[2] The density of goods, people, and activity made South Water Street virtually impassable for much of the day and left a mess of refuse in their wake.[3] Moreover, lines of waiting market-destined delivery wagons backed up beyond the market area and thwarted movement of trolleys and vehicles on surrounding streets.[4] Police Chief George M. Shippy tried to tackle this problem in 1907, proposing that horses and carts move in continuous loops up and down South Water Street, pausing only long enough to pick up and deposit their cargo. He argued that this would systematize the currently chaotic process of doing business at the market, allowing everyone equal access to desired goods. Though never implemented, Chief Shippy's proposal demonstrates the extent of the market's popularity and the real traffic implications of its site.[5]

Street congestion impacted other areas of the city, most notably in the Loop and along nearby routes across the river. Passengers from elevated railroads, streetcars, and passenger rail lines joined pedestrians, teamsters, and private vehicles on the streets and sidewalks of the Loop district, compelling the *Chicago Daily Tribune* to label this area the "Busiest Spot on Earth" in a 1907 headline.[6] Freight and commercial vehicles shouldered much of the blame for these conditions.[7] Officials proposed solutions that included the extension of elevated rail service, increased street regulations, parking prohibitions, and new through streets. Without coordinated action, however, such piecemeal solutions made little impact on the area's congestion.

Figure 3.2 South Water Street produce market, Chicago, circa 1906. (Library of Congress. Chicago, Ill.—South Water Street—produce market, ca. 1906. Photograph. https://www.loc.gov/item/2006679952/.)

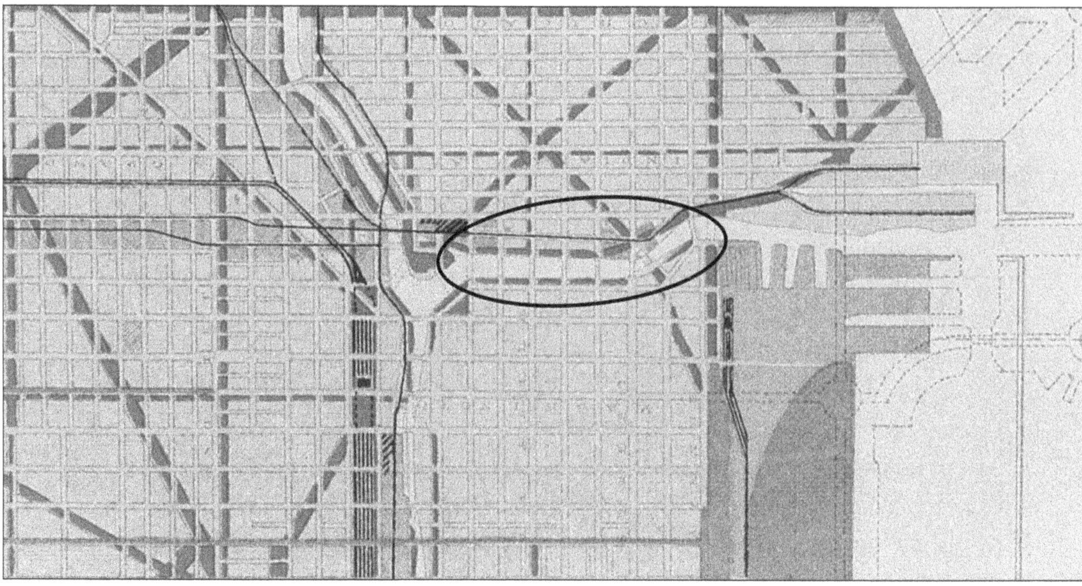

Figure 3.3 Map detail, *Plan of Chicago*'s proposed street widenings for central business district, with proposed riverside boulevards highlighted, 1909 (ellipse added). (Burnham, Daniel H., and Edward H. Bennett. *Plan of Chicago.* Edited by Charles Moore. Chicago: The Commercial Club, 1909. Reprint, Princeton, NJ: Princeton Architectural Press, 1993. Plate 111. Image courtesy Princeton Architectural Press.)

Given the mounting volume and concentration of street users, adequate links between the city's two halves on both sides of the Chicago River gained greater importance. Calls for a new, wide boulevard across the river dated to at least 1900, and the city council commenced a study of various solutions beginning in 1904. Most proposals envisioned such a connection in the vicinity of Michigan Avenue, located just east of the Loop and already established as an important center for commercial, arts, and civic institutions.[8] As Daniel Burnham and Edward Bennett began to prepare the Chicago plan in 1906, they naturally integrated issues already under discussion, including this proposed north-south link. Their final 1909 report, the *Plan of Chicago*, merged the extension of Michigan Avenue across the Chicago River with a comprehensive recasting of neighboring South Water Street (figs. 3.3–3.4). These new east-west and north-south traffic corridors would encircle the business district, simultaneously upgrading access to the urban core and providing an aesthetic blueprint for the entire waterfront.

Three critical beliefs underwrote Burnham and Bennett's recommendations for the Chicago riverfront. First, they recognized the Chicago River's integral role in the city's growth and success, for it "gave to the city its location and fostered its commerce."[9] Second, they regretted the ad hoc development and lack of upkeep along its shores. Finally, they argued that comprehensive planning could bring order, functionality, and beauty to the river's banks.[10] These ideals informed their formal introduction to the scheme that would ultimately become Wacker Drive.

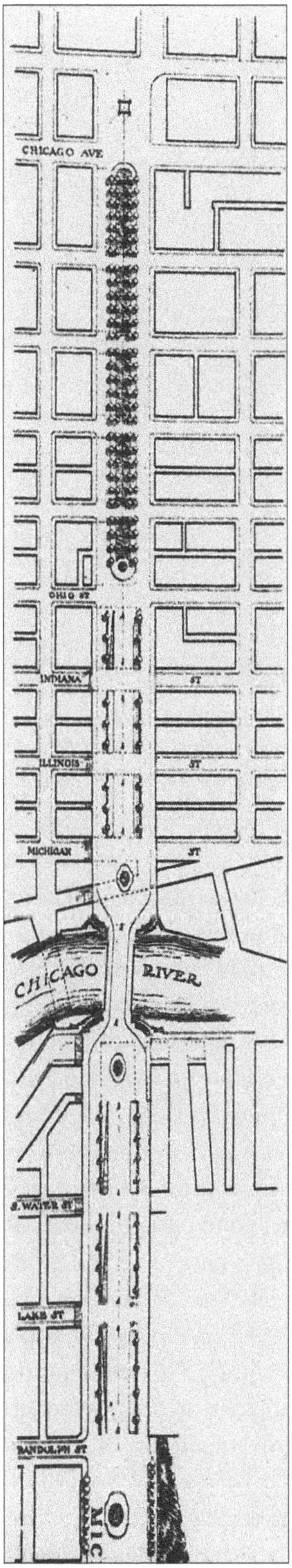

Figure 3.4 Michigan Avenue widening, as cast in *Plan of Chicago*, plate 113. (Burnham, Daniel H., and Edward H. Bennett. *Plan of Chicago*. Edited by Charles Moore. Chicago: The Commercial Club, 1909. Reprint, Princeton, NJ: Princeton Architectural Press, 1993. Plate 113. Image courtesy Princeton Architectural Press.)

They proposed new boulevards on both sides of the river running from Lake Michigan to North Avenue at the north and Halsted Street at the south. These roads would "be raised above the normal traffic level in order to afford greater facility of circulation, and to allow warehouses to be constructed below the roadway."[11] After describing the resulting benefits for the area's traffic relief and mercantile congestion, the *Plan of Chicago* also touted the leisure component of the boulevards as offering "the most delightful route to the Lake."[12] Although the suggestion for elevating these new boulevards seems almost casual at first, the ramifications of such a choice were far more significant. More than simple traffic corridors, the new riverfront roads would be three-dimensional vessels for multiple components of urban life. They would create new travel corridors while sorting different types of traffic, providing better connections to existing infrastructure and redefining the riverfront's appearance.

Burnham and Bennett's accompanying illustrations provided appealing, if not also vague, depictions of the beauty and efficiency of this scheme (figs. 3.5–3.6). Renderings forecast shores lined with buildings of uniform heights and connected by a network of bridges and two-story riverside streets. This landscape offered distinct accommodations for each group of its users: loading facilities for boats that connected to lower-level streets reserved for freight traffic, which in turn accessed the basements of adjoining buildings; an upper-level road for horses, carriages, and a few fledgling automobiles; and a pedestrian promenade along the upper street.[13] Beaux Arts architectural principles defined the design's practical and aesthetic posture. The sorting and funneling of different types of users epitomized the essence of the École's focus on the organization of and movement through a given space. Its classical architectural vocabulary of rusticated ma-

Figure 3.5 Proposed arrangement of riverside streets and freight facilities, *Plan of Chicago*, 1909. (Burnham, Daniel H., and Edward H. Bennett. *Plan of Chicago*. Edited by Charles Moore. Chicago: The Commercial Club, 1909. Reprint, Princeton, NJ: Princeton Architectural Press, 1993. Plate 107. Image courtesy Princeton Architectural Press.)

sonry, arcades, and balustrades linked these different levels to one another, creating an orderly urban waterfront far removed from current conditions.

The idyllic nature of this imagery did not ensure the plan's implementation, and these riverfront ideas lingered on paper for many years. The Chicago Plan Commission, the official municipal body founded to review, develop, and champion projects outlined in the 1909 plan, focused its early efforts on building public support for the *Plan*—which really meant votes for bonds to finance gradual implementation of its proposed projects. The commission's first major project was the widening of Twelfth Street, an east-west road stretching from Lake Michigan eastward across the Chicago River. Burnham and Bennett had cast this road as one of the major boulevards to encircle and define the city's new civic and commercial center, and so its existing sixty-foot width was to be expanded to over one hundred feet. Voters approved financing for the project in 1912, but legal battles over property seizures delayed the start of construction until 1916. As ongoing litigation, World War I, and the need for additional funding repeatedly postponed completion of Twelfth Street until the late 1920s, improvements for Michigan Avenue and South Water Street gained momentum.[14]

The widening and extension of Michigan Avenue northward across the Chicago River established an important precedent for the South Water Street improvement.

Figure 3.6 Boulevard Link proposal (Michigan Avenue), *Plan of Chicago*, 1909. (Burnham, Daniel H., and Edward H. Bennett. *Plan of Chicago*. Edited by Charles Moore. Chicago: The Commercial Club, 1909. Reprint, Princeton, NJ: Princeton Architectural Press, 1993. Plate 112. Image courtesy Princeton Architectural Press.)

Michigan Avenue provided a critical north-south connection between the shores of Lake Michigan and Chicago's central business district, the Loop. Its northern terminus at River Street was just southeast of the Rush Street Bridge, which crossed the Chicago River and connected to the lake's northeastern shores (fig. 3.7). The idea of a simplified and enlarged north-south connection across the river dated to the late 1880s, with varying on-grade, elevated, and subterranean plans resurfacing through the 1890s.[15] In 1904 the *Chicago Tribune* reignited debate about Michigan Avenue when the paper indicted it and the existing Rush Street Bridge as unfit to

Figure 3.7 Rush Street Bridge, Chicago, looking north from Water Street, 1890. (Chicago History Museum, ICHi-093376.)

handle contemporary traffic demands. The *Tribune* called for the widening and extension of Michigan Avenue across the river and the construction of a new bridge. The newspaper's call-to-arms had great weight, and after further investigation the Chicago City Council approved this design and authorized the Board of Local Improvements to begin to acquire necessary properties along the road's widened path. However, these plans ultimately stalled when necessary legal ordinances did not materialize, and the project lay fallow until Daniel Burnham integrated them into his work on the *Plan of Chicago* beginning in 1906. Burnham advocated making Michigan Avenue a two-level street for the three blocks south of the river, which would then connect to a new two-level bridge. This bridge would funnel traffic across the river and deposit it onto an expanded version of the existing Pine Street, creating a continuous traffic corridor. Burnham revised this design in 1907 and 1908 and ultimately published it as part of the *Plan of Chicago* in 1909.[16]

As cast in the *Plan*, the new Michigan Avenue was to be a 246-foot-wide boulevard with a gentle incline rising from Randolph Street toward the river to accommodate a lower level (see fig. 3.6). The boulevard's main roadway would be divided into three sections: two lanes in each direction for through traffic, flanking lanes for turning and stopping, and central ramps to the lower street level. Trees were to punctuate the center islands and the bounding sidewalks, with great plazas marking the two sides of the new bridge.[17] As such, Burnham and Bennett's scheme united engineering-oriented strategies for transportation efficiency with popular ideas about civic beautification. In its separation of local from freight traffic, its sorting of surface traffic, and its provision of below-grade service access to adjoining buildings, the design echoed basic principles of railroad management and adapted them to urban road design. At the same time, the boulevard's proposed breadth, architectural regularity, and systematic order recalled that of Paris's Champs Élysées, a popular reference for City Beautiful practitioners like Burnham and Bennett. Michigan Avenue's grade separation would functionally ease traffic, while its broad street surface would bring practical and aesthetic poise to Chicago's shores.

In addition to providing traffic relief, the proposed boulevard was to recast the programmatic and architectural tones of Michigan Avenue and Pine Street. As they stood in 1900, both Michigan Avenue and Pine Street housed an array of warehouses, saloons, and industrial buildings. Michigan Avenue's geographic importance was already well-established, and Pine Street's connection to new speculative development along the northeastern shores of Lake Michigan heightened its import from a planning perspective. Planners sought to redirect the practical purposes of these areas to better match their strategic locations and their related prospects for growth. Office buildings, hotels, upscale retail shops, and banks were to replace the mundane functions that currently busied these streets, ultimately creating a new upscale business center outside of the Loop.[18]

With this programmatic reform came a new vision for architectural grandeur and unity. The *Plan of Chicago*'s portrayal of the new Michigan Avenue belied any of the street's existing architectural fabric, instead forecasting blocks of new commercial buildings with common heights, cornice lines, and classically based architectural vocabularies. The new bridge was to carry this parlance across the river, using rusticated stone arcades, balustrades, and four classically adorned towers to define the river's shores. The entire *Plan of Chicago* spoke in this architectural language, casting major road intersections, a proposed civic center, and a series of lakefront parks in the same manner. The most direct precedent for this unified vision was Baron Georges-Eugène Haussmann's recasting of Paris in the second half of the nineteenth century. Haussmann, driven by the political and social aspirations of Napoleon III, had systematically replaced the city's tangle of medieval streets with the huge boulevards, plazas, and uniform blocks of buildings that define today's Paris. Divorced from the social discord and urban disruption wrought by Haussmann's projects, Paris's resulting clear organization and unified architectural beauty set an appealing model for Burnham and his contemporaries. Especially when compared with the Chicago River's existing shores full of dilapidated warehouses and wharves, the *Plan*'s vision of Michigan Avenue forecast an idyllic new landscape for Chicago seemingly exempt from existing conditions and deeply steeped in the European Beaux Arts tradition.

The fate of the Michigan Avenue proposal remained uncertain for many years because of objections to two major facets of its design: its elevated component and its projected disruption to existing property. Local business owners along the existing Michigan Avenue were the most vocal opponents of the double-deck scheme. They formed an advocacy group called the Michigan Avenue Improvement Association and argued that the proposal was no different from a typical bridge viaduct. The association maintained that the elevated street and its accompanying supports would negatively impact the accessibility, visibility, and success of their businesses and only would benefit "automobilists and owners of carriages."[19] The *Chicago Evening Journal* agreed with these conclusions, calling the proposal "abhorrent to any citizen who does not happen to be a man of leisure and to own an automobile" and indicted the city council as corrupt in trying to make local property owners suffer the costs and consequences of the road's construction.[20] The *Journal* continued:

> Chicago does not want a viaduct over Michigan boulevard, or anywhere else, and the park commissioners should be prevented from building one. Such a structure would cut off the view of the lake and would be an eyesore to the whole city. It might be a convenience to automobile owners, but it would be an injury to the citizens as a whole.[21]

Despite these criticisms, none of the objectors questioned the need for immediate action to combat traffic woes or the specific necessity of a north-south thoroughfare. Instead they urged adoption of solutions like a tunnel under the river or a single-level boulevard and bridge. Advocates contended that these alternatives would be less costly than Burnham's double-deck design and would increase the value of property along Michigan Avenue.[22]

To combat such objections, the Chicago Plan Commission undertook a prodigious publicity campaign to generate enthusiasm for the proposed Michigan Avenue Bridge and to bolster general enthusiasm for the *Plan of Chicago*. This included publishing an abridged version of the plan in 1911 and releasing a focused plea for the Michigan Avenue project in 1913. Paired with the lectures, slide presentations, and school curricula, these efforts convinced Chicago's city council and its citizens to proceed with the double-deck iteration of the Michigan Avenue improvement. In 1913 the Chicago City Council passed an ordinance authorizing the project, and citizens approved a bond to finance construction in the next general election. Legal battles over the properties to be claimed for the road delayed the start of construction until April 1918, when demolition finally began. Construction took an additional two years, and the new Michigan Avenue Bridge opened on May 14, 1920.[23]

The progress on Michigan Avenue fueled enthusiasm for related street improvements from the *Plan of Chicago*. The Chicago Plan Commission's annual report for 1917 touted Michigan Avenue as just the start of major projects for the city and swiftly turned to the South Water Street Improvement as its next urgent focus.[24] The commission's chairman, Charles H. Wacker, pitched South

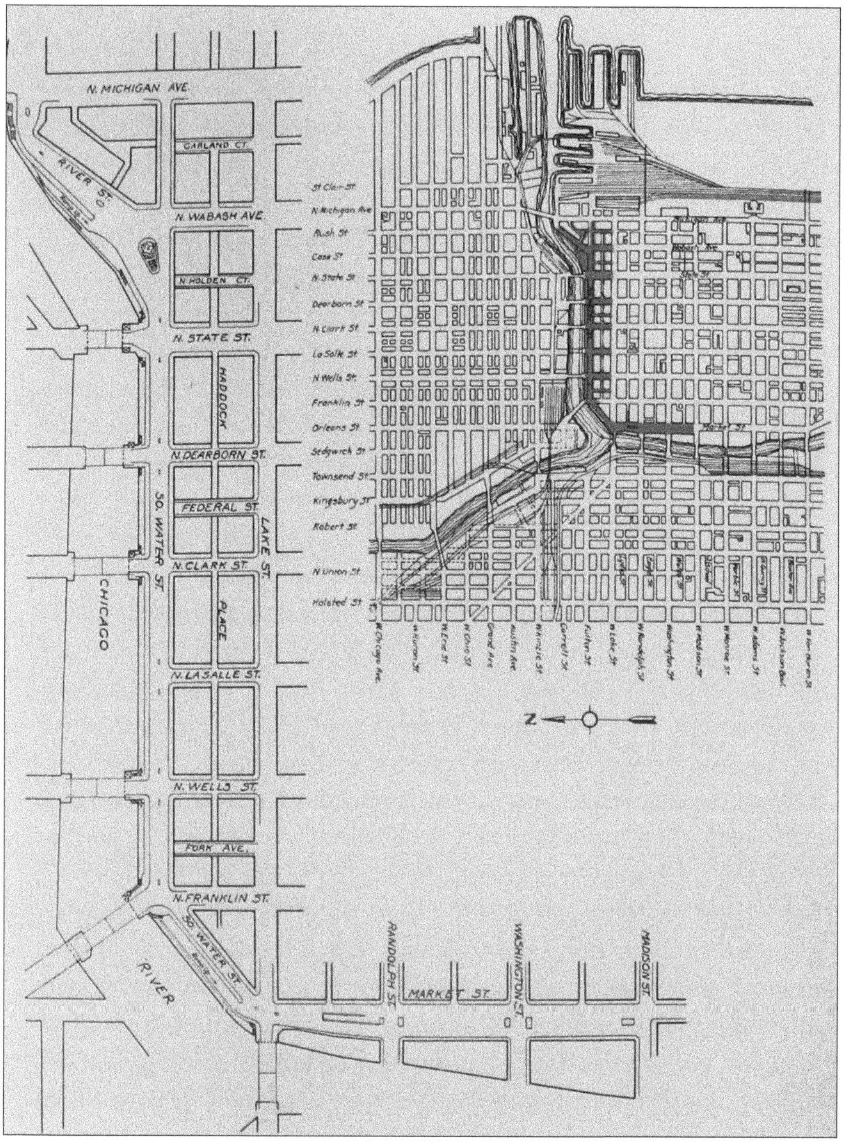

Figure 3.8 Map of proposed South Water Street Improvement, 1923 (shading in original). (Prior, J. H. *Report to the Board of Local Improvements: The Work of M. J. Faherty, Associates and Staff, 1915–23.* [Chicago]: n.p., 1923. Fig. 21, 14. Chicago Public Library, Municipal Reference Collection.)

Water Street's existing conditions as dangerous for the city, calling it "an economic waste; a burdensome charge on all the people; a drawback to Chicago's progress; obstructive to its prosperity; and a conflagration danger to the whole Loop district."[25] The Chicago Plan Commission issued a full report on the proposed project in 1917, establishing the basic design and the social, economic, and aesthetic arguments that would be used to lobby for its implementation.

Three issues underwrote the plan for reinventing South Water Street. First, the progress (and projected completion) of a double-deck Michigan Avenue was going to affect the elevations, connections, and traffic flows of adjoining roads. South Water Street ran east-west along the river's southern shore, crossing Michigan Avenue just south of the projected new Michigan Avenue bridge (fig. 3.8). This meant that changes to Michigan Avenue would directly impact its intersection with South Water Street. Similarly, because of new federal regulations for bridge types and heights, the city was building (or planning to build) at least four other new bascule bridges across the Chicago River. The structural requirements of this swinging bridge model necessitated greater elevations at their points of approach. South Water Street ran just south of the sites of these four bridges, meaning that it soon would face additional grade incongruities. Piecemeal accommodation of these bridges would inevitably produce a sequence of odd hills at each intersection—the antithesis of the civic grandeur and orderly traffic flow sought by city leaders. Instead, Wacker, Bennett, and the commission proposed to reconstruct South Water Street at a higher elevation suited to meet the new bridge connections. Rather than using earth to provide the necessary height, they reasoned that a constructed, multilevel roadway would provide the required elevation and the additional benefit of more road space. In this one act, a multilevel South Water Street would connect multiple civic improvement projects, heal ruptures in the street pattern, and increase traffic capacity along the river's southern shore.[26]

The second major factor fueling the South Water Street plan was the road's present condition and purpose. Chicago leaders saw South Water Street's current chaos and prime location as inefficient for the market and inconvenient for surrounding areas of the city. They reasoned that they could relocate the market to a bigger site near the river, provide better rail connections, and remove market-destined traffic from the streets of the Loop. They supported these claims with persuasive traffic statistics. City Engineer Henry A. Goetz contended that 10 percent of the daily vehicles in the Loop were actually related to the market. Furthermore, he reported that market vendors made four thousand daily trips between the market and local freight yards to fetch their goods.[27] The Plan Commission used these figures to underscore not only the congestion in the market itself but also its consequences for the surrounding business district. The relocation of the market, they reasoned, would remove the health and fire dangers of the existing market, improve traffic flow, and liberate the corridor for redevelopment as an expanded east-west thoroughfare along the river—a beautiful and poised complement to the adjoining Loop district.[28]

The Plan Commission's third argument for changing South Water Street rested on the contention that the street's existing conditions imposed significant costs on the citizens of Chicago. They first argued that the market's current site and operational patterns inflated the costs of goods. Since the existing market was located far from major railroad lines, merchants had to transport goods across the city over bumpy cobblestone streets and often in less-than-ideal weather conditions. This translated to considerable damage to or loss of produce en route to the market, which compelled merchants to compensate for their losses by raising their prices.[29] Secondly, the traffic delays caused by the market's congestion cost everyone in the city time and money. Engineer Goetz called South Water Street "useless" from a traffic perspective,[30] and Bennett cautioned, "Over-burdened streets result in stagnation of traffic and costly delays for which the consumer ultimately pays."[31]

The Plan Commission quantified these losses with persuasive statistics in its official reports and supporting publicity efforts. It projected that reclaiming South Water Street would save Chicago citizens $2,620,800 in wasted food, $1,624,800 in reduced handling of food, $563,000 in savings to businesses, $160,000 in reduction of street delays, and would generate $169,800 in new municipal revenue annually. The Plan Commission slickly implied that these savings of over $5 million were tangible enough to actually pay for the projected cost of the South Water Street improvement (just over $6 million). Mainstream periodicals repeated such figures, reinforcing the Plan Commission's assertion that the South Water Street project was the obvious practical and economic solution to Chicago's traffic and financial concerns.[32]

To solve these three categories of problems and reinvent South Water Street, the Chicago Plan Commission proposed a double-decked version of the roadway stretching from Michigan Avenue to Market Street (figs. 3.9–3.11). The plan suggested using eminent domain proceedings to seize all existing buildings on the street's river side, then to demolish them, and finally to use their sites to expand the road's width from 80 to 135 feet. The widened road's upper level would match the elevation of new neighboring bridges and would serve local, light traffic. Its lower level would host heavy freight traffic and would afford subterranean connections to the warehouses, manufacturing facilities, and railroad yards along the shores of Lake Michigan. It also would provide basement-level access to new buildings projected along the riverfront corridor. The design called for a second subterranean level, envisioned as a flexible space that could be used for either additional freight purposes or as a public parking facility for automobiles—both assuaging parking concerns and generating income for the city.[33]

Bennett envisioned a sheath of rusticated arcades, balustrades, promenades, and statue-laden plazas to unite these distinct levels and functions, creating an orderly riverfront façade for the multilayered thoroughfare. Edward Bennett's description of this treatment emphasized its architectural cohesion and rejection of typical highway design models:

> The upper level in no sense resembles an elevated structure. West from State Street it is carried on a masonry wall of fine architectural treatment with arched openings for lighting the lower level and surmounted with a granite balustrade, conforming to those of the new bridge approaches. The improvement will offer opportunity for a splendid architectural treatment in connection with the new bascule bridges, the first of which is being constructed at Franklin Orleans Streets.
>
> A scheme of decorative lighting similar to that of Michigan Avenue is a part of the plan.[34]

The visual distinction between this forecast of South Water Street and its existing condition could not have been more striking. The Plan Commission repeatedly

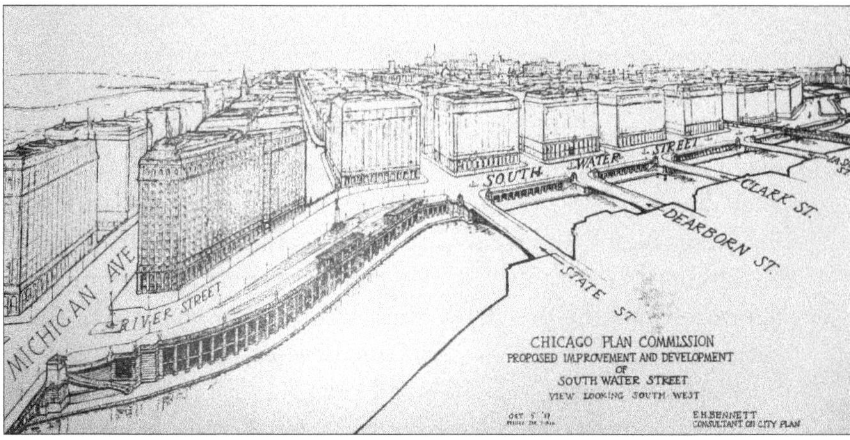

Figure 3.9 Proposed South Water Street Improvement, 1921. (Chicago [Ill.] Board of Local Improvements. *A Report to the Hon. William Hale Thompson by the Board of Local Improvements for the Past Six Years*. Chicago: Board of Local Improvements, 1921. 20. Chicago Public Library, Municipal Reference Collection.)

Figure 3.10 Proposed new riverfront elevation and projected buildings along South Water Street, 1922. (Chicago [Ill.] Board of Local Improvements. *Chicago Plan*. Chicago: Board of Local Improvements, 1922. 7–8. Ryerson and Burnham Libraries, Art Institute of Chicago.)

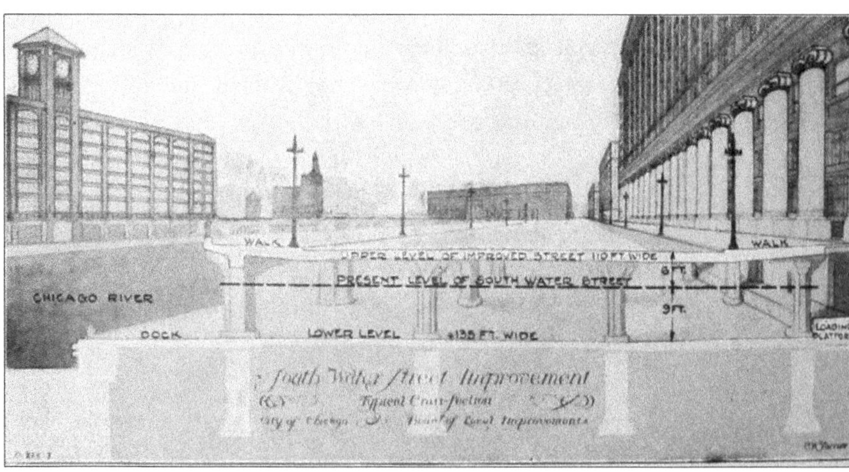

Figure 3.11 Sectional rendering, proposed South Water Street Improvement, 1923. (Prior, J. H. *Report to the Board of Local Improvements: The Work of M. J. Faherty, Associates and Staff, 1915–23*. [Chicago]: n.p., 1923. Fig. 26, 18. Chicago Public Library, Municipal Reference Collection.)

emphasized this contrast in its reports. It published pictures of the market's contemporary chaotic conditions, the related traffic congestion, and the decrepit masonry buildings that presently defined the riverfront's southern shore (fig. 3.12). The renderings of the South Water Street scheme magically healed these ills, instead showcasing a new waterfront of grand scale with tall, uniform buildings strung together by the arcaded march of the proposed double-deck boulevard (fig. 3.13). This transformed South Water Street from a transportation channel to an essential piece of the city's armature. It would act as building and thoroughfare, connector and border, mediating between the different components of the city's fabric. The renderings also projected the ease with which different constituencies would use the improved road. Boats moved fluidly through the river and unloaded their cargo onto broad loading areas along the road's lower level, and automobiles and horses and carriages had plenty of space as they circulated along the road's upper level and across the new Michigan Avenue Bridge.[35] South Water Street was to epitomize the City Beautiful, bringing functional fluidity and aesthetic bravado to Chicago's run-down riverfront.

Edward Bennett provided the main design voice and ongoing advocacy for the South Water Street improvement. As consulting architect for the Chicago Plan Commission, Bennett designed and promoted most projects from the *Plan*. He worked with Plan Commission engineer Hugh E. Young on the details of the project—though the basic parameters of the design had been established (with Daniel Burnham) in the original 1909 plan. Bennett and Young's collaboration reflects a common trend in the leadership and development of major urban planning projects in the 1910s and 1920s. Bennett, as the nationally recognized design authority, authored the major design elements and lent esteem to the project; while others—including Bennett's employees and Young, the local engineer—were responsible for the detailed articulation of the plan. Similar professional hierarchies later underwrote elevated highway construction in both New York and Boston.[36]

Whatever the architectural embellishments, the South Water Street plan had a very direct functional precedent in Chicago's elevated railroads. As discussed in chapter 1, elevated railroads arrived in Chicago much later than in New York, but they penetrated the city's core more deeply than in other cities. Without a subway, Chicago relied almost exclusively on the "El" for public transit to, around, and through the Loop until the mid-twentieth century. The El had contradictory legacies. It at once delineated the most convenient, and thus prestigious, downtown locations; but also inflicted its massive underpinnings, shadows, and noise on neighboring properties. These negatives notwithstanding, most discussion of the El in the 1910s and 1920s centered on streamlining and expanding its service, not questioning its very basic model for multitiered movement. Citizens expressed particular interest in additional through service. They argued that concentrating distinct types of users on dedicated cars would effectively increase the El's capacity and would speed passengers' arrivals at their final destinations. Therefore, Mich-

Figure 3.12 Existing conditions, Chicago River waterfront, early twentieth century, looking southeast from Wolf Point. ([Chicago River]. Kaufmann & Fabry, photographer. Edward H. Bennett Collection, Ryerson and Burnham Archives, The Art Institute of Chicago. Digital File #197301_151023-157.)

Figure 3.13 Proposed new riverfront conditions, from same vantage point as Figure 3.12. (Prior, J. H. *Report to the Board of Local Improvements: The Work of M. J. Faherty, Associates and Staff, 1915–23*. [Chicago]: n.p., 1923. Fig. 25, 18. Chicago Public Library, Municipal Reference Collection.)

igan Avenue and the new South Water Street, both as major thoroughfares and as multilevel streets, logically evolved from the local traffic segregation model of the elevated railroad.[37]

Despite its roots in the pre-automobile era, the 1917 publication of the *South Water Street Plan* coincided with surging automobile usage in Chicago. The city had one motor vehicle for every sixty-one people in 1915; ten years later, the ratio had increased to one to eleven.[38] This meant that the *Plan*'s approaches to civic beauty, organization, and circulation now had to accommodate the new variable of the automobile. However, since Burnham and Bennett had structured their plan to improve street-bound circulation, the automobile changed the means, but not the routes, of urban movement. If anything, the automobile congestion, paired with post–World War I reconstruction efforts, empowered the Chicago Plan Commission to lobby all the more stridently for implementing *Plan* projects. Chairman Wacker implored: "'That this plan, which will reduce loop congestion 16 per cent, is an urgent necessity, must now be clearly apparent to all our citizens.'"[39] Six months later the *Chicago Tribune* reported optimistically about the public's response to these ideas: "The plan of Chicago is taking citywide hold of the people as never before. In every quarter it is realized that the great public improvements the platform proposes should be carried to completion speedily."[40]

Official action did proceed quickly. In July 1919 the Chicago City Council voted to ask for public approval of $28.6 million in bond issues during the upcoming November election. In October, the Board of Local Improvements approved the South Water Street plan, meaning that if the bond issues passed the next month, the project could begin soon thereafter. The citizens of Chicago approved the bonds on November 4, 1919, which assigned $3.8 million to the South Water Street improvement. New assessments on nearby properties were to provide the balance of the projected $6 million cost.[41]

Despite such official approval, it would be nearly five years before construction actually began on South Water Street. Property owners on and around South Water Street created this delay with a series of objections and legal battles over the proposed project. Their complaints officially focused on the rightful impact and distribution of the project's physical and financial costs, but there were larger social issues in play. Weeks after the November 1919 bond approval, owners of north-facing property on South Water Street lobbied to move the market one block south of its current location. While their properties were not slated to be demolished for the project, the construction would prevent access to their buildings for a number of years. Instead of questioning the South Water Street improvement itself, they lobbied for the widening of an alley behind their properties that would give access to their buildings and provide a new site for market peddlers. They argued that it was beneficial to keep the market close to the Loop and that their alternate scheme would save adjoining property values from the depreciation expected from relocating the market to a different part of the city.[42]

The resulting discourse about this proposal revealed contrasting perceptions of civic space, class, and public welfare. The complainants clearly perceived the market as a public amenity and felt that preserving local businesses and maintaining the market's close proximity to the downtown core were in the public's best interest. But the Chicago Plan Commission, and specifically Chairman Wacker, argued that the public's welfare would be served best by recasting this whole area. The *Chicago Tribune* documented Wacker's indignance about the alley scheme, which he argued would thwart the efficacy of the South Water Street improvement: "'Imagine. . . such a condition as South Water street two blocks from the Grand Opera house in Paris—two blocks from Trafalgar square in London—or next to the Waldorf-Astoria in New York.'"[43] The intended absurdity of Wacker's comparisons reveals a perceived class distinction between the daily transactions of the city's mercantile population and the leisure activities of the elite. His comments also imply related value judgments about the different types of buildings used to support each constituency. The buildings of the Loop were likened to cultural icons of other major cities, with the South Water Street fabric cast as a second-class, costly, and disgraceful neighbor.[44] The lawyer for the South Water Street merchants tried to highlight the prejudice of such sentiments in his appeals to the Board of Local Improvements:

> Mr. Kraus told the board that 'certain gentlemen who don't like the smell of limburger cheese, and are not in favor of having the kind of chickens which lay eggs on streets near the loop' are backing the move to drive the produce market away from the downtown district.
>
> 'Charles H. Wacker, chairman of the Chicago plan commission, is trying to drive away a landmark which made Chicago as famous as Wall Street has made New York,' Mr. Kraus said.[45]

Despite this declarative stance, the Board ruled against the alley-widening scheme this very same day.

In January 1922, the Chicago Plan Commission sought to boost enthusiasm and action for the South Water Street project by issuing a new project profile. It urged immediate action on this improvement program, citing again the market's present wasteful conditions and the rejuvenation promised by the redevelopment scheme. But the new report also published updated cost estimates for the project that far exceeded those originally projected in 1917. Officials attributed this change to a broader project scope, which now included additional street widenings, and also to increased property values for areas slated to be seized for the road. This increase, paired with growing public awareness of plans to finance the project through tax assessments on neighboring properties, sparked a new round of objections that delayed the project for another two years.[46]

Jointly led by Loop business owners and another group of South Water Street merchants, this debate centered on the equitable distribution of project costs among local property owners and the City of Chicago. In the spring of 1922, Michael J. Faherty, president of the Board of Local Improvements, announced his intentions to finance the South Water Street improvement through new tax assessments on an area of properties bounded by Lake Michigan, North Avenue, Des Plaines Street, and Roosevelt Road. This segment included all of the skyscrapers in the Loop district, houses in the up-and-coming "Gold Coast" area north of the river, and manufacturing properties on the west side. Faherty argued that these locations would benefit significantly from the project's completion, thus justifying their liability for a significant portion of project costs.[47] The affected property owners called this approach "confiscatory" and "beyond the bounds of reason," and filed a lawsuit in September 1922 to contest Faherty's approach.[48]

This legal battle, which consumed most of the next two years, revolved around trying to quantify the benefits of the South Water Street improvement to different groups of citizens. The city wanted local tax assessments to compose 65 percent of the project's funding, with city bonds financing the balance. The angry property owners argued that the project would not only benefit them but also would improve conditions for the entire city. This, they claimed, meant that the whole city should shoulder a greater percentage of the project's costs. As litigation proceeded, there were repeated attempts to reach mutually agreeable settlements. Between November 1922 and January 1923, the two sides negotiated to equally split the costs of the project, but soon thereafter city attorney Samuel A. Ettelson convinced Mayor Thompson to renege on the previous settlement. Ettelson subsequently argued that the property owners should fund 100 percent of the project's costs, infuriating his opponents, who pledged to continue their legal battle indefinitely.[49]

In the spring of 1923, new municipal leadership changed the tone of these negotiations. On April 16, 1923, William Emmett Dever (1862–1929) became Chicago's forty-second mayor. Elected on a platform of reform, Dever immediately questioned the prior administration's previous cost estimates and negotiations about the South Water Street project. He postponed any action on the improvement pending full evaluation of the existing plans and available funds and subsequently retracted previous offers for splitting the cost with property owners. But despite Dever's reputed indignation about the property owners' continued pursuit, the two parties finally reached an agreement in April 1924. The city would carry 48 percent of the project cost through city bonds, with the other 52 percent gathered through tax assessments on the neighboring properties. This was a compromise for both sides, as the merchants had won a previous judgment where the court had mandated that property assessments compose only 35 percent of the project's funding. However, the city had appealed this ruling and was awaiting the judge's new decision when the parties reached their final compromise.[50]

Events moved quickly after this agreement. In June 1924 the citizens of Chicago approved $10 million in bond issues to finance the city's share of the agreed-upon terms, and the city began to acquire properties by late summer. In September local merchants filed two last-minute lawsuits trying to postpone the project's start pending the selection and preparation of a new market site, but their efforts failed. After seven years of debate, on October 2, 1924, the start of demolition of existing market buildings marked the official beginning of the South Water Street improvement.[51]

Notably, during all of these years of scrutiny for the South Water Street project, little discussion questioned its necessity or design. Most citizens, including the objecting merchants, agreed with predictions that the improvement would relieve local congestion and provide necessary connections to other important roads. Project supporters typically cast the Beaux Arts design as a virtuous foil to the dilapidated buildings along the present riverfront. In so doing, the road's constructed nature became almost more important than its role as a traffic artery. Such support speaks to the success of the Chicago Plan Commission's robust publicity efforts, which had entrenched the South Water Street program as an integral piece of the city's long-term plans. With a unified architectural voice, multiple levels, and direct connections to adjoining buildings, the new South Water Street would visually proclaim Chicago's leadership in modern architecture, transportation, and commerce.

4

ART DECO NEW YORK

> Traffic is now seeking New York, rather than New York traffic. It will continue to do so unless we should utterly fail to rise to our opportunity and provide increased facilities to meet a steadily increasing demand. Our facilities at the present time are about taxed to the limit, but the opportunities for adding to them are almost limitless. (1907)
>
> —*New York Times*, "Is New York to Lose Commercial Supremacy?"

NEW YORK'S WEST SIDE HIGHWAY MATERIALIZED after more than three decades of discussion about how to improve the city's Hudson River waterfront. Most of the years of debate centered on accommodating railroad and shipping interests, not those of automobile users. Manhattan's western shore had long been a natural focus for commercial and mercantile interests because of its geographic location. It served as a major port on the Atlantic coast and also welcomed intracontinental deliveries from New Jersey and northern points along the Hudson River (fig. 4.1). The Hudson River Railroad Company (established 1846) brought rail service to the area beginning in 1847, when it constructed a freight railroad line stretching along Manhattan's western shore from the island's northern tip to Canal Street. The only other rail connection to Manhattan was the New York Central Railroad's passenger line, which ran along the center of the island and terminated at Grand Central Station (fig. 4.2). When the New York Central Railroad and the Hudson River Railroad merged in 1869, they created a monopoly over all railroad transportation to and from Manhattan.[1] This monopoly significantly hampered the port's efficient operation and growth over the next fifty years.

The railroad monopoly aggravated the limited capacity of New York's existing port facilities. The port's finger piers were too small to accommodate many large shipping vessels, and ever-rising land prices and metropolitan population growth rendered expansion unlikely if not impossible. Moreover, the disconnect between railroad lines terminating in New Jersey and ocean-shipping facilities on the Hudson's New York shore greatly complicated port operations.[2] New Jersey-based railroad companies bought and operated docks along the Manhattan waterfront and then employed huge marine fleets to shepherd goods between the Hudson's

Figure 4.1 Existing conditions along Manhattan's West Street, circa 1900. Note piers for railroad freight transfers at left (with ship mast visible behind); early automobile in street; rail line toward right; existing buildings at far right. (Photographer unknown/Museum of the City of New York. X2010.11.3698.)

shores. This created greater congestion within the waters of the port itself and prolonged the time it took for goods to reach their final destinations, neither of which benefitted the long-term health of the port's economy.[3]

The route and physical presence of the New York Central Railroad's existing freight line were also problematic. Its waterfront tracks ran on-grade along a city-granted right-of-way from the tip of Manhattan through Riverside Park until Sixtieth Street, after which the railroad ran on the street surfaces of Eleventh Avenue, Tenth Avenue, West Street, and Canal Street. This created disruptive visual, auditory, and physical juxtapositions between the railroad, the park, the waterfront, and adjoining streets. As early as 1907 residents were complaining about the continuous noise and street congestion created by the train line.[4] In addition to the railroad's smoke, noise, and visual disruptions, its path on city streets posed real physical dangers to other vehicles and pedestrians. The steam engines' sizes and power far surpassed those of the streetcars, wagons, horses, and pedestrians with whom they shared the street surface. Accidents were frequent and often deadly, garnering Eleventh Avenue the nickname of "Death Avenue" by the early twenti-

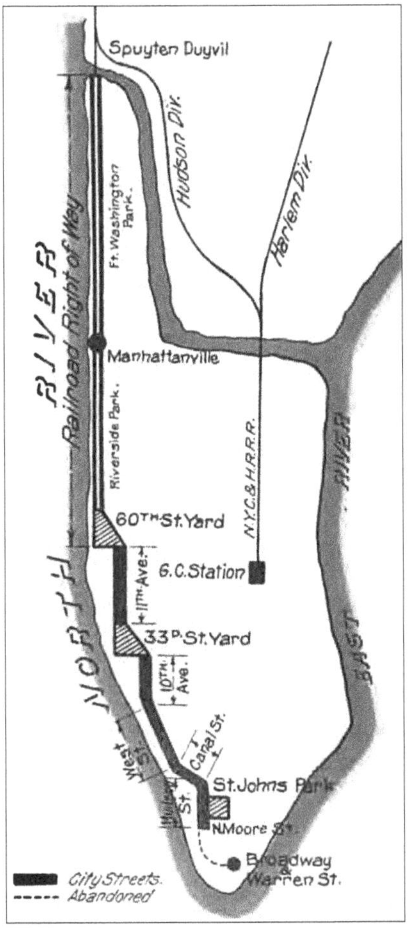

Figure 4.2 Map of Manhattan, showing rail connections, 1908. (Wilgus, William J. *Proposed New Railway System for the Transportation and Distribution of Freight by Improved Methods in the City and Port of New York.* New York: Amsterdam, 1908, 8.)

eth century. The tragic deaths of schoolchildren received particular attention. When a seven-year-old boy was crushed by a New York Central freight train in 1908, local residents marched five hundred schoolchildren through the streets of New York to protest the continued use of the on-grade tracks, citing 198 previous deaths under trains along this corridor in the previous decade.[5] At the time of this particular accident, efforts to change these conditions had already been underway for four years, but legal battles had stymied any action. This situation remained in deadlock for the next thirty years as the New York Central Railroad negotiated with the city, the state, and local advocacy groups over the legal rights and design approaches for restructuring the railroad's route, efficiency, and physical impact.[6]

The diverse concerns over the New York Central's tracks cultivated a wide series of design proposals, some of which provided important precedents for the subsequent development of the West Side Highway. Proposals for versions of vertical traffic separations were particularly popular, including schemes for street overpasses across the tracks, elevating the railroad so that streets could pass beneath, and an underground freight railroad from New Jersey to New York connecting to a subterranean railroad encircling the island of Manhattan. William J. Wilgus (1865–1949), chief engineer for the New York Central and Hudson Railroad between 1899 and 1907 and later independent consulting engineer, authored the latter scheme in 1908. Because of his position with the railroad, Wilgus had an unparalleled understanding of the complexity of railroad operations in general and of the distinct issues facing rail transportation in Manhattan in particular. His report, *Proposed New Railway System for the Transportation and Distribution of Freight by Improved Methods in the City and Port of New York* (1908), offered a comprehensive plan for rail service for the entire port of New York, including the gnarly west side freight line. Wilgus proposed to create a new freight subway beneath the streets of Manhattan that would share tunnel space with new passenger subway lines. This dedicated freight line could make

Figure 4.3 William J. Wilgus's proposal for a new freight subway in Manhattan, 1908. (Wilgus, William J. *Proposed New Railway System for the Transportation and Distribution of Freight by Improved Methods in the City and Port of New York.* New York: Amsterdam, 1908, 27.)

direct deliveries to the basements of nearby buildings, streamlining the freight delivery process (fig. 4.3). The freight subway would be fed by larger freight terminals at Sixtieth Street and on the New Jersey shore, to be reached by a tunnel under the river. This proposal simultaneously removed the railroad tracks from the shore and the city streets and provided more room for shipping traffic at the piers by relieving the need for harbor lighterage. Wilgus also suggested that elevated passenger rail service could be developed in concert with the freight railway. His diagram of such a scheme on West Street showcased an elevated railroad running down the center of the street between waterfront piers and uniformly sedate commercial buildings (fig. 4.4). Flanked by trees on either side, the elevated railway left the street surface free for pedestrian and vehicular traffic while freight cars could make direct subterranean connections to neighboring piers.[7] Despite early enthusiasm for this plan, the railroad and the city were too distracted by legal battles over the details of land ownership to fully consider the plan, and it did not materialize.

Other proposals for solving New York's railroad and port problems echoed Wilgus's enthusiasm for vertical traffic separations. Designers typically distinguished their suggestions for the railroad's path through Riverside Park from those for its route south of Seventy-Second Street. As early as the 1890s, proposals had been made to submerge the park-side railroad tracks in a cut in the earth that could then be covered with a roof. Some suggested constructing an elevated roadway atop the roofed tracks, thereby removing the blight of the railroad while creating a new traffic corridor along the water. Another variant advocated roofing over the tracks with a four-hundred-foot-wide classical waterfront terrace extending north from Seventy-Second Street through Riverside Park. In 1910 Docks Commissioner Calvin Tomkins proposed creating an elevated freight railroad south of Seventy-Second Street that would connect to a new terminal facility at Thirtieth Street, to be jointly operated by multiple railroads. This proposal again garnered some attention from city officials and the popular press, but the legal and practical ramifications of a jointly held terminal facility discouraged serious action on the proposal.[8]

As the city of New York and the railroad company battled over land ownership and development rights through the 1910s and 1920s, their conciliatory proposals revisited aspects of previous designs. In 1911 the railroad suggested the roofing of the railroad tracks in Riverside Park, the creation of a new road atop the track

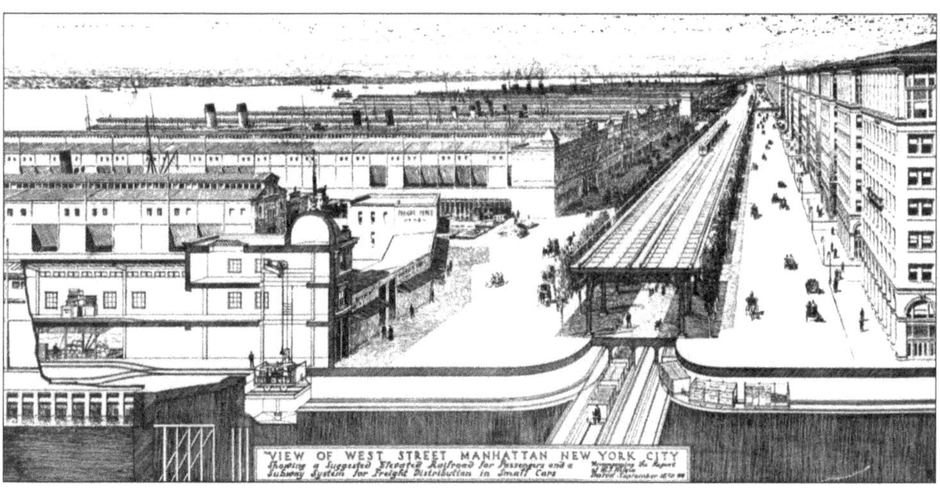

Figure 4.4 William J. Wilgus's proposal for Manhattan's western waterfront along West Street, 1908. (Wilgus, William J. *Proposed New Railway System for the Transportation and Distribution of Freight by Improved Methods in the City and Port of New York.* New York: Amsterdam, 1908, 28.)

tunnel, and the erection of elevated tracks south of Seventy-Second Street along the marginal way bordering the pier facilities. The city and the railroad agreed on the major elements of this design but differed on their conceptions of who would pay for the improvements, who owned the land on which the tracks presently ran, and whether multiple railroad companies should have access to the improved freight infrastructure. These complex legal issues, paired with the interruption of World War I, deferred adoption and implementation of any improvement scheme until July 1929. The final products of these thirty years of deliberation came to fruition in the 1930s. They included the covering of the railroad tracks through Riverside Park until 126th Street and the construction of a new freight terminal at St. John's Park (the former end of the Hudson River Railroad), both of which opened in June 1934; and the relocation of Eleventh Avenue's on-street tracks to a walled cut between Thirty-Fourth and Sixty-Fourth Streets opened in 1937. All of the options for elevated railroad lines, however, were noticeably absent from the final projects.[9]

The rejection of elevated railroad options for the west side reflected waning enthusiasm for this transit model citywide. While American cities had initially celebrated the speed, efficiency, and experiential qualities of elevated rail travel, by the early twentieth century the elevated trains' route limitations, noise, dangers, and crowding were generating public complaints. Initially *New York Times* editorials and articles called only for service upgrades, including additional rail cars, route extensions, and facility improvements. But the launch of New York City's subway system in 1904 upset the elevated railroad's monopoly over high-speed public transit. By 1913, subway ridership was growing at a faster rate than that of the elevated railroads. The growth of automobile usage provided another alternative to the elevated systems, and by the early 1920s it was widely held that the drawbacks of elevated railroads far outweighed their benefits. New York police commissioner Richard Enright was one of the earliest officials to call for the demolition of elevated railways—not just because of their blighting impact, but to make more room on city streets for automobiles. In 1923 residents along New York's Sixth Avenue urged the city to replace their elevated railroad with a subway and even offered to pay for its removal themselves. Politicians then celebrated the demolition of elevated lines as major accomplishments for their political records.[10] Thus, while the New York Central Railroad and the city of New York were locked in legal battles over the west side between 1911 and 1929, elevated railroads experienced a radical decline in reputation, devolving from sublime demonstrations of engineering efficiency to blighting relics of an outmoded transportation model. This shift, paired with the legal ruling that the New York Central's elevated freight line would prevent competing railroad companies from subsequently constructing their own connections to the waterfront, quashed early enthusiasm for elevated freight solutions along the west side.[11]

Meanwhile, the motor car had introduced new options for moving goods that both helped and complicated port operations. As detailed earlier, the existing structure of New York's port yielded convoluted exchanges between rail, water, and land transportation. The popularization of the automobile, and of the motor truck in particular, offered an option for circumventing these patterns. By the onset of World War I, motor trucks were playing an increased role in moving goods to and from the port. Not subject to the exhaustion, illness, or unpredictable behavior that typified their horse-drawn predecessors, trucks' speed, flexibility, and low cost of operation made them a popular choice for short-distance hauling, and experts predicted that their market-share would only grow in the coming years.[12] This was both a relief and a new problem for port interests. Motor trucks clearly offered merchants alternatives to expensive lighterage and rail transfers, which superficially relieved some of the freight congestion along the waterfront. But port operators were loath to see their dominance challenged, which magnified their resolve for rail-based port upgrades. Truck operators, of course, felt otherwise, since freight rail improvements would challenge their growing importance.[13]

The freight situation compounded worsening traffic conditions citywide. Trucks, with their formidable size and weight, were hard to maneuver on city streets and inflicted damage to street surfaces. Additionally, truck drivers needed to navigate around the ever-increasing number of automobiles now joining horses, carts, trolleys, trains, and omnibuses on city streets. The volume of automobiles was truly overwhelming. While New York City sported only 116,858 registered motor vehicles in 1916, by 1923 that statistic had more than tripled to 371,003. New York's greater metropolitan area housed an additional 480,801 vehicles, many of which commuted daily to Manhattan for business.[14] The volume, speed, and self-direction of this automotive constituency led to increasing accidents, unprecedented traffic congestion, and chaotic street conditions. In 1913 one New Yorker called out the irony of the previous community outrage about fatalities on Death Avenue compared to the relative silence on the more erratic danger of the automobile, quipping, "the automobile zig-zags through our city streets in many instances as fast as the Twentieth Century Limited, killing on an average over 200 human beings a year, and there is no cessation, no one adequately punished."[15] Census statistics confirm these observations, with annual automobile fatalities steadily climbing from 197 in 1915, to 368 in 1919.[16]

Traffic congestion, while more mundane than traffic accidents, created frustrated drivers and inefficient business operations. New York's own mayor, Brooklyn resident John Hylan, became both victim and temporary savior of such conditions in June 1923 when, faced with a horrible traffic jam approaching the Williamsburg Bridge, he got out of his automobile and directed traffic himself.[17] While this bottleneck related specifically to bridge access, similar congestion thwarted passenger and commercial vehicles throughout the city. Local business advocacy groups tried to quantify the emotional and economic ramifications of such congestion. One such report claimed that area trucks spent one half of their travel time stuck in traffic, costing the business community $100 million annually.[18] Countless organizations and individuals used similar complaints to support pleas for traffic relief. Railroad officials called for expanded passenger and freight service to relieve pressure on city streets. Traffic engineers suggested arcaded sidewalks, pedestrian bridges, directional restrictions, and widened roadways to facilitate easier street passage. And government officials promised new roads, new regulations, and final resolution of the ongoing dispute with the New York Central Railroad.[19] While the railroad debate raged until 1929, by 1925 a hybrid of some of these ideas had emerged in the proposal for an elevated express highway along the Hudson River—what would become the West Side Elevated Highway.

An elevated highway for Manhattan's west side evolved from the rail-based focus of earlier west side transportation plans. As discussed previously, the New York Central Railroad's 1911 plan was the first to envision a road atop a new freight railroad line. This idea lingered during the intervening years of deliberations, and by 1924 Manhattan borough president Julius Miller (1880–1955) was advocating a similar plan: the construction of an elevated motor road atop a new elevated freight line running from Seventy-Second Street to Canal Street. This scenario was particularly advantageous for the city of New York, as the New York Central Railroad was to shoulder the entire cost of the new motor road in exchange for revised property rights and easements along its existing property. While the railroad initially expressed interest in this plan, it ultimately opted to build its new freight line along a different inland route. This left the automotive highway issue unresolved, which President Miller saw as problematic.[20]

Miller subsequently made the elevated motor highway his personal crusade. In January 1926 he presented a plan to the Board of Estimate and Apportionment for an $11 million elevated express highway to run along the Hudson waterfront from Canal Street to Seventy-Second Street. The highway was to be built entirely on city property but was designed to connect to a new express road through Riverside Park to be built from Seventy-Second Street north to 129th Street atop the depressed railroad tracks still planned by the New York Central Railroad (fig. 4.5). Designed by Arthur S. Tuttle, chief engineer of the Board of Estimate and Apportionment (but incorporating elements of previous proposals for the joint elevated freight railroad and highway), the highway was to be sixty-five feet wide and to sit twenty feet above street level (figs. 4.6–4.7). It would carry three lanes of traffic in each direction, with a projected capacity of five thousand vehicles per hour moving at thirty miles per hour. The road was to have an internal steel frame but was to be clad in cement. The design anticipated future expansion, envisioning the eventual addition of a second deck and the segregation of north and southbound traffic on dedicated levels.[21]

Aesthetically, this rendition of the elevated highway evoked some aspects of the superstructures of existing elevated railroads. A simple steel frame was to carry the road, with regular panels syncopating the road's street-facing sidewalls (figs. 4.8–4.9). Arched brackets would mark the junctions between vertical supports and the roadbed, and light stanchions would feature floriated brackets reminiscent of the Victorian period. In the era of the elevated railroad, a similar architectonic vocabulary defined the lengths of track running through city streets. But the aes-

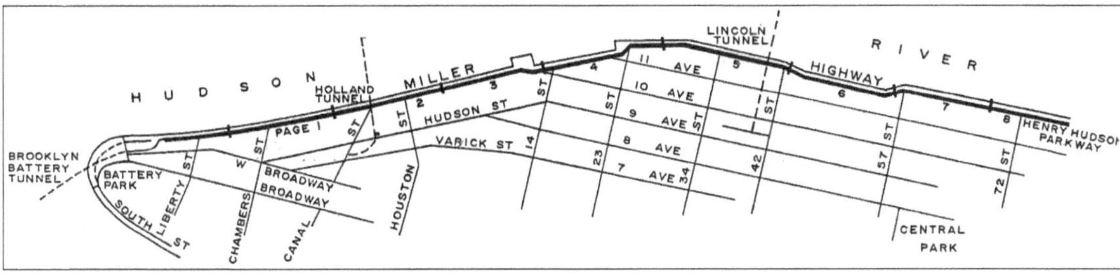

Figure 4.5 Route of Miller Highway, aka West Side Elevated Highway, as built. (Borough President of Manhattan, and Triborough Bridge and Tunnel Authority, *Miller Highway West Side Elevated Improvement.* New York: n.p., February 4, 1957, 2. Courtesy NYC Municipal Archives.)

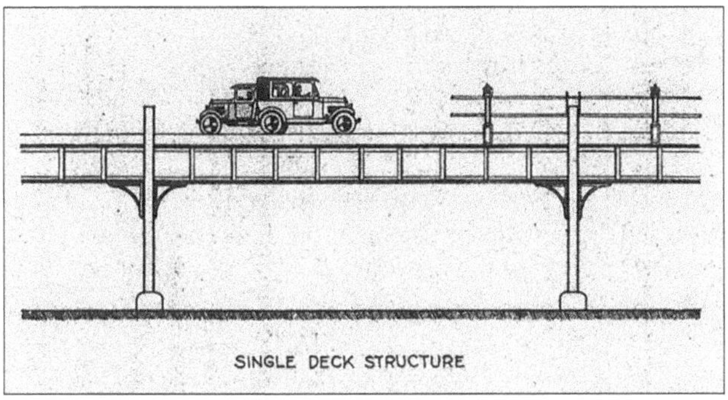

Figure 4.6 Side elevation, single-deck structure, proposed elevated express highway. (New York Board of Estimate and Apportionment. *Report of the Chief Engineer of the Board of Estimate and Apportionment of the City of New York for the Year 1926.* New York: Hickey & Kischel, 1926, 34. Courtesy NYC Municipal Archives.)

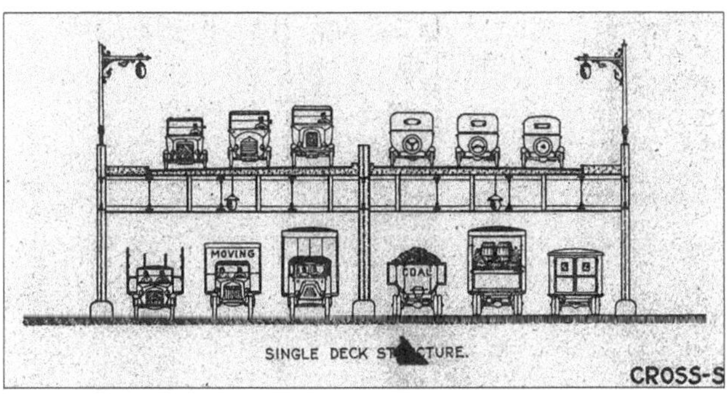

Figure 4.7 Section, single-deck structure, proposed elevated express highway. (New York Board of Estimate and Apportionment. *Report of the Chief Engineer of the Board of Estimate and Apportionment of the City of New York for the Year 1926.* New York: Hickey & Kischel, 1926, 34. Courtesy NYC Municipal Archives.)

thetic focus of the elevated railroad system had been the passenger stations, with staircases, ticket windows, and waiting platforms embellished with decorative ironwork, gingerbread gothic tracery, and intricate railings. Since an automobile road did not need such passenger stations, there were fewer obvious opportunities for similar treatment.

Government officials and local business advocates lauded the highway proposal. In April 1926 New York governor Alfred E. Smith empowered the New York City Board of Estimate and Apportionment to authorize construction of the elevated highway. By June, the Board of Estimate had approved President Miller's plan and was preparing to hold hearings about the project. Two months later, surveys of the existing property and infrastructure along the route were underway.[22] Mercantile and trade organizations supported this rapid progress, citing the highway as "vitally necessary to the welfare of the city."[23] Writing to express their enthusiasm for the project, a group of local business organizations authored a letter and official resolution that linked worsening traffic congestion to business concerns and then

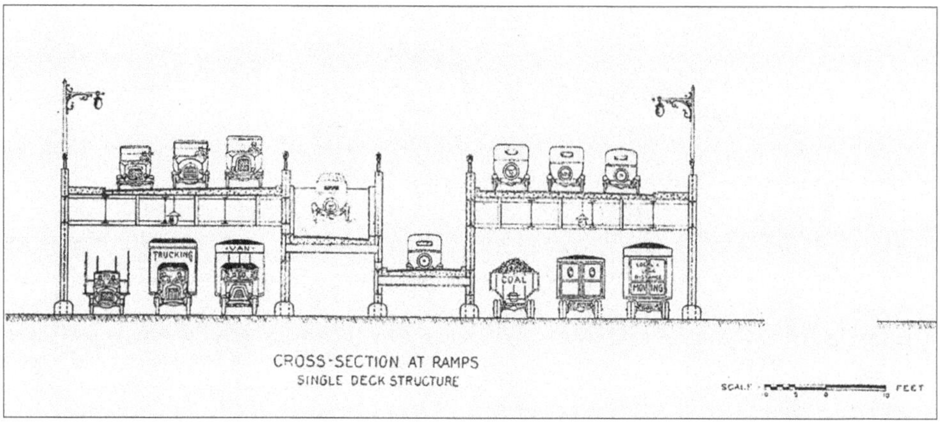

Figure 4.8 Sections at ramps for single and double-deck options, proposed elevated express highway, 1926. (New York Board of Estimate and Apportionment. *Report of the Chief Engineer of the Board of Estimate and Apportionment of the City of New York for the Year 1926.* New York: Hickey & Kischel, 1926, 31. Courtesy NYC Municipal Archives.)

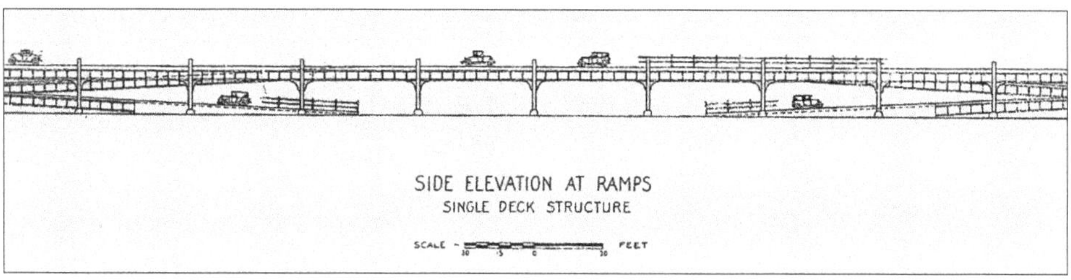

Figure 4.9 Side elevation, single-deck option, proposed elevated express highway, 1926. (New York Board of Estimate and Apportionment. *Report of the Chief Engineer of the Board of Estimate and Apportionment of the City of New York for the Year 1926.* New York: Hickey & Kischel, 1926, 31. Courtesy NYC Municipal Archives.)

lauded the proposed elevated highway as the "logical remedy" to the "hardships which the existing traffic conditions are inflicting upon our City's civic and commercial welfare."[24] This argument was a popular rationale for supporting major infrastructure projects. Nonetheless, the west side's preexisting conditions and the predicted impact of an elevated highway provided many opportunities for dissent.

The Committee on the Regional Plan of New York and Its Environs was one of the first groups to express concern over the elevated highway proposal. In March 1927 the committee sent a memorandum to the Board of Estimate explaining that while it did not oppose the construction of an elevated highway on the west side, it wanted to call attention to issues of "design, situation, and time of erection for the proposed structure."[25] The committee was worried that an elevated road would interfere with present functions on the street surface and would not alone provide a long-term solution for west side problems. The memorandum urged the incorporation of the highway proposal into a larger comprehensive plan for west side development, including the reconstruction of the New York Central

Railroad tracks. It advocated for the primacy of the needs of the port over those of local traffic and encouraged maximizing existing space before adding any new elements. Most importantly for this discussion, the committee called for architectural consideration of a prospective highway so that "its design would make it an attractive feature in the structural development of the City."[26] They continued:

> An elevated road of steel construction, having the same appearance as the existing elevated railroads, would be unpopular and have the effect of depreciating property. If, however, it were designed in a manner that would be appropriate for its position at the chief entrance to the City from the Harbor, it would probably cost a great deal more money than could be spent at present. With property it would be a permanent improvement, would add to the value of the adjacent property, and, in the end, would be the least costly.[27]

Prominent New York architect Chester Holmes Aldrich echoed the committee's plea for architectural sensitivity in a letter of March 25, 1927:

> It goes without saying, that the preparation of the plans of such an elevated highway should be undertaken only in collaboration with the most expert architectural advice. I cannot conceive of anything more disastrous than to build an elevated road of steel construction which would in any way suggest the existing elevated railroads in the City, and I hope very sincerely that nothing will be undertaken in the way of authorizing the preparation of these designs without taking advantage of the expert architectural knowledge available.[28]

The nuances of the above arguments bear special attention. First, both letters avoid complete dismissal of the elevated highway project but encourage careful reconsideration in light of historical events. Second, their cited historical perspective is to be found in the elevated railroads, which both letters invoke as the antithesis of sensitive urban improvements. Both authors allude to a common understanding of elevated railroads' negative functional and environmental impacts, and suggest that architectural counsel could define elevated highway construction differently. Such invocations would significantly impact the final highway design.

Other objections focused on existing street conditions, the legacy of elevated railroads, and the need for comprehensive planning on the west side. During a speech to the Municipal Art Society in April 1927, Thomas Adams, general director of plans and surveys for the Regional Plan of New York and Its Environs, suggested that clearing the impromptu carts, shacks, and stands from the marginal street along the west side piers would provide enough street space to significantly speed travel on the west side, eliminating the need for an elevated highway. The Fine Arts Federation, composed of sixteen artistic and architectural societies, echoed Adams's call for the clearing and widening of the existing waterfront street.[29] The Municipal Art Society registered its own dissatisfaction with the elevated highway scheme, calling it "'unsightly and calculated to interfere with surface traffic.'"[30] In a letter of May 14, 1927, the City Club of New York emphasized the waterfront's primary function as a freight-oriented seaport and questioned the highway's role as an impedance to this function: "Freight comes first. And yet it is proposed to hem in this long line of piers with a giant barrier in the form of an elevated highway, resting on its myriad legs, like a long cement centipede, to the infinite disturbance and distress of the freight-carrying trucks struggling to get about on the surface of the street below."[31] Atop this functional incongruity, the City Club also distrusted the wisdom of emulating the elevated railroad model and indicted the highway's prioritization of private automobile interests, quipping, "The luxury of a few persons who like to come downtown to business in their own private cars is interesting but secondary."[32] In sum, these commentaries showcased distinct but interrelated concerns about similarities between elevated highways and elevated railroads, port operations, unobstructed streets, urban beauty, and the perceived elitism of automobiles gaining prominence in the urban transportation melée.

Perhaps the most surprising figure to oppose the elevated highway was the mayor of New York City, James J. Walker (1881–1946, served as mayor 1925–1932). Walker objected to the highway on the grounds that its fate was inextricably linked to ongoing negotiations with the New York Central Railroad regarding Eleventh Avenue. He argued against committing to the highway until the completion of relevant engineering studies and the resolution of the railroad issue. So even as Borough President Miller continued to push the elevated highway scheme, Mayor Walker tried to slow its progress. In April 1927 Walker succeeded in forestalling public hearings about the highway on these grounds. Hearings did happen in June 1927, but on the Mayor's urging, the Board of Estimate and Apportionment deferred a decision on the elevated highway and created a special committee to study the west side problems in more detail. The committee, charged with developing approaches for financing the project, negotiating with the New York Central Railroad, and evaluating the technical requirements of the elevated highway plan, worked through the summer and fall of 1927. The winter of 1927 and early spring of 1928 saw little progress, with extensions to the committee's timeframe and repeated efforts from President Miller and Mayor Walker to advance and postpone the plan, respectively.[33]

The spring and summer of 1928 brought a series of changes to the dialogue. First, in May 1928 the city and the New York Central Railroad finally reached agreement on matters of property ownership and development rights for the west side. Though financing for west side improvements was not yet resolved, this was a major milestone in the ongoing negotiations with the railroad. Second, in June 1928 the New York City Committee on Plan and Survey presented Walker with a much-anticipated report about the city's long-term planning needs. Their central recommendation was for the creation of a permanent city planning board to oversee and coordinate the city's growth. This enabled Walker to envision a governmental structure that would systematically address issues of traffic, economy, and sanitation, and instilled confidence that individual projects could be coordinated within a comprehensive planning purview. Third, Tuttle swayed Walker's opinion of the elevated highway proposal, stating that its benefits would far outweigh its drawbacks. This led to Walker's ultimate endorsement of the project, and in August 1928 the Board of Estimate approved the first section of the elevated highway from Fifty-Ninth Street north. Negotiations about the highway's southern route over the New York Central Railroad's proposed railroad yards continued into the fall, but on October 18, 1928, the Board of Estimate and Apportionment gave final approval to the entire elevated highway scheme.[34] Reflecting on this victory, Miller reiterated that the new road would "undoubtedly relieve vehicular traffic congestion in Manhattan to a marked degree. It will take much of the traffic from the central avenues of the borough and send it north and south along the riverfront." Miller also predicted that travel on the road would provide "charming views of the river and the opposite shores."[35]

These events did not dissuade dissent from other members of the community, who continued to question three elements of the elevated highway: its practical necessity, physical consequences, and visual impact. The City Club of New York was one of the most vocal advocacy groups, arguing for the postponement of the highway project pending the creation and oversight of an official city planning board. Miller tried to assuage these concerns at a November 1928 meeting of the organization, but the City Club grew even more troubled. On January 8, 1929, the club presented a letter to Walker that pleaded for reconsideration of the project based on five main claims: that the new highway would not save enough time to be worth the huge expense; that the city was failing to undertake improvements to local streets that might alleviate the need for the highway; that the highway was distracting attention from proposals for the Triborough Bridge, which the club saw as a more pressing need; that the route and presence of an elevated highway would be detrimental to the economic vitality, future growth, and visual appeal of the Manhattan waterfront; and finally, that the highway would not help congestion but instead would magnify it significantly.[36]

Merchants operating in the Gansvoort and Washington Street market also objected to the highway plan when they learned that its path was going to require the eviction of tenants and demolition of buildings in their neighborhood. Though Miller initially responded to these complaints by citing the necessary "inconveniences" of public improvement projects, he agreed to work with a local committee to minimize the road's disruption to the neighborhood. These efforts ultimately yielded a compromise whereby the highway would only cross a small corner of the market, compelling the local merchants to retract their objection.[37]

Separate from the highway's necessity or its practical impact, the view of the road troubled another contingent of local advocacy groups. Building on their objections from 1927, a number of arts and civic beautification organizations lobbied for the consultation of artists, architects, and landscape architects in the design of all improvements for the west side. At an April 1928 hearing in front of the Board of Estimate, representatives from the Fine Arts Federation, the Committee on Civic Design of the New York chapter of the American Institute of Landscape Architects, the Municipal Art Society, the Citizens Union, the City Club, and the Port of New York Authority all made presentations urging the consultation of design professionals. Reporting on Walker's reaction to these efforts, the *New York Times* recounted: "Mayor Walker assured them that the board would welcome the cooperation of artists and architects, but that the problem basically was an engineering one and that nothing should be permitted to delay its advancement unnecessarily."[38] The Fine Arts Federation underscored its displeasure by registering an official objection to the elevated highway at a May 1928 Board of Estimate meeting. The City Club's aforementioned efforts to stop the highway, which peaked in the fall of 1928, echoed these sentiments. But while the City Club's attempts to halt the elevated highway failed (the Board of Estimate approved the final nuances of the highway design just three days after the City Club's January 8, 1929, correspondence), the appeal for professional design advice did yield results. On February 26, 1929, the *New York Times* announced that the Board of Estimate and Miller had retained the Manhattan architecture firm of Sloan and Robertson to consult on and embellish the design of the elevated highway.[39]

The engagement of an architecture firm to contribute to the elevated highway design marked a major milestone for the project. It acknowledged the physical impact that the road would have on its surroundings and discredited Walker's previous characterization of the road as solely an engineering challenge. The choice of Sloan and Robertson was also significant, as the firm then was designing some of Manhattan's premier Art Deco skyscrapers. Their projects epitomized New York real estate development in the pre-Depression years, balancing lucrative rental-income prospects with the desire for architectural distinction at both street level and in the city skyline. Sloan and Robertson's resulting cadre of buildings showcased setback massing empowered by steel skeletons with stylized decoration in terra-cotta, bronze, and stone distinguishing ground floors, entrances, and the very tops of towers. The duo became especially well-known for their incorporation of architectural sculpture in many projects, an approach that they would eventually bring to the West Side Elevated Highway. The city's retention of Sloan and Robertson not only underscored the importance of the elevated highway project overall but also acknowledged the project's complexities as a new functional and visual element in the city and demonstrated the city's willingness to invest in both of these perspectives.

John Sloan (1888–1954) and T. (Thomas) Markoe Robertson (1878–1962) established their architectural partnership in or around 1924. A native of New York

City, Sloan studied architecture at New York University and then practiced briefly in New York and the Philippines before serving as an architect, construction worker, and advisor for the American military during World War I. Following the war he practiced independently in Manhattan until establishing the partnership with Robertson. Sloan's most significant commission during this time was the Pershing Square Building in New York, a classically referenced protoskyscraper completed in 1923. Robertson, also a native New Yorker, studied at Yale University and the École des Beaux Arts before joining his father's architectural practice in 1908.[40] His father's designs mirrored the major stylistic trends of the era, evolving from a loose Romanesque approach in the late nineteenth century to a more classically referenced style by the early twentieth century. Following his father's death in 1919, Robertson brought this stylistic flexibility and his Beaux Arts training to the new partnership with Sloan.[41]

The new firm of Sloan and Robertson quickly gained distinction in New York with a series of notable office buildings in the late 1920s. Their approach synthesized their historicist training with the popular Art Deco style. Indicative of this was the Graybar Building at 420 Lexington Avenue, a thirty-two-story office building completed in 1927.[42] Reflecting the impact of the 1916 New York zoning ordinance, the Graybar Building presents a series of setback towers rising from a solid base at ground level (fig. 4.10). Buff Indiana limestone clads the lowest three floors, while light gray brick covers the balance of the structure. Dark bricks define the regularly spaced window spandrels, creating vertical stripes that emphasize the building's upward thrust. Stylized carvings, inset decorative panels, and metal grillwork decorate the building's monumental entrances and provide the most overt instances of Art Deco ornamentation. However, the building's interior lobby provides a surprising contrast to this architectonic vocabulary, featuring a stone-clad concourse of classically referenced arcades and vaults. The Graybar Building's direct connection to nearby Grand Central Terminal could explain this departure, as the architects may have emulated the station's classical vocabulary to create continuity between the two structures. Even without this reason, the contrast demonstrates the architects' fluency with both historic and modern approaches, if not also their inconsistency within a single structure.[43]

Two other buildings demonstrate the firm's rising prominence and its more integrated synthesis of historic and contemporary design motifs: The Fred F. French Building and the Chanin Building. The Fred F. French Building at 551 Fifth Avenue, a contemporary of the Graybar Building, was completed in 1927 for a real estate developer by the same name (fig. 4.11). The Fred F. French Company had established itself as a leading real estate developer of residential apartment buildings and planned the project on Fifth Avenue as its new corporate headquarters—the company's first commercial project. Rather than relying solely on his own architectural staff for the design, as he did for other projects, Fred French engaged Sloan and Robertson as consulting architects for the new building. Sloan and

Figure 4.10 Graybar Building, New York City. Sloan and Robertson, Architects, 1927. (Irving Underhill [–1960]/Museum of the City of New York. X2010.29.144.)

Robertson worked with French's in-house architect, H. Douglas Ives, to design a distinctive skyscraper that would proclaim the company's arrival on the booming Fifth Avenue business corridor.[44]

The architects' solution was one that used bright colors, opulent materials, and exotic iconography to distinguish an architectural form not dissimilar from many other contemporary Manhattan skyscrapers. The thirty-eight-story design consists of a three-story limestone base carrying an intermediary block of eight brick-clad floors. A pyramidal recession of setbacks tops this block, carrying a megalithic brick tower above. Two small setbacks crown this tower, defining the

Figure 4.11 Fred F. French Building, New York City. Sloan and Robertson, Architects, 1927. (Wurts Bros. [New York, N.Y.]/Museum of the City of New York. X2010.7.2.6031.)

penthouse level and rooftop water storage tank, respectively. This recessional setback massing, like that of the Graybar Building and most other contemporary New York skyscrapers, was indebted to the 1916 zoning ordinance's proportional requirements for building height and area. Instead of a series of gradual setbacks, however, Ives and Sloan and Robertson placed a slender tower atop a bulkier base at the French Building, showcasing the tower as a singular statement of corporate power. They then used colorful materials and lavish ornamentation to accentuate the building's street façades, entrances, and tower—the areas that would command the most visual attention.[45]

The architects chose a Mesopotamian decorative vocabulary to convey both historical allusion and modern ostentation. At the ground level, they placed a bronze frieze atop the first level of limestone-clad window bays. Vaguely evocative of Greco-Roman architectural friezes, winged Assyrian beasts fill metopes flanked by stylized lotus and papyrus stalks (an Egyptian reference), bordered on the bottom by a geometric molding and above by a row of round-headed studs crowned by a rosette molding. The building's bronze-clad entrances echo this treatment, offering intricate arches carried atop coffered bronze piers and framed by panels of stylized human figures representing architecture and building, and industry. The Fifth Avenue entrance frames a barrel-vaulted vestibule with a multicolored stone floor, bronze-framed display windows, and a set of revolving glass doors flanked by bronze bundle-shaft columns. The intricacy of this treatment and the quality of the materials conveyed a sense of stature and luxury to the French Building's tenants and visitors.[46]

On the upper levels of the French Building the architects magnified this decorative treatment to a scale appropriate to the building's broader urban audience. They topped the building's midsection and setbacks with strips of red and black geometric faience (glazed terra-cotta architectural decoration), in turn framed by bands of limestone trim. Black terra-cotta panels define the window spandrels. The orange brick tower rises from this base. Green faience panels evoke capitals atop the tower's piers, and bands of orange and green faience wrap the tower's uppermost levels. Huge faience panels mark all four sides of the building's summit (fig. 4.12). The identical north and south reliefs depict a rising sun, symbolizing progress, flanked on either side by winged griffins, representing integrity and watchfulness. Beehives and golden bees frame this ensemble, intended to represent industry and thrift. The panels on the short east and west sides portray the head of Mercury, mythological Roman messenger and god of commerce. Visible from afar, the color, size, and imagery of these panels differentiated the French Building from neighboring skyscrapers in midtown Manhattan and reinforced tenets of progress, efficiency, and commerce that were important to Fred French. The building's use of multiple historic references, affinity for stylized Near Eastern forms, and diverse material palette also situated it firmly within the emerging Art Deco movement.[47]

Figure 4.12 Crowning tower details, Fred F. French Building, New York City. (Janet Adams, New York City Landmarks Preservation Commission, Research Department.)

Sloan and Robertson's most widely acclaimed commission was the Chanin Building (fig. 4.13), a fifty-six-story Art Deco skyscraper built for Irwin S. Chanin, one of Fred French's rival developers.[48] Like French, Chanin sought to establish an iconic corporate headquarters for his real estate empire in midtown Manhattan. Perhaps in an effort to snub his competition, Chanin hired Sloan and Robertson in 1927 when the Fred F. French Building was under construction. Sloan and Robertson's design for the Chanin Building demonstrated their growing maturity as designers. Because of the site's enclosure by three streets, the architects were bound to accommodate three distinct sets of zoning requirements. This ultimately yielded a building of buff brick in three parts: a street-level mass rising sheer to the seventeenth floor, topped by a series of pyramidal setbacks between the seventeenth and thirtieth floors, leading to a single tower stretching from the thirtieth floor to the building's summit. Instead of using colorful surface decoration to articulate the transitions between these elements, as they had at the French Building, Sloan and Robertson defined the Chanin Building's aesthetic as the play of sunlight and artificial nighttime illumination on the building's surfaces. Masonry buttresses at the top of the tower play an important role in this effect, accentuating the building's masonry bulk by day but creating shadowy recesses by night that highlight the tower's vertical stacks of windows reaching high into the sky. A smaller set of buttresses between the fifth and six stories mimic this effect for the lower portion of the tower. Such treatment evinced very progressive architectural sensibilities at

Figure 4.13 Chanin Building, New York City. Sloan and Robertson, Architects, 1927. (Irving Underhill [–1960]/Museum of the City of New York. X2010.29.192.)

the time. It proclaimed that the building's geometry was itself of visual interest, and relied on the modern marvel of electric illumination as an essential component of the structure's visual potency.[49] Both of these elements clearly resonated with New York architect Hugh Ferriss, who featured the Chanin Building in his 1929 book, *Metropolis of Tomorrow*, as a positive example of contemporary skyscraper developments in America.[50]

Elaborate exterior and interior decoration complement the Chanin Building's form. Sloan and Robertson developed this ornamental program in collaboration with noted architectural sculptor Rene Chambellan (1893–1955) as well as the head of the Chanin Company's internal architecture staff, Jacques Delamarre. They sought to engage passersby with distinctive materials and stylized ornamentation on the building's lower stories and at its entrances (fig. 4.14). The ground floor, intended for shops, offers large plate-glass windows framed in bronze and set in black marble. Crowning this level is a bronze frieze depicting the story of evolution, told through a visual progression from basic plant forms to increasingly advanced marine animals, birds, and fish. Limestone piers topped by terra-cotta capitals unite the second and third floors, with groups of bronze-framed windows running in between. Bronze spandrel panels decorated with abstract geometric forms connect the windows of the second and third stories, allowing them to read as single visual units.

The fourth floor crowns the street-level decorative program. Here, a pattern of sumptuous stylized plant forms envelops the full expanse of the fourth story. Rendered in terra-cotta, the relief reads as a mottled horizontal band from afar but as a detailed exaltation of natural forms from closer proximity. It marks the transition from more detailed architectural treatment below to the stacks of office windows rising rhythmically above. This ornamentation reconciles the building's enormous scale with its street-level presence: at once providing visual distinction between the tower's base and its upper stories, while also providing visual stimulation for street-goers below. Smaller pieces of terra-cotta ornamentation extend this decorative vocabulary into the balance of the brick tower above, occasionally marking the tops of the building's setbacks.[51]

The Chanin Building's entrances and lobbies transpose the exterior's decorative approach into abstract geometric patterns, decorative grilles, and figural reliefs. Chambellan and Delamarre placed walls of colorful marble striated by bronze ribs atop multihued terrazzo floors with triangular patterning. Decorative bronze wraps internal storefronts and moderne patterns of bronze and glass define their doors. Intricate bronze ventilation grates present scenes of stylized skylines and vegetation. Marble relief panels illustrating "the city of opportunity" adorn the entry vestibules, telling a story similar to that of Irwin Chanin, where a man's hard work can carry him from humble beginnings to wealth and power. At Chanin's offices on the fifty-second floor, Chambellan crafted entrance gates of wrought iron and bronze that demonstrate this ascension less subtly: lightning bolts, cogs and wheels, and stacks of coins allude to the capitalist power of Chanin and his company. Thus, a person's experience in the Chanin Building was opulent,

Figure 4.14 Street-level decoration, Chanin Building, New York City. (Edmund Vincent Gillon/Museum of the City of New York. 2013.3.2.930.)

inspiring, and didactic, demonstrating the wealth and prestige that hard work had earned for the building's owner and that others might reach by following his model.[52]

Sloan and Robertson's progression from the Graybar Building to the Chanin Building narrates the evolution of the Art Deco style in the mid- to late 1920s, culminating with the synthesis of abstracted stylistic references, modern materials, and astylar geometries.[53] The firm's succession of commissions from competing Manhattan developers quickly advanced their reputation and generated additional commissions. Many of their affiliates were instrumental in other major Manhattan building projects: the owner of the Graybar Building subsequently developed Rockefeller Center; and Chambellan completed architectural sculpture at Radio City Music Hall, Rockefeller Center, and the East Side Airline Terminal.[54] This context, paired with John Sloan's local political activism, likely brought Sloan and Robertson to the attention of Julius Miller as he was fighting to advance the West Side Highway plan. Though clearly hired as a postscript to the development of the highway's major route and structural elements, Sloan and Robertson's retention by the Board of Estimate demonstrated the desire to synthesize modern transportation, modern engineering, and modern architecture in the public realm.

At this late stage in the process, Sloan and Robertson's response to this charge was necessarily oriented toward superficial decoration. Their ultimate design choices testify to an acute awareness of the road's physical presence, the distinct constituencies of people affected by it, and the potential for using tenets of modern design to express the excitement of automobile travel. These first two items are integrally linked. For pedestrians, ground-level vehicles, and occupants of neighboring buildings, the elevated highway would be a new physical and visual obstacle, its piers straddling streets and its roadbed interrupting the visual connectivity of the surroundings. Dressing the road's substructure was a response to these "bystanders," trying to diminish the road's negative impact by making it more visually palatable to its nonuser public. Sloan and Robertson designed the highway's steel guardrails and side panels according to this goal. They envisioned balustrades of vertical metal strips alternating between short and tall, abstracting the profile of modern skyscrapers (fig. 4.15). Larger rectangular plaques were to syncopate this pattern, sometimes left blank and other times adorned by official seals of the city of New York. A regular pattern of rectangular steel panels was to cloak the actual roadbed beneath the balustrade. At cross streets, these panels were to carry large decorative sculptures citing the name of the street or pier (respectively) on the other side of the highway (figs. 4.16–4.17). These sculptures

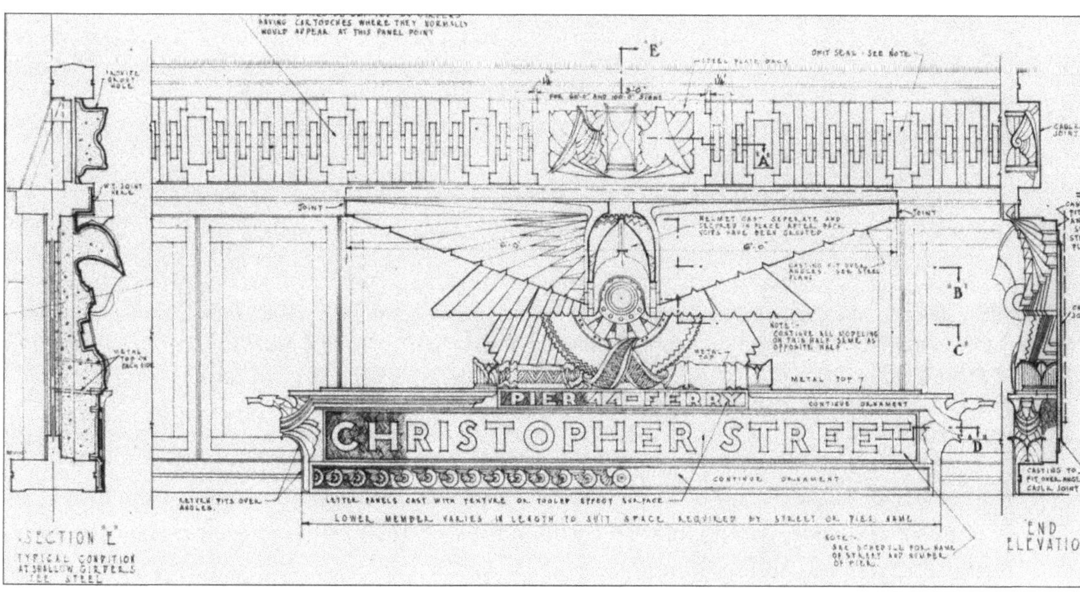

Figure 4.15 Superstructure sidewall and embellishment details featuring name of cross street, West Side Elevated Highway, New York City, May 1929. (Borough President of Manhattan Photograph Collection, negative 334–2. Courtesy NYC Municipal Archives.)

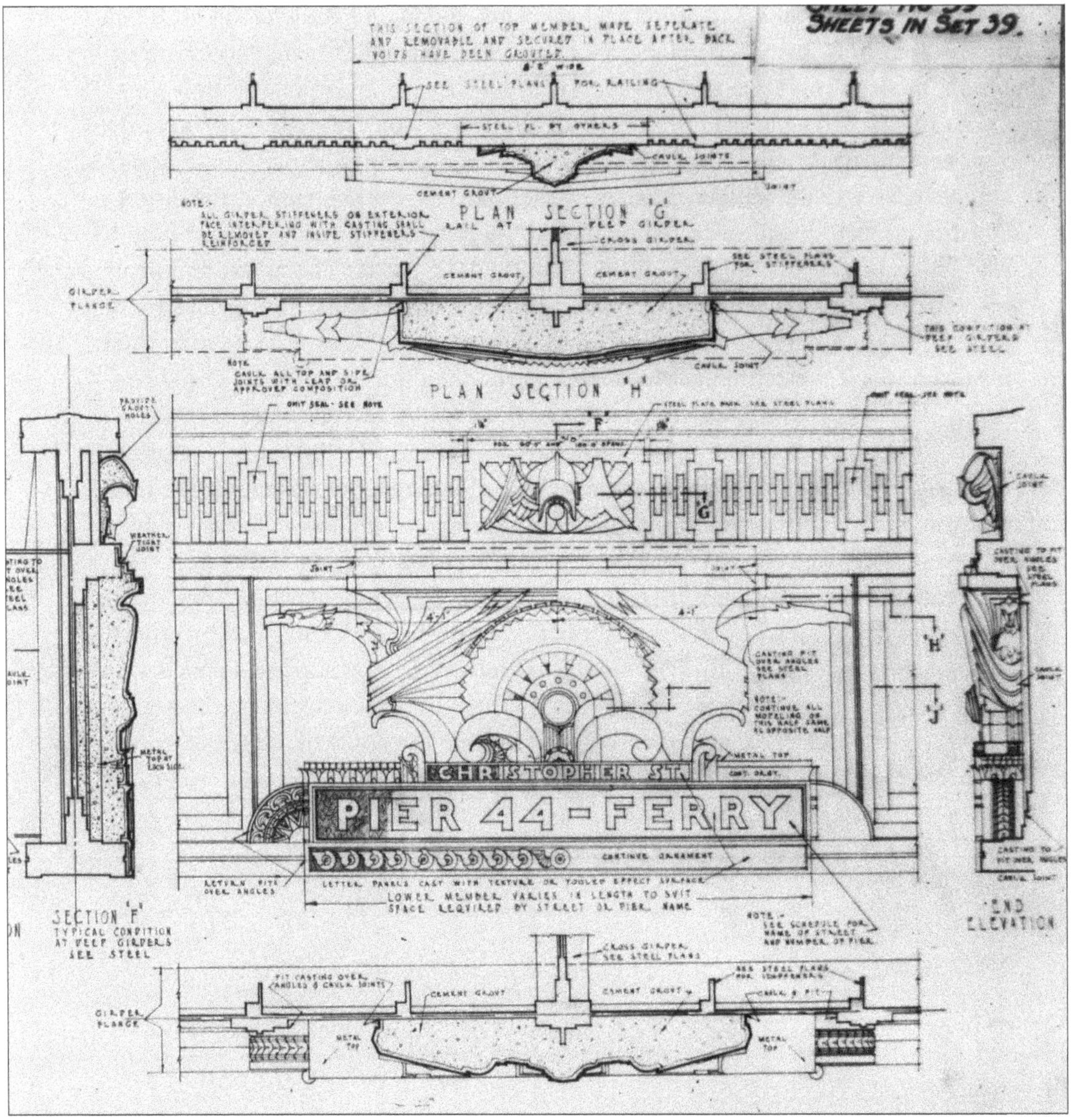

Figure 4.16 Superstructure sidewall and embellishment details featuring pier name, West Side Elevated Highway, New York City, May 1929. (Borough President of Manhattan Photograph Collection, negative 334–2. Courtesy NYC Municipal Archives.)

integrated winged allusions to eagles with abstracted wheel forms and Art Deco geometries. This program of exterior embellishment made the road legible to its nonuser audience, pacing its path through the city and celebrating the mechanized travel that it was to facilitate.[55]

Sloan and Robertson also planned a decorative program geared toward those driving on the road. Entrance and exit ramps were to be marked by decorative sculptures that would mimic the iconography of wings and wheels on the road's substructure. The road's balustrade was to be punctuated by small stepped posts

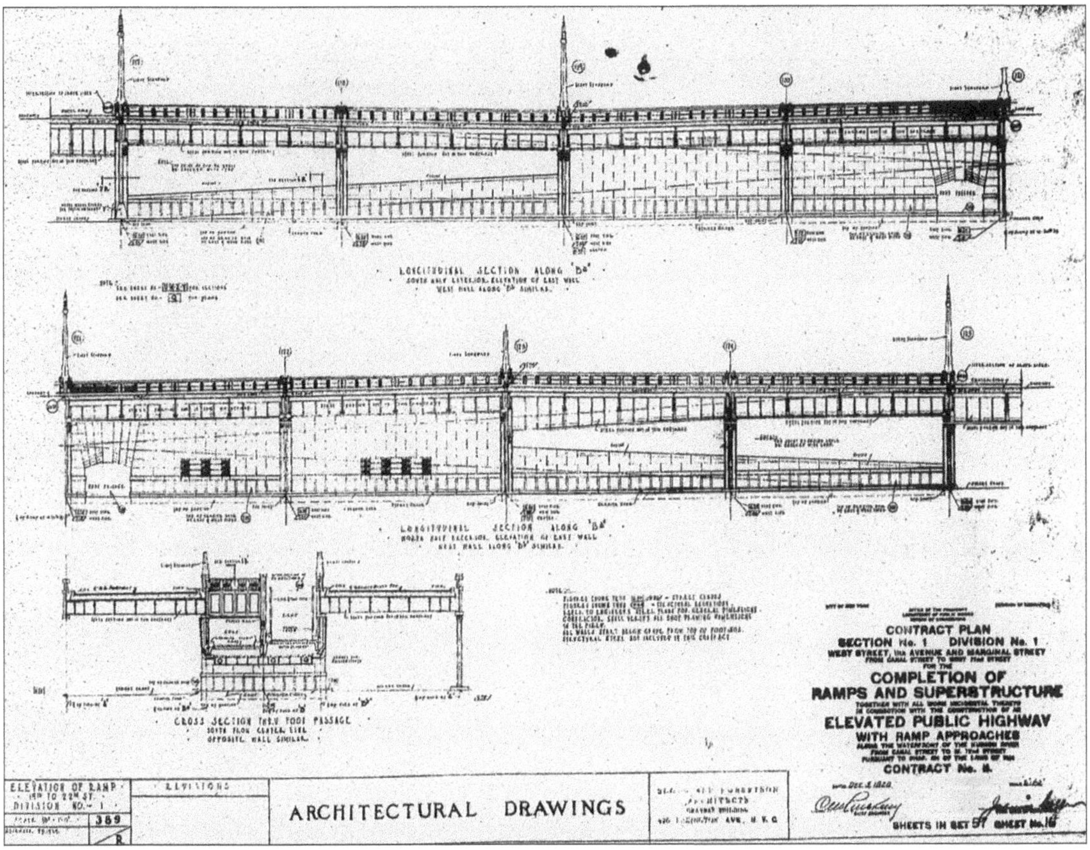

Figure 4.17 Side elevations, showing posts and lamp standards, West Side Elevated Highway, New York City, May 1929. (Borough President of Manhattan Photograph Collection, Microfilm 755. Courtesy NYC Municipal Archives.)

along its length, emulating the forms of nearby setback skyscrapers. The lamp standards were to magnify this iconography, using gradually stepped steel plates to create tall, slim, pyramid-topped forms (see fig. 4.17). This was a simple vocabulary aimed at motorists, with railing posts and lamp standards echoing the forms of nearby architecture and syncopating one's movement on the road. At the highway's entrances and exits, slower-moving traffic would be able to appreciate more detailed sculpture ceremonially marking these junctions.[56] Thus, Sloan and Robertson acutely understood the different views from, and of, the elevated highway and chose relative scales and levels of decoration for each. They extended the road's construction materials into its architectonic vocabulary, reveling in the planar layers created by individual pieces of steel and crafting geometric patterns and symbolic imagery out of them. This approach mirrored their previous designs for Manhattan skyscrapers, where they showed a similar interest in simple geometries and the use of sculptural decoration to distinguish important elements. With these designs, in the spring of 1929 the West Side Elevated Highway arrived on the cusp of realization.

5

STREAMLINED BOSTON

> Between the North and South stations existing streets are indirect, and at many points inadequate even for present needs. A crosstown traffic street between these important points has been urged by merchants and teamsters for many years. (1911)
>
> —Massachusetts Joint Board on Metropolitan Improvements, *Final Report of the Joint Board on Metropolitan Improvements*

LIKE NEW YORK AND CHICAGO, Boston's elevated highway emerged from long-standing debate about the city's needs for efficient freight transportation, commercial exchange, and personal movement. And as with the preceding two cities, Boston's geography, shifting economic base, and existing infrastructure significantly colored the city's ability to respond effectively to these issues in the early twentieth century. However, Boston's situation differed from those in Chicago and New York in that it took more than a half-century for the city to actually complete its elevated highway. Over this time, interest in and responsibility for a crosstown elevated road shifted from city, to state, and then to federal jurisdiction. This sequence literally empowered the Central Artery, as postwar state and federal funding financed the project. In addition, this progression also abstracted the original hopes for the highway and removed design authority from those it directly affected.

Three main stages trace Boston's course to the Central Artery. Boston's pre- and early automotive eras define the first phase, when the city established an organic settlement pattern that responded to local topography and commercial necessity. While this trend satisfied local growth needs for some time, by the late nineteenth century the narrow, meandering streets were already struggling to accommodate growing masses of street traffic. Increasing automobility in the first two decades of the twentieth century compounded this congestion. The second phase of growth, between the late 1910s and the mid-1940s, measured these circumstances in reports on economic welfare, street conditions, and traffic congestion, with corresponding proposals for major urban improvements. Many of these ideas originated locally with prominent businessmen and political leaders who saw traffic-relief measures as integrally related to Boston's survival as a commercial center. Professional planning advisors integrated these findings into subsequent proposals for comprehensive metropolitan and regional planning, which drastically changed the scope of previous discussions. The third phase, from the mid-1940s through the mid-1950s, brought these different scales of government, planning, and activism into conflict with one another. When the state of Massachusetts integrated the Central Artery into its vision for a regional highway network, it overrode the city of Boston's local aspirations for the road. It ensnared the project in postwar state and federal highway-building initiatives and changed its financial and ideological foundations, and it also drew citizens and municipal government into adversarial relationships with highway planners. Over the course of its gestation period, therefore, the Central Artery experienced a significant transformation, morphing from a locally initiated scheme for crosstown transportation into the only link to downtown Boston in a state-sponsored regional highway network.

Boston's topography laid the groundwork for the city's early successes and later traffic conundrums. The city was founded in 1630 on a hilly, amoeba-shaped peninsula connected to the mainland by a narrow neck. The city's maritime bias emerged as a direct result of this strategic location, as did its byzantine street pattern, which accommodated the originally mountainous local topography. The singular land connection was defensively advantageous, though problematic in the long term since it severely limited access to the city. Planning efforts in the eighteenth and nineteenth centuries largely focused on refining these natural qualities to better suit the needs of a growing city. Locals cut down the hills and used the earth to expand Boston's footprint, creating the South End and Back Bay neighborhoods and widening the strip of land connecting the city to the mainland. While these efforts did significantly enlarge Boston's geographic area and improve access to it, they did not alter the city's irregular street pattern. As Boston tried to maintain (or even expand) its preeminence as a commercial city, this proved increasingly problematic.[1]

Boston's economic conditions were also changing. The city had established itself as a mercantile center during its first three centuries, which had created a supporting infrastructure of docks, piers, shipbuilding facilities, and warehouses. By the early years of the twentieth century, however, other East Coast cities like New York, Philadelphia, and Baltimore were outpacing Boston's shipping capacity and support facilities. Boston remained a shipping center for wool, leather, shoes, and boots through World War I, but its total shipping charges declined all the while. Among U.S. ports, Boston ranked sixth in foreign shipping by 1920, down from fourth place in 1908 and second place in 1901. Federal and local officials tried to sustain these industries with new amenities including a new shipping channel and the world's largest stone and concrete drydock, but by the early 1920s declining port traffic was upending the city's identity and financial stability, sending large portions of the working waterfront into decline.[2] Local leaders started to expand their advocacy to include attracting new types of businesses, and they saw major civic improvement projects as visible means of doing this. By the mid-1920s they

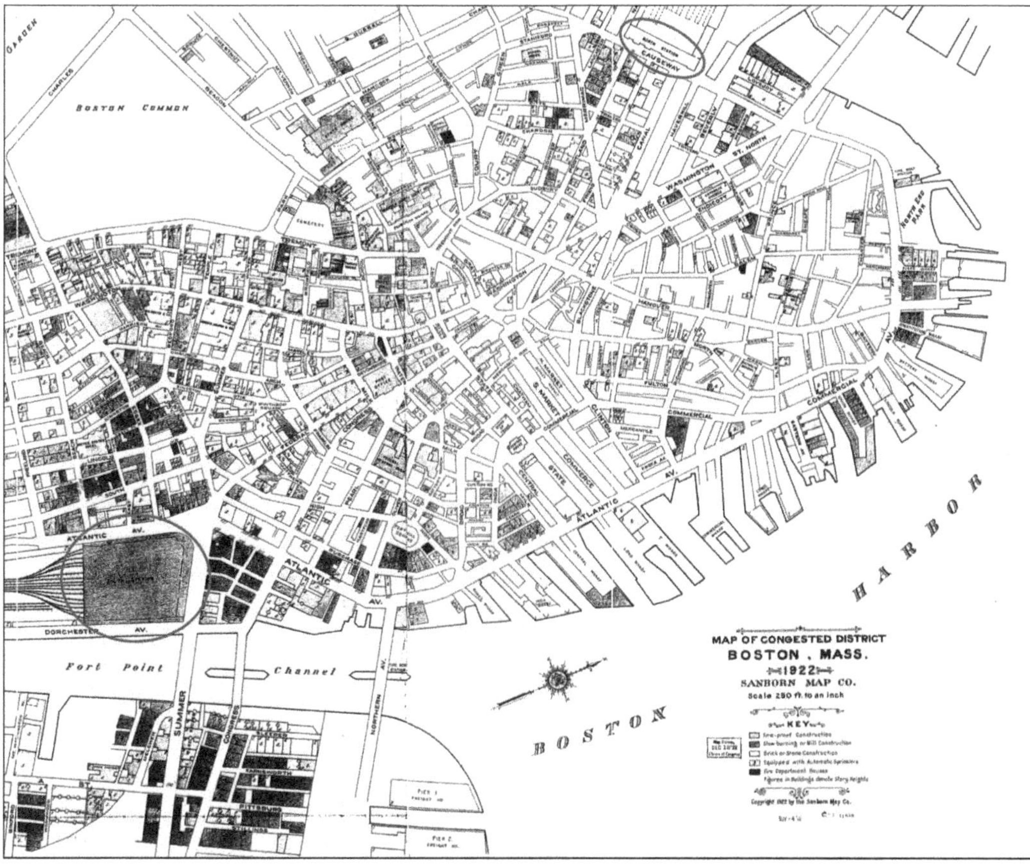

Figure 5.1 Boston's Central Business District, 1922, with South and North stations circled for reference (markings added). (Sanborn Map Company, Insurance Maps, Boston, Massachusetts. [Sanborn Map Company, 1922], Sheets 0–0a. Digital Sanborn Maps, http://sanborn.umi.com [accessed June 14, 2019]).

could refer to a growing list of reports and design proposals offered by local advisory boards and government committees promising to empower Boston's future.

Many such reports targeted Boston's rail and street infrastructure. Like most American cities, Boston experienced significant railroad development in the nineteenth century, boasting seven different rail lines by midcentury with corresponding stations throughout the city. By the early twentieth century these lines had been consolidated to focus on two major downtown stations on opposite sides of the congested business district: North Union Station (at the north, typically called North Station) and South Station (fig. 5.1). These stations reflected the architectural grandeur of the late Victorian and City Beautiful eras, with an eclectic pairing of Second Empire and Renaissance elements at North Station and a more pure rendition of classicism at South Station. However, their stately appearances did not compensate for the lack of rail connection or easy street passage between the two terminals. This functional shortcoming complicated shipping transfers and added to local street congestion, something lamented by merchants as early as 1902. By 1910 some had proposed the idea of a tunnel between North and South Stations.[3]

The following year, these two ideas came together via a report jointly authored by a board of railroad, harbor, transit, and park authorities that proposed both a new rail tunnel and a surface highway between the two stations. The Massachusetts Joint Board on Metropolitan Improvements envisioned the tunnel as a speedy new connector for freight and passengers transferring between the two rail stations and also lauded the expected relief of street congestion thanks to the absence of previously street-bound vehicles.[4] Leaders thought that solving rail congestion would stimulate sequential changes throughout the city—finessing street-level movement and liberating downtown areas for profitable redevelopment.

The highway component of the 1911 proposal reflected a separate, though related, set of problems. The dense, irregular streets of the business district proved inhospitable routes not only for the goods and passengers moving between the two rail stations but also for Boston's nonrail constituencies. The indirect routes and poor surfaces of downtown streets thwarted easy movement for the increasingly diverse assemblage of horses, carts, streetcars, pedestrians, and early automobiles that daily jockeyed for space on them. Street widening and paving upgrades typified the first line of defense against such problems. Boston saw ongoing efforts to upgrade street materials in the 1910s, with the addition of wood block, granite, and asphalt paving in various parts of the city.[5] But the more grandiose—and therefore less frequently realized—proposals to combat Boston's worsening traffic congestion were schemes for new streets.

Suggestions for new streets and street improvements intensified as automobility increased. As early as 1902 Boston merchants had already approached two successive mayors with a plan for "highway" connections between the key mercantile centers of North Station, South Station, the market district, and the waterfront. While the specific route of this proposal differed from that ultimately implemented for the Central Artery, the petitioners' argument for creating direct paths for fast movement of people and goods across the city presaged those used in subsequent campaigns for road improvements.[6] In 1912 the Boston Real Estate Exchange proposed a highway running from the downtown retail district southwest to Copley Square, though Mayor John F. Fitzgerald's financial concerns about the project reportedly quashed its prospects. Controversy swirled around a 1915 proposal to claim land from the Boston Common to widen Tremont, Park, and Boylston Streets, which served as main thoroughfares between the business district, Beacon Hill, and Back Bay. A public referendum defeated this effort, though it reappeared (unsuccessfully) in 1919. In 1923 William Stanley Parker, architect and member of the Boston City Planning Board, proposed the construction of three concentric thoroughfares in the city core, each one-hundred-feet across, to provide wide, direct routes across the otherwise dense downtown fabric. One of Parker's three roads, which became known as the "Intermediate Thoroughfare" or "Loop Road," did receive serious consideration in the following two years.[7] Industrial promoter William J. McDonald proposed an aerial highway in 1929 that followed a route similar to that of Parker's. It was to run above steam and elevated railroad tracks around the downtown business core and would connect to seven terminals around the city's perimeter. Despite the distinctions between these unrealized proposals, their succession demonstrates a shared conviction that the city's economic health depended on better transportation connections between the mercantile and commercial centers.[8]

In addition to routes *through* Boston, leaders also contemplated better routes *around* and *to* the city. In a 1909 report by the Massachusetts Commission on Metropolitan Improvements, landscape architect Arthur A. Shurtleff argued that the routes of existing radial highways necessarily funneled most traffic directly to Boston even when it was not the travelers' chosen destination. In response, Shurtleff proposed a circumferential highway around the city to link suburban communities to one another and relieve unnecessary downtown traffic. He suggested that this circumferential road, paired with improvements to existing radial thoroughfares and widening of major downtown streets, could effect a comprehensive and efficient street system for the entire metropolitan Boston area. Though Shurtleff's proposal was unsuccessful, subsequent design ideas echoed his findings. In its 1911 report, the Joint Board on Metropolitan Improvements recommended new boulevard and highway connections between Boston and the surrounding cities of Somerville and Cambridge. Leaders from Boston and outlying cities debated a variety of new street connections and improvements through the 1910s, with little measurable progress.[9] While all of these schemes provided exciting and seemingly easy solutions to traffic problems, government leaders disliked the lack of coordination between the various studies and continuously postponed action pending better integration. In 1921 the Boston City Planning Board officially recommended the development of a "comprehensive city plan," and the following year Mayor James Michael Curley allocated funds to the board for this purpose.[10] On May 1, 1922, the board engaged Nelson P. Lewis, former chief engineer of the New York City Board of Estimate and Apportionment, to fulfill this role.[11]

Concurrent with Lewis's appointment, Boston achieved a quick succession of planning milestones that eventually led to the design of the Central Artery. First was Lewis's own assessment of the city's situation, which lamented Boston's lagging response to the countless individual reports already on hand, encouraged collaborative planning on a regional scale, and suggested the immediate completion of an aerial survey and map for reference in city planning efforts. Lewis's death in 1924 cut short his Boston consultancy, though his advice still heavily influenced the City Planning Board's efforts to craft a city plan and a zoning code. That same year also marked the adoption of Boston's first zoning code. These efforts took flight in 1922 with the appointment of Arthur C. Comey, a landscape architect and city planner (and a founding member of the American City Planning Institute), as director of zoning. The City Planning Board worked with Comey, Lewis, and Edward M. Bassett to produce the final law, which eliminated the city's previous restrictions on tall buildings and divided the city into typological districts. The authors hoped that the guidelines would encourage new commercial investment, systematize future growth, and predict areas for future infrastructure improvement.[12]

Other efforts focused on measuring and relieving street congestion. The Boston Chamber of Commerce conducted successive traffic counts of passenger and vehicular traffic entering and leaving the downtown area in 1924 and 1926, the latter in conjunction with the City Planning Board. The comparative results showed a 21 percent increase in the number of vehicles in the area during business hours, with the heaviest increase wrought by passenger cars.[13] Fueled by these statistics, in November 1926 incoming Mayor Malcolm E. Nichols appointed a Street Traffic Advisory Board to study the situation further. Nichols preferred traffic regulation to isolated street improvement projects and therefore favored comprehensive analysis that would inform such action.[14] He retained Miller McClintock, director of the Erskine Traffic Bureau of Harvard University and renowned traffic consultant, to direct the study. The resulting report, issued in 1928, advocated improvements in traffic regulations, traffic signals, and parking facilities as the major methods for easing street congestion.[15]

The final planning milestone for Boston involved retaining an expert planning advisor and preparing a thoroughfare plan. The City Planning Board successfully proposed this measure in 1926, arguing that only a planning consultant could orchestrate the synthesis of the maps, census data, zoning code, and traffic counts recently compiled by the city. In 1927 the board retained city planning consultant Robert Whitten to develop the plan. Whitten was a statistician by training who rose to become an authority on traffic and city planning in the 1920s. President of the American City Planning Institute at the time, Whitten had worked previously with Nelson P. Lewis and Edward Bassett on planning efforts for New York City, and with his wife, had befriended Boston city planning board secretary Elisabeth M. Herlihy at the 1924 National Conference on City Planning in Los Angeles.[16] Building on these personal connections, Whitten directed the City Planning Board's preparation of the thoroughfare plan between 1927 and 1930. The project's investigative depth and synthesis of previous research distinguished it from earlier traffic studies and street improvement schemes. It integrated concurrent research from Miller McClintock and the Street Traffic Advisory Board, as well as the state's Division of Metropolitan Planning. Whitten's team sought to provide a comprehensive network of through streets in the city of Boston connecting to larger highways in the metropolitan region and also to respond to associated plans for zoning, port improvements, parks, recreation spaces, and public buildings. Issued in 1930 as the *Report on a Thoroughfare Plan for Boston*, Whitten's final report outlined ten major and fifty-six minor transportation projects classified by relative urgency, all aimed to provide adequate traffic capacity for at least the next twenty-five years (fig. 5.2). At the epicenter of Whitten's vision was a dual-level highway running through downtown Boston and connecting to regional highways—the Central Artery.[17]

As cast by Whitten, the Central Artery would be a two-level express road extending one and a half miles from South Station to North Station. Beginning

Figure 5.2 Detail of downtown Boston showing proposed principal express roads (numbered) as detailed in *Thoroughfare Plan*, 1930. Central Artery is marked as #2 through the downtown corridor. (City Planning Board, Robert Whitten, consultant. *Report on a Thoroughfare Plan for Boston.* Boston: City Planning Board, 1930: fig. 4. City of Boston Archives.)

at Kneeland Street at the south, it was to run parallel to but inland from Atlantic Avenue until Commercial Street, after which it turned northwest to terminate at North Station at Nashua Street (fig. 5.3). Its northern terminus was to connect with a projected north shore highway and a new tunnel to east Boston, and its southern boundary was to join a south shore radial highway. The road's full corridor was to be a minimum of one hundred feet wide, with the elevated roadway occupying the central fifty-four feet. Six lanes would accommodate long distance traffic on the elevated section of the road, while local traffic could flow separately beneath on a surface road. Planners estimated that the high-speed upper roadway would accommodate sixty thousand vehicles per day at speeds averaging thirty miles per hour. They predicted that the elevated road would absorb 40 percent of the traffic that presently clogged downtown streets.[18]

Whitten's team projected the Central Artery as a broad open corridor surrounded by dense commercial buildings and centered by the sparse steel and concrete ribbon of the elevated superstructure (figs. 5.4–5.5). The elevated structure received little articulation in these early renderings, cast as a simple viaduct carried by sets of three piers and punctuated by rectangular light stanchions along the road's guardrails. The imaginary corridor of buildings surrounding the Central Artery was cast in a vague but modern light. Austere commercial buildings of uniform heights line the street, with multistory entrances and large storefront windows defining their ground levels. The vanishing points of the perspectival renderings focus on distant geometric skyscrapers, their pyramidal silhouettes evoking contemporary Art Deco forms. Pedestrians dot the flanking sidewalks,

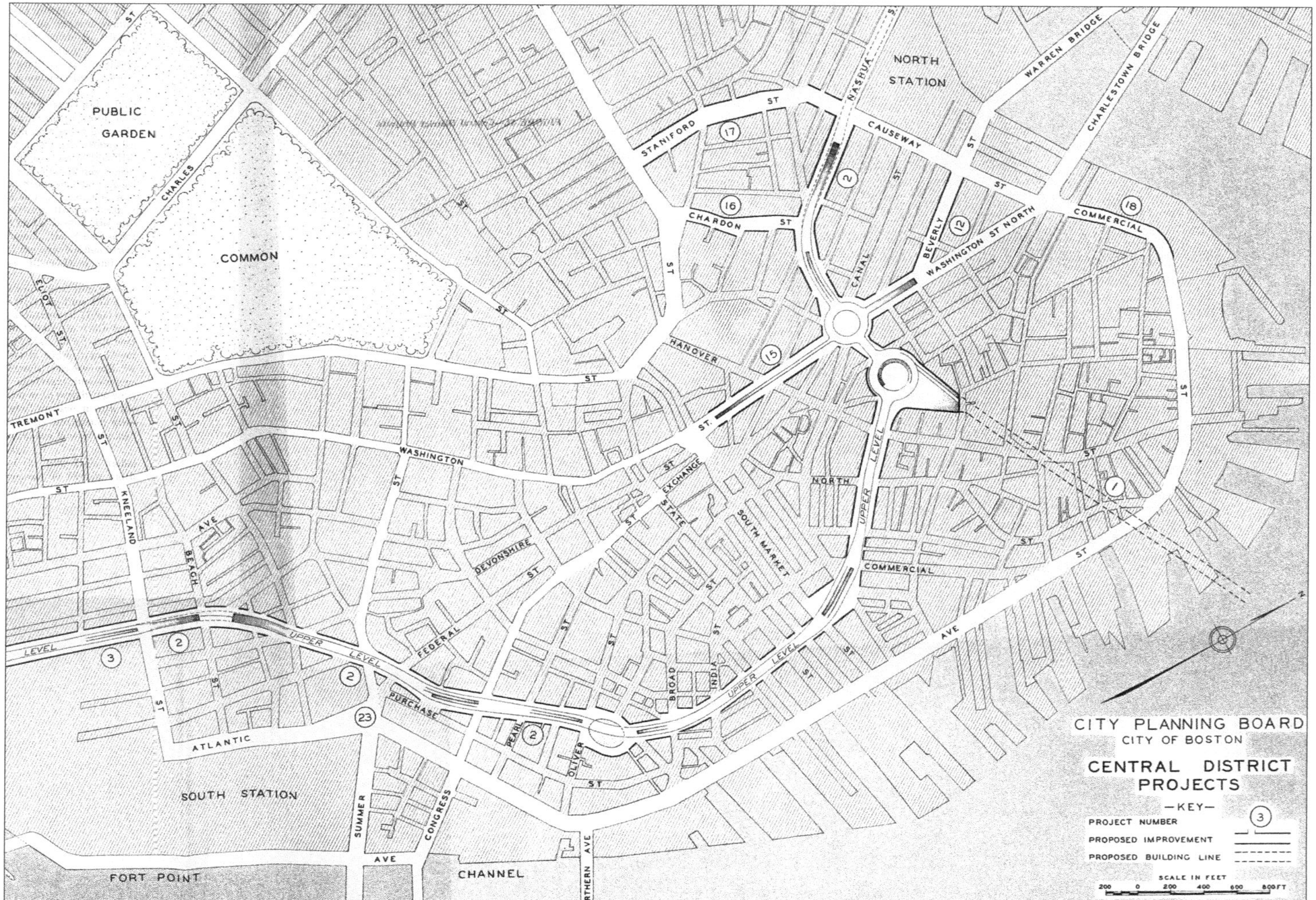

Figure 5.3 Proposed Central Artery route through downtown core, 1930. (City Planning Board, Robert Whitten, consultant. *Report on a Thoroughfare Plan for Boston*. Boston: City Planning Board, 1930: fig. 51. City of Boston Archives.)

Figure 5.4 Sectional perspective, proposed Central Artery corridor. (City Planning Board, Robert Whitten, consultant. *Report on a Thoroughfare Plan for Boston*. Boston: City Planning Board, 1930: fig. 46. City of Boston Archives.)

Figure 5.5 Sectional perspective at typical ramp, Central Artery corridor. (City Planning Board, Robert Whitten, consultant. *Report on a Thoroughfare Plan for Boston*. Boston: City Planning Board, 1930: fig. 47. City of Boston Archives.)

apparently unaffected by the multiple levels of traffic surrounding them. Automobiles and buses are the only types of vehicles present, reflecting the growing dominance of the internal-combustion vehicle and the implied rejection of older types of transportation.

The Central Artery's projected route and relationship to the surrounding urban fabric synthesized local traffic needs with those of long-distance through traffic, elements which had been evaluated separately in the preceding decades. Rather than independently fulfilling calls for crosstown streets between Boston's mercantile centers as suggested in 1902 and 1912, or constructing the regional highway connections advocated in 1909, 1911, or 1923, the Central Artery conflated two distinct needs and two different families of design proposals. The *Thoroughfare Plan* explained, "There is an undoubted need for a new north-south highway by-passing present centers of congestion. There is also need for an elevated express road to carry through traffic across the downtown district. By combining these two requirements a much more adequate facility can be secured than by attempting to solve them separately."[19] The Central Artery's proposed route almost exactly mimicked that of the so-called "Intermediate Thoroughfare" proposed by William Stanley Parker in 1923—the middle rung of the three concentric roads that Parker claimed would heal the city's local and metropolitan traffic snarls. Its elevated component reflected contemporary enthusiasm for vertical traffic separations and futuristic motor speedways, including that proposed by William J. McDonald the year before the publication of the *Thoroughfare Plan*. Thus, Whitten's plan was not altogether new in its ideas but built on those already being discussed within the local and national design communities.

The Central Artery scheme also contradicted contemporary backlash against elevated structures in the urban realm. As explained in relation to New York City's West Side Elevated Highway, the popularity of elevated railroads had severely declined in the 1910s and 1920s, leading to their demolition in many cities. As discussed in chapter 1, Boston's elevated railroads emerged fairly late and had limited coverage within the city. The Atlantic Avenue Elevated (1901) was the main line, providing the only public transit link along the city's waterfront. Whitten acknowledged the visual and functional similarities of the proposed Central Artery to existing elevated railroads, but argued "that great care will be taken in its design to make it attractive and to reduce noise and vibration; that it will be used by motor vehicles and not by railroad trains."[20] In addition to these experiential factors, Whitten rejected common design alternatives, noting that a tunnel version of the road would interrupt sewer and subway prospects, and that continued reliance on surface streets came with onerous experiential and economic costs.[21]

The *Report on a Thoroughfare Plan for Boston* also anticipated questions about utilizing Atlantic Avenue and its existing elevated railroad as the basis for the proposed Central Artery. Atlantic Avenue's waterfront location and roughly circumferential path from southeast to northwest largely met the strategic needs for route and efficiency desired by the City Planning Board. Expanding Atlantic Avenue could be seen as a more expedient and less disruptive alternative to bulldozing existing structures in order to construct an entirely new road. Some also wondered if the superstructure of the existing elevated railroad might be adapted to carry the proposed elevated highway, thus sparing great expense. The *Thoroughfare Plan* methodically debunked these alternatives. It maintained that less than one-fourth of the existing railroad structure would be reusable for an elevated roadway, that the height of the elevated railroad was unnecessarily high for a roadway and that this height would create extra expense in constructing ramps to the lower street surface, and that the construction of such ramps would greatly hinder existing traffic flow along the waterfront. Moreover, it questioned the practicality of removing the sole option for public transit to the waterfront and contended that the Atlantic Avenue route would not be as attractive to through traffic as that proposed for the Central Artery. Whitten and his team even developed mathematical equations to substantiate the temporal and economic savings afforded by the Central Artery design.[22] Such statistics, paired with the comparative evaluation of alternate proposals, lent scientific credence and diligence to the *Thoroughfare Plan*.

As the first official plan of such comprehensive breadth, the *Thoroughfare Plan* elicited great excitement and quick action from local leaders. More than twenty local civic, mercantile, and architectural advocacy groups endorsed the plan's trajectory for city improvements. In May 1930, just one month after the plan's publication, the state legislature authorized Mayor James Michael Curley (now serving his third term after defeating Malcolm Nichols) to adopt the *Thoroughfare Plan* as a guide for future development in Boston. Curley then submitted a bill authorizing the Central Artery (considered to be the most urgent project in the plan) to the 1931 legislative session, but this measure ultimately failed. Its failure partially can be attributed to the project's astounding cost estimate of $28 million, which was clearly implausible given the nation's worsening financial depression. But the tense relationship between city and state affairs in Boston also complicated matters. The city did not have enough money to finance a major project like the Central Artery without borrowing from the state; and the state legislature's mistrust of reputedly corrupt (and subsequently convicted) Curley compounded its financial objection to the project (and led to heavy-handed regulation of local affairs in general).[23] Thus, within two short years, the forecast for the Central Artery turned from theoretical optimism to financially mandated postponement.[24]

For the next twenty years, the Central Artery, and public improvements in general, remained a focus for civic, engineering, and design leaders. Curley pursued a course of action reflective of his populist leadership style. He directed what city funds he could to constructing small street improvements that would ultimately be part of the Central Artery and initiated small public construction projects to provide his constituents with new amenities like parks, wider streets, golf courses, and libraries. These efforts not only provided necessary improvements to the city landscape but also provided employment for local citizens at a desperate economic time, and by extension, reinforced Curley's popularity with his constituents.[25] Meanwhile, the City Planning Board continued to advocate for implementation of the Central Artery. Their annual reports from the 1930s repeatedly returned to Whitten's *Thoroughfare Plan* as the best solution for local transportation woes and cited the Central Artery as the most pressing project from the plan. In 1938 the board suggested overcoming the project's huge price tag through joint funding from city, metropolitan, and state coffers, but leaders in each of these sectors were loath to cooperate in such a manner.[26] Four members of the City Planning Board, Elisabeth M. Herlihy, Henry H. Harriman, Frederic H. Fay, and William Stanley Parker, carried their local agenda to the state level when they became members of the newly established State Planning Board in 1935. Their influence likely contributed to the state's growing coordination of state and municipal improvements in the late 1930s and 1940s and to the state's subsequent adoption of the Central Artery proposal in the mid-1940s.[27]

Advocacy groups and individuals also revisited the Central Artery scheme during the 1930s, proposing on-grade options and alternate routes through the downtown core. In 1936 the Traffic Commission of the Boston Real Estate Exchange advocated for the removal of the Atlantic Avenue Elevated and the subsequent widening and transformation of Atlantic Avenue into a major thoroughfare. The real estate executives felt that only a major road project would relieve Boston's business district from the congestion choking its streets and argued that Atlantic Avenue offered a latent opportunity for improving an existing street and relieving traffic. They reasoned that removal of the railroad superstructure and repaving of the street surface would quickly increase Atlantic Avenue's capacity from four to six lanes, thereby providing greater capacity along a direct crosstown route and increasing the values of adjoining properties.[28] Developer William J. McDonald, who had proposed an elevated highway atop existing rail structures in 1929, offered another proposal in 1937. McDonald envisioned a double-deck highway stretching from the Back Bay to South Station, where it would connect to a reconfigured version of the existing elevated railroad superstructure. The highway would then follow the paths of the existing Atlantic Avenue, Commercial, and Causeway Streets to North Station, where it would connect to the Charlestown Bridge. McDonald wanted the highway to be a toll road, thus liberating taxpayers from the associated costs of its construction. Because McDonald's proposed route used existing streets instead of new rights-of-way, the estimated cost for his plan was $12.5 million—less than half that of the 1930 Central Artery proposal.[29] These privately generated ideas stirred conversation within the city but sparked little else.

Between the late 1930s and late 1940s, interest in the Central Artery shifted from the municipal to the state level. Massachusetts, as part of a Works Progress Administration project, initiated a traffic survey of the Boston metropolitan area in 1938. A special legislative commission was appointed to consider the report's findings and made its own presentation to the state legislature in 1940. Its conclusions reframed Boston's traffic congestion as a state and regional issue and positioned its remedy as essential to the entire region's health.[30] When city agencies had initiated previous calls for a comprehensive metropolitan highway network (and for the Central Artery, in particular), their proposals had faltered largely because of the tremendous costs that the city could not shoulder alone. But state support for the Central Artery as a regional traffic lynchpin marked a critical turning point. As a result, in 1941 city, state, and regional authorities jointly filed the Central Traffic Artery Bill with the state legislature. Estimated to cost $10.5 million, this version of the Central Artery was cast as a double-deck highway primarily following the path of Atlantic Avenue, without any widening of the existing road and connecting to surface improvements already constructed by the city. The elevated road would not reuse any of the existing structure from the Atlantic Avenue Elevated. Four lanes of traffic would flow on the elevated deck, and three lanes of traffic would run along either side of the elevated highway's center road supports.[31] Despite the joint effort, and likely because of the United States' growing involvement in World War II, the legislature did not approve the bill but instead created a new legislative committee to evaluate Boston traffic congestion, the Legislative Recess Commission on Postwar Highways.[32]

Successive state reports on postwar redevelopment advocated for the Central Artery as part of larger highway improvement plans. The Massachusetts Postwar Highway Commission, formed in 1943, offered a report in 1945 that reiterated previous conclusions that a new north-south street was "necessary to relieve the congested conditions existing in the downtown retail, office and market districts."[33] The second volume of this report provided parody-like illustrations of Massachusetts's existing road conditions compared with modern transportation solutions in other parts of the country. Among other examples, it contrasted Boston's Atlantic Avenue with the streamlined entrance to New York's Triborough Bridge, hoping to stimulate change by visually demonstrating the comparatively provincial nature of Boston's infrastructure.[34] Using the commission's report as its foundation, the State Department of Public Works proposed a bill to authorize the Central Artery in December 1945. This version of the highway plan was to occupy a sequence of small existing streets, creating a more direct linear connection between North and South Stations. Mayor Curley, newly inaugurated for his fourth term, objected to the joint city-state financial structure proposed by the Department of Public Works, which left Boston responsible for $13 million. Additionally, he argued against the property damages that the new route would inflict and instead favored an alternate route offered by William J. McDonald, the real estate developer who had previously offered two distinct elevated highway schemes in 1929 and 1937, respectively. Echoing his 1937 proposal, McDonald's scheme would run along Atlantic Avenue for a good part of its length, sparing the significant property damage assured by the Department of Public Works' plan. These financial and route considerations compelled the state legislature to reject the bill as proposed. Governor Robert F. Bradford then authorized the preparation of a master highway plan for the entire metropolitan area, the first state plan of such scope.[35]

The resulting report, issued in 1948, secured the Central Artery's realization but not its final route. The Joint Board for the Metropolitan Master Highway Plan, composed of the commissioner of Public Works, the chairman of the State Planning Board, and the chairman of the Metropolitan District Commission, developed the plan in association with an engineering firm, Charles A. Maguire and Associates. Their design, *The Master Highway Plan for the Boston Metropolitan Area*, proposed a network of eight radial highways leading to an inner belt highway encircling downtown Boston (fig. 5.6). The Central Artery was to become a piece of this inner belt, acting as a distributor road for local traffic *and* a bypass road for through travel. The projected route for the Central Artery was not significantly different from that proposed previously. From south to north, it was to occupy a new right-of-way through the Chinatown and leather districts to align

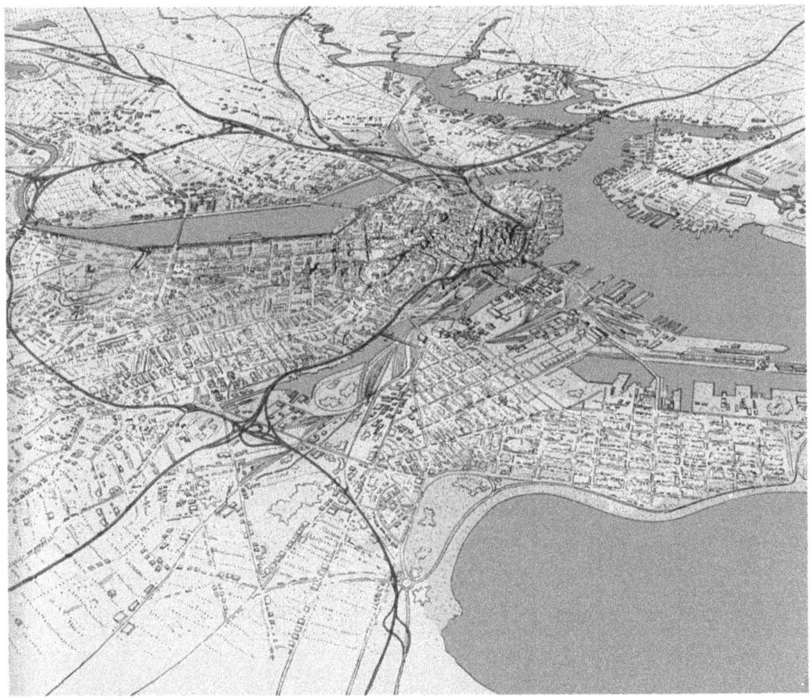

Figure 5.6 Aerial rendering of proposed metropolitan highway network, with Central Artery at center as single route through the downtown core, 1948. (Charles A. Maguire and Associates, engineers, with J. E. Greiner Company and De Leuw, Cather and Company. *The Master Highway Plan for the Boston Metropolitan Area*. Boston: Joint Board for the Metropolitan Master Highway Plan, 1948: inside cover rendering.)

with Atlantic Avenue from Summer Street to Northern Avenue, after which point it would turn northwest and run parallel to Cross Street through Haymarket Square to North Station and a bridge to Charlestown.[36] The Massachusetts Legislature approved these plans and issued $100 million in highway bonds in 1949. From these bonds the Department of Public Works and the Metropolitan District Commission jointly received $45 million for Boston-area improvements, and the Central Artery was the top priority for the allocation of these funds.[37]

The *Master Highway Plan*'s projection of the Central Artery reflected larger stylistic shifts since Robert Whitten's 1930 scheme. It forecast the elevated highway as a fluid, streamlined form flowing through a broad swath of land (figs. 5.7–5.8). No longer constrained by dense urban fabric as it had been in the Whitten version, it appeared as an almost sculptural object in the urban landscape. Cars, trucks, and buses of similarly sleek forms dot the road's bare deck and surrounding surface roads, alluding to the unimpeded travel and high speeds that the new road would afford to its users. This imagery projected the road's aesthetic and physical presence as totally divorced from the surrounding urban context, a strong modern foil to the modest commercial buildings and pedestrian scale of the downtown core. Taken at face value, the Central Artery's visual contrast with its surroundings would be notable. However, the road's route and requisite demolition of existing buildings brought its impending presence into alarming focus for Boston residents, businesses, and, surprisingly, its city government. This ultimately provoked more than five years of debates and design revisions among community activists, city, and state leaders, even as construction began on portions of the Artery.

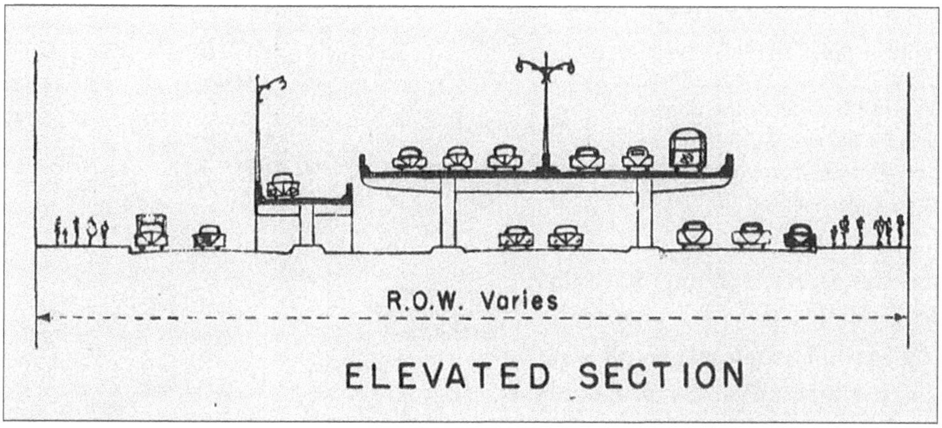

Figure 5.7 Typical elevated highway section as cast by 1948 plan. (Charles A. Maguire and Associates, engineers, with J. E. Greiner Company and De Leuw, Cather and Company. *The Master Highway Plan for the Boston Metropolitan Area.* Boston: Joint Board for the Metropolitan Master Highway Plan, 1948: 46.)

Figure 5.8 Central Artery as projected by 1948 plan. (Charles A. Maguire and Associates, engineers, with J. E. Greiner Company and De Leuw, Cather and Company. *The Master Highway Plan for the Boston Metropolitan Area.* Boston: Joint Board for the Metropolitan Master Highway Plan, 1948: 47.)

Two distinct sections of the Central Artery's route elicited controversy. The first was its relationship to the North End, one of Boston's oldest, most vibrant, and most ethnically diverse neighborhoods, occupying the northernmost tip of the city's peninsula. Like all of the official highway plans before it, the *Master Highway Plan* plotted the Central Artery's path between the North End and the downtown business core. The highway's intended trajectory to North Station would interrupt the North End's main street, Hanover Street, and would necessitate the seizure and demolition of commercial and residential structures in its way. Experts estimated that this would disrupt ten thousand jobs and cost the neighborhood \$10 million in land damages.[38] When this became apparent to neighborhood residents in early 1950, they rose in opposition. They argued for a highway route *around* the North End following the existing paths of Atlantic Avenue and Com-

Figure 5.9 Route options for Central Artery, 1950. ("North End Skyway Battle," *Christian Science Monitor* [1 May 1950]: 2. From The Christian Science Monitor. © 1950 Christian Science Monitor. All rights reserved. Used under license.)

mercial Street, echoing William McDonald's previous proposals (fig. 5.9). Though the route was 780 feet longer than that proposed by the state, its financial cost and accompanying destruction of local buildings would be much less. The North End activists voiced their concerns at a public hearing in front of the State Public Works Department on February 21, 1950; and on March 29, launched a publicity campaign throughout the effected neighborhoods where they literally labeled the buildings slated to be torn down for the highway. The activists also personally appealed to Mayor John Hynes in May of 1950.[39] However, these efforts ultimately failed to change the state's plans.

Both city and state officials supported the original Maguire scheme because of three distinct perceptions of projected traffic needs and existing conditions. First, they believed that traffic needed to get *to* the heart of the city, not around it.[40] The City Planning Board concurred with this assessment, arguing in an April 1950 advisory report to Hynes that the proposed alternate route would be so far from downtown that it would "defeat the purpose of the highway."[41] State officials maintained that getting traffic from such a highway route to the central business district would require additional street widenings and demolition that would equal if not surpass the predicted demolition for the crosstown option.[42]

Second, city and state officials argued that Atlantic Avenue and Commercial Street were important waterfront roads whose service to the city's maritime industries should not be disrupted. The City Planning Board had expressed this opinion more than a decade earlier when suggestions were first made for an alternate Atlantic Avenue route for the highway.[43] All of the traffic plans from the preceding twenty years had shared the board's conclusions about Atlantic Avenue and had supported a crosstown route instead. But it is important to recognize that these plans evaluated traffic congestion as it specifically pertained to local economic problems. Statistical traffic counts and business studies confirmed that the majority of vehicles were trying to access the downtown business core, and that the resulting traffic congestion was threatening the city's economic vitality. Thus, the state's Central Artery route responded directly to these findings. Even with potential savings in land and construction costs, the Atlantic Avenue option appeared misguided and impractical by comparison.

Third, this economic focus extended to the government's evaluation of the North End's physical infrastructure and economic vitality. Asked about the property seizures that the crosstown route would affect, Public Works aid Gordon McLean commented, "'No historic landmarks or monumental buildings are affected. . . . Many small business must be relocated, practically all of which are in obsolete uneconomic buildings.'"[44] This evaluation of existing structures evinced the planning profession's growing dismissal of old, dense, mixed-used neighborhoods in the 1940s and 1950s. One of Boston's oldest neighborhoods, the North End offered modest historic masonry buildings with commercial and retail spaces on the ground floors and residential spaces above. Different socioeconomic and ethnic groups comingled here, keeping streets busy with business patrons and local activity that thrived thanks to the area's close proximity to the waterfront and downtown business districts. This messy vitality, however, appeared chaotic, outdated, and prime for redevelopment to high-style architects and planners then enamored by superblocks and skyscraper-strewn visions of urban order. Jane Jacobs, the prophetic New York activist who rallied against such trends, described the North End with sardonic wit in her 1960 call to arms, *The Death and Life of Great American Cities*. Jacobs quipped, "Instead of super-blocks, or even decently large blocks, it has very small blocks; in planning parlance it is 'badly cut up with wasteful streets.' Its buildings are old. Everything conceivable is presumably wrong with the North End."[45] As Jacobs predicted, such conventions informed official evaluations of the North End. Compared to city and state plans for economic stimulation and urban highway construction, the North End's unpretentious buildings and disheartened constituents appeared trivial casualties. Therefore, even though Mayor Hynes and Governor Dever did review and authorize further evaluation of the Atlantic Avenue route, they ultimately sided with the Department of Public Works' original scheme. The Department of Public Works awarded the project's first construction contracts in September 1950, and initiated eminent domain proceedings for fifty-four parcels of North End land on November 10, 1950. Construction on the first piece of the Central Artery, a new bridge over the Charles River near North Station, began in January 1951.[46]

The second controversy over the Central Artery's route pertained to its southern reach from Fort Hill Square south of South Station and its impending relationship to the adjoining leather manufacturing and Chinatown districts. Early plans had shown the Artery in various proximities and routes to South Station, but the state did not announce publicly a final route until 1953, soon after the legislature allocated funds to construct this section. The state's plan was to create a new right-of-way extending south from Atlantic Avenue at Fort Hill Square across the leather district (just west of South Station) and continuing south through four full blocks of Chinatown between Hudson and Tyler Streets. The highway would terminate at its intersection with expressways approaching the city from the south. This path would necessitate $9 million in land seizures in the Chinatown district and would destroy a large portion of the local leather manufacturing district.[47] Mayor John Hynes, Massachusetts governor Christian Herter, the Boston City Planning Board, and residents and business owners in the affected areas all expressed alarm at this scheme, and over the next two years, engaged in lengthy debates, design reviews, and project revisions.

As with the contested North End route, distinct conceptions of local commerce, transportation efficiency, and architectural value fueled objections to the proposed Chinatown path. But in this case, local officials aligned more closely with area residents and business owners. Hynes rendered his opposition to the scheme in March 1953, followed by official objections from the City Planning Board and Boston City Council in the following months. All of these dissenters cited as their primary complaint the road's destruction of Boston's leather and garment districts. They predicted that this would be a major blow to the city's economy and would drive these industries to relocate to other cities.

Numerous design proposals and meetings about alternative routes stretched from the fall of 1953 through the spring of 1954. The City Planning Board conducted a two-month study that suggested shifting the proposed route to the east. Soon thereafter, the city and state jointly hired a New York engineering firm, Parsons, Brinckerhoff, Hall and MacDonald, to evaluate route options. Their report recommended constructing a portion of the highway in a tunnel that would run underneath the leather district and shifting the route one block west of the original scheme. This would have spared the leather district but still slighted Chinatown. The City Planning Board firmly disagreed with this proposal and engaged a separate engineering consultant to review the plan.[48] This firm, John Clarkeson Engineering, rejected the Parsons Brinckerhoff scheme. In January 1954, Clarkeson recommended carrying the road as an elevated highway along Atlantic Avenue and across the South Station rail yards, avoiding the leather and Chinatown areas entirely. They estimated that this route would save the state $15 million in construction costs and $12 million in property seizures.[49] However, State Public Works commissioner John A. Volpe was not enthusiastic about this alternative. He argued that the Artery was not supposed to bypass the congested parts of the city but was geared to bring people directly to and from these areas. Moreover, Volpe maintained that the Clarkeson scheme, which offered only six ramps along the corridor (compared to the state's proposal for twelve to fourteen), would be inadequate for necessary traffic flow. According to his rationale, this design complicated access to the downtown core instead of relieving it, which was contrary to the road's underlying premises of transportation efficiency and economic stimulation.[50]

Although the state initially seemed unwilling to consider an alternative to its consultant's recommendations, early 1954 brought some compromises. On February 9, Governor Herter, Mayor Hynes, and Commissioner Volpe agreed to revise the Central Artery's path to either skirt or tunnel under one of Chinatown's most prized structures, the four-year-old Chinese Merchants' Building, a neighborhood recreation center and headquarters for a community outreach organization. The Chinatown community took great pride in the new building, which they had financed themselves and which had been designed by a Chinese architect. The state's initial plan would have required the complete demolition of the Merchants Building, so subsequent ideas for relocating the structure or rerouting the road seemed promising by comparison. However, the salvation of the Merchants' Building did not translate to significant changes in the state's final plans. On February 11, Volpe announced that the state would proceed according to a slightly modified version of the Parsons Brinckerhoff scheme. The Central Artery would flow through an underground tunnel between Congress and Kneeland Streets, after which it would become a depressed surface road. The depressed road would run along Albany Street, slightly east of its originally proposed location, until its connection with regional highways. This route would still require land seizures but would not cut through the heart of the district to the same extent as the state's initial plan. Hynes ultimately endorsed this route, lamenting the state's unwillingness to adopt the city's alternate scheme, but crediting the city's efforts with compelling revisions of the state's original plans.[51]

While the Chinese community was pleased to see the Merchants' Building spared, they still disapproved of the state's plan. Dr. Stanley Chin, spokesman for the Chinese community and chairman of the Save Downtown Boston Committee, characterized the plan as "'just Commissioner Volpe's original plan with slight modifications.'"[52] Over the next three months, however, the community's dissention turned to compromise. Still faced with serious loss of homes and businesses with the state's plan, the community volunteered to sacrifice a section of the Chinese Merchants' Building to save most of the neighborhood's other threatened properties. Eliminating part of the Merchants' Building provided enough street space to move the highway 504 feet east and to make it a surface road, preventing many of the major property removals associated with the previous iteration. Commenting on this decision in August 1954, Chin evinced a decidedly more positive reaction: "'The Chinese people wholeheartedly support this plan in the interest of the public as a whole. Commissioner Volpe's 14-month waiting period showed democracy in action, and we benefitted as much as our friends in the area.'"[53]

Chin's allusion to the public's "interest" highlights an important undercurrent in highway rhetoric of this era. Lobbyists used such phraseology to justify arguments both for and against urban highways. Highway advocates like Robert Whitten and John Volpe argued that the new roads were for the public good by easing traffic and bolstering local business revenues. They qualified the costs of highway construction, including properties seized and neighborhoods fractured, in the same terms. But highway opponents like those in the North End and Chinatown saw these same factors as burdensome, maintaining that such expenses did not serve the social and economic health of their communities. Chinatown's ultimate compromise with the Merchants' Building evinced a middle ground between these two extremes, trading one evil for another perceived to be less vile. Thus, urban highways—and the Central Artery in particular—acquired layers of sociopolitical rhetoric that simultaneously celebrated, justified, and damned them.

Design Details

The design of the Central Artery's substructure received much less public attention than its route. Robert Whitten's 1930 *Thoroughfare Plan* had established the road's basic form as a simple elevated platform supported by rectangular piers. Whitten recognized that the road's scale and proximity to adjoining buildings had the potential to be architecturally awkward, if not altogether overwhelming and ugly. Whitten addressed this very issue in his 1930 report, qualifying the elevated highway proposal with reassurances that its position above the middle of a wide road would mediate its visual and auditory impact, and that designers would take "great care" to ensure the road's attractiveness.[54] Whitten even sent pictures of the nearly complete West Side Elevated Highway to the Boston City Planning Board in November 1930. These images were to be given to Boston newspapers to illustrate positive elevated highway precedents in other cities.[55] However, a decorative program comparable to that of the West Side Highway never materialized in Boston. Rather, the Central Artery's holding pattern during the 1930s and early 1940s focused on the road's promised traffic relief, financial implications, and projected route. Once the project secured state funding in 1950, the City Planning Board urged that "'eminent architectural consultants be engaged to assist in the preparation of adequate designs to enhance . . . (the arterial highway) structure.'"[56] The final design process for the Central Artery partially engaged this recommendation, but only through the filter of the engineering firms tasked with overseeing the road's design.

A joint venture between Fay, Spofford & Thorndike, a Boston-based engineering firm, and Charles A. Maguire and Associates, the engineering firm responsible for the 1948 *Master Highway Plan*, authored the final Central Artery design. Fay, Spofford & Thorndike had notable connections to the Boston City Planning Board and the local academic community. One of the firm's founders, Frederic H. Fay (1873–1944), was a founding member and chairman of the Boston City Planning Board and also a member of the Massachusetts State Planning Board. Fay was one of the earliest supporters of the Central Artery and advocated for the project during his tenure on both boards. Though he died before the project secured approval, it is likely that his connection influenced the state's ultimate retention of his firm. One of Fay's partners, Charles Milton Spofford, imbued the firm with a close connection to the Massachusetts Institute of Technology (MIT) where he was a professor of civil engineering. Spofford's colleague at MIT, John B. Wilbur, served as project director overseeing the entire Central Artery design process beginning in 1949. Wilbur subsequently recruited MIT students and recent graduates to work for Fay, Spofford & Thorndike on the Central Artery design.[57]

According to Cranston R. Rogers and Bruce Campbell, engineers who worked on the project for Fay, Spofford & Thorndike, the Central Artery design mediated between the precedent of the Whitten plan, state and federal standards for highway design, local urban context, and mandated thrift. As outlined in the 1948 *Master Highway Plan*, the state's decision to associate its highway improvement efforts with the federal government's Interstate highway program necessitated adherence to certain national design standards. These standards outlined appropriate widths for highway rights-of-way, routing methodologies, and basic design parameters for elevated structures, underpasses, and surface roads. The 1948 plan included a generalized profile for elevated roads (see fig. 5.7) that laid the basic formula for the Central Artery's substructure.[58] As Fay, Spofford & Thorndike and Maguire Associates developed the project's specific parameters, they worked to plan the road's columns to interfere as little as possible with existing street patterns. Aesthetic considerations received the least priority.[59]

Nevertheless, an architect did collaborate with the joint-venture partnership on the Central Artery design. Harold C. Knight (1902–1989) worked for Fay, Spofford & Thorndike between 1946 and 1953 as architect associate. A native of Somerville, Massachusetts, Knight trained at the Wentworth Institute of Technology and then at the Boston Architectural School. He worked as a draftsman in a number of architectural offices before serving as architect for the Prudential Insurance Company between 1934 and 1946. By the mid-1940s, Knight was building his own architectural practice while also beginning to work for Fay, Spofford & Thorndike.[60] While at the engineering firm, Knight's colleagues report that he was the sole architectural consultant for the Central Artery design. Knight advised on design details for sign bridges (holding signs over the road) and light standards, and also on the road's ramps and overall profile. The highway's ramps and substructure evinced the most overt architectural details with horizontal stripes laid in the ramps' concrete sidewalls and similar horizontal banding in the steel of the road's guardrails (fig. 5.10). This allusion to modern streamlined forms expanded on the Central Artery's basic materials and utilitarian forms without adding significant cost—which was very important to project leaders.[61]

Knight's personal architectural practice reflected midcentury-modern design trends. Initially called Harold C. Knight Architects and then rebranded Knight, Bagge & Anderson in 1953, Knight's firm specialized in the design of schools and churches, though also developed an extensive repertoire of administrative, hospital, and residential buildings for area military installations and private companies.

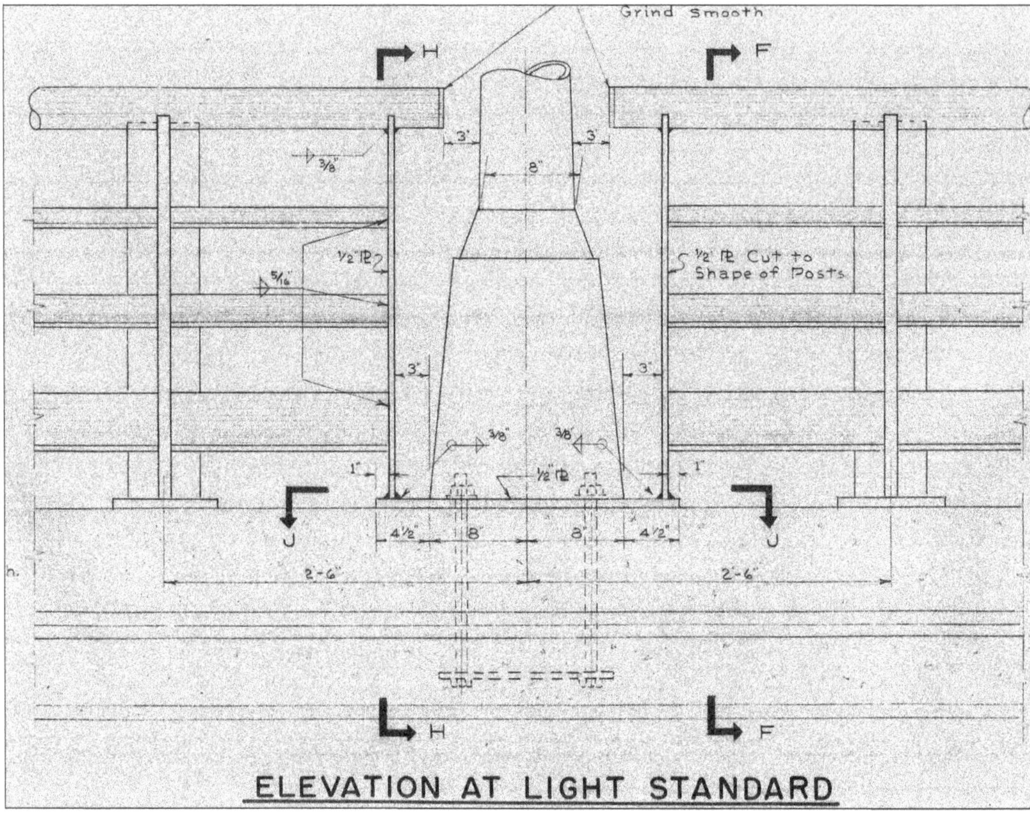

Figure 5.10 Typical handrail elevation at light standard, Central Artery. Charles A. Maguire & Associates and Fay, Spofford & Thorndike, engineers. ("John F. Fitzgerald Expressway." Architectural drawings, Sheet 110. July 18, 1956. Courtesy Fay, Spofford & Thorndike.)

The firm's design vocabulary contrasted sparse rectilinear forms with soaring gabled rooflines, sculptural bell towers, and flat-roofed colonnaded entrances (figs. 5.11–5.12). Materials were most often brick with contrasting trim of light-colored stone or concrete facing.[62]

Though little of this oeuvre relates directly to Knight's previous work at Fay, Spofford & Thorndike, it illustrates Knight's stylistic tendency toward modern geometric forms and a simple materials palette. This arguably would have suited Knight's role at Fay, Spofford & Thorndike quite well since he was working within the parameters of utilitarian engineering projects. Any architectural articulation needed to honor a project's utility and economy. The horizontal banding for the Central Artery accommodated this goal, growing directly and easily from the steel and concrete materials that would compose the road. This notwithstanding, as construction began on the Central Artery, Knight's horizontal stripes eventually paled in comparison to the overwhelming architectural contrasts provoked by juxtaposing the new highway with Boston's existing urban fabric.

Figure 5.11 First Baptist Church, Waltham, MA. Harold C. Knight, circa 1958. (Courtesy Knight/Turek family and KBA Architects.)

Figure 5.12 Fisk Memorial Church, Natick, MA. Harold C. Knight, circa 1963. (Courtesy Knight/Turek family and KBA Architects.)

III

BRIDGES AND DIVIDES

6

THE REALITIES AND CONSEQUENCES OF CONSTRUCTION

The throng stared as though hypnotized. Five thousand pounds of pear-shaped steel swinging from a crane cable hammered the sole remaining structure blocking the path of the $60,000,000 Central Artery between North Station and Haymarket sq. (1952)

—A. S. PLOTKIN, "Biggest Wrecking Job in Bay State History"

Modernistic pylons, rustications, plaques and volutes are carved on the granite masonry of the ramps. The supports of the elevated road have been placed in the street below in such a way as to cause the least interference with surface traffic. (1930)

—*New York Times*, "First Autos Travel Express Road Unit"

STARK CONTRASTS characterized the construction process for elevated highways. Harsh demolition activity clashed with the passivity of surrounding contexts; construction activity simultaneously overwhelmed and awed observers; and the new roads' scales and materials outpaced those of neighboring structures. While the finished roads did meet some predictions for traffic relief, economic stimulation, and physical redemption, their long-term reputations never matched the enthusiasm of early forecasts, and local responses to the highways typically reflected more conflicted feelings. This mixed reception derived from the juxtaposition of new elevated highways with existing structures and neighborhoods. While all three cities had long anticipated the promised rewards of new highways, they never could have foreseen fully the changes in scale and urban continuity that these projects would wreak. This chapter traces the evolution and revelation of this physical impact through the construction and completion phases for each highway. It contends that each road revealed its architectural and spatial import not only in its physical details but also in its relationship to, and cultivation of, changes in the surrounding urban fabric. Such impacts included population displacement, demolition of old buildings, construction of new architectural landmarks, and the creation of automobile-centric landscapes, all of which lingered as key factors in defining each road's legacy in the following years.

Figure 6.1 Start of demolition for Wacker Drive, October 2, 1924. ("Unroof Building over Heads of S. Water Firms," *Chicago Daily Tribune*, October 3, 1924, 23.)

Chicago

The construction of Wacker Drive began with haste and pickaxes, not pomp and circumstance. The scene unfolded on October 2, 1924, at 346–352 West South Water Street, an unremarkable commercial building along the riverfront used by Chicago's produce-market vendors. Slated for demolition to make way for the new South Water Street, the building's tenants had spent years trying to postpone or stop its demolition, asking for additional time and compensation for their relocation to a new venue. When a federal judge refused to respond to their latest legal petition, demolition crews leapt into action. Tenants refused entry to the workers, so the crew scaled the fire escapes and took pickaxes to the roof, showering those still inside with tar paper and debris (fig. 6.1).[1] "Progress" had arrived along the Chicago River.

This dramatic scene starkly pitted the merchants, representative of the old market and the city's antiquated waterfront, against government officials, demolition crews, and the "forward" march of mercantile, architectural, and automotive progress. The crew's ascension to and destruction of the rooftop clearly asserted progress's triumph. Chicago Plan Commission chairman Charles Wacker, relieved to see demolition finally underway, called the project's start "'the most important event in Chicago's history.'"[2]

Demolition and construction on South Water Street echoed and magnified the social, technological, and architectural contrasts evinced on this very first day of construction. Socially, the project's progress signaled the city's prioritization of commercial and traffic concerns over those of local market vendors. The literal seizure and demolition of South Water Street's modest buildings proved the most blaring indication of this choice. These buildings were unassuming masonry structures of four and five stories (see fig. 3.2). Gently arched windows syncopated their facades and brick cornices marked their peaks. Even as they shared party walls, building heights varied, giving South Water Street an irregular profile. Deep awnings knit the ground floors together, sheltering merchants and their goods in the adjoining street. The might of modern demolition equipment quickly leveled this unpretentious fabric on the north side of South Water Street, leaving the opposing buildings awkwardly exposed.[3] The swift imposition of such devastation demonstrated not only the technological power of modern construction but also more subtle messages about the comparative importance of the mercantile community and the value of their vernacular structures.

Just as this demolition began, there erupted a related debate over renaming South Water Street in honor of Wacker. A local businessman suggested the name change in May 1924, even before the fate of the South Water Street project was secured. He positioned the new name as a fitting tribute to Wacker's tireless advocacy for the city's modernization and beautification. The city council subsequently approved the name change in the summer of 1924.[4] In late 1924 and early 1925, however, successive editorials and letters-to-the-editor urged city leaders to reconsider their decision. These objections rested on South Water Street's rich history as a riverfront market and its contributions to Chicago's unprecedented growth in the nineteenth and early twentieth centuries. The *Chicago Tribune* editorialized about this in particular, lamenting the potential loss of historical continuity that would come with a name change: "Chicago is not so rich in the memories and traditions which great cities cherish that we can afford to give up, one after another, as we are doing, those ties with our past which old street and place names preserve."[5] Even as the *Tribune* and local voters approved of the physical recasting of South Water Street, they clung nostalgically to its nomenclature as an important vestige of the past. Notably, city leaders used similar reasoning to reach the opposite conclusion. If the produce market was to be removed and replaced by a gleaming double-deck boulevard, it followed that the new street should receive a similarly new and modern name. By removing the physical and intangible remnants of old South Water Street they would signal the area's complete rebirth. This approach ultimately prevailed, and by June 1925 the new name of Wacker Drive was increasingly common parlance.[6]

From a technical perspective, Wacker Drive's scale, materials, and rate of construction far outpaced existing conditions along the river. The interruption of existing buildings and streets signaled the first indication of this change. Preparatory demolition claimed fourteen feet from Market Street building fronts between Randolph and Lake Streets and twelve feet from sidewalks in the same area. It seized the entire Lind block at the corner of Randolph and Market Streets, one of the few structures to survive the Great Fire of 1871.[7] The Hibbard, Spencer, Bartlett & Co. Building, a ten-story masonry warehouse next to the State Street Bridge, was the largest structure to succumb to demolition.[8] As these older streets and structures literally fell victim to progress, these changes edified Chicago's intended transition from a nineteenth-century industrial city to a twentieth-century business hub.

Construction scenes confirmed the awe-inspiring breadth of the improvement. Swarms of workers dotted the river's shore, first digging caissons for the road's footings and then laying an intricate web of steel bars to reinforce the concrete roadbed. On August 10, 1925, over 150 workers poured twelve hundred cubic yards of concrete—reportedly the largest recorded concrete pour in a single day. Twelve days later the contractor broke its own record, pouring the same amount of concrete in an hour's less time.[9] As workers prepared the roadbed along the waterfront, its width and reach quickly dwarfed the workers themselves (fig. 6.2). Atop this foundation crews built the wooden forms for the road's concrete columns. This pattern of wooden supports and strapping initially appeared spindly and crude, but as the march of the monolithic columns emerged, they foreshadowed the rigor and scale of the finished streetscape (fig. 6.3). Workers, perched atop the formwork, seemed small and fragile by comparison, as did the existing buildings in the background. One journalist called the project "the most interesting and instructive exhibit in civic engineering to be viewed on this continent today."[10]

The pace of construction matched the promised speed and modernity of the finished road. City leaders divided the project into twelve sections and awarded contracts for each portion separately. Construction began at the road's two extremes and worked inward toward the midpoint. Officials predicted that their technically savvy, diligent, and efficient approach to construction (even in difficult weather conditions) would allow early completion of the project. They were right. The first

Figure 6.2 Workers laying steel rebar for Wacker Drive's roadbed. (Chicago Plan Commission, *Souvenir of Wacker Drive* [Chicago: Chicago Plan Commission, 1926], 14. Courtesy Herlihy Mid-Continent Construction Co.)

Figure 6.3 1926 view of Jewelers' Building under construction, Chicago. Dinkelberg and Giaver, 1925–1927. Wacker Drive under construction in foreground. (DN-0080157, *Chicago Sun-Times/ Chicago Daily News* collection, Chicago History Museum.)

portion of Wacker Drive (between Lake and Franklin Streets) opened on August 31, 1925—less than a year after construction began. Successive blocks opened in the following months until the project's official completion and dedication on October 20, 1926. Seventy-five thousand people gathered to celebrate the new thoroughfare, which Mayor Dever called "'the greatest improvement of its kind in the world's history.'"[11] By the end of its first day, local police officers credited Wacker Drive with already affecting noticeable improvements in Loop traffic congestion.[12]

Visions of Beauty and Efficiency

As built, Wacker Drive stretched eight blocks east to west, from Michigan Avenue to Market Street, for a total distance of just over one mile (fig. 6.4). The new road offered three levels: a basement level for parking (stretching only from Michigan to Wabash Avenues), a lower level for through traffic, and the upper level for local surface travel. The lower level's 135-foot width accommodated six lanes of traffic, a sidewalk along its southern edge, and docks and loading areas along the water (fig. 6.5). The upper level's surface was 114 feet wide, with seventy-two feet for the

Figure 6.4 Completed Wacker Drive and riverfront, 1931. Top level of Wacker Drive visible along the right (south) side of the river, flanked by the completed Jewelers' Building at far right. Ramp to lower Wacker Drive, and accompanying balustrades and arcades, define the river's southern edge. (Chicago History Museum, ICHi-005777.)

road, twenty-four feet for a sidewalk on its southern edge, and eighteen feet for a riverside promenade on the northern side. Traffic flowed seamlessly from existing surface streets to Wacker Drive's upper level, making the road's multilevel nature invisible from its land side.

From the river and its northern shores, however, it was clear that the multistory street had dramatically recast the riverfront. A new, crisp concrete girdle wrapped the shoreline, stringing the Loop's buildings along a grand arcade (figs. 6.6–6.7; see also figs. I.1–I.2 in introduction). Lower Wacker Drive ran behind the arcade, receiving light and air through its broad concrete arches. The arcade's chamfered piers carried volute-topped concrete brackets that supported the upper-level roadway. This pairing created the illusion of classical columns with bases, shafts, and capitals. The surface road flowed atop these columns, bordered by a concrete balustrade. Rectilinear pedestals syncopated the balustrade, aligning with the columns below. Concrete obelisks topped these pedestals at major intersections, connoting pauses in the road's march. These obelisks carried groups of spherical lights at key intersections and pedestrian destinations (fig. 6.8). Benches and overlooks occasionally interrupted the balustrade, providing places for pedestrians to stop and enjoy the view of the river beyond. Staircases abutted each of the seven bridges that joined Wacker Drive, allowing pedestrians to descend to

Figure 6.5 1926 view of automobiles and horse and carriage driving on still-unfinished ramp between lower and upper levels of Wacker Drive. Octagonal structural support and lower level are visible at left. (DN-0082061, *Chicago Sun-Times/Chicago Daily News* collection, Chicago History Museum.)

the waterfront promenades and docks below. The lower road assumed a more ornamental architectural vocabulary between Wabash and Michigan Avenues, with rectangular openings replacing the arcade, smooth rustications on its piers and walls, and a small dentil molding and cornice defining the transition to the upper level's balustrade (fig. 6.9). The combined effect of these details was a unified and majestic shoreline far removed from South Water Street's decrepit conditions.

Wacker Drive's functional model also outshined its predecessor. Because of its multiple levels, the road was able to separately accommodate different types of needs. The upper-street surface, which offered on-grade intersections with neighboring streets, carried local traffic. The lower level channeled freight and long-distance traffic and also connected directly to waterfront shipping areas and the basement-level loading zones of neighboring buildings. At Michigan Avenue, where the road had three levels (the lowest for parking), the middle deck provided a freight station connecting to the city's sixty-two-mile underground tunnel network.[13] These components streamlined the relationship between different functions and modes of transportation in the city. River deliveries could now move

WEST WACKER

Figure 6.6 (facing page, top) Wacker Drive, looking east from Franklin Street Bridge, 2008. (Courtesy Hope Dinsmore.)

Figure 6.7 (facing page, bottom) Lower Wacker Drive arcade detail, from Wells Street Bridge. (Courtesy Hope Dinsmore.)

Figure 6.8 (right) Upper Wacker Drive obelisk and light detail. (Courtesy Hope Dinsmore.)

Figure 6.9 (below) Wacker Drive between Wabash and Michigan Avenues, from Wabash Bridge. (Courtesy Hope Dinsmore.)

directly from boats to freight trucks, which then could travel at uninterrupted high speeds through the city on Lower Wacker Drive. Freight could also move directly from boats or freight trucks to the tunnel system. Separate from these functional advantages, Wacker Drive absented the delivery and service needs of commercial buildings from public view. Freight trucks could unload their wares to basement-level loading docks on Lower Wacker Drive and then easily continue on to other destinations. In effect, by subtracting one constituency of vehicles from surface streets, Wacker Drive both lessened street congestion and beautified the surrounding environment. This practical model gave the riverfront an unprecedented system of coordinated urban movement.

The promise of Wacker Drive's efficiency and amenities stimulated new development along the waterfront. The completion of the Michigan Avenue improvement in 1920 had laid the groundwork for the Loop's expansion to and across the Chicago River. When the *Chicago Tribune* built its iconic gothic-inspired skyscraper on North Michigan Avenue (Raymond Hood and John Mead Howells, 1922–1925), it boldly declared the viability of major commercial development on the river's northern shore. Wacker Drive, because of its connection to Michigan Avenue, only broadened the possibilities for, and promise of, future riverside growth.[14]

The forty-story Jewelers' Building (built 1925–1927) at the corner of Wabash Avenue and South Water Street (now 35 East Wacker Drive) evinced early confidence in the potential for this area (see figs. 6.3–6.4). In 1924 the Chicago Jewelers' Association hired Chicago architect Frederick P. Dinkelberg and engineer Joachim G. Giaver to design a new building uniquely suited to their needs. The duo, who had spent most of their careers working for D. H. Burnham and Company, designed a classically inspired skyscraper with a twenty-three-story monolithic base topped by a setback tower, crowned in turn by a round cupola. Its stately terra-cotta exterior belied the building's most unusual feature: an internal parking garage at the core of its first twenty-three stories. The integrated garage allowed vendors and clients to securely enter and leave the building in their automobiles, alleviating concerns about thefts during travel to and from jewelry transactions. Offices surrounded the garage and filled the setback tower.[15] Such marriage of classical grandeur and modern programmatic practicality mirrored similar intentions for Wacker Drive. The building embraced the automotive public and integrated it into its organizational rationale, setting a modern new trend for the Chicago River waterfront.

A slew of major land transactions and construction announcements followed on the heels of the Jewelers' Building. In January 1925 developers announced plans for a new eight-hundred-seat theater along then-called West South Water Street. The summer and fall of 1925 saw successive land purchases, compelled by hastening progress on the street's construction. After its completion, buzz intensified about construction along Wacker Drive and the north side of the river. Neighborhood businesses and advocacy groups lobbied for the construction of new public buildings on the north side; car magnate Alonzo C. Mather announced his plans to build the world's tallest twin towers on Wacker Drive and Michigan Avenue; the University of Chicago projected a new Loop skyscraper; and Marshall Field and Company decided to consolidate all of its wholesale, warehouse, and manufacturing facilities into a mammoth new building on the river's north bank—what would become the Merchandise Mart (Graham, Anderson, Probst and White, built 1928–1930).[16] All of these plans validated the Chicago Plan Commission's predictions that Wacker Drive would attract new types and volumes of development to the area.

This groundswell of real estate activity also raised concerns about the architectural character of new buildings along Wacker Drive. As cast in a front-page cartoon by the *Chicago Tribune* on August 27, 1926, the new Wacker Drive skyline had the potential to be a "jumble" or a "joy" (fig. 6.10). The cartoon projected the "jumble" option as an array of buildings of dissonant heights and styles, while the alternative of "joy" offered unified blocks of commercial buildings with common heights, cornice lines, and architectural vocabularies.[17] The latter image strongly resembled the renderings used by the Chicago Plan Commission to lobby for the South Water Street improvement. The ideal of such imagery could not be guaranteed in the context of private capitalist development, however, nor was it clear if such uniformity was even desirable.

Edward H. Bennett had first called attention to this issue with a March 1926 statement urging property owners to erect buildings that complemented the architectural style of Wacker Drive and the Michigan Avenue Bridge.[18] Mayor Dever formalized this call in August 1926 when he and the municipal art commission initiated a meeting of local property owners, city officials, and architects to discuss Wacker Drive's architectural future. In his comments at the meeting, Dever urged, "'A unified plan of building construction should be worked out and instead of a hodge-podge of architecture rising with two story buildings alongside of skyscrapers, there should be a coordinated set of beautiful, dignified structures along the entire drive.'"[19] While few disagreed that Wacker Drive had great potential for civic beauty, many questioned the viability, legality, and desirability of holding private property owners to a common design standard. Even the *Tribune*, who had earlier editorialized on the promise of uniform building styles and heights, modified its stance to support more moderate coordination of building materials and sill lines. It reasoned: "By itself, a Tribune Tower is a thing of beauty. A row of them, side by side, would lack distinction. Better to let each architect have a free hand in designing his building, provided only that certain minimum restrictions are accepted."[20] The mayor's committee met to establish such standards during late 1926 and early 1927. Early ideas included developing a coordinated building program for the entire waterfront to which property owners would be asked to voluntarily adhere. The committee later agreed that it would not be feasible to affect the heights or designs of structures, but that uniform cornice and balcony lines might sufficiently bind structures together.[21]

Bennett tried to navigate a middle ground between ideas of staid repetition and

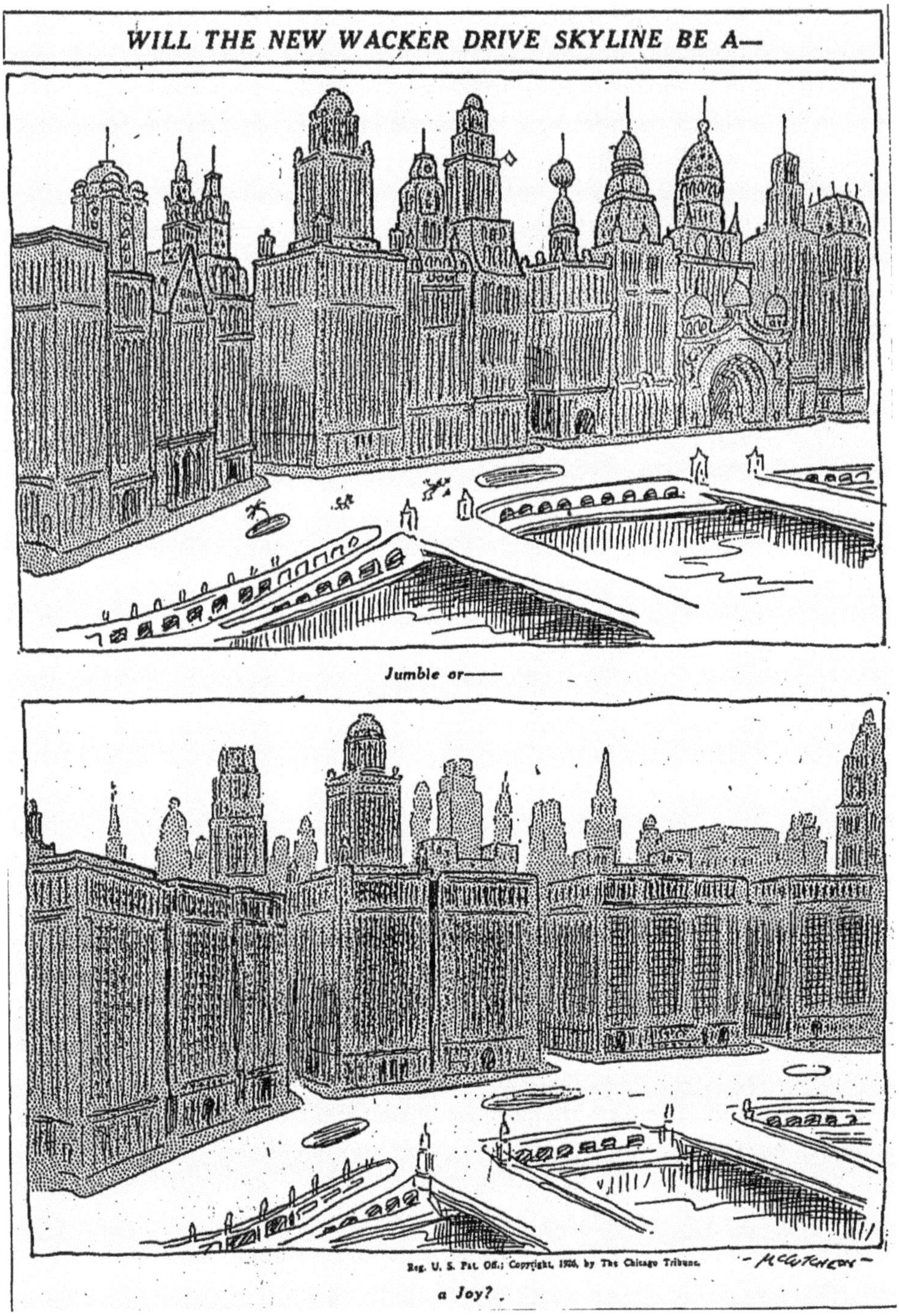

Figure 6.10 *Chicago Tribune* cartoon questioning the direction of architectural development along the new Wacker Drive, August 1926. ("Will the Architecture of Wacker Drive Be a Jumble or a Joy" *Chicago Tribune* (27 August 1926): 1. From Chicago Tribune. © 1926 Chicago Tribune. All rights reserved. Used under license.)

complete design independence. Speaking to the mayor's committee in December 1926, he advocated for finding a way to "bind the blocks and entire street into a whole," while still allowing the individual buildings to singularly express their search for height.[22] Bennett envisioned clusters of higher buildings at major intersections (which were already beginning to evolve on their own) and the use of common belt courses to create visual continuity between individual buildings. He was wary of overly simplistic interpretations of codes regulating skyscraper design, balking at the prospect of a row of simple rectangular masses topped by singular protruding towers. Rather, Bennett called for "variety to the architectural front and a feeling of substantiality in the architecture rather than the impression . . . of a screen of no depth or simply a flat wall pierced with holes of various sizes." [23] Bennett's position therefore struck a careful midpoint between the architectural unity of his own design for Wacker Drive, the banal repetition of box-like buildings, and the endless possibilities of free market capitalism.[24] He wanted Wacker Drive to foster modern architectural invention while respecting the connective armature of the road itself.

In spite of the efforts by Bennett and Dever, it was difficult and legally impossible to enforce any kind of architectural cooperation among Wacker Drive property owners. By August 1927, the *Chicago Tribune* was already lamenting the undistinguished quality of the new buildings along the drive, and it predicted that soon "no one with an eye for line and composition will be able to walk down Wacker Drive without a shudder."[25] The local chapter of the American Institute of Architects, upon urging of the *Tribune*'s aforementioned editorial, convened a committee to advise Loop property owners on design issues in September 1927. This extended the responsibilities of the organization's municipal art committee, which already had been advising the city of Chicago on the ornamentation of its new bridges. In its expanded role, the municipal art committee would offer property owners free evaluation of proposed architectural designs. Officials positioned such a dialogue as in the public's best interest, and though any recommendations would not be binding, they predicted that owners would be receptive to such feedback.[26] Despite such optimism, the municipal art committee saw minimal activity in 1927.[27] Wacker Drive's individual blocks, though birthed by a commonly held and publicly financed vision for urban beauty, would be rendered by unregulated private enterprise.

The architectural inconsistencies of its emerging skyline notwithstanding, Wacker Drive's completion and attraction of new development stimulated enthusiasm for similar redevelopment of other areas of the city—most notably opposite Wacker Drive along the northern shore of the Chicago River. In the 1909 *Plan of Chicago,* Burnham and Bennett had envisioned two facing-riverside boulevards, and so the completion of Wacker Drive implied the necessary construction of its foil on the opposite bank. Local property owners and city officials had begun to lobby for this improvement soon after construction of Wacker Drive had commenced. However, their reasoning for this campaign was quite different from that advanced for Wacker Drive. Because of the market on South Water Street and its proximity to the Loop, city officials had positioned its riverside improvement as a sorely needed remedy to existing problems regarding sanitation, transportation, and commerce. The north side, however, hitherto a less commercial and less accessible part of the city, did not provoke the same justification. Instead, petitioners lamented the presently unsavory view, arguing that "unless something is done across the river to improve conditions, the outlook from Wacker drive will be a dreary and unpleasant one."[28]

While architects and business leaders repeatedly returned to ideas for a "North Wacker Drive" between 1925 and 1930, only a small section of the road ever materialized. This fragment stretched between North Wells and North Orleans Streets on the river side of Marshall Field and Company's Merchandise Mart (completed 1930). Marshall Field and Company, when it had first announced its development plans in 1927, had promised to donate enough land in front of its new building to allow construction of the first portion of a riverside drive. It appears that the retail giant fulfilled this promise and that city coffers funded the construction of the road itself.[29] The public interest and mutual benefits of this public-private partnership, however, did not replicate themselves elsewhere along the river's north shore. City officials directed their attention to more pressing street improvements that directly benefited the mature parts of the city. Notably this included Lake Shore Drive, Burnham and Bennett's stately lakeside road and accompanying parks from the 1909 plan, whose construction south of Grant Park stretched from 1917 until 1932. Other concurrent *Plan of Chicago* projects involved widening downtown streets—including Roosevelt, La Salle, Ogden, Ashland, Damen, and Western—and the extension of other streets into adjoining areas. These improvements provided more immediate relief to downtown traffic concerns, thereby minimizing the urgency of a north riverside road by comparison. Mounting municipal debt and the Great Depression slowed the improvement program in the late 1920s, and the north river drive project never reemerged as a major priority.[30] Today, the small road fronting the Merchandise Mart (now renamed Merchandise Mart Plaza) stands as a fragment of the ideal waterfront originally envisioned by Burnham and Bennett (fig. 6.11).

With its displacement of existing buildings and tenants, creation of a unified architectural identity, and stimulation of new business sectors and geographies, Wacker Drive fulfilled its sponsors' intentions of changing the physical and architectural character of the Chicago River waterfront. In October 1927 *Architectural Record* applauded this transformation, describing it as "a broad, beautiful, double-decked drive (the first of its kind), built to the water's edge, across which lofty skyscrapers now cast tall shadows to mirror their jeweled towers in the clear water below."[31] But the majesty and unity of Wacker Drive's architectural features belied more complicated and troubling undercurrents about the local economy, social

Figure 6.11 Riverfront road in front of the Merchandise Mart, Chicago. Graham, Anderson, Probst, and White, 1930. (Courtesy Hope Dinsmore.)

welfare, and the merits of existing urban forms. Whatever the legitimate traffic, fire, and health concerns, Chicago's leaders' indictment of South Water Street's ramshackle buildings and impromptu market format connoted value judgments about the propriety and desirability of these conditions. To compete with more established cities in an increasingly global economy, Chicago chose to literally remove these vestiges of its commercial heritage and to replace them with a new icon of transportation efficiency and architectural modernity. This selective editing of local history and physical form smacks of the legacy of Baron Georges-Eugène Haussmann in nineteenth-century Paris, who similarly sought to reframe Paris's physical form to reflect a curated version of French identity.[32]

With this lineage in mind, it becomes clear that Wacker Drive was born of both traditional and modern aspirations. Because of its highly visible definition of the shoreline, Beaux Arts vocabulary, and multiple levels of movement, Wacker Drive proclaimed a radical departure from existing conditions and a clear endorsement of popular City Beautiful principles. However, this same model also situated the project within a tradition of lower-class disenfranchisement that set a troubling standard for subsequent decades of urban improvement projects—both in Chicago and elsewhere. As built then, Wacker Drive simultaneously demonstrated the aesthetic panache, functional efficiency, and social paradoxes of modern urban planning.

New York City

During Wacker Drive's design and construction, Chicago leaders repeatedly stressed its redemptive role in recasting the riverfront's physical and architectural character. By contrast, in New York, the West Side Elevated Highway's promised traffic relief overshadowed full comprehension of its physical presence virtually until its completion. During eight long years of construction, scenes of dramatic contrast emerged between the new road's mechanized superstructure and the more varied utilitarian features of the Hudson River shore, but the public dialogue remained focused on the highway's predicted efficiency. The project's scale, route, and environmental context profoundly colored this situation. So even as high-style architects designed a rich program of architectural embellishments for the superstructure, it was the utility and magnitude of the road's physical presence that ultimately affected New Yorkers the most.

Three underlying factors impacted the construction process and ultimate reception of the West Side Elevated Highway. First was the project's scale. As opposed to Wacker Drive's length of just over one mile, the West Side Highway stretched more than four miles, from Canal Street at the south to Seventy-Second Street. This breadth meant that construction necessarily proceeded more gradually. Officials divided the highway into seven distinct sections—each with its own unique set of challenges and ramifications. With this staggered construction pattern, scenes of construction beginning and ending repeated themselves over the life of the project. This not only meant that final completion of the highway took much longer but also that its construction impacted a larger mass of citizens, properties, and traffic than its Chicago counterpart.

Second, the West Side Highway's route along existing rights-of-way precluded the controversies about property seizures and demolition that had so tarnished Wacker Drive's evolution. Marching up West Street and the marginal way adjoining the waterfront piers, the West Side Highway necessitated demolition of only two buildings along its path. This made its construction less emotionally charged than that in Chicago and infused its progress with a sense of awe more than one of resentment.

Nevertheless, the highway did significantly impact street patterns and surface traffic, which constitutes its third defining characteristic. In Chicago, Wacker Drive's functional and architectural ethos depended on the road's integration into the river shoreline such that its multitiered nature was visible only from the river and its northern shores. In Manhattan, however, the highway's constructed nature atop the street surface affected both highway users and viewers. The gradual emergence of its steel superstructure dramatically announced the arrival of a new era of urban transportation. Simultaneously, this iteration of modern urbanism differed both from neighboring buildings and infrastructure and from other contemporaneous improvement projects happening elsewhere in Manhattan. This made the West Side Highway a midpoint of sorts, straddling distinct definitions of architectural, landscape, urban, and transportation modernity.

Segments of a Whole

Construction of the West Side Elevated Highway began on May 24, 1929, with the groundbreaking for the road's first section between Canal Street and Twenty-Second Street. Work progressed quickly here, reaching completion in November 1930.[33] During these eighteen months, scenes along the route illustrated shifting norms for transportation, urban scale, and architecture. The motley crew of vehicles along the Hudson River shore clearly evinced the transportation changes (fig. 6.12). This single corridor hosted huge mercantile and passenger ships, the on-grade tracks of the New York Central Railroad, horses and carts, automobiles, trucks, and pedestrians—not to mention the new assemblage of cranes and excavators now working on the highway itself. The new highway's dominant location

Figure 6.12 West Side Elevated Highway under construction, looking north from Canal Street, June 12, 1929. (Borough President of Manhattan Photograph Collection, negative 408a. Courtesy NYC Municipal Archives.)

Figure 6.13 View north from Canal Street of West Side Elevated Highway under construction, March 14, 1930. Compare to previous view from same location in figure 6.12. (Borough President of Manhattan Photograph Collection, negative 477b8. Courtesy NYC Municipal Archives.)

Figure 6.14 West Side Elevated Highway under construction. View north from south of Charleton Street, February 22, 1930. (Borough President of Manhattan Photograph Collection, negative 477c02. Courtesy NYC Municipal Archives.)

straddling the middle of West Street clearly signaled the growing primacy of automotive transportation among these options. The road's comparative scale to the adjoining pier buildings reinforced this trend. Little previously had challenged the dominance of the piers and their visiting ships, but the highway's long, lofty march presented a strong new rival. This was magnified at street level for pedestrians and vehicles, which were dwarfed and literally overshadowed by the tall superstructure (figs. 6.13–6.14). At the level of the road deck, workers had the unusual opportunity to walk parallel to the upper stories and roofs of adjoining buildings, surely a sublime experience (figs. 6.15–6.16). People atop the roadbed appeared small in comparison to both the neighboring buildings and the highway's breadth and seemingly infinite reach.

The highway's materials also questioned norms of architecture along the shore. As discussed previously, a menagerie of piers, docks, and warehouse buildings defined this corridor, all of modest masonry or wood construction and in various stages of benign neglect. The arrival of the highway's slender steel supports and gridded underpinnings provided a strong mechanized contrast to these surroundings. The superstructure appeared as a mechanized snake slowly creeping through the street corridor. Where stone lintels, masonry walls, cornices, and occasional pediments composed the existing architectural vocabulary, the highway's materials and geometric regularity asserted a definitive tone of change (figs. 6.17–6.18).

Construction of the successive sections of the West Side Highway replicated these contrasts but also more clearly reflected the competing interests and visions for the Hudson River waterfront. The fact that construction did not automatically proceed northward from Twenty-Second Street demonstrates the nuances of these conditions. Work began on the second section of the highway, from Fifty-Ninth to Seventy-Second Streets, in September 1930. This portion involved careful negotiation and collaboration with the New York Central Railroad, whose Sixtieth Street rail yard was to be spanned by the elevated road (fig. 6.19). The highway's columns needed to interfere as little as possible with existing (and proposed) railroad tracks, which ultimately compelled the choice of caisson construction for the highway's footings instead of more typical (and more disruptive) pile-driving. The railroad company opted to build this section for the city so that it could control all of these variables, effectively trading its contractor services for city-owned land needed for its track relocation project. This advanced the highway while also setting the stage to upgrade the New York Central Railroad tracks and Riverside Park north of Seventy-Second Street, an effort led by Robert Moses beginning in 1934 and subsequently named the West Side Improvement. This northernmost portion of the West Side Elevated Highway, which connected to Riverside Drive at Seventy-Second Street, opened to the public on March 9, 1932.[34]

Due to lagging resolution of other west side issues, the remaining stretch of highway between Twenty-Second and Fifty-Ninth Streets was subdivided into four

Figure 6.15 Workers laying granite block paving on West Side Elevated Highway, September 19, 1930. (Borough President of Manhattan Photograph Collection, negative 472f. Courtesy NYC Municipal Archives.)

Figure 6.16 Looking north at Nineteenth Street ramp, West Side Elevated Highway under construction, August 21, 1930. (Borough President of Manhattan Photograph Collection, negative 477f31. Courtesy NYC Municipal Archives.)

Figure 6.17 West Side Elevated Highway under construction, view from Clarkson Street, 1929. (Milstein Division, The New York Public Library.)

Figure 6.18 Workers atop West Side Elevated Highway during construction, piers visible in background, 1929. (Milstein Division, The New York Public Library.)

Figure 6.19 West Side Elevated Highway passing over New York Central Railroad yard, June 23, 1933. (Borough President of Manhattan Photograph Collection, negative 0692-457. Courtesy NYC Municipal Archives.)

smaller segments. Work between Twenty-Second and Thirty-Eighth Streets began on August 19, 1931, following long-awaited agreement between city and federal officials over the construction of new piers along the Hudson River. Between 1928 and 1931 there had been at least three different proposed locations for these new piers: between Forty-Eighth and Fiftieth Streets, Twenty-Third and Twenty-Ninth Streets, or Forty-Eighth and Fifty-Eighth Streets. In each case, the city's desire to berth large ocean liners needed to be weighed against potential disruption to the flow of vessels along the river and interference with proposed land-borne projects, including the elevated highway. The U.S. War Department held jurisdiction over the pier decision because of its impact on water transportation, thus progress on the highway above Twenty-Second Street could not proceed until finalization of the pier plans. Partial resolution came on January 14, 1931, when the War Department approved the erection of two new piers at Forty-Eighth and Fiftieth Streets. This effectively freed more southern portions of the shore from consideration, thereby allowing construction of the elevated highway to proceed north from Twenty-Second Street. Accordingly, construction began on June 20, 1932, and the new section from Twenty-Second to Thirty-Eighth Streets opened on January 5, 1933.[35]

The next section of the highway between Thirty-Eighth and Forty-Sixth Streets progressed rapidly. The city opened bids for this segment in November 1933, and construction began in early March 1934. By the following August it welcomed its first users.[36] However, the remaining stretch between Forty-Sixth and Fifty-Ninth Streets did not begin for almost an additional two years. The main problem was the New York Dock Department's aforementioned pier construction project. While site selection had been partially resolved in 1931, subsequent negotiations revised the plans to include piers at Forty-Sixth, Forty-Eighth, Fifty-Second and Fifty-Fourth Streets. Site preparations at these locations included excavations, foundations, and realignment of surface streets, all of which needed to happen before pier construction could even begin. The extent of these site improvements affected the West Side Highway, whose planned route between Forty-Eighth and Fifty-Eighth Streets ultimately needed to shift one block east to run along Twelfth Avenue. This change, in turn, required the seizure and demolition of two buildings, including a large trash incinerator at Twelfth Avenue and Fifty-Sixth Street, which further delayed the project. All told, these factors delayed actual pier construction until November 3, 1934, and construction of the final highway segment until February 13, 1936.[37]

After almost another full year of construction, city leaders dedicated the complete four-and-one-half-mile West Side Elevated Highway on February 9, 1937. Mayor Fiorello La Guardia and Borough President Samuel Levy marked the occasion by conducting a good-humored automobile race between City Hall and Fiftieth Street. The mayor traversed three miles on the new highway, reaching his destination in twelve minutes and forty-six seconds. Levy, on the other hand, used existing surface streets to travel the same distance and arrived more than twenty minutes after the mayor. The mayor's victory, a foregone conclusion, provided compelling evidence of the new time savings afforded by the completed highway.[38]

These dedicatory events marked the completion of Julius Miller's original conception of the highway, running from Canal Street to Seventy-Second Street. But during the many years of construction, the highway's popularity had created new congestion that subsequently spurred an addition to the highway. This pertained to the highway's original southern terminus at Canal Street. New congestion had

Figure 6.20 Looking north at Duane Street, West Side Elevated Highway, May 31, 1938. (Borough President of Manhattan Photograph Collection, negative 1245e. Courtesy NYC Municipal Archives.)

developed there as a result of vehicles clamoring for access to the ramp to the West Side Highway. Levy hoped to alleviate this congestion by extending the highway further south to Battery Place. In August 1934 he secured approval and funding for this extension, but construction of the first segment of this link, from Canal to Duane Streets, did not begin until January 1938.[39] The reasons for this delay are not entirely clear, though fiscal issues were likely part of the problem. The city had reported worsening financial conditions in the previous years, which had slowed other portions of the highway's construction. Design details were the other component of this delay, as the Holland Tunnel's path beneath Canal Street prevented typical continuation of the road's structural supports. Instead, engineers had to develop a bridge to span this section. The bridge design received approval and funding in July 1937, and construction began in early 1938. The connection between Canal and Duane Streets opened to traffic on February 4, 1939 (fig. 6.20).[40]

World War II delayed completion of the highway's remaining leg between Duane Street and Battery Place. Construction resumed in March 1948 and focused on the segment between Duane and Carlisle Streets, which opened the following November. The section between Carlisle Street and the new Brooklyn-Battery Tunnel was completed on May 25, 1950.[41] After more than twenty years, the full stretch of the West Side Elevated Highway was finally complete.

The Finished Product

Despite the varying times and circumstances of its construction, the West Side Elevated Highway presented a remarkably consistent engineering and architectural vocabulary.[42] The highway offered two thirty-foot-wide roadways threaded up to twenty-five feet in the air for four and a half miles along the Hudson River shore. This provided three travel lanes in each direction, interrupted by center-entrance ramps between Nineteenth and Twenty-Third Streets, and at Fortieth, Forty-Sixth, Fifty-Fourth, and Fifty-Seventh Streets. A repeating structural module paced the road's path, consisting of steel bents supporting a steel-clad roadbed of concrete and granite block (fig. 6.21; see also figs. I.3–I.4 in the introduction). Horizontal bands of light and dark paint adorned the lower halves of the structural supports, foreshadowing the play of light and dark on the railing above. Small decorative steel plates, projecting from the I-beams' exterior surfaces, marked the columns' junctions with the roadbed and their termination at the top of the road's guardrails. Sloan and Robertson were responsible for these and other nuances of the highway's design.

Tall rectangular steel panels sheathed the roadbed's exterior, accentuated by the patterns of rivets holding the pieces together. A railing topped this sequence, composed of flat, vertical metal strips as balusters, which alternated with smaller, vertically centered rectangular strips. Rectangular panels, the same height but twice as wide as the balusters, interrupted the railing after each sequence of five

Figure 6.21 West Side Elevated Highway, as built, at Watts Street, 1974. (Library of Congress, Prints and Photographs Division, Historic American Engineering Record, Reproduction number HAER NY,31-NEYO,88-22. http://www.loc.gov [accessed December 5, 2019]).

Figure 6.22 Sidewall detail, West Side Elevated Highway at Hubert Street, 1974. (Library of Congress, Prints and Photographs Division, Historic American Engineering Record, Reproduction number HAER NY,31-NEYO,88-5. http://www.loc.gov [accessed December 5, 2019]).

Figure 6.23 Ornamental seal of the city of New York, West Side Elevated Highway, 1974. (Library of Congress, Prints and Photographs Division, Historic American Engineering Record, Reproduction number HAER NY,31-NEYO,88-7. http://www.loc.gov [accessed December 5, 2019]).

small strips and four balusters (fig. 6.22). Larger square panels subsequently interrupted every fourth iteration of this pattern, providing a backdrop for ornamental cast-iron seals honoring New York's history (fig. 6.23). These eighteen-inch circular ornaments featured five different historical incarnations of the seal of the city of New York. More than two thousand of these seals, designed and cast by sculptor Rene Paul Chambellan, Sloan and Robertson's frequent collaborator, adorned the highway.[43]

Sloan and Robertson developed an Art Deco vocabulary for the highway's light standards, signage, and ramp entrances. The light standards echoed the geometric clarity and simple use of modern materials found on the highway's guardrails (fig. 6.24). Intersecting vertical steel plates stepped back as they rose to form slender pyramidal light posts. These three-dimensional pyramid shapes

Figure 6.24 Typical light standard, West Side Elevated Highway, 1974. (Library of Congress, Prints and Photographs Division, Historic American Engineering Record, Reproduction number HAER NY,31-NEYO,88-9. http://www.loc.gov [accessed December 5, 2019]).

echoed the profiles of nearby New York setback skyscrapers. Single horizontal cross-members carried two lamps atop each post. The regular march of these light standards echoed the vertically punctuated landscape of tall buildings that drivers saw from the highway.

Twenty-one cast-iron cartouches mounted on the exterior of the road's guardrails marked the highway's passage over surface streets. These cartouches featured more elaborate iconography and mediated the highway's obstruction of views to the river by providing clear indications of the cross streets and adjoining piers at each intersection. Sloan and Robertson used Art Deco artistry to fuse this factual information to symbols of speed, mechanization, and American identity. At Hubert Street and Pier 27, for example, geometrically abstracted winged forms created the shape of a five-pointed star as the cartouche's focal point (see fig. 6.22). The top of this star was formed by three propellers set against abstract geometric shapes. Another set of wings lay behind this star, fronted by a set of mechanical gears. Grounding this composition was a small podium bearing the cartouche's factual information. It featured bold san-serif capital letters set against a subtle basket-weave pattern. Winged wheels framed the pedestal's lettering, set against stepped horizontal bands suggestive of speed and movement. The cartouche at Desbrosses Street (Piers 29–31) featured similar iconography, notably adding two stylized eagle heads to flank the central text (fig. 6.25). All of these elements referenced icons of American identity, the eagle and the star; while the gears and propellers clearly celebrated modern technology and transportation.

Short granite walls framed each of the highway's entrance ramps and echoed the cartouches' decorative vocabulary (fig. 6.26). An abstracted wheel centered the composition, with three layers of wings unfurling to one of its sides. A thick semicircular band spiraled out of the wheel to wrap the wall's rounded outer edge and continued as a horizontal band along its top. These walls signaled a visual and

Figure 6.25 Ornamental cartouche at Desbrosses Street, and view under highway to Hudson River, West Side Elevated Highway, 1974. (Library of Congress, Prints and Photographs Division, Historic American Engineering Record, Reproduction number HAER NY,31-NEYO,88-8. http://www.loc.gov [accessed December 5, 2019]).

Figure 6.26 Granite ramp detail at Canal Street, West Side Elevated Highway, 1974. (Library of Congress, Prints and Photographs Division, Historic American Engineering Record, Reproduction number HAER NY,31-NEYO,88-4. http://www.loc.gov [accessed December 5, 2019]).

experiential transition for viewers. As the wings stretched away from the wheel, they mimicked the movement and increasing speed that drivers experienced as they merged onto the highway.

The amalgamation of symbolic imagery, modern materials, and stylized forms in the West Side Elevated Highway's ramps, cartouches, light standards, and superstructure echoed Sloan and Robertson's approach to architectonic decoration in their Manhattan skyscrapers. The detailed articulation of certain elements worked in service of the larger composition—in this case, the highway superstructure—in much the same way that sculptural relief and decorative metalwork accentuated critical elements in their office buildings. Moreover, Sloan and Robertson scaled this decoration to suit the highway's two distinct constituencies: the automobile drivers on the elevated surface; and the drivers and pedestrians navigating beneath and around it at ground level. They had approached skyscraper design similarly, considering a building's composition as part of an urban skyline while also providing human-scale details to relate to its users. All told, the highway's level of articulation confirmed its physicality and architectural importance. Straddling the street surface, the public had no choice but to interact with the thoroughfare in some capacity, even if they were not specifically driving on it.

Confusion and Reception

Three major factors colored the public's response to the West Side Highway's progress and completion. First, the highway's path through existing commercial streets negated the concerns about property seizures and context that so defined the elevated expressway dialogues in Chicago and Boston. The riverfront streets housed industrial and mercantile wharves and warehouses, elements far removed from the everyday experiences of New York's middle and upper classes who were planning the highway and who stood to benefit most from its completion. As a result, the highway's impending arrival did not incite great public outcry. Instead, the public accepted the highway as a fait accompli, and newspaper coverage reinforced this sentiment with regular accounts of the highway's progress, its promised traffic relief, and the predicted infusion of new business and real estate activity that its completion would bring to the west side.[44]

Second, the long-standing debate over upgrading the New York Central Railroad tracks and Riverside Park confused comprehension of the elevated highway as a separate entity. This was not as much of an issue during the early years of its construction, as the majority of the West Side Improvement did not begin until 1934. As construction dragged on, however, and as Robert Moses (1888–1981)—New York City's infamous Parks Commissioner from 1934 to 1968—spearheaded rapid completion of the West Side Improvement (stretching north from Seventy-Second Street to the tip of the island), the press sometimes referred to Julius Miller's elevated highway as part of Moses's initiative.[45] Though this was primarily an issue of nomenclature, it stood to confuse the distinction between the elevated highway and the Henry Hudson Parkway, which offered a very different highway aesthetic and driving experience than the West Side Highway. As further evidence, even though the West Side Highway (from Canal to Seventy-Second Streets) had opened in February 1937, the following October's headlines about the completion of the West Side Improvement proclaimed "West Side Highway to Open," and then reported about the Henry Hudson Parkway.[46]

Third, separate from the name confusion, the fact that the West Side Improvement included highway, railroad, park, and recreation components gave it greater relevance to a larger constituency of New Yorkers than did the elevated highway. The roofing of the railroad tracks removed the previous noise and soot from Riverside Park; extensive landfill facilitated acres of new parkland and recreation spaces; and the Henry Hudson Parkway provided a meandering riverside path along a newly planted backdrop. The scale and comprehensive quality of this landscape was unsurpassed. Thus, the West Side Improvement received front-page newspaper billing on the day of its dedication while the West Side Highway's similar festivities only garnered page twenty-three.[47] Similarly, multiple architecture and engineering journals featured in-depth profiles of the West Side Improvement's completion, but the West Side Elevated Highway received only scant coverage, largely during its early years of construction.[48]

A major force fueling this disparity was Robert Moses himself. Ever the opportunist, Moses took ownership of west side redevelopment ideas that had languished on paper and in boardrooms for decades and applied federal work-relief funds to realize their speedy implementation as the West Side Improvement. Moses's leadership style garnered great public attention, as did the projects that he championed. Therefore, since Moses's tenure began in 1934 while the West Side

Elevated Highway was still under construction, and because the elevated road abutted Moses's project, and since the two projects concluded within months of each other, many mistakenly grouped the two together.[49]

This social and circumstantial context ultimately cast the West Side Elevated Highway as a utilitarian improvement focused on efficiency and speed, with little attention to its aesthetic or physical ramifications. Even in its incomplete stages the highway generated so much use that traffic quickly overloaded its facilities. In November 1930, just days after the inauguration of the highway's first segment, the temporary ramps at its truncated end proved too narrow to accommodate the throngs of automobiles clamoring to use it.[50] As construction proceeded, merchants petitioned city officials to construct additional ramps to streamline highway access and thereby relieve local street congestion. Property owners and merchants in the vicinity of Thirty-Fourth Street pursued such action for more than three years, arguing that the nearest ramps at Twenty-Third Street and Fortieth Street were too far away to truly benefit their neighborhood. Nothing ever came of their efforts.[51]

As the full length of the highway neared completion, local authors marveled at its efficient channeling of traffic and predicted boon to local industrial businesses. The *New York Times* corroborated officials' predictions of time savings, growth for the waterfront, and expected tax revenue.[52] Students from Miller McClintock's Bureau for Street Traffic Research at Harvard University used statistical analyses to proclaim that the new highway, paired with the Henry Hudson Parkway, sped travel along the west side by between 25 and 40 percent.[53] One realtor predicted that the west side's rail and road improvements would bolster the area's established success as an industrial center, noting that "'a steady influx of business may be looked for in the next few years. The area will remain primarily industrial because its buildings and transportation facilities were especially designed for that purpose.'"[54] This last comment, reflecting the west side's intentional industrial caste, underscores why local businesses primarily saw the highway as a benefit instead of a problematic intrusion on their landscape.

If one of the highway's key features was its efficiency, then another was the experiential quality of driving on it. Two days after the road's dedication, a short article in the *New York Times* called the new road "the scenic highway out of the city and in," and lauded the fact that a car passenger riding south on the West Side Elevated Highway "need hardly see a brick wall until he gets down to ground at Canal Street."[55] This commentary provided contrasting impressions of the city. On the one hand, drivers escaped the city while they were on the highway, saved from the street congestion and accompanying noise, crowding, and filth. Simultaneously, however, the highway provided a thrilling vantage point from which to observe the city and the water. This abstracted the urban environment, making it an element to observe instead of one in which to participate. In both cases, there is implied social judgment about the experience of the city itself. The author saluted the privilege of those able to circumvent modern urban conditions, while still

Figure 6.27 Aerial view of West Side Elevated Highway, looking south from Forty-Second Street, circa 1957. (Borough President of Manhattan, and Triborough Bridge and Tunnel Authority, *Miller Highway West Side Elevated Improvement.* [New York: n.p., February 4, 1957], 9. Courtesy NYC Municipal Archives.)

suggesting the value of the city as something to experience—albeit from atop the perch of a moving vehicle. This duality would continue to characterize arguments in support of urban highways in the coming decades and foreshadowed the long-term implications of mass automobility on a global scale.

Surprisingly, there is scant contemporary evidence of citizens commenting about their street-level interaction with the West Side Highway. This was not for lack of cause, as contemporary photographs clearly show dramatic contrasts between the road's hulking mass and the scale of the pedestrians, automobiles, trucks, and ships operating around its fringes (fig. 6.27). The highway's marginal location may explain this omission, as only industrial and waterfront workers had occasion to interface with it daily and may not have felt compelled to record their experiences. Only years after its completion, with the waning prominence of New York's port facilities in the post–World War II era, did locals articulate resentment of the noise, shadows, and waterfront disruption wrought by the steel and concrete viaduct.

Finally, from the perspective of planning trends, the West Side Elevated Highway fueled the conception of urban highways (elevated and surface) as visible solutions to social, economic, and planning problems. Over the long course of its construction, people questioned not the utility of the road but the timeline for its completion and the possibilities for its extension. With a waterfront and economy in decline, New Yorkers saw this project as creating new accessibility and new possibilities for growth. Its raised nature, surely born partially of expedience and economy, provided tangible evidence of the city's attention to local conditions. The road's architectural embellishments, though window dressing to some degree, simultaneously celebrated the new (uniquely American) automobile age while trying to mediate its physical impact on the human-scaled environment of the city. These features were all admirable in many ways, which fed subsequent emulation of this development model.

Boston

Of this study's three examples, the construction of Boston's Central Artery yielded the most dramatic contrasts between old and new conditions. Two major factors contributed to this. First was the highway's path through the city. Since the new road not only traversed the existing right-of-way of Atlantic Avenue but also cut across densely populated residential neighborhoods, it necessarily heightened the personal, political, and environmental stakes. Second, even as the highway design remained fairly constant during the two decades between its conception and its realization, Boston's political, transportation, and architectural climates changed significantly. This context set an unstable foundation for the Central Artery's success both as a transportation solution and as a visible measure of urban progress.

Two subsidiary issues demonstrate how the Central Artery's route so fundamentally shaped its evolution and reception. First, the Central Artery meant very different things to distinct constituencies. For downtown commercial businesses and struggling waterfront merchants, the elevated highway promised a new level of accessibility and, thus, the potential for increased profitability. Literally located on the highway's fringes, these groups stood to gain much from the new road without direct injury to their personal properties. For those neighborhoods directly in the highway's path, the impending thoroughfare had more dire personal consequences. Not only would it claim individual homes and businesses, it also stood to divide the remaining portions of their neighborhoods from the rest of the city. For residents of the northern and southern suburbs who daily commuted to and from the city, the Central Artery was to empower particularly streamlined movement because of its connections to new expressways at the north and the south. Instead of previous circuitous routes through the city's dense urban core, drivers would be able to move swiftly and directly to their final destinations, thereby saving time and money. The wide range of these sets of expectations necessarily complicated the reality and reception of the new highway.

Second, the highway's path along and through existing urban fabric necessarily heightened its comparative physical impact. The physical and social fab-

Figure 6.28 1952 view toward North End from Custom House tower. Early demolition preceding Central Artery construction visible at far left. (Courtesy of the Boston Public Library, Leslie Jones Collection.)

rics of the waterfront, North End, and Chinatown districts laid the bases for this contrast. Along the waterfront streets of Atlantic Avenue and Commercial Street, a motley crew of wharves, warehouses, and commercial buildings testified to Boston's mercantile past. These included some of the best examples of mid-nineteenth-century granite wharf buildings of the so-called Boston Granite School. The nearby North End accommodated both commercial and residential uses in modest five- and six-story masonry buildings. Simple but stately, these buildings offered an assortment of brick quoins, stone window lintels, stringcourses, keystones, and muted mansard roofs, all representative of early and mid-nineteenth-century eclecticism (fig. 6.28). These structures were often multifunctional, housing retail shops on the ground floor with assorted businesses and apartments above. Handmade signs labeled the businesses tucked inside. Both the North End and Atlantic Avenue reflected Boston's heritage as a small mercantile city with local business interests.

Boston's South Cove neighborhood of Chinatown offered a similar combination of residential and commercial uses as the North End. A product of landfill in the 1830s, the South Cove sported a mix of nineteenth-century commercial blocks and tenement buildings. Other immigrant groups had lived in the area previously, but deteriorating building conditions and encroaching industrial development had eroded its appeal by the last quarter of the nineteenth century. As Chinese immigrants arrived in Boston at this same time, they gravitated to the area's inexpensive rents. By 1890 they had clearly established themselves as the neighborhood's dominant ethnic group.[56] Together, the existing conditions of the waterfront, the North End, and Chinatown magnified the audacity of the Central Artery's arrival.

Construction of the Central Artery officially began in January 1951 with work on a new bridge over the Charles River at the highway's northernmost terminus. Property seizures and demolition in the North End provided the most visible early sign of the Central Artery's approach. The Massachusetts Department of Public Works initiated eminent domain proceedings to acquire fifty-four parcels of North End land in November 1950. They made subsequent announcements in February 1951, and demolition stretched from the spring of 1951 to May 1952.[57] Demolition photographs powerfully illustrate the physical and emotional impact this process brought to the neighborhood (figs. 6.29–6.32). Gaping holes suddenly interrupt the continuity of building facades, with mountainous piles of rubble foreshadowing the fate of adjoining structures. Storefronts have been vacated, though abandoned signs in some windows suggest the activities of now-displaced businesses. Half-demolished buildings flank others that are as-yet undisturbed, while tall cranes broodingly hover nearby. Lone pedestrians on the sidewalks and streets pause to observe the activity, providing poignant human foils to the buildings, machinery, and destruction nearby.

Demolition and construction proceeded south from the North End through Haymarket Square to Fort Hill Square. Though this section of the highway did not require the same extent of building seizures, it still imposed a very visible mark on the wharf and warehouse buildings that had once dominated the waterfront. The construction of Atlantic Avenue in the late 1860s had already affected much of the old fabric of this area, notably removing a series of warehouses on India Wharf designed by Charles Bulfinch.[58] Instead of claiming entire buildings here, the elevated highway literally bisected them (fig. 6.33). Particularly startling examples are the State Street Block (Gridley J. Fox Bryant, 1858) and Central Wharf (credited to Charles Bulfinch, 1816–1817), both located just southeast of Boston's Custom House. Contemporary photographs dramatically capture the violent truncation of these structures. Severed joists and infill masonry party walls flank open wounds in both buildings. The highway's web of underpinnings creeps between, a stark mechanized contrast to the warehouses' masonry and wood forms. The corner of Commercial and Cross Streets showcased comparable conditions where Mercantile Wharf and two neighboring structures to the north had suffered similar injuries. All told, the demolition and interruption of buildings provided some of the most dramatic visual evidence of the arrival of modern automobility and modern highway construction in the city (fig. 6.34). One New York journalist provided an especially vivid account:

Figure 6.29 1953 view toward North End from Custom House tower, showing significant clearing for Central Artery. Compare to view from same vantage point in figure 6.28. (Courtesy of the Boston Public Library, Leslie Jones Collection.)

Figure 6.30 1954 view toward North End from Custom House tower, showing construction of Central Artery. Compare to views from same vantage point in figures 6.28 and 6.29. (Courtesy of the Boston Public Library, Leslie Jones Collection.)

Figure 6.31 Demolition in process, North End, Boston, February 5, 1952. (TC4.07 1277x Box 5 Photo no. 17–2 February 5, 1952. Massachusetts State Archives.)

Figure 6.32 Demolition in process, Hanover Street, North End, Boston, February 5, 1952. (TC4.07 1277x Box 5 Photo no. 18 February 5, 1952. Massachusetts State Archives.)

Figure 6.33 Central Artery under construction, bisecting wharf buildings, November 1, 1954. (TC4.07 1277x Box 1 Photo no. 17 November 1, 1954. Massachusetts State Archives.)

Figure 6.34 Central Artery under construction, October 1, 1954. (TC4.07 1277x Box 1 Photo no. 13 October 1, 1954. Massachusetts State Archives.)

> Sentimentalists who like to think that Boston never changes should see the old place now.
>
> From the rubble of gaping holes in the Faneuil Hall market district, concrete ramps and supports for a $40,000,000 central aerial traffic artery are rising in place of buildings that looked down on early American history.[59]

This commentator went on excitedly to report on the city's material modernization as well, lauding the removal of old brick and mortar to make way for new forms in concrete and steel. Clearly, the visual weight of downtown destruction was understood as evidence of major approaching change.

In addition to these clashes with the existing built environment, construction of the Central Artery strongly proclaimed the might and magnitude of machine over man. Its tall piers rose thirty to forty feet into the air, easily dwarfing both workers and pedestrians. The geometric regularity of its steel and concrete appeared all the more pristine in relation to the irregular piles of earth and discarded lumber that littered construction sites (figs. 6.35–6.36). The construction machinery itself was loud, powerful, and awe-inspiring. Locals would gather to watch the excavation and construction, marveling at the might and rhythmic progress of construction equipment. One observer contrasted the pace and progress of a one-hundred-ton pile driver with his memories of the horse-powered versions that had enabled previous city construction projects.[60] As the construction crews progressed southward, scenes of machine-empowered progress repeated themselves in Fort Hill Square, Dewey Square, and Chinatown.

Completion of the Central Artery happened in stages over nearly a decade, with each successive milestone marking a different set of implications for distinct parts of the city. The first section to be completed stretched from the Charles River to the entrance of the Sumner Tunnel on North Street (fig. 6.37).[61] This section traversed the controversial corridor of the North End where residents had so vocally—and unsuccessfully—opposed the highway's path. As predicted, demolition had taken a particularly visible physical and emotional toll on the neighborhood. But when the road opened on October 29, 1954, the public dialogue focused exclusively on the resultant reductions in travel time. State and municipal officials drove the first vehicles over this stretch of highway, notably timing their journeys with a stopwatch to demonstrate their speed. Local Democratic politicians voiced their own interpretation of the day's significance by driving a truck bedecked with signs reading "Central Artery Dedication, Planned and Built by Democrats, Speeches and Music by Republicans" into the middle of the dedication festivities. Their commentary reflected the dominantly Republican leadership then overseeing the project's implementation, even as Democrats had actually directed most of its planning. Despite this hiccup, the road's efficiency carried the day. After the first full day of operation, drivers proudly reported that the Artery reduced

Figure 6.35 Construction worker and Central Artery support, April 29, 1954. (TC4.07 1277x Box 5 Photo no. 128 April 29, 1954. Massachusetts State Archives.)

Figure 6.36 Beneath Central Artery, May 3, 1955. (TC4.07 1277x Box 5 Photo no. 212 May 3, 1955. Massachusetts State Archives.)

Figure 6.37 Completed section of Central Artery, near Haverhill Street, November 2, 1954. (TC4.07 1277x Box 5 Photo no. 179 November 2, 1954. Massachusetts State Archives.)

the trip from the Mystic River in Charlestown to the Sumner Tunnel from twenty-five-minutes to two minutes.[62]

The Central Artery's next milestone was its southward extension to Fort Hill Square. This section stretched south from the North End to east of Faneuil Hall and Quincy Market, then turned southeast to merge with the existing path of Atlantic Avenue. Moving south along a widened Atlantic Avenue corridor, the highway claimed the aforementioned wharf and warehouse buildings and terminated at Fort Hill Square.[63] The southbound portion of this extension opened on November 1, 1955, with the northbound lanes following in December 1955. This completed the elevated portion of the highway. Officials expected that this segment would particularly benefit traffic between North and South Stations. State Public Works commissioner John Volpe predicted that the completion of this segment would propel vehicle usage from eighty thousand vehicles per day to one hundred thousand.[64] This is particularly notable in light of Robert Whitten's original prediction in his 1930 *Thoroughfare Plan* of the road's capacity at only sixty thousand vehicles daily.

The final stretch of the Central Artery's cross-city route was the much-disputed leg from Dewey Square (at South Station) through Chinatown connecting with the Southeast Expressway. As detailed in chapter 3, residents and business owners from the Chinatown and leather districts had fought the state's original route for the area, resulting in agreement on a revised trajectory in May 1954. With this decision, engineers needed to plan for transitioning the road from the elevated viaduct to the surface and then underground. Construction had begun on this transition piece by late fall 1955, with completion of the tunnel following in November 1958. Crews then focused on the link between the tunnel and the Southeast Expressway, which they completed in June 1959.[65] After more than eight years of construction and a cost of $110 million, the Central Artery had reached completion.[66]

Receptions and Perceptions

City, state, and federal officials dedicated the Central Artery and its link to the Southeast Expressway on June 25, 1959. This milestone not only marked project completion but also realized the full extent of the highway's utility as a connection to regional expressways at both its northern and southern termini. State Attorney General Edward J. McCormack characterized the new road as "'the vein through which will flow the economic lifeblood of our cities and towns.'"[67] In addition to other city and state leaders, executives from Boston's two major department stores, William Filene's Sons Company and Jordan Marsh Company, addressed the crowd. Edward R. Mitton, president of Jordan Marsh, remarked that the highway gave city merchants "'renewed confidence'" in Boston's economic future.[68]

Newspaper coverage underscored the new regional accessibility. On the day after the Central Artery's inauguration, three *Boston Globe* reporters, each from different suburban towns, reported on the ease of their commutes using the new expressways. Nye Rosa, from the western suburb of Sudbury, reported time savings of ten minutes. Leonard Lerner, a resident of the southern suburb of Holbrook, reduced his travel time by thirty-five minutes.[69] Ronald Wysocki, of the northern suburb of Peabody, saved fifteen minutes, recounting, "With the Expressway there were no nerve-wracking traffic jams, no twisting and turning, no mapping of battle strategy to find the quickest way home. It was just straight ahead all the way."[70] The only mention of the road's implications for local Bostonians pertained to the newsboys who previously sold newspapers at major city intersections. They had been very successful when city streets were jammed, but the opening of the Central Artery relocated so much traffic that their business suddenly plummeted.[71]

Although most of the public dialogue immediately surrounding the dedication of the Central Artery focused on its ramifications for travel routes and speed, locals could not help but notice the new reality of the Central Artery in downtown. The completed highway stretched 1.7 miles from the Charles River at North Station to its junction with the Southeast Expressway in Chinatown (see fig. I.5). The elevated structure stopped just north of Dewey Square where it descended into the Dewey Square Tunnel and emerged in Chinatown as a surface artery. The elevated viaduct ranged from one hundred to two hundred feet wide, including entrance and exit ramps, and climbed thirty to forty feet into the air. This height paralleled the second and third floors of most adjoining buildings. Large green steel I-beams composed both the vertical and horizontal members of the structure, interrupted only by occasional concrete piers. The same enormous beams carried the underbelly of the road and created the exterior face of the roadbed. Thus the roadbed's façade was a wide I-beam syncopated by smaller vertical "T" supports and rivets along its length (see fig. 6.37). The guardrails above this level provided

Figure 6.38 Local traffic under Central Artery, 2002. (Author photograph.)

the highway's main architectonic features. Here a sheath of flat green steel clad the lower half, while the steel folded to create four inset horizontal bands above. A simple rectilinear railing topped the steel, carried by short cylindrical supports. Streetlights, composed of tall thin poles topped by gentle arcs carrying mercury vapor lights, provided the only vertical foils to the structure's horizontal march.[72]

The road's physical presence greeted drivers, local building tenants, and pedestrians quite differently. For automobile drivers on neighboring surface streets, the highway appeared as a shadowy overpass that obstructed views but did little to dissuade travel beneath or around it since most through streets still passed under the elevated superstructure (fig. 6.38). Drivers on the artery enjoyed not only direct and high-speed movement but also the sublime experience of overlooking the city from a moving elevated perch. For tenants in adjoining buildings, the highway proved

Figure 6.39 View west from waterfront area toward Boston's financial district, looking across surface streets and interrupted by Central Artery, 2002. (Author photograph.)

a duplicitous neighbor. It was an exciting spectacle for the lucky few in buildings tall enough to look over the road; while for those parallel to or below its roadbed, its shadows and noise seriously affected everyday activities. Ironically, the highway impacted pedestrian circulation most of all. The expressway's green form created a literal and metaphorical barrier between distinct parts of the city, serving as the dominant sight at the end of local streets and dividing downtown Boston from its waterfront (figs. 6.39–6.42). Its murky undercroft discouraged crossing beneath it, and a cave-like pedestrian underpass at Hanover Street did not attract great patronage. These circumstances not only substantiated predictions that North End residents had made years earlier but also confirmed Boston traffic commissioner Timothy J. O'Connor's own characterization of the project as a "Chinese wall."[73]

Some national publications initially lauded the Central Artery as an example of progressive urban transportation approaches. In the January 24, 1955, issue of *Time*, the magazine featured a picture of the Central Artery to illustrate strides in traffic management occurring across the country. The caption read, "New high speed Central Artery slices through old, narrow streets of Boston's Hub."[74] Though the highway was still incomplete, *Time* clearly positioned it as indicative of the most current urban planning approaches. *American City* reported similarly in July 1958, lauding the Central Artery's essential role as a connector for the area's new metropolitan highway network and as a stimulus for new business development

Figure 6.40 View west from aquarium area toward financial district, interrupted by Central Artery, 2002. (Author photograph.)

Figure 6.41 View east toward Boston Harbor from State Street, interrupted by Central Artery, 2002. (Author photograph.)

Figure 6.42 Pedestrian walking between Central Artery off-ramp and One International Place, 2002. (Author photograph.)

downtown.[75] These commendations surely pleased Boston officials who had hoped for just such endorsement of and investment in the city's future.

However, it did not take long for Central Artery conditions to provoke more resentment than optimism. Approximately 114,000 vehicles traversed the road the day after it opened, far exceeding its predicted capacity of ninety thousand. A week later, nightly rush-hour traffic jams were already dampening driver experiences. Two weeks into the highway's full operation, people were complaining about the traffic created by so many entrance and exit ramps and also about the high rates of speed of those merging onto the highway from these ramps.[76] These circumstances highlighted the artery's critical foible as a traffic solution: it tried to solve too many problems. As discussed in chapter 5, Robert Whitten originally did envision the Central Artery as both a through road and a high-speed bypass for local traffic. But between Whitten's 1930 plan and the 1948 *Master Highway Plan*, automobile usage expanded so exponentially that this approach became less sound. The *Master Highway Plan* also expected the Central Artery to provide the sole downtown connection to its planned regional highway network. Together, these three charges saddled the artery's short span with a huge number of vehicles, which quickly led to frequent accidents and frustrating traffic jams. In October 1959, only months after the Central Artery's full opening, the *Boston Globe* characterized the road as in need of its own congestion relief.[77]

Although traffic conditions largely dominated public discourse about the Central Artery, its aesthetic appearance also provoked some polarizing responses. The *Boston Herald* referred, in passing, to the Central Artery as "the beautiful overhead highway" in July 1959, but this was one of few positive comments.[78] One of the earliest and most lengthy critiques of the highway appeared in *Architectural Forum* in October 1959. With subtitles including "The box-girdered hell," author Richard A. Miller launched a scathing indictment of the new expressway, chiding, "it is a wonder that this most expensive of urban expressways could have possibly been made so ugly."[79] Miller editorialized about how the superstructure might have been designed differently to lengthen its spans and reduce its street-level impact, even going so far as to include his own illustrations. Although most people were not equipped with the knowledge to make such specific observations, Miller clearly struck a chord with those who knew the road. The December 1959 issue of *Architectural Forum* included a reader's response to Miller's commentary:

> Your recent article on Boston's Central Artery . . . was welcome to one who has spent more time under, than on, it. Critics have begun to point out that elevated freeways nearly always are much bigger than antiquated rapid-transit elevateds, and the illustrations in your article would seem to confirm this.[80]

Within a short time, laypeople, architects, and architectural critics seemed to agree that the Central Artery had created a new cadre of urban problems. In April

1964, *New York Times* architecture critic Ada Louise Huxtable called the project "a conclusive exercise in how to dismember and blight a city."[81] At less than five years of age, the Central Artery was already considered passé and problematic.

Four critical issues complicate this conclusion. First, the Central Artery's evolution from city, to state, and then federal stewardship successively distorted its originally local focus. Initiated by city leaders in the 1920s, then absorbed into state highway plans in the 1940s, and garnering federal support after the 1956 Federal-Aid Highway Act (for the Dewey Square Tunnel), the Central Artery morphed into a project with many additional charges, decision-makers, and fiscal responsibilities than originally intended. This progression moved the decision-making authority further and further away from the affected community, redirecting the planning dialogue to focus on issues of expediency and economy more than on sensitive urban design.

Second, while these operational shifts did reframe responsibility for the Central Artery, there were never similar efforts to reevaluate the basic capacity and design of the highway given the changes in automobile ownership and travel patterns that happened between 1930 and 1948. Richard Miller directly addressed this issue in his October 1959 *Architectural Forum* article: "Without doubt, the plan [from 1930] was prescient and valid—at least through World War II. But by the middle fifties the entire scale of the urban traffic problem had changed, as is clearly apparent in a comparison of the 1930 proposal with the 1955 result."[82] The Central Artery's quickly overwhelmed traffic capacity was the prime indication of this misalignment. Larger cars and new traffic engineering standards in the 1950s necessitated a more extensive ramp system and bulkier physical structure than that originally forecast. Paired with the fact that the highway corridor never benefited from the coordinated redevelopment projected in Robert Whitten's plans, the completed Central Artery emerged as a mismatched compilation of ideas from two distinct eras.[83]

Third, even despite these shortcomings, the Central Artery did contribute to Boston's survival and, arguably, resurgence, as a desirable business center. In the years coinciding with and following the highway's construction, the city successfully recruited and implemented a series of major new building projects. The first was the new Prudential Center development in the Back Bay, courted by Mayor Hynes beginning in 1952. Hynes, eager to encourage the Back Bay as a secondary business center, offered tax incentives to the Prudential Insurance Company for building a new business and shopping center atop twenty-eight acres of abandoned rail yards. The Prudential's eventual acceptance of this offer, despite the fact that the Back Bay was far from the Central Artery itself, evinced improving perceptions of Boston's economic future.[84] The second major project was the replacement of Scollay Square with a new collection of city and federal government buildings. Scollay Square was one of Boston's more tawdry areas, filled with movie houses, tattoos parlors, and burlesque theatres. Hynes saw it as an ideal candidate for increasingly popular "urban renewal" approaches. As the nearby Central Artery approached completion in the late 1950s, Hynes successfully negotiated widespread demolition and redevelopment of the area. The result was Government Center, a huge civic complex hosting a plaza, new city hall, and two new federal office buildings, completed in the late 1960s. Although critics subsequently derided this development approach, Government Center's geographic and temporal proximity to the Central Artery marked significant reinvestment in Boston's downtown core.[85]

Finally, the Central Artery's emotional and financial costs and complicated traffic legacy motivated greater community awareness and responsiveness to later highway proposals. This applied most specifically to the unrealized concept of the so-called Inner Belt, a highway proposed in the 1948 *Master Highway Plan* as an inner concentric companion to the existing circumferential highway of Route 128. The state intended to thread the Inner Belt through significant sections of the South End, Cambridge, Somerville, Roxbury, and Jamaica Plain, thereby providing a high-speed route *around* the city, instead of *through* it. The 1956 Federal-Aid Highway Act inflated the state's aspirations, inciting the addition of a five-story interchange in the South End to connect with a proposed southwest expressway. Most problematic, the Inner Belt's route was to march through vibrant but low-income neighborhoods and displace more than five thousand families. With the fresh memory of the Central Artery's impact on the North End and Chinatown, residents from the affected communities rallied together and staunchly fought the plan. Officials continued to champion, revise, and negotiate aspects of the design through the 1960s before completely abandoning it in the early 1970s. The communities' ultimate success must be understood as an outgrowth of the emotional and financial costs of the Central Artery.[86] At the same time, since the Inner Belt would have provided an alternate route around the city, it stood to relieve some of the traffic congestion on the Central Artery itself. Therefore, defeat of the Inner Belt simultaneously evolved from the Central Artery's shortcomings and solidified its amplified traffic burdens.

7

AFTERSHOCKS

Interstates and Interventions

> Wacker Drive is arguably the most important artery within that hub [the Chicago central business district], in terms of both traffic flow and goods movement and delivery. The condition of Wacker Drive is of national importance. (1999)
>
> —THOMAS R. WALKER, CDOT Transportation Commissioner, as quoted in "Congress Snubs Chicago's Wacker Drive Rehab Plan"

> In 43 years, the divided highway . . . has metamorphosed—from a proud symbol of the future to what some observers see as a vivid example of the failure of New York City to deal with its problems and a symbol of civic procrastination by several city administrations. (1974)
>
> —ROBERT LINDSEY, "West Side Highway: 43 Years, All Downhill"

> Just imagine, the greatest "green monster" in Boston, 30 feet up in the sky, emitting toxins and obstructing everything in reach or in view. Below it, nothing but dark shade, an inert swath where pedestrians stumbled through their exhausted and ruptured city. (2002)
>
> —MARIA BELLALTA, "Another Shade of Green"

IN THE YEARS since their respective completions, Wacker Drive, the West Side Elevated Highway, and the Central Artery have endured serious reevaluation of their social, transportation, and architectural legacies. Wacker Drive, long discounted as a mere traffic thoroughfare by Chicagoans, benefited from reconstruction and restoration efforts that renewed its architectural features. The West Side Elevated Highway, overwhelmed by traffic, physically unstable, and socially unpopular, succumbed to a new on-grade highway. Boston's Central Artery, reviled almost immediately for its inadequate traffic capacity and blighting urban impact, gave way to a new underground tunnel system. There are three common narratives within these stories. First, mounting midcentury automobile usage compelled reevaluation of each roadway. Second, such traffic volumes precipitated nationwide legislation for new highway construction that offered a new model of urban highway design for the late 1950s and 1960s. Third, backlash against this latter era of highway construction fueled subsequent revision to urban expressway typologies, notably including all three cities' highways. Together, this sequence illustrates the contemporary relevance of early elevated highways and also their cohesiveness as a unique group in the pre-Interstate era.

Chicago

Chicago's experience revolved around the limitations of Wacker Drive's capacity more than its form. When Daniel Burnham and Edward Bennett published the *Plan of Chicago* in 1909, the city boasted only 7,110 registered automobiles. By the time construction of Wacker Drive began in 1924, however, the city hosted over 260,000 automobiles; and by the time of its completion, 317,000 automobiles called Chicago home.[1] Burnham and Bennett never could have anticipated this kind of surge, let alone that which continued in the following decades. Wacker Drive's physical features and accommodation of both travel and parking needs further complicated matters. In 1931 the *Chicago Tribune* reported on the almost comedic parking conditions along Lower Wacker Drive. With cars parked two and three deep along the road's perimeter, frustrated drivers would commandeer space between the road's mid-lane support piers for parking spaces, leaving other motorists to weave their way around the parked vehicles. Returning drivers for other cars would sometimes have to push errant vehicles out of the way to leave their legal spaces, sometimes scratching car fenders.[2] Clearly, the road's overwhelming popularity quickly taxed its facilities.

In fact, Wacker Drive proved such a popular route that city officials sought to extend it. In 1938 Mayor Edward Kelly unsuccessfully lobbied for Public Works Administration funds to extend Wacker Drive south along the southern branch of the Chicago River. This extension eventually did proceed in the late 1940s, funded jointly by the city, Cook County, and the state.[3] Completed in 1958, this extension followed a slightly inland route that negated the possibility of an architectural presence along the waterfront, and its upper street surface abandoned the Beaux Arts vocabulary of the original road.

The fate of the southern extension of Wacker Drive was closely tied to that of the modern-day Eisenhower Expressway—originally called the Congress Expressway. Foreshadowed generally as a major western road in the 1909 plan and then formalized in a 1927 highway plan by the Chicago Plan Commission, final planning and construction of the expressway began in earnest after World War II. Financing for the road derived primarily from city, county, and state sources, though federal aid did eventually play a role. The expressway's path targeted low-income slum areas and required widespread demolition, which presaged a growing trend in urban highway construction. Municipal leaders argued that such destruction seemed negligible compared to the regional accessibility, commercial opportunities, and redevelopment promised by such high-speed automotive access.[4] The Eisenhower Expressway connected to the southern extension of Wacker Drive, heightening the latter road's importance in channeling regional traffic to and through Chicago's urban core.

Figure 7.1 Eastern extension of Wacker Drive, from Michigan Avenue Bridge, February 2009. (Courtesy Hope Dinsmore.)

Wacker Drive's eastern extension followed a similar functional rationale, providing a trilevel waterfront connection to the city's main lakeside thoroughfare, Lake Shore Drive. A partnership between the Illinois Central Gulf Railroad and state and federal authorities financed construction of this segment during the 1970s.[5] While this portion of the road does front directly on the river, it does not offer the same integrated functional and aesthetic presence along the river as does its 1920s predecessor (fig. 7.1).

By the 1990s, the physical condition of the original length of Wacker Drive was aesthetically haggard and functionally problematic. Water and salt had corroded the road's concrete, deteriorating supporting columns and leaving chunks missing from the roadbed. The lane widths, clearance heights, and turns had suited the scale of the Ford Model A of the 1920s but had limited the road's capacity and safety for larger and faster vehicles in later years. This had compelled weight restrictions for vehicles on the upper deck and height restrictions for those below, all of which compromised Wacker Drive's intended streamlining of riverside traffic. In addition, instead of great civic amenities, the road's lower levels and promenades had become havens for many of the city's homeless population.[6]

In the late 1990s, these conditions induced city leaders to secure federal support for rebuilding the east-west portion of Wacker Drive. The project targeted two distinct issues. First, it sought to improve traffic circulation by rebuilding the road's structural system; and second, it sought to preserve and extend the drive's architectural vocabulary and civic amenities further along the waterfront. Construction of the improvement stretched from 2001 to 2002, with the federal government providing $125 million of the $200 million project cost and the balance shared by city and state coffers. The project entirely rebuilt Wacker Drive: crews replaced the bulky octagonal support columns with smaller modern versions; expanded the vertical clearance on the lower drive; removed, restored and reinstalled its limestone facing and details; and constructed new riverfront amenities east of Michigan Avenue.[7] Given Chicago's midcentury focus on high-speed direct highways, the integrated approach of this incarnation reflected an ironic shift in public road-building efforts. It demonstrated a modern appreciation of Wacker Drive's functional and aesthetic model and marked a new direction in urban highway planning. In the years since 2009, Chicago has undertaken a series of improvement projects geared toward creating pedestrian and recreational engagement along Wacker Drive's riverfront promenades. Championed by Mayor Rahm Emanuel and funded in part by federal loans, the so-called "Chicago Riverwalk" provides new walkways, parks, art installations, and riverside shops that empower a degree of multitiered riverside activity that mimics that first forecast by Burnham and Bennett over a century ago.[8]

New York

Like Wacker Drive, the West Side Elevated Highway was the first in a series of major expressway projects to revolutionize automobile access to and through its city. And as with its Chicago counterpart, the West Side Elevated Highway differed substantially from many of its successors. Over the long course of the West Side Highway's construction, the local and national culture of highway-building changed. The local shift happened under the leadership of Robert Moses, metropolitan New York's veritable public works czar from 1934 until 1968. During Moses's leadership as parks commissioner, he implemented meandering parkway projects like the Henry Hudson Parkway. As his responsibilities extended to a regional level, however, and as federal funds became available for urban highways beginning in 1944, he increasingly focused on untangling as much of New York City's automotive congestion as possible. This manifested itself in a series of broad, straight expressways pushed through and across the metropolitan region. While these roads came to form the basis of New York's contemporary highway system, they typically sacrificed urban continuity in low-income and minority districts—setting a very problematic precedent. This cultivated public outcry against such projects and led to Moses's own denigration in the later years of his career.[9]

The national shift, which largely was tied to federal funding, followed a similar trajectory. Before 1900, local and regional authorities bore responsibility for road construction. As automotive use increased, however, individual states created road departments: thirty-nine states had done so by 1915, and all states had highway bureaus by 1917. The first federal highway bill, the Federal Highway Act of 1916, codified the national importance of road building by allocating $75 million for road construction over the next five years. The federal investment model required contributions from local and regional authorities that would then be matched by federal dollars. As an example, the 1941 Defense Highway Act promised to match $10 million state investments in road development. Such financial arrangements necessitated the distribution of responsibilities among local, state, and federal agencies, a balance that often complicated project logistics and also left a great deal of authority with local officials.[10]

However, the Federal-Aid Highway Act of 1956 changed the terms and scale of any previous financing. Enacted on June 29, 1956, President Dwight D. Eisenhower's highway legislation earmarked more than $33 billion for a forty-one-thousand-mile network of highways to link all states and most cities with populations over fifty thousand. The structure of the financial support was particularly advantageous for cities and states, who had to supply only 10 percent of a project's cost in order to qualify for federal support of the remaining balance.[11] Cities clamored to take advantage of these funds, with urban highways planned for countless cities nationwide. Nonetheless, the highway bill sported two fundamental problems. First, it transposed the impetus for road construction from local to regional and national sources. This was not just an issue of purview but one of comparative awareness of and interest in local conditions. Second, nationwide design standards usurped design authority from local officials and homogenized design details. These factors set the Interstate highway program on shaky ground regarding community and design issues, even as other constituencies lauded increasing automotive accessibility.

The synthesis of Moses's personal approach and the federal highway funds proved a trying combination in New York City. Moses successfully constructed a series of new highways following the new standards, including the New England Thruway (1958), Major Deegan Expressway (1961), Cross-Bronx Expressway (1963), Whitestone Expressway (1963), and Staten Island Expressway (1964). He also extended the elevated Brooklyn-Queens Expressway, which had been in a stage of partial completion since the late 1930s.[12] While these highways systematized metropolitan travel to an awe-inspiring degree, their community costs were high. The Cross-Bronx Expressway, for example, cut a wide swath through residential areas of the borough, which was doubly alarming given the possibility of a less destructive alternative just blocks away. Moses fought community objections to the route, citing the potential delays and cost increases of negotiating a new path, and advocated for the additional "benefit" of reducing housing density in an area deemed unsavory and overpopulated by planning professionals. Moses ultimately prevailed, but the ill repute of such projects colored subsequent public awareness of and advocacy against his planning approach.[13]

The defeat of two elevated highway proposals for Manhattan demonstrate this trend. The *Regional Plan of New York and its Environs* had forecast four crosstown expressways for Manhattan in its 1920s planning recommendations. City planning officials, including Moses, incorporated these ideas into their long-term visions for city transportation. Moses officially began to lobby for the so-called Lower Manhattan Expressway in 1940. The Lower Manhattan Expressway was to have been an elevated viaduct thirty to forty feet in the air connecting the Holland Tunnel on the western shore to the Williamsburg Bridge at the east. Its direct cross-island route, touted to be the least disruptive by Moses, was to have evicted 1,972 families and 804 businesses. The Mid-Manhattan Expressway, proposed in 1950, followed a similar rationale. It was to have connected the Lincoln Tunnel with the Queens Midtown Tunnel via an elevated six-lane highway along Thirtieth Street. To secure the necessary right-of-way for the road, Moses proposed to demolish all buildings on the south side of the street. For both the Lower Manhattan Expressway and Mid-Manhattan Expressway, the specter of such widespread destruction provoked community uproar and, ultimately, project cancellation.[14] Even as renderings of these elevated highways showcased exciting urban landscapes with roads skirting through skyscrapers and stacked atop one another—much like those offered in the 1920s—concern for the human scale and livability of American cities began to trump the seductiveness of automobile infrastructure.

As these national and regional shifts evolved, the West Side Elevated Highway faced ever-increasing amounts of traffic. The resulting traffic jams and deteriorating conditions demonstrated several key issues. First, like Wacker Drive, the West Side Elevated Highway's route, form, and width proved troublesome for evolving volumes, speeds, and sizes of vehicles. The highway's series of sharp turns, dictated by the locations of adjoining buildings and piers, proved difficult for drivers to navigate—especially at high speeds—and by 1941 had already resulted in thirty-three deaths.[15] In addition, the highway's narrow lanes and left-hand entrance and exit ramps meant that breakdowns could quickly cripple a large section of the highway. City officials recognized this as early as 1947 when they initiated a "jeep tow patrol" service to cruise the length of the highway looking for disabled vehicles and safely tow them off the road.[16] Beneath and near the elevated highway, thanks to the highway's prohibition of trucks, freight traffic struggled to move through ever-more-congested area streets, leading to widespread frustration.[17]

Finally, there was the structure itself. The highway's long approach ramps demanded significant street space, limiting the visual and physical permeability of the areas beneath the highway. The forest of supporting columns dissuaded access to the waterfront, as did the parking lots that filled the road's shadowy undercroft (fig. 7.2). Waning industry left many of the waterfront piers empty and decaying, providing few reasons for locals to venture beyond the highway to the water. The

Figure 7.2 As-built conditions under the West Side Elevated Highway adjacent to Hudson River piers, as captured by Berenice Abbott, April 18, 1936. (Berenice Abbott [1898–1991] for Federal Art Project/Museum of the City of New York. 43.131.1.644.)

road's Art Deco embellishments appeared paltry in the face of such large-scale decline. On the highway surface, heavy usage wore the granite paving blocks smooth, making them very slippery when wet. In addition, deicing salts corroded the concrete beneath the blocks, making the roadbed unstable. These conditions spurred piecemeal repairs from the late 1940s through the early 1970s, during which time citizens and leaders began to question the road's future.[18]

Although the borough president of Manhattan promised large-scale rehabilitation and reconstruction of the West Side Elevated Highway as early as 1954, patchwork repairs succeeded in postponing full confrontation of these larger issues. In December 1973, however, the physical reality of the highway literally crashed down on Manhattan as a section of the road collapsed under the weight of a loaded dump truck bringing asphalt to fix part of the road (fig. 7.3).[19] This accident compelled closure of major sections of the highway and spurred acute reevaluation of the road. From the time of the highway collapse until the mid-

Figure 7.3 The literal downfall of the West Side Elevated Highway, December 15, 1973, as the roadbed collapsed under the weight of a loaded dump truck bringing asphalt to repair the road. (Ted Cowell. Courtesy Cowell family.)

1990s, controversy raged about the prognosis for west-side redevelopment. For many years public discourse focused on the so-called Westway proposal, a design for replacing the West Side Elevated Highway with a tunneled highway through new landfill along the Hudson River shore, which would have been topped by huge public parks and residential developments. This option, which qualified for federal Interstate support, was eventually defeated on environmental grounds. Over the following decade, city leaders and experts evaluated a series of smaller and less expensive alternatives, including variations on repairing or demolishing the elevated highway. The ultimate decision, reached in close consultation with adjoining neighborhood groups, opted to demolish the elevated road and replace it with an on-grade roadway south of Fifty-Seventh Street. The new "urban boulevard" would carry between six and eight lanes and would be regulated by traffic lights. Its medians would offer small planting strips, and regular east-west crosswalks would facilitate pedestrian access to the river. A sixteen-foot-wide bike and pedestrian path would flank the western side of the new street, lined by a riverside swath of new trees and landscaping. Above Fifty-Seventh Street, a new viaduct would carry traffic to a connection to the Henry Hudson Parkway at Seventy-Second Street (figs. 7.4–7.5).[20] Construction of this landscape, termed

Figure 7.4 New West Side Highway Viaduct, looking south from Seventy-Second Street. (Author photograph.)

Figure 7.5 Remaining arcaded segment of West Side Elevated Highway at Seventy-Second Street, at former junction with Henry Hudson Parkway. New highway viaduct is visible to the south. (Author photograph.)

the "West Side Highway Reconstruction Project," reached completion in 2001.[21] The ongrade physical presence of the new West Side Highway was derived not just from pressing traffic needs but also in response to the collective memory of the looming physical presence of its elevated predecessor.

Boston

The physical form of the original Central Artery, because of its direct route through downtown, had the most dramatic and lasting impact of the three roads. Moving east through the streets of the financial district past entrances to modern office towers, people came upon a massive steel and concrete skeleton straddling surface roads and shouldering traffic overhead. The Central Artery's underpinnings dominated views at the ends of streets and dwarfed adjoining modest buildings (see figs. 6.39–6.42). Its structure and corresponding shadow literally blocked all views of the city's waterfront, replacing them with the machined starkness of the highway's green guardrails. Crossing underneath this green giant was itself unpleasant, requiring navigation of both the local traffic and the pigeons who called its murky underside home. Drivers were not fans of the highway either. By the mid-1980s, 180,000 vehicles used the highway daily—twice its original estimated capacity. Its numerous entrance and exit ramps complicated traffic patterns and slowed speeds, creating frequent traffic jams.

These conditions spurred a variety of responses. Some suggested adding a second deck to the highway, which would have doubled its capacity but only worsened its experiential and environmental impacts. Others proposed widening the road by claiming additional adjoining properties, but community activism prevented serious consideration of this concept.[22] By the early 1970s, attention increasingly focused on the idea of putting the Central Artery underground. In 1975 the Boston Redevelopment Authority prepared a feasibility report for state and federal authorities that examined the plausibility of accomplishing such a huge feat. The report called the Central Artery's underpinnings "the most conspicuous eyesore in downtown Boston today," and lamented the isolation of the North End "behind an intimidating barrier of steel and concrete." It continued on to label the elevated highway as "a mistake" and "an ugly scar across the urban landscape."[23] This report, evincing a pronounced shift in attitude about the Central Artery from an official Boston planning agency, marked the start of a long journey for the city of Boston. In 1983 the Boston Redevelopment Authority authored a full design for depressing the artery, and local politicians convinced the federal government to integrate the proposed highway into the Interstate system—yielding significant funding from the federal government.[24]

The complete design for burying the Central Artery involved threading a new, expanded highway underneath the existing highway corridor. The existing elevated Central Artery was to remain functional during the construction process,

Figure 7.6 Aerial view of completed surface parks created by the Big Dig, today known as the Rose Kennedy Greenway, occupying the corridor previously filled by the elevated Central Artery, June 2017. (Kyle Klein Photography.)

after which it would be dismantled and replaced by a surface network of public parks and civic amenities. This approach would simultaneously remove the visual, physical, and auditory barriers of the elevated highway, expand traffic capacity, reconnect the North End to the rest of the city, provide views of and access to the waterfront, and heal the wound in the urban fabric wrought by the elevated Central Artery. It would also require unprecedented engineering skill, funds, and public patience. Construction of the resulting project, known as the Central Artery/Tunnel Project (or colloquially, the Big Dig), stretched from 1991 to 2007 (fig. 7.6).

The Big Dig rejected its predecessor's physical presence in the city in two main ways. First, it offered a solution that is invisible and silent on the surface. High-speed vehicles flow uninterrupted beneath downtown Boston, separated from local traffic on the surface. Second, it returned the former highway corridor to the city fabric. Bright sunlight floods land and buildings that had been in shadow for the previous half century, and all types of street traffic now move easily between the waterfront and the downtown core (figs. 7.7–7.10). Whereas the elevated Central Artery derived its modernity from its stark forms and brute focus on direct travel connections, the Big Dig responded with an inverse model of modernity that removed both elements from public view.[25]

Figure 7.7 (above) Decommissioned Central Artery underpinnings, roadbed removed, January 2004. (Author photograph.)

Figure 7.8 (left) Partially demolished elevated Central Artery, showing remaining supports and missing roadbed, looking south from Clinton Street area, March 2004. (Author photograph.)

Figure 7.9 (facing page, top) Completed Rose Kennedy Greenway corridor, looking south from Clinton Street area, July 2008. Exit ramp from new Central Artery tunnel is visible at left. Compare to view from similar vantage point in figure 7.8. (Author photograph.)

Figure 7.10 (facing page, bottom) Completed Rose Kennedy Greenway corridor, looking north from Clinton Street area, July 2008. Central Artery tunnel runs beneath parks to emerge before Charles River to connect to Leonard P. Zakim Bunker Hill Memorial Bridge, visible at top. (Author photograph.)

MERCANTILE MALL

Modern Intentions; Modern Problems

In 1920, when leaders in Chicago, New York, and Boston were beginning to contemplate elevated highways, the United States boasted 8.1 million registered automobiles nationwide. Five years later, that number had more than doubled to 17.5 million. Twenty-five years later, as Boston prepared to finally start construction of the Central Artery, that figure had reached 40.4 million automobiles.[26] This progression challenged not only the norms of everyday life but also the physical structure of American cities. Elevated urban highways manifested a specific response to these conditions.

The ideological, technical, and spatial ramifications of automobiles did not gel with the existing fabric of early twentieth-century cities. Whereas existing urban frameworks offered shared streets and public transportation, the automobile introduced a privatized resource that demanded independence within this communal framework. The automobile's display of modern technology not only empowered such freedom but also presented a new aesthetic reference for artists and designers. These factors collided as engineers, planners, architects, and municipal leaders struggled to adapt existing landscapes to these new norms.

Elevated-highway designers drew on the precedent of the elevated railroad but fused it with a new conception of the entire urban landscape as functionally and architecturally modern. In their ideal scenarios they envisioned elevated roadways as more than practical viaducts. They saw them as threads of modern travel and communication woven into the very fabric of new urban landscapes. When faced with implementing such schemes, they adapted this vision to solve common problems, even as their topographical and logistical challenges differed. Chicago, New York, and Boston faced similar economic concerns related to faltering trade, accessibility, and civic identity. In each case the constructed presence of the new highway—rendered through its scale, reach, and architectural details—acted as a messenger of larger civic aspirations for economic, architectural, and transportation modernity. Local conditions then determined the aesthetic terms of this shared approach. In Chicago, this meant Beaux Arts classicism; in New York, Art Deco flourishes; and in Boston, bare, horizontally banded steel. This evinced the malleability of the artistic definition of modernity even as its logistical framework remained the same. These projects shared a philosophical definition of modernity predicated on denigrating, removing, and replacing urban fabric of the past but engaged different aesthetic approaches in their new additions to their respective cities.

Building and using these thoroughfares provoked stark realizations of new contrasts in the urban landscape. The breadth and technological empowerment of construction sites mocked the scale and materials of surrounding structures. Automobiles escaped the muck and congestion of on-grade streets to whiz aboveground through their cities. Especially in New York and Boston, pedestrians found themselves literally overwhelmed by the scale and physicality of the elevated superstructures. Over time, the long-term ramifications of these conditions grew more complex. New automobile sizes, speeds, and volumes challenged the capacity of these roads, making their experiential qualities more frustrating than sublime. Removed from the modern utopian frameworks envisioned by designers, the elevated highways became disconnected from their immediate contexts, standing as solitary projections of modern urbanism.

In a broader context, this evolution planted the seeds of our current car-focused culture. These early constructed roadways stoked the automotive accessibility of urban centers, begetting ever-increasing demand for broader networks of roads to connect suburban and urban landscapes. The 1956 Federal-Aid Highway Act endorsed this growth pattern, incentivizing urban highway construction as national policy. The Interstate highways, however, derived from national policy and financial incentives, not from the consideration of local economies, local traffic bottlenecks, and worn urban fabric that had fueled the plans for the projects in this study. Instead of utopian-inspired visions of synchronized modern urban form, the Interstates brought paths of regional importance to downtown areas, empowering automotive movement to and through urban centers, with little focus on movement within them. In so doing, the Interstate Highway System normalized the public's expectations for geographic mobility and reinforced the appeal of automotive transportation as especially convenient, flexible, and direct. The exponential growth and reinforcement of this model is visible in America's overwhelmingly dominant car culture, and we should all be concerned about the compounded impact of this pattern on social isolation, community fragmentation, and environmental pollution.

From an architectural perspective, the roots of these current conditions are clearly visible in the reconsiderations of urban form and mobility encapsulated by the elevated urban highways of the first half of the twentieth century. Distinctly different from their midcentury progeny, these highways evolved from dreams of integrated urban landscapes suited to the scale and pace of the automobile. Their designers imbued them with modern architectural intent that was as strong, if not as prominent, as their ultimate physical impacts on their surroundings. This disparity fueled late twentieth-century denigration of elevated highways but should now inform new appreciation of their idealistic roots in the formative years of the automobile age.

NOTES

INTRODUCTION

1. See, for example, William F. Streich, "A Plan for Multiplying the Utility of Business Thoroughfares," *American City* 8 (March 1913): 275–276; "Proposed Plan to Relieve Traffic Congestion in St. Paul and Provide Parking Space for 3,000 Automobiles," *American City*, April 1928, 87; John Irwin Bright, "The Plan of Philadelphia," *Annals of the American Academy of Political and Social Science* 116 (November 1924): 231–235.

2. Margy Sweeney, "Reworking Wacker," *Grid* 7, no. 3 (September 2001): 32; Blair Kamin, "They're Making the City Riverfront a Place for People," *Chicago Tribune*, September 18, 2016, 2; Blair Kamin, "Riverwalk Stretches East to Repair the Design Divide," *Chicago Tribune*, May 19, 2019, 1.

3. Dennis J. O'Brien, "The West Side Highway Reconstruction Story," *Public Works* 128 no. 1 (January 1997): 28–30.

4. For more on the development of the Interstate Highway System, see Mark H. Rose, *Interstate: Express Highway Politics, 1939–1989,* rev. ed. (Knoxville: University of Tennessee Press, 1990); Tom Lewis, *Divided Highways: Building the Interstate Highways, Transforming American Life.* (New York: Viking, 1997).

5. Leo Marx, *The Machine in the Garden: Technology and the Pastoral Ideal in America* (New York: Oxford University Press, 2000), 220–222.

CHAPTER 1

1. For further discussion, see Spiro Kostof, "The Urban Skyline," chap. 5 in *The City Shaped: Urban Patterns and Meanings through History* (Boston: Bulfinch Press, 1991), 279–335.

2. Charles W. Cheape, *Moving the Masses: Urban Public Transit in New York, Boston, and Philadelphia—1880–1912* (Cambridge: Harvard University Press, 1980), 3–5. For more on the role of the omnibus in early intra-urban movement see Kenneth T. Jackson, *Crabgrass Frontier: The Suburbanization of the United States* (New York: Oxford University Press, 1985), 33–35.

3. Cheape, *Moving the Masses*, 5–7, 104, 118–120.

4. "Women of Nerve: They Remain in a Street Car While All the Men Run," *New York Times*, April 19, 1889, 8.

5. Robert M. Fogelson, *Downtown: Its Rise and Fall, 1880–1950* (New Haven, CT: Yale University Press, 2001), 46.

6. Robert A. M. Stern, Thomas Mellins, and David Fishman, *New York 1880: Architecture and Urbanism in the Gilded Age* (New York: Monacelli Press, 1999), 69–75; Cheape, *Moving the Masses*, 8–9. For more on the vast array of nineteenth-century proposals for elevated railroads in New York see Robert C. Reed, *The New York Elevated* (New York: A. S. Barnes, 1978), 22–30.

7. Steam power was not ideal for urban applications because of its predisposition to explosion, droppings of hot ashes, and pollution of smoke and soot. Early elevated railroads tried to rely on other means of propulsion—cable, pneumatic, or early electric—but the power and imminence of steam technology compelled New York, Chicago, and Boston to ultimately use steam power on some of its elevated lines.

8. "Establishing Rapid Transit," *New York Times*, June 6, 1878, 8; "Opening of a New Elevated Steam Railway in New York City," *Scientific American* 38, no. 20 (May 18, 1878): 315; "Rapid Transit and Trade," *New York Times*, June 18, 1878, 8. Of course, as business activity increased near elevated lines there were corresponding decreases in activity farther away, leading to complaints from affected businesses.

9. Harold M. Mayer and Richard C. Wade, *Chicago: Growth of a Metropolis* (Chicago: University of Chicago Press, 1969), 208–214.

10. "Running on the L," *Chicago Daily Tribune*, June 7, 1892, 9.

11. Moses King, ed., *King's Handbook of New York City: An Outline History and Description of the American Metropolis*. 2nd ed. (New York: Benjamin Blom, 1972), 1:138.

12. Such effects were not unanticipated in the planning phases for elevated railroads. Many citizens and design professionals expressed their concerns about these results, but city officials generally felt that the elevated railroads' benefits to the public outweighed their injuries to individual property owners. Only after construction was complete did larger constituencies appreciate the environmental dissonance created by the elevated railroads. See "Elevated Railway Noises: A Grievous Nuisance That Comes with Warm Weather," *New York Times*, June 3, 1879, 8; "'L' Roads and Property Owners," *Chicago Daily Tribune*, January 27, 1890, 6; "Views Differ Regarding the L Loop," *Chicago Daily Tribune*, February 10, 1893, 3.

13. T.A.J. "Elevated Railways: Objections to Their Introduction into Chicago—Experience of New York," *Chicago Daily Tribune*, June 16, 1879, 2.

14. "For Rapid Transit," *Chicago Daily Tribune*, September 17, 1893, 25.

15. "For True Rapid Transit," *New York Times*, December 1, 1892, 3.

16. "For True Rapid Transit," 3; Cheape, *Moving the Masses*, 8–9. For more on the development of New York's subway system see Clifton Hood, "Subways, Transit Politics, and Metropolitan Spatial Expansion," in *The Landscape of Modernity: Essays on New York City, 1900–1940*, eds. David Ward and Olivier Zunz (New York: Russell Sage Foundation, 1992), 191–212.

17. Cheape, *Moving the Masses*, 104–110. Although Bostonians had proposed an elevated railway as early as 1879, they did not construct any until the early twentieth century. Whereas New York and Chicago posited elevated railroads as the first stage of response to urban congestion, Boston repeatedly rejected elevated schemes for many years, instead opting for the subway as the primary response to nineteenth-century traffic woes. See also Lawrence W. Kennedy, *Planning the City upon a Hill: Boston since 1630* (Amherst: University of Massachusetts Press, 1992), especially 99–102.

18. Fogelson, *Downtown*, 56–60.

19. Fogelson, *Downtown*, 56–60; Cheape, *Moving the Masses*, 130–140; Brian J. Cuda-

hy, *Change at Park Street Under: The Story of Boston's Subways* (Brattleboro, VT: Stephen Greene Press, 1972), 13–15.

20. Kennedy, *Planning the City upon a Hill*, 99–102.

21. Kennedy, *Planning the City upon a Hill*, 99–102; Cheape, *Moving the Masses*, 130–145; Cudahy, *Change at Park Street Under*, 10–13.

22. "The Boston Subway," *Scientific American* 73, no. 9 (August 31, 1895): 135; "The Boston Electric Subway," *Scientific American* 75, no. 10 (September 5, 1896): 197; "Completion of Part of the Boston Subway," *Scientific American* 78, no. 12 (September 18, 1897): 177, 184.

23. "Now for Speed," *Boston Daily Globe*, September 1, 1897, 1.

24. "Every Car Crowded," *Boston Daily Globe*, September 2, 1897, 1.

25. Kennedy, *Planning the City upon a Hill*, 101.

26. Kennedy, *Planning the City upon a Hill*, 101; Sam Bass Warner, Jr., *Streetcar Suburbs: The Process of Growth in Boston, 1870–1900*, 2nd ed. (Cambridge: Harvard University Press, 1978), 25–28.

27. There is a wealth of primary documentation and secondary scholarship on the complexities of nineteenth-century industrialization and immigration. See, among others, Jacob A. Riis, *How the Other Half Lives: Studies among the Tenements of New York* (New York: Penguin, 2001); Jane Addams, *Twenty Years at Hull House with Autobiographical Notes* (New York: Signet, 1960); Stanley K. Schultz, *Constructing Urban Culture: American Cities and City Planning, 1800–1920,* Technology and Urban Growth Series. (Philadelphia: Temple University Press, 1989); and Peter Hall, *Cities of Tomorrow: An Intellectual History of Urban Planning and Design in the Twentieth Century* (Malden, MA: Blackwell, 2002), especially 36–47.

28. For primary sources see Andrew Jackson Downing, *Victorian Cottage Residences* (New York: Dover, 1981); Catharine Esther Beecher and Harriet Beecher Stowe, *The American Woman's Home: or, Principles of Domestic Science: Being a Guide to the Formation and Maintenance of Economical, Healthful, Beautiful and Christian Homes.* (Watkins Glen, NY: American Life Foundation, 1979). Secondary sources: Jackson, *Crabgrass Frontier*; Warner, *Streetcar Suburbs*; Dolores Hayden, *Building Suburbia: Green Fields and Urban Growth, 1820–2000* (New York: Pantheon, 2003).

29. Daniel Bluestone, *Constructing Chicago* (New Haven, CT: Yale University Press, 1991), 105–109, 114–115; David M. Scobey, *Empire City: The Making and Meaning of the New York City Landscape* (Philadelphia: Temple University Press, 2002), 5, 70, 104; Sarah Bradford Landau and Carl W. Condit, *Rise of the New York Skyscraper 1865–1913* (New Haven, CT: Yale University Press, 1996), 5. For more on the abstract definition of a skyscraper see Winston Weisman, "New York and the Problem of the First Skyscraper," *Journal of the Society of Architectural Historians* 12, no.1 (March 1953): 13–21. For more on the business and economic changes that fueled the construction of office buildings see Olivier Zunz, *Making America Corporate, 1870–1920* (Chicago: University of Chicago Press, 1990), especially chapters 2 and 3; and Eric Hobsbawm, *The Age of Capital, 1848–1875* (New York: Vintage, 1996).

30. Landau and Condit, *Rise of the New York Skyscraper*, 83–90; Lee E. Gray, "Type and Building Type: Newspaper/Office Buildings in Nineteenth-Century New York," in *The American Skyscraper: Cultural Histories*, ed. Roberta Moudry (New York: Cambridge University Press, 2005), 86–87, 92–95; Gail Fenske and Deryck Holdsworth, "Corporate Identity and the New York Office Building: 1895–1915," in *The Landscape of Modernity*, eds. Ward and Zunz, 131–132.

31. Fenske and Holdsworth, "Corporate Identity and the New York Office Building," 130.

32. Fenske and Holdsworth, "Corporate Identity and the New York Office Building," 135–139. For more on the economic forces that drove skyscraper construction see Carol

Willis, *Form Follows Finance: Skyscrapers and Skylines in New York and Chicago* (New York: Princeton Architectural Press, 1995), especially 145–155.

33. Landau and Condit, *Rise of the New York Skyscraper*, 19–23, 146–148.

34. The Monadnock Building is well documented in many strong sources. For a particularly clear and succinct explanation of these issues see Leland M. Roth, *American Architecture: A History* (Boulder, CO: Westview Press, 2001), 271–273.

35. Landau and Condit, *Rise of the New York Skyscraper*, 30–33, 37–38.

36. Landau and Condit, *Rise of the New York Skyscraper*, 35–37. Elevators have been the subject of much scholarly debate, as some have positioned them as essential forerunners to the development of the skyscraper, while others have lauded them as empowering but not critical assets in skyscraper progress. This book favors the latter interpretation. As has been shown earlier in this chapter, socioeconomic changes created the need and opportunity for office buildings, and economic competition drove them skyward. See Landau and Condit, *Rise of the New York Skyscraper*, 19–23, 146–148.

37. For more on the corporate culture of skyscrapers, including the use of telephones and typewriters and their supporting social hierarchy, see Zunz, *Making America Corporate, 1870–1920*, 113–124.

38. "A Retrospect of the Year 1896," *Scientific American* 76, no. 1 (January 2, 1897): 4.

39. Fogelson, *Downtown*, 251–254; "Topics of the Times," *New York Times*, June 14, 1899, 6.

40. Flink, *The Car Culture*, 5–7.

41. Clay McShane, *Down the Asphalt Path: The Automobile and the American City* (New York: Columbia University Press, 1994), 81–103.

42. James J. Flink, *America Adopts the Automobile, 1895–1910* (Cambridge, MA: MIT Press, 1970): 12–15; McShane, *Down the Asphalt Path*, 103–105; Flink, *The Car Culture*, 15–17.

43. Flink, *The Car Culture*, 7–8; McShane, *Down the Asphalt Path*, 54–56, 62–66; and John B. Rae, *The Road and the Car in American Life* (Cambridge, MA: MIT Press, 1971), 23–37. For more on early road improvement efforts see Bruce E. Seely, *Building the American Highway System: Engineers as Policy Makers* (Philadelphia: Temple University Press, 1987), especially chap. 1, "The Early Good Roads Movement," 11–23.

44. Flink, *America Adopts the Automobile*, 278–281; Flink, *The Car Culture*, 50–51.

45. Flink, *American Adopts the Automobile*, 262–268.

46. Flink, *The Car Culture*, 75–78; Flink, *America Adopts the Automobile*, 268–278; McShane, *Down the Asphalt Path*, 135; and Rae, *The Road and the Car*, 45–47.

47. "From 'Horseless Carriage' to Palace Motor Car," *New York Times*, January 12, 1913, XX1.

48. "A Marvelous Automobile Record—103 ½ Miles an Hour." *Scientific American* 91, no. 7 (August 13, 1904): 115; "Vanderbilt Race Won by Hemery," *New York Times*, October 15, 1905, 1; "Master of the Highway" Paige-Detroit Motor Car Company advertisement, *Los Angeles Times*, May 1, 1921, VI11; "Stock Car Record for Mile Broken in South," *Washington Post*, April 23, 1921, 11; "Stock-Car Record Falls," *Los Angeles Times*, May 1, 1921,VI9; "Roamer Breaks World's Stock Chassis Record" Roamer Motor Car Company Advertisement, *Chicago Daily Tribune*, May 5, 1921, F9.

49. McShane, *Down the Asphalt Path*, 119–122; Flink, *America Adopts the Automobile*, 97–98; "The Future of the Motor Car." *Scientific American* 77, no. 3 (July 17, 1897): 35.

50. McShane, *Down the Asphalt Path*, 125–134; Rae, *The Road and the Car*, 133–134; David Blanke, *Hell on Wheels: The Promise and Peril of America's Car Culture, 1900–1940* (Lawrence: University Press of Kansas, 2007), 27.

51. Rae, *The Road and the Car*, 137–146; McShane, *Down the Asphalt Path*, 128–134, 147–148; Blanke, *Hell on Wheels*, 70. See also Michael L. Berger, "The Car's Impact on the

American Family," in *The Car and the City: The Automobile, the Built Environment, and Daily Urban Life*, eds. Martin Wachs and Margaret Crawford (Ann Arbor: University of Michigan Press, 1992), 57–74.

52. "Walnut Park" advertisement, *Los Angeles Times*, May 30, 1919, I5. Bolding in original.

53. Jackson, *Crabgrass Frontier*, 175.

54. Schultz, *Constructing Urban Culture*, 176–177.

55. McShane, *Down the Asphalt Path*, 62–67. See also Peter D. Norton, *Fighting Traffic: The Dawn of the Motor Age in the American City,* Inside Technology Series. (Cambridge, MA: MIT Press, 2008).

56. U.S. Bureau of the Census, *Historical Statistics of the United States, Colonial Times to 1970, Bicentennial Edition, Part 2* (Washington, DC: U.S. Government Printing Office, 1975), 727.

57. Willis, *Form Follows Finance*, 34, 9; Marc A. Weiss, "Density and Intervention: New York's Planning Traditions," in *The Landscape of Modernity*, eds. Ward and Zunz, 50–51.

58. Kennedy, *Planning the City upon a Hill*, 78–84, 112–115; Michael Holleran, *Boston's "Changeful Times": Origins of Preservation and Planning in America* (Baltimore: Johns Hopkins University Press, 1998), 165–187. For more on the impact of fire on Boston and other cities see Christine Meisner Rosen, *The Limits of Power: Great Fires and the Process of City Growth in America* (New York: Cambridge University Press, 1986).

59. U.S. Bureau of the Census, *Statistical Abstract of the United States: 1970.* 91st ed. (Washington, DC: U.S. Government Printing Office, 1970), 22.

60. U.S. Bureau of the Census, *Historical Statistics of the United States, Colonial Times to 1970, Bicentennial Edition, Part 2*, 716.

61. McShane, *Down the Asphalt Path*, 104–106.

62. U.S. Department of Commerce, *Statistical Abstract of the United States: 1920.* 43rd ed. (Washington, DC: U.S. Government Printing Office, 1921), 316.

63. U.S. Bureau of the Census, *Historical Statistics of the United States, Colonial Times to 1970, Bicentennial Edition, Part 2*, 720.

64. William P. Helm, "Motor Traffic Problem," *Washington Post*, June 9, 1924, 8.

65. "The Dance of Death That Goes on Between the Sidewalks of New York," *American City* 35, no. 3 (September 1926): 317.

66. "Likens Traffic to a Giant Cobra," *New York Times*, November 25, 1923, RE2.

67. "Where Traffic Crawls," *Boston Traveler*, October 1, 1929, n.p. Massachusetts State Transportation Library, 1930s Newspaper Scrapbook Collection.

68. "Motor Official Declares War on Loop Congestion," *Chicago Sunday Tribune*, February 7, 1926): A6.

69. Sidney A. Reeve, "Congestion in Cities" *Geographical Review* 3, no. 4 (April 1917): 293.

CHAPTER 2

1. Clay McShane, *Down the Asphalt Path: The Automobile and the American City* (New York: Columbia University Press, 1994), 184–188.

2. McShane, *Down the Asphalt Path*, 184–187, 190, 197.

3. Clay McShane, "The Origins and Globalization of Traffic Control Signals," *Journal of Urban History* 25, no. 3 (March 1999): 381–383; McShane, *Down the Asphalt Path*, 199–201.

4. McShane, "The Origins and Globalization of Traffic Control Signals," 383–384.

5. Robert M. Fogelson, *Downtown: Its Rise and Fall, 1880–1950* (New Haven, CT: Yale University Press, 2001), 257; "New Rules of the Road," *New York Times*, January

28, 1914, 7; "One-Way Rule Aids in Clearing Traffic," *New York Times*, February 1, 1916, 9; "One-Way Street," *Washington Post*, September 2, 1917, 12; "One Way Traffic to Get Tryout on the Rialto," *Chicago Daily Tribune*, March 27, 1921, 5; Winfield M. Thompson, "Many Narrow Streets. Philadelphia Traffic Needs Much Like Those Pressing in Boston," *Boston Globe*, December 11, 1915, 12; Irving C. Moller, "Guiding the Traffic Flow," *Annals of the American Academy of Political and Social Science* 133 (September 1927): 119.

6. Fogelson, *Downtown*, 284–285; "Announces New Traffic Rules," *Boston Globe*, December 3, 1922, 6.

7. Fogelson, *Downtown*, 287–295; Paul Barrett, *The Automobile and Urban Transit: The Formation of Public Policy in Chicago, 1900–1930*. Technology and Urban Growth Series. (Philadelphia: Temple University Press, 1983), 158–161; "Boylston-St. Merchants Want Parking Allowed," *Boston Globe*, June 27, 1923, 7; "Auto Parking Problem Grows," *Boston Globe*, July 9, 1923, 5; "Ban on Parking Near Greensward on Commonwealth Avenue," *Boston Globe*, April 25, 1924, 1A. For more on Los Angeles' particular response to automobiles and parking regulations see Richard Longstreth, "Perils of a Parkless Town," in *The Car and the City: The Automobile, the Built Environment, and Daily Urban Life*, eds. Martin Wachs and Margaret Crawford (Ann Arbor: University of Michigan Press, 1992), 141–153.

8. Fogelson, *Downtown*, 287–288, 295–296; "20-Minute Parking Rule to Aid Traffic," *New York Times*, June 5, 1924, 5; "One-Hour Parking Limit Downtown Advocated," *Washington Post*, January 12, 1924, 5; "Long Beach Places New Parking Limit," *Los Angeles Times*, November 28, 1923, I20; "It's Expensive to Park Too Long," *Los Angeles Times*, May 9, 1926, G15.

9. This will be revisited in chapter 3 in relation to Wacker Drive.

10. McShane, *Down the Asphalt Path*, 206–207; Fogelson, *Downtown*, 296–297; Irving C. Moller, "Guiding the Traffic Flow," *Annals of the American Academy of Political and Social Science* 133 (September 1927): 119; "Jordan Marsh to Park Autos," *Boston Daily Globe*, June 14, 1924, 1, 10; John Ihlder, "Automobile Use in Many Cities at Maximum of Street Facilities," *New York Times*, June 24, 1923, XX9.

11. John S. Crandell, "Shall We Abolish Sleep? The 24-Hour Street as a Means of Reducing Traffic Congestion," *The American City* 38 (February 1928): 82.

12. Diana Rice, "Truck Delivery by Night Studied," *New York Times*, August 7, 1927, X16; "New York's Truck Experiment," *Washington Post*, November 16, 1927, 6; "Delivery Schedule Revision Heralded," *Washington Post*, November 18, 1926, A7; Harper Leech, "Freight Trucks Held to Blame for Loop Delay," *Chicago Daily Tribune*, March 7, 1926, A18; "Subways Suggested for Carrying Mail," *New York Times*, November 11, 1928, 3; "Elevated Freight Highways Seen as Need in Cities," *Chicago Daily Tribune*, January 24, 1926, A8; B. F. Fitch, "The Place of the Motor Truck in the Modern City Plan," *Annals of the American Academy of Political and Social Science* 133 (September 1927): 200–226.

13. In this context I am specifically differentiating singular designs for transportation improvements from comprehensive city plans and imaginary utopias that also incorporated innovative transportation approaches. By "Engineering" projects, I encompass the evolution of street construction and paving technologies, the widening of streets, the erection of bridges and overpasses, construction of elevated railroads and subways, and the assorted individual proposals for the likes of elevated streets, sidewalks, moving platforms, and subterranean pathways. The city plans (real or utopian) that subsequently incorporated similar ideas into comprehensive ideologies for urban form will be treated separately, later in this chapter.

14. McShane, *Down the Asphalt Path*, 216–217; Nelson P. Lewis, "The Automobile and the City Plan," *Proceedings of the Eight National Conference on City Planning, Cleveland, June 5–7, 1916* (New York: Conference on City Planning, 1916): 41–42.

15. Lewis, "The Automobile and the City Plan," 49.

16. McShane, *Down the Asphalt Path*, 217.

17. Asha Elizabeth Weinstein, "The Congestion Evil: Perceptions of Traffic Congestion in Boston in the 1890s and 1920s" (Ph.D. diss., City and Regional Planning, University of California, Berkeley, 2002), 173–175; "Mayor Discusses Street Widening," *Boston Daily Globe*, January 29, 1912, 2; "Favors Widening around Common," *Boston Daily Globe*, November 15, 1919, 10; "$14,000,000 for Wider Streets," *Boston Daily Globe*, December 28, 1922, 8; "Tremont Street to Be Widened," *Boston Daily Globe*, October 15, 1924, 23A; "Famed Ancient Hub Street Given Sunshine Once More," *Washington Post*, May 11, 1924, ES3.

18. Barrett, *The Automobile and Urban Transit*, 143–147, McShane, *Down the Asphalt Path*, 217; Fogelson, *Downtown*, 259–260.

19. Lewis, "The Automobile and the City Plan," 53; Ernest P. Goodrich, "The Urban Auto Problem," *Proceedings of the Twelfth National Conference on City Planning, Cincinnati, Ohio, April 19 to 22*. (New York: Conference on City Planning, 1920), 79, 82, 84; Fogelson, *Downtown*, 261–262.

20. Robert A. M. Stern, Thomas Mellins, and David Fishman. *New York 1880: Architecture and Urbanism in the Gilded Age* (New York: Monacelli Press, 1999), 61–63; "Municipal Affairs," *New York Times*, February 2, 1868, 8; "Miscellaneous," *New York Times*, June 28, 1868, 4; "Board of Assistant Aldermen," *New York Times*, January 19, 1869, 2; "Minor Topics," *New York Times*, January 21, 1869, 4; "Letters to the Editor—The Loew Bridge," *New York Times*, December 20, 1868, 5.

21. "Minor Topics," 4.

22. Weinstein, "The Congestion Evil," 342–344; Clifford Donald Ellis, "Visions of Urban Freeways, 1930–1970" (Ph.D. diss., University of California, Berkeley, 1990), 44–45.

23. "Shall We Have Double-Decked Streets?," *Scientific American* 88, no. 17 (April 25, 1903): 310.

24. "Transit by Moving Platform," *New York Times*, February 28, 1904, SM2.

25. "Double-Deck Streets as a Relief for Traffic Congestion," *Scientific American* 96, no. 25 (June 22, 1907): 505, 510.

26. "To Have Streets in the Air," *New York Times*, March 22, 1908, M5; "For Beauty and Utility in New York City," *New York Times*, November 29, 1908, SM3.

27. E. Hénard, "The Cities of the Future," *American City* (January 1911): 27–31; "City of the Future: Paris Architect Forecasts the Coming Municipality," *Washington Post*, November 20, 1920, E4; Wolf Von Eckardt, "Man for All Seasons," *Washington Post*, August 10, 1969, 155.

28. "Subways for Foot Travel," *Boston Daily Globe*, October 21, 1911, 12.

29. "A New Airship Runabout," *Washington Post*, March 8, 1908, M3.

30. "Start Airship Line in Spring," *Chicago Daily Tribune*, February 4, 1912, 7; "It Will Be the Dirigible," *Los Angeles Times*, May 26, 1919, II4; "Plans Airplane Line on Coast," *Los Angeles Times*, January 30, 1920, II7; Rear Admiral William A. Moffett, "ZR-1 is Hailed as the Pioneer of a New Era in Transportation," *New York Times*, September 16, 1923, XX12; "Air Highways Just Opening, Eckener Says," *Chicago Daily* Tribune, November 1, 1924, 7; Lewis G. Simmons, "The Solution of Big Cities' Traffic Problems," *Illustrated World* (October 1917): 269.

31. "A Sunken Boulevard for Automobiles," *Scientific American* (October 23, 1923): n.p. Vertical Files, Francis Loeb Library, Harvard Graduate School of Design.

32. "Traffic and City Streets," *Public Works* 55, no. 2 (February 1924): 45–46.

33. Raymond S. Tompkins, "Are We Solving the Traffic Problem?," *American Mercury* (February 1929): 155.

34. "Super-Streets and Subways: Tentative Details of a Traffic Plan Recommended for New York City," *Scientific American* (September 1924): 149; T. Kennard Thomson, "Drastic Changes in Traffic Facilities Will Alone Meet Manhattan's Needs," n.p. (January 1927):

10–11. Clippings file, Vertical files, Francis Loeb Library, Harvard Graduate School of Design; "Raised Sidewalks and Traffic Separation Urged for Chicago." *American City* 35, no. 3 (September 1926): 334–336; Hugo Gernsback, "Solving Metropolitan Traffic Congestion," *Science and Invention* 14, no. 11 (March 1927): 1002–1003, 1057; "And This? Dr. John A. Harriss Proposes Six-Deck Streets," *American City* 36, no. 6 (June 1927): 803–805.

35. Joan E. Draper, "Paris by the Lake: Sources of Burnham's Plan of Chicago," in *Chicago Architecture 1872–1922; Birth of a Metropolis*, ed. John Zukowsky (Munich: Prestel Verlag [in association with The Art Institute of Chicago], 1987), 108.

36. Merchants' Association of New York Committee on Control of Street Traffic, *Control of Street Traffic.* (New York: Merchants' Association of New York Committee on Control of Street Traffic, 1924); Boston Special Commission on Intermediate Thoroughfare, "Final Report of Special Commission on Laying Out and Constructing New Thoroughfare and the Extension and Widening of Certain Streets in Connection Therewith," *Supplement to Current Affairs* 16, no. 32 (December 21, 1925): 1.

37. See William H. Wilson, *The City Beautiful Movement* (Baltimore: Johns Hopkins Press, 1989).

38. Mel Scott, *American City Planning since 1890: A History Commemorating the Fiftieth Anniversary of the American Institute of Planners* (Berkeley: University of California Press, 1969), 37–39, 101; Harold M. Mayer and Richard C. Wade, *Chicago: Growth of a Metropolis* (Chicago: University of Chicago Press, 1969), 274–276.

39. "A Plan for a Boston Plan" as published in Paul U. Kellogg, "Boston's Level Best: The '1915 Movement' and the Work of Civic Organizing for Which it Stands," *Survey* (June 5, 1909): 396.

40. Edward A. Filene to Daniel H. Burnham, October 14, 1909, Daniel H. Burnham Archives, Ryerson and Burnham Libraries, Art Institute of Chicago.

41. "Prospectus of the '1915' Boston Exposition; To be Held in the Old Art Museum, Copley Square, November 1 to 27, 1909." Daniel H. Burnham Archives, Ryerson and Burnham Libraries, Art Institute of Chicago; "Explaining 1915 Movement," *Boston Daily Globe*, October 25, 1909, 7; "Exposition is Viewed by 4000," *Boston Daily Globe*, October 31, 1909, 11; "Two Deliver Addresses," *Boston Daily Globe*, November 6, 1909, 6; "Address by B. C. Marsh," *Boston Daily Globe*, November 14, 1909, 15; Kim McQuaid, "An American Owenite: Edward A. Filene and the Parameters of Industrial Reform, 1890–1937," *American Journal of Economics and Sociology* 35, no. 1 (January 1976): 80–81; Scott, *American City Planning since 1890*, 110–113; Lawrence W. Kennedy, *Planning the City Upon a Hill: Boston since 1630* (Amherst: University of Massachusetts Press, 1992), 124–126.

42. Scott, *American City Planning since 1890*, 113–117.

43. Scott, *American City Planning since 1890*, 44, 57; Robert A. M. Stern, Gregory Gilmartin, and John Montague Massengale, *New York 1900: Metropolitan Architecture and Urbanism 1890–1915.* (New York: Rizzoli, 1983), 27–30; "To Improve the City," *New York Times* (December 2, 1902): 8.

44. New York City Improvement Commission, *The Report of the New York City Improvement Commission to George B. McClellan, and to the Board of Aldermen of the City of New York.* (New York: New York City Improvement Commission, 1904), 1–2, 6–18; *The Report of the New York City Improvement Commission to the Honorable George B. McClellan, Mayor of the City of New York and to the Honorable Board of Aldermen of the City of New York.* (New York: Kalkhoff, 1907), 7–11.

45. Keith D. Revell, "Regulating the Landscape: Real Estate Values, City Planning, and the 1916 Zoning Ordinance," in *The Landscape of Modernity*, eds. Ward and Zunz, 27; Stern, et al., *New York 1900*, 30–31; Scott, *American City Planning since 1890*, 57.

46. Daniel H. Burnham and Edward H. Bennett, *Plan of Chicago*, ed. Charles Moore (Chicago: The Commercial Club, 1909), 9–30, 31–42.

47. Scott, *American City Planning since 1890*, 139–140. It is notable that the activities of the Chicago Plan Commission were heavily subsidized by private funding from the Commercial Club, continuing the joint public-private sponsorship that defined the development and adoption of the *Plan of Chicago*. See Chicago Plan Commission, *Ten Years Work of the Chicago Plan Commission, 1909–1919* (Chicago: Chicago Plan Commission, 1920), 21.

48. Chicago Plan Commission, *Ten Years Work*, 12; Chicago Plan Commission, *Thirteenth Annual Report of the Chicago Plan Commission* (Chicago: Chicago Plan Commission, 1923), 1186; Chicago Plan Commission, *Sixteenth Annual Report of the Chicago Plan Commission for the Year 1925* (Chicago: Chicago Plan Commission, 1926), 8; Chicago Plan Commission, *Eighteenth Annual Report of the Chicago Plan Commission for the Year 1927* (Chicago: Chicago Plan Commission, 1927), n.p.

49. For more on the efforts to promote the 1909 plan see Carl Smith, *The Plan of Chicago: Daniel Burnham and the Remaking of the American City* (Chicago: University of Chicago Press, 2003), especially chap. 7, "Promotion," 111–129.

50. Boston Society of Architects Committee on Municipal Improvement, *Report Made to the Boston Society of Architects by its Committee on Municipal Improvement* (Boston: Alfred Mudge and Son, 1907), 3.

51. The Joint Board on Metropolitan Improvements focused on tackling conditions that jointly affected the city of Boston and its surrounding metropolitan region. As such, its tone was less about Boston's comparative relationship to competing cities and more about the creation of synchronized planning efforts for the city and its surrounding suburbs. Notably, this report spent considerable time discussing the creation of a new highway between North and South stations in conjunction with the construction of a railway tunnel along the same route. The tunnel project aimed to finesse passenger- and freight-rail transport, which were significantly hampered by the lack of connection between Boston's two rail terminals. The highway proposal was an opportunistic addition to the scheme, capitalizing on the railway tunnel construction to simultaneously facilitate a surface highway. This forerunner to the Central Artery will be discussed in more detail in chapter 5. See Massachusetts Joint Board on Metropolitan Improvements, *Final Report of the Joint Board on Metropolitan Improvements, Pursuant to Chapter 113 of the Resolves of 1909, and Chapters 112 and 134 of the Resolves of 1910* (Boston: Wright and Potter, 1911), especially 37–46.

52. Boston City Planning Board, *Seventh Annual Report of the City Planning Board for the Year Ending January 31, 1921* (Boston: City of Boston Printing Department, 1921), 3–4; Boston City Planning Board, *Eighth Annual Report of the City Planning Board for the Year Ending January 31, 1922* (Boston: City of Boston Printing Department, 1922), 3–23; Boston City Planning Board, *Ninth Annual Report of the City Planning Board for the Year Ending January 31, 1923* (Boston: City of Boston Printing Department, 1923), 3.

53. See New York Board of Estimate and Apportionment, Committee on the City Plan, *Development and Present Status of City Planning in New York City, Being the Report of the Committee on the City Plan, December 31, 1914, Together with Papers Presented at a Meeting of the Advisory Commission on City Plan, December 17, 1914* (New York: Board of Estimate and Apportionment, Committee on the City Plan, 1914).

54. Kennedy, *Planning the City Upon a Hill*, 124–126; Blaine A. Brownell, "Urban Planning, the Planning Profession, and the Motor Vehicle in Early Twentieth-Century America," in *Shaping an Urban World,* ed. Gordon E. Cherry (New York: St. Martin's Press, 1980), 61.

55. Don S. Kirschner, *The Paradox of Professionalism: Reform and Public Service in Urban America, 1900–1940*. Contributions in American History no. 19 (New York: Greenwood Press, 1986), 6–10.

56. Brownell, "Urban Planning, the Planning Profession," 63–64; Scott, *American City Planning since 1890*, 163–166.

57. Nelson P. Lewis, *The Planning of the Modern City: A Review of the Principles Governing City Planning*, 2nd ed. (New York: John Wiley and Sons, 1923), 1–2, 412–419. See also Jeffrey K. Stine, *Nelson P. Lewis and the City Efficient: The Municipal Engineer in City Planning during the Progressive Era*. Essays in Public Works History, no. 11 (Chicago: Public Works Historical Society, 1981), 13.

58. Mark Foster, "City Planners and Urban Transportation: The American Response," *Journal of Urban History* 5, no. 3 (May 1979): 371; "Predicts Motor Viaduct: Elevated Road for Automobile Traffic Favored by Nelson P. Lewis," *New York Times*, May 23, 1920, XX8; "New York Engineer to Aid Committee," *Boston Globe*, June 11, 1922, 6; "City Planning. Abstract of Lecture Delivered by Miss Elisabeth M. Herlihy, Secretary of the City Planning Board at the Boston Public Library, Thursday, March 1, 1923." (Boston: City of Boston Printing Department): 1. Elisabeth May Herlihy Papers, Box 9: EMH Correspondence 1923+; Folder: City Planning Lecture 1923—EMH. Massachusetts Historical Society.

59. Donald A. Krueckeberg, "From the Autobiography of Edward M. Bassett," in *The American Planner: Biographies and Recollections,* ed. Donald A. Krueckeberg (New York: Methuen, 1983), 102–103, 112–113; Scott, *American City Planning since 1890*, 154–155.

60. Robert H. Whitten to Elisabeth M. Herlihy, 15 November 1930, Robert Harvey Whitten Papers, Special Collections, Frances Loeb Library, Harvard Graduate School of Design.

61. "Robert Whitten, City Planner, Dies," *New York Times*, June 7, 1936, 46; Robert H. Whitten, "Unchoking Our Congested Streets." *American City* 23 (October 1920): 351–354. See also Cleveland City Plan Commission, *The Cleveland Thorofare Plan.* ([Cleveland?], 1921); and Boston City Planning Board, Robert Whitten, Consultant, *Report on a Thoroughfare Plan for Boston.* (Boston: City Planning Board, 1930).

62. Thomas Sugrue, "Miller McClintock," *Scribner's Magazine* 102, no. 6 (December 1937): 9, 12–13; "Dr. Miller McClintock Dies at 65; Ex-Head of Mutual Broadcasting," *New York Times*, January 11, 1960, 45; Ellis, "Visions of Urban Freeways," 327–331; "Arcades Urged to Ease Congestion," *New York Times*, August 4, 1929, N48; "Stagger Hour Plan Praised," *Los Angeles Times*, August 6, 1931, A10; Hal Foust, "Report Shows Superhighway to be Necessity," *Chicago Daily Tribune*, February 6, 1933, 5. See also Miller McClintock, *Street Traffic Control* (New York: McGraw-Hill, 1925).

63. Thomas S. Hines, *Burnham of Chicago: Architect and Planner* (New York: Oxford University Press, 1974), 346–348. Note that all of the details discussed here are heavily documented in multiple sources on Burnham's life. See also Carl Smith, *The Plan of Chicago: Daniel Burnham and the Remaking of the American City* (Chicago: University of Chicago Press, 2006); and Kristen Schaffer, *Daniel H. Burnham: Visionary Architect and Planner*, ed. Scott J. Tilden (New York: Rizzoli, 2003).

64. Hines, *Burnham of Chicago*, 348; David L. A. Gordon, "A City Beautiful Plan for Canada's Capital: Edward Bennett and the 1915 Plan for Ottawa and Hull," *Planning Perspectives* 13 (1998): 279–280.

65. *Proceedings of the Fifth National Conference on City Planning, Chicago, Illinois, May 5–7, 1913* (Boston: n.p., 1913), 94.

66. E. H. Bennett, "Expert Report in Chicago Plan Commission," *South Water Street Plan* (Chicago: Chicago Plan Commission, 1917), 38–50. Edward H. Bennett Collection, Ryerson and Burnham Libraries, Art Institute of Chicago.

67. David A. Johnson, "Regional Planning for the Great American Metropolis: New York between the World Wars," in *Two Centuries of American Planning*, ed. Daniel Schaffer (Baltimore: Johns Hopkins University Press, 1988), 170–173; Edward H. Bennett, "Raised Walk and Crossing Plan Urged," Edward H. Bennett Collection, Ryerson and Burnham Libraries, Art Institute of Chicago, n.d.; Edward H. Bennett, "Loop is Key to Traffic, Says

Expert," *Chicago Herald and Examiner*, January 14, 1926, 1; "Double Decked Congress St. Project Revived," *Chicago Daily Tribune*, September 22, 1927, n.p. Edward H. Bennett Collection, Ryerson and Burnham Libraries, Art Institute of Chicago.

68. Joseph J. Corn and Brian Horrigan, *Yesterday's Tomorrows: Past Visions of the American Future*, ed. Katherine Chambers (Baltimore: Johns Hopkins University Press, 1996), 4; Carol Willis, "Skyscraper Utopias: Visionary Urbanism in the 1920s," in *Imagining Tomorrow: History, Technology, and the American Future*, ed. Joseph Corn (Cambridge, MA: MIT Press, 1986), 169.

69. Corn and Horrigan, *Yesterday's Tomorrows*, 5–10; Willis, "Skyscraper Utopias," 169.

70. Willis, "Skyscraper Utopias," 166.

71. Willis, "Skyscraper Utopias," 166–170; Howard P. Segal, "The Technological Utopians," in *Imagining Tomorrow: History, Technology, and the American Future*, ed. Joseph Corn (Cambridge, MA: MIT Press, 1986): 122–123; Moses King, comp., *King's Views of New York 1896–1915 & Brooklyn 1905* (repr., New York: Arno Press, 1980): especially coverplates of 1909 and 1915 editions. See also Howard P. Segal, *Technological Utopianism in American Culture.* (Chicago: University of Chicago Press, 1985).

72. Edgar Chambless, *Roadtown* (New York: Roadtown Press, 1910), 19–22, 29–31, 35–36, 42, 53, 57.

73. See Le Corbusier, *The City of Tomorrow and its Planning*, trans. Frederick Etchells (1929; repr., Cambridge, MA: MIT Press, 1971); and Le Corbusier, *Urbanisme* (Paris: G. Cres, 1925); and Robert Fishman, *Urban Utopias in the Twentieth Century: Ebenezer Howard, Frank Lloyd Wright, and Le Corbusier* (New York: Basic Books, 1977), 192–201.

74. Le Corbusier, *The City of Tomorrow and its Planning*, 164–167, 182–183, 188–189.

75. Willis, "Skyscraper Utopias," 171; Jonathan Barnett, *The Elusive City: Five Centuries of Design, Ambition and Miscalculation* (New York: Harper and Row, 1986), 124; and Hugh Ferriss, "A New Architecture," *New York Times*, March 19, 1922, 53.

76. Willis, "Skyscraper Utopias," 172–173.

77. Hugh Ferriss, *Metropolis of Tomorrow* (1929; repr., New York: Princeton Architectural Press, 1986), 15–16, 59–66, 109, 128–130; Willis, "Skyscraper Utopias," 175; Barnett, *The Elusive* City, 124.

78. Harvey Wiley Corbett, "The Problem of Traffic Congestion, and a Solution," *The Architectural Forum* 46, no. 3 (March 1927): 201–208; "Harvey Corbett, Architect, Dead," *New York Times*, April 22, 1954, 29; Robert A. M. Stern, Gregory Gilmartin, and Thomas Mellins, *New York 1930: Architecture and Urbanism Between the Two World Wars* (New York: Rizzoli, 1987): 26–39; Willis, "Skyscraper Utopias" 172.

79. Robert A. M. Stern, *Raymond Hood.* Institute for Architecture and Urban Studies 15 (New York: Rizzoli, 1982), 16–17; Stern, et al., *New York 1930*, 575–578; Raymond Mathewson Hood and Carol Willis, *Raymond Hood, City of Towers [catalog]: January 7—March 7, 1984* (New York: Whitney Museum of American Art at Philip Morris, 1984).

80. Willis, "Skyscraper Utopias," 175; Stern, *Raymond Hood*, 16.

81. Fishman, *Urban Utopias in the Twentieth Century*, 122–124. See also Frank Lloyd Wright, *Modern Architecture, Being the Kahn Lectures for 1930*, Princeton Monographs in Art and Archaeology (Princeton, NJ: Princeton University Press, 1931); and Frank Lloyd Wright, *The Disappearing City* (New York: W. F. Payson, 1932).

82. Fishman, *Urban Utopias in the Twentieth Century*, 124–128, 131–134; Corn and Horrigan, *Yesterday's Tomorrows*, 50–51.

83. Fishman, *Urban Utopias in the Twentieth Century*, 127, 131; Corn and Horrigan, *Yesterday's Tomorrows*, 51.

84. Stern, *Raymond Hood*, 19; Richard Guy Wilson, Dianne H. Pilgrim, and Dickran

Tashjian, *The Machine Age in America, 1918–1941* (New York: Brooklyn Museum of Art, 1986), 70–72, 193–194.

85. David Gelernter, *1939: The Lost World of the Fair* (New York: Free Press, 1995), 4, 19–22; Wilson, et al., *The Machine Age in America*, 72–75. See also Norman Bel Geddes, *Magic Motorways* (New York: Random House, 1940).

86. "Shall We Have Double-Decked Streets?," 310.

CHAPTER 3

1. Harold M. Mayer and Richard C. Wade, *Chicago: Growth of a Metropolis* (Chicago: University of Chicago Press, 1969), 24–40.

2. "South Water Street Busy," *Chicago Daily Tribune,* November 16, 1910, A6.

3. Mayer and Wade, *Chicago*, 38, 124, 310–312; John W. Stamper, *Chicago's North Michigan Avenue: Planning and Development, 1900–1930*, Chicago Architecture and Urbanism Series (Chicago: University of Chicago Press, 1991), 18–20; Henry A. Goetz, "Expert Report: Results of Extended Expert Study of Chicago's Street Traffic Problem in the Central Business District," in Chicago Plan Commission, *South Water Street Plan* (Chicago: Chicago Plan Commission, 1917), 18, 31–37. Edward H. Bennett Collection, Ryerson and Burnham Libraries, Art Institute of Chicago.

4. "Teams Overrun a Street," *Chicago Daily Tribune*, May 15, 1903, 15.

5. "Carts in Endless Chain," *Chicago Daily Tribune*, August 24, 1907, 5.

6. "Chicago's Loop is the Busiest Spot on Earth," *Chicago Daily Tribune*, April 28, 1907, F2.

7. "Traffic Delayed by Carelessness," *Chicago Daily Tribune*, May 25, 1907, 2.

8. "Council Wants Boulevard Link," *Chicago Daily Tribune*, May 17, 1904, 1.

9. Daniel H. Burnham and Edward H. Bennett, *Plan of Chicago*, ed. Charles Moore (Chicago: The Commercial Club, 1909), 97.

10. Burnham and Bennett, *Plan of Chicago*, 97.

11. Burnham and Bennett, *Plan of Chicago*, 97.

12. Burnham and Bennett, *Plan of Chicago*, 97.

13. Burnham and Bennett, *Plan of Chicago*, 96–97.

14. Carl Smith, *The Plan of Chicago: Daniel Burnham and the Remaking of the American City.* (Chicago: University of Chicago Press, 2006), 133–134; Paul Barrett, *The Automobile and Urban Transit: The Formation of Public Policy in Chicago, 1900–1930,* Technology and Urban Growth Series (Philadelphia: Temple University Press, 1983), 76–77.

15. Stamper, *Chicago's North Michigan Avenue*, 1–4.

16. Stamper, *Chicago's North Michigan Avenue*, 4–8; "Council Wants Boulevard Link," *Chicago Daily Tribune*, May 17, 1904, 1.

17. Burnham and Bennett, *Plan of Chicago*, 96–97, 99–107; Stamper, *Chicago's North Michigan Avenue*, 8.

18. Stamper, *Chicago's North Michigan Avenue*, 3–4, 23–24.

19. F. H. Fox, as quoted in, "High Boulevard Foes Find Ally," *Chicago Daily Tribune*, July 23, 1923, 9.

20. "No Boulevard on Stilts Wanted," *Chicago Evening Journal*, May 28, 1907, as reprinted in *Chicago Daily Tribune*, May 29, 1907, 8.

21. "No Boulevard on Stilts Wanted."

22. William Nelson Pelouze, "Voice of the People: Tunnel for Boulevard Link," *Chicago Daily Tribune*, July 27, 1908, 6; One of the Common People, "Voice of the People: Opposed to High Boulevard Link," *Chicago Daily Tribune*, July 27, 1908, 6; "Prepared for Final Fight Against Raised Boulevard," *Chicago Daily Tribune*, October 13, 1908, 20; "Fight Double Deck 'Link': Michigan Ave. Property Owners Protest Against Boulevard," *Chicago Daily Tribune*, July 12, 1911, 7; Stamper, *Chicago's North Michigan Avenue*, 9–10.

23. Chicago Plan Commission, *Chicago's Greatest Issue: An Official Plan* (Chicago: Chicago Plan Commission, 1911); Charles H. Wacker, *Argument in Favor of Plan for the Proposed Michigan Avenue Connecting Link Improvement* (Chicago: Chicago Plan Commission, 1913); "Council Passes Boulevard Link Ordinance, 51 to 7," *Chicago Daily Tribune*, July 15, 1913, 1; Henry M. Hyde, "No Beginning on Boulevard Link for Three Years," *Chicago Daily Tribune*, May 6, 1915, 13; "Today's Program for Opening of the 'Link' Bridge," *Chicago Daily Tribune*, May 14, 1920, 1; Stamper, *Chicago's North Michigan Avenue*, 11–17.

24. Charles H. Wacker, *Annual Report for 1917 to the Chicago Plan Commission* (Chicago: Chicago Plan Commission, 1918), 4.

25. Wacker, *Annual Report for 1917*, 8.

26. E. H. Bennett, "Expert Report: Chicago Plan Commission Report on a Plan for the Improvement and Development of South Water Street," in Chicago Plan Commission, *South Water Street Plan* (Chicago: Chicago Plan Commission, 1917), 38–40. Edward H. Bennett Collection, Ryerson and Burnham Libraries, Art Institute of Chicago; Helen Whitehead, *Outline of the History of Wacker Drive* (N.p.: August 28, 1952), 1. Municipal Reference Collection, Chicago Public Library.

27. Goetz, "Expert Report," 33.

28. Mayer and Wade, *Chicago*, 38, 124, 310–312; Stamper, *Chicago's North Michigan Avenue*, 18–20; Goetz, "Expert Report," 18, 31–37.

29. Goetz, "Expert Report," 33–35.

30. Goetz, "Expert Report," 35–36.

31. Bennett, "Expert Report," 45. Underlining original.

32. Charles H. Wacker, "South Water Street Plan: Traffic, Revenue and Economic Benefits," in Chicago Plan Commission, *South Water Street Plan* (Chicago: Chicago Plan Commission, 1917), 7, 10, 12–14. Edward H. Bennett Collection, Ryerson and Burnham Libraries, Art Institute of Chicago; Chicago Plan Commission, *Reclaim South Water Street for All the People* (Chicago: Chicago Plan Commission, November 1917), 3. Edward H. Bennett Collection, Ryerson and Burnham Libraries, Art Institute of Chicago; "South Water Street Improvement as Proposed by Chicago Plan Commission," *Chicago Commerce*, November 22, 1922, 14–15.

33. Wacker, "South Water Street Plan," 8; Bennett, "Expert Report," 40–41.

34. Bennett, "Expert Report," 41.

35. Chicago Plan Commission, *Reclaim South Water Street*, 1; Wacker, "South Water Street Plan," 15; Goetz, "Expert Report," 18; Bennett, "Expert Report," 38; Chicago Plan Commission, *Ten Years Work of the Chicago Plan Commission, 1909–1919* (Chicago: Chicago Plan Commission, 1920), 52–55.

36. R. Stephen Sennott, "'Forever Inadequate to the Rising Stream': Dream Cities, Automobiles, and Urban Street Mobility in Central Chicago," in *Chicago Architecture and Design, 1923–1993: Reconfiguration of an American Metropolis*, ed. John Zukoswky (Munich: Prestel-Verlag [in association with The Art Institute of Chicago], 1993), 56; Joan E. Draper, *Edward H. Bennett: Architect and City Planner, 1874–1954* (Chicago: Art Institute of Chicago, 1982), 17–22.

37. Mayer and Wade, *Chicago*, 208–214; "Ask an End to 'L' Congestion; Wide Demand," *Chicago Daily Tribune*, May 1, 1913, 1; Barrett, *The Automobile and Urban Transit*, 147–148.

38. Barrett, *The Automobile and Urban Transit*, 130.

39. Charles H. Wacker, as quoted in "Wacker Urges South Water Improvement," *Chicago Daily Tribune*, June 2, 1918, A6.

40. "Whole City Aroused to Plan; Stirred to a New Civic Epoch," *Chicago Daily Tribune*, December 28, 1918, 4.

41. Oscar E. Hewitt, "Vote this Fall on $28,600,000 Loan Is Asked," *Chicago Daily*

Tribune, July 12, 1919, 14; "Vote to Rebuild Water Street to Rival Boul Mich," *Chicago Daily Tribune*, October 18, 1919, 5; Charles H. Wacker, "Chicago Spirit Reborn by Vote, Wacker Says," *Chicago Daily Tribune*, November 5, 1919, 2; "Faherty Tells When, Where Dirt Will Fly," *Chicago Daily Tribune*, November 5, 1919, 1.

42. "Seek to Widen Alley to Save South Water Street," *Chicago Daily Tribune*, November 28, 1919, 13; Al Chase, "Loop to Have New Street for Produce Market," *Chicago Daily Tribune*, March 4, 1920, 2; "Produce Firms Fight to Stay on S. Water St.," *Chicago Daily Tribune*, August 4, 1920, 16.

43. Charles H. Wacker, as quoted in "Wacker Clashes with Lawyer on Plan for Plaza," *Chicago Daily Tribune*, January 8, 1921, 4.

44. Eye Witness, "Mere Good Luck Saves City from Water St. Peril," *Chicago Daily Tribune*, April 16, 1919, 12.

45. "Produce Mart Must Move from South Water St.," *Chicago Daily Tribune*, May 17, 1921, 9.

46. *South Water Street Facts: Why the Improvement Should Go Forward Without Delay* (Chicago: Plan Commission, 1922), 3–4, 8–9. Municipal Reference Collection, Chicago Public Library; "Faherty to Tax Gold Coast for S. Water Street," *Chicago Daily Tribune*, May 2, 1922, 14.

47. "Faherty to Tax Gold Coast for S. Water Street," 14.

48. "South Water St. Merchants War on Levy by City," *Chicago Daily Tribune*, July 8, 1922, 13; "Objections to S. Water St. Job Over $6,000,000," *Chicago Daily Tribune*, September 13, 1922, 14.

49. "S. Water Street Owners Protest Big Assessment," *Chicago Daily Tribune*, November 1, 1922, 19; "Protest Bears Fruit," *Chicago Daily Tribune*, November 21, 1922, 1, 10; "Agree City Pay $10,000,000 of So. Water Cost," *Chicago Daily Tribune*, January 16, 1923, 3; "Ettelson Jams Cogs on S. Water Plan; War Ahead," *Chicago Daily Tribune*, February 9, 1923, 5; "City Lines Up Experts in S. Water Contest," *Chicago Daily Tribune*, February 27, 1923, 18.

50. "Mayor Stirs Up Hornets' Nest on South Water," *Chicago Daily Tribune*, March 9, 1924, 17; "Dever Cancels All So. Water Street Parleys," *Chicago Daily Tribune*, March 11, 1924, 3; "Mayor Puts End to S. Water St. Plan Squabble," *Chicago Daily Tribune*, June 10, 1923, 9; "Agree on So. Water Street Plan at Last," *Chicago Daily Tribune*, April 23, 1924, 1; *Outline of Wacker Drive Dedication Speech*. N.p., i–ii. Box 1, Folder 6, William Emmett Dever Collection, Chicago History Museum.

51. Oscar Hewitt, "Voters O.K. All Bond Issues by 2 to 1 Majority," *Chicago Daily Tribune*, June 3, 1924, 5; "Dever Acts to Speed S. Water Street Project," *Chicago Daily Tribune*, July 16, 1924, 14; "Ask U.S. to Halt Building Razing on So. Water St," *Chicago Daily Tribune*, September 30, 1924, 4; "Unroof Building Over Heads of S. Water Firms," *Chicago Daily Tribune*, October 3, 1924, 3; *Outline of Wacker Drive Dedication Speech*, i–ii.

CHAPTER 4

1. William J. Wilgus, *Proposed New Railway System for the Transportation and Distribution of Freight by Improved Methods in the City and Port of New York* (New York: Amsterdam, 1908), 7–8; Josef W. Konvitz, "William J. Wilgus and Engineering Projects to Improve the Port of New York, 1900–1930," *Technology and Culture* 30, no. 2 (April 1989): 401.

2. Konvitz, "William J. Wilgus," 401.

3. Konvitz, "William J. Wilgus," 401–402; Carl W. Condit, *The Port of New York*, vol. 2, *A History of the Rail and Terminal System from the Grand Central Electrification to the Present* (Chicago: University of Chicago Press, 1981), 101–108; Keith D. Revell, *Building*

Gotham: Civic Culture and Public Policy in New York City, 1898–1938 (Baltimore: Johns Hopkins University Press, 2003), 60–63.

4. John J. Rooney, as quoted in "Say Tracks Hurt Riverside Park," *New York Times*, March 31, 1907, 5.

5. "Children Parade against Death Ave," *New York Times*, October 25, 1908, 9.

6. Wilgus, *Proposed New Railway System*, 8; Condit, *The Port of New York*, vol. 2, 140–141.

7. Konvitz, "William J. Wilgus," 404–410; Wilgus, *Proposed New Railway System*, 5, 7–11; Condit, *The Port of New York*, vol. 2, 141.

8. Ann L. Buttenwieser, *Manhattan, Water-Bound: Planning and Developing Manhattan's Waterfront from the Seventeenth Century to the Present* (New York: New York University Press, 1987), 159–161; Robert A. M. Stern, Gregory Gilmartin, and John Montague Massengale, *New York 1900: Metropolitan Architecture and Urbanism 1890–1915* (New York: Rizzoli, 1983), 42–43; Condit, *The Port of New York*, vol. 2, 141; "Riverside Park Improvement Scheme to Follow Lines Adopted in Vienna," *New York Times*, October 9, 1910, RE1; "Plans $1,00,000,000 Dock-Side Railway," *New York Times*, July 15, 1910, 1.

9. "Waterfront Plan of New York Central," *New York Times*, September 29, 1911, 7; Condit, *The Port of New York*, vol. 2, 141–151. The intricacies of the legal battles and logistical negotiations between the city of New York and the New York Central Railroad are important stories unto themselves, but are beyond the scope of this study. Carl W. Condit's *The Port of New York*, vol. 2, remains the definitive narrative of this story.

10. John F. Hylan, *Seven Years of Progress: Important Public Improvements and Achievements by the Municipal and Borough Governments of the City of New York, 1918–1925*. (New York: M. B. Brown, 1925), 12–13.

11. "Opposition Developing," *New York Times*, January 27, 1893, 10; John D. Bowne, "Elevated Road Conditions," *New York Times*, December 14, 1902, 32; "Elevated Travel Changing," *New York Times*, November 17, 1912, 18; "Subway Gains Fast, Elevated Slowly," *New York Times*, October 17, 1913, 20; "West Side Improvement," *New York Times*, May 16, 1916, 12; "Says Traffic Here is Beyond Control," *New York Times*, November 15, 1922, 1; "Ask for Removal of Elevated Spur," *New York Times*, March 2, 1924, E1; Robert M. Fogelson, *Downtown: Its Rise and Fall, 1880–1950* (New Haven, CT: Yale University Press, 2001), 277–278.

12. A. B. Cordner, "Motor Trucks to Supplant Horse Drawn Vehicles," *New York Times*, March 20, 1910, S4; "Motor Transport Grows," *New York Times*, September 11, 1921, 86; "Specially Built Roads for Trucks," *New York Times*, July 2, 1916, XX10.

13. "Truckmen to Fight Freight Subway," *New York Times*, November 8, 1908, 8; "Motor Trucks Help Traffic Conditions," *New York Times*, March 24, 1912, XX3; "Gives the Statistics of Truck Superiority," *New York Times*, April 4, 1915, X9; "Trucks to Supplant Water Freight Service," *New York Times*, September 27, 1926, 34.

14. Ernest P. Goodrich and Harold M. Lewis, "Projects for Relief of Traffic Congestion in New York and Its Environs," *The American City*, July 1924, 29.

15. George P. Le Brun, "Killings in Streets," *New York Times*, November 3, 1913, 8.

16. U.S. Department of Commerce, *Statistical Abstract of the United States: 1920*. 43rd ed. (Washington, DC: U.S. Government Printing Office, 1921), 316.

17. "Hylan Untangles Big Traffic Jam," *New York Times*, June 18, 1923, 2.

18. Committee on Control of Street Traffic, Merchants' Association of New York, *Control of Street Traffic*. (New York: n.p., 1924), 20.

19. Harold M. Lewis, "The New York Motor Traffic Problem," *Annals of the American Academy of Political and Social Science* 116 (November 1924): 214–223; "Traffic Congestion Remedies," *New York Times*, September 10, 1923, 16; "20-Minute Parking Rule to Aid Traffic," *New York Times*, June 5, 1924, 5; "Want Wider Motor Roads for Future

Traffic Needs," *New York Times*, July 6, 1924, XX9; "Traffic Relief Plan: Mr. Bossom Advocates Second-Story Walk on Busy Streets," *New York Times*, August 10, 1924, RE2; Silas Bent, "Great Triple Problem Presses on City," *New York Times*, September 28, 1924, XX1.

20. "Orders Motors for $24,000,000 Highway," *New York Times*, February 3, 1925, 23; "Miller Proposes Biggest Boulevard to Ease West Side," *New York Times*, January 21, 1926, 1.

21. *Report of the Chief Engineer of the Board of Estimate and Apportionment of the City of New York for the Year 1926* (New York: Hickey and Kischel, 1927): 27–35; "Miller Proposes Biggest Boulevard to Ease West Side," 1; "Sees No Obstacle to West Side Drive," *New York Times*, January 24, 1926, E2; "New York to Build Elevated Highway," *New York Times*, April 25, 1926, XX1.

22. "New York to Build Elevated Highway," *New York Times*, April 25, 1926, XX1; "The West Side Elevated Highway," *New York Times*, June 16, 1926, 24; "West Side Highway Surveys Under Way," *New York Times*, August 8, 1926, E2.

23. Listed Civic Organizations to the Board of Estimate and Apportionment, October 27, 1927, James J. Walker papers, Subject File 1926-32-W-283, Folder 1927-32-Walker-Miscellaneous-2, New York City Municipal Archives.

24. Listed Civic Organizations to the Board of Estimate and Apportionment.

25. The Committee on the Regional Plan of New York and Its Environs, *Proposed Elevated Highway on West Side of Manhattan* (N.p.: March 18, 1927), 1. James J. Walker papers, Subject File 1926-32-W-283, Folder 1927-32-Walker-Miscellaneous-2, New York City Municipal Archives.

26. Committee on the Regional Plan of New York and Its Environs, *Proposed Elevated Highway*, 4.

27. Committee on the Regional Plan of New York and Its Environs, *Proposed Elevated Highway*, 4.

28. Chester Holmes Aldrich to Board of Estimate and Apportionment, March 25, 1927, James J. Walker papers, Subject File 1926-32-W-283, Folder 1927-32-Walker-Miscellaneous-2, New York City Municipal Archives.

29. "West Side Highway Project Criticized," *New York Times*, April 8, 1927, 48; "Raised Highway Opposed," *New York Times*, June 6, 1927, 10.

30. As quoted in "Strongly Opposes Elevated Highway," *New York Times*, May 12, 1927, 20.

31. The City Club of New York to the Board of Estimate and Apportionment, May 14, 1927, 2–3, James J. Walker papers, Subject File 1926-32-W-283, Folder 1927-32-Walker-Miscellaneous-2, New York City Municipal Archives.

32. The City Club of New York to the Board of Estimate and Apportionment, May 14, 1927, 1–2, James J. Walker papers, Subject File 1926-32-W-283, Folder 1927-32-Walker-Miscellaneous-2, New York City Municipal Archives.

33. "Walker Beats Move by Miller to Push Express Highway," *New York Times*, April 5, 1927, 1; "Plans to Improve West Side Held Up," *New York Times*, June 17, 1927, 25; "Protests Activity for West Side Plan," *New York Times*, January 27, 1928, 23.

34. "Railroad Agrees to West Side Map," *New York Times*, May 11, 1928, 34; "Walker Gets Plan to Check Haphazard Growth of the City," *New York Times*, June 6, 1928, 1, 14–15; See City Committee on Plan and Survey, *Report of the City Committee on Plan and Survey* (New York: City Committee on Plan and Survey, 1928); "Elevated Highway along Hudson Shore Is Ordered by City," *New York Times*, August 17, 1928, 1, 7; "Elevated Speedway Is Approved in Full," *New York Times*, October 19, 1928, 1, 14.

35. "Elevated Speedway Is Approved in Full," *New York Times*, October 19, 1928, 14.

36. "Elevated Highway Urged before Foes," *New York Times*, November 15, 1928, 15; The City Club of New York to the Honorable James J. Walker, January 8, 1929, James J.

Walker papers, Subject File 1926-32-W-283, Folder 1927-32-Walker-Miscellaneous-1, New York City Municipal Archives.

37. "Elevated Highway to Oust Merchants," *New York Times*, October 31, 1928, 61; "Express Highway Wins Final Vote," *New York Times*, January 11, 1929, 28.

38. "Says Road Invades City's Land Again," *New York Times*, April 27, 1928, 27. It should be noted that Mayor Walker's comments were rendered within the context of a hearing about general west side improvements, not about the road in particular, therefore explaining his general support for continued advancement of "the project" even while his specific support for the elevated highway was not yet assured.

39. "Miller's Road Plan Draws Art Protest," *New York Times*, May 16, 1928, 47; "City Club Opposes Elevated Highway," *New York Times*, October 22, 1928, 33; "Express Highway Wins Final Vote," *New York Times*, January 11, 1929, 28; "Miller Gets Architects," *New York Times*, February 26, 1929, 51.

40. T. Markoe Robertson's father was Robert Henderson Robertson (1849–1919).

41. "John Sloan Dead; Architect was 66," *New York Times*, June 26, 1954, 13; "T. Markoe Robertson, 84, Dies; Founder of Architectural Firm," *New York Times*, August 3, 1962, 23; City of New York, Landmarks Preservation Commission, *Upper East Side Historic District Designation Report*, vol. 2 (New York: The Commission, 1981): 1326–1328, 1346–1347; F. S. Laurence, "The Pershing Square Building," *American Architect and the Architectural Review* 124 (October 10, 1923): 319–324.

42. "The Graybar Building, New York City," *Architecture and Building* 59, no. 6 (June 1927): 179.

43. "The Graybar Building, New York City," 179–182; "Graybar Building, 420 Lexington Avenue, New York City, Sloan and Robertson, architects," *The Architect* 9, no. 2 (November 1927): 197–202.

44. New York City Landmarks Preservation Commission, *Fred F. French Building Landmark Designation Report.* (March 18, 1986): 1, 4, 7; Carol Herselle Krinsky, "The Fred F. French Building: Mesopotamia in Manhattan," *The Magazine Antiques* 121 (January 1982): 286–287.

45. New York City Landmarks Preservation Commission, *Fred F. French Building*, 9, 12, 11.

46. New York City Landmarks Preservation Commission, *Fred F. French Building*, 12–15.

47. New York City Landmarks Preservation Commission, *Fred F. French Building*, 13, 19; Krinsky, "The Fred F. French Building," 288.

48. For more on Irwin Chanin and his importance as an artistic patron and developer in New York City, see Diana Agrest, ed., *A Romance with the City: Irwin S. Chanin.* (New York: Cooper Union Press, 1982).

49. New York City Landmarks Preservation Commission, *Chanin Building Landmark Designation Report* (November 14, 1978), 1, 3–4; "The Chanin Building, New York City," *Architecture and Building* 61, no. 2 (February 1929): 39–40; "Fifty-Six Stories of Modern Americanism," *Through the Ages* 7 (August 1929): 23–26.

50. Hugh Ferriss, *Metropolis of Tomorrow* (1929; reprint, New York: Princeton Architectural Press, 1986), 50–51.

51. Matlack Price, "The Chanin Building, Sloan & Robertson, Architects," *Architectural Forum* 50, no. 5 (May 1929): 699; New York City Landmarks Preservation Commission, *Chanin Building*, 3; Susan Tunick and Theodore Prudon, "The Chanin Building, New York City," *Friends of Terra-cotta* 1, no. 4 (Fall/Winter 1982/1983): 1.

52. "Fifty-Six Stories of Modern Americanism," 26–28; Wendy Kaplan, "'The Filter of American Taste': Design in the USA in the 1920s," in *Art Deco 1910–1939*, eds. Charlotte Benton, Tim Benton, and Ghislaine Wood (London: V and A Publications, 2003), 338–339.

53. For more on the Art Deco period, see Benton, Benton, and Wood, eds., *Art Deco 1910–1939*; Richard Guy Wilson, Dianne H. Pilgrim, and Dickran Tashjian, *The Machine Age in America, 1918–1941* (New York: Brooklyn Museum of Art, 1986); and Alastair Duncan, *American Art Deco* (London: Thames and Hudson, 1986).

54. New York City Landmarks Preservation Commission, *Chanin Building Landmark Designation Report*, 3; New York City Landmarks Preservation Commission, *Fred F. French Building Landmark Designation Report*, 7–8.

55. Sloan and Robertson, Architects, "Architectural Drawings: Contract Plan, Section No. 1, Division No. 2, Footings and Superstructure, Elevated Public Highway, Contract No. 3." Drawing 389, Sheet 39. Borough President of Manhattan Photograph Collection, New York City Municipal Archives.

56. Sloan and Robertson, Architects, "Architectural Drawings: Contract Plan, Section No. 1, Division No. 2, Footings and Superstructure, Elevated Public Highway, Contract No. 3." Drawing 389, Sheet 39. Borough President of Manhattan Photograph Collection, New York City Municipal Archives.; Sloan and Robertson, Architects, "Architectural Drawings: Contract Plan, Section No. 1, Division No. 1, Completion of Ramps and Superstructure, Elevated Public Highway, Contract No. 6." Borough President of Manhattan Photograph Collection, New York City Municipal Archives.

CHAPTER 5

1. For authoritative sources on Boston's early history and land reclamation efforts see Walter Muir Whitehill and Lawrence W. Kennedy, *Boston: A Topographical History*, 3rd ed. (Cambridge, MA: Belknap Press of Harvard University Press, 2000); Lawrence W. Kennedy, *Planning the City upon a Hill: Boston since 1630* (Amherst: University of Massachusetts Press, 1992); and Jane Holtz Kay, *Lost Boston*, rev. ed. (Boston: University of Massachusetts Press, 2006).

2. Kennedy, *Planning the City upon a Hill*, 109–111. For more on local proposals for improving Boston's harbor facilities see Massachusetts Joint Board on Metropolitan Improvements, *Final Report of the Joint Board on Metropolitan Improvements*, 15–25. See also Boston City Planning Board, *Eighth Annual Report of the City Planning Board for the Year Ending January 31, 1922* (Boston: City of Boston Printing Dept., 1922), 21.

3. "Plan for Direct Highway to Relieve Congested Traffic," *Boston Daily Globe*, January 18, 1902, 14; "Byrnes Urges Tunnel Plan," *Boston Daily Globe*, March 8, 1910, 10.

4. Massachusetts Joint Board on Metropolitan Improvements, *Final Report of the Joint Board on Metropolitan Improvements*, 37, 40–41.

5. "Boston's Bad Streets," *Boston Daily Globe*, August 7, 1903, 6; "Favor Wood Blocks for Street Paving," *Boston Daily Globe*, July 22, 1915, 16; "Heart-to-Heart Talk on Paving," *Boston Daily Globe*, July 25, 1916, 9; "Timilty Gets Contract," *Boston Daily Globe*, July 29, 1916, 14; Clay McShane, *Down the Asphalt Path: The Automobile and the American City* (New York: Columbia University Press, 1994), 216–217.

6. "Plan for Direct Highway to Relieve Congested Traffic."

7. For more on William Stanley Parker's proposal see City Planning Board, *Progress Report on Proposed Intermediate Thoroughfare* (Boston: City Planning Board, 1925); Special Commission on Intermediate Thoroughfare, *Final Report of Special Commission on Laying Out and Constructing New Thoroughfare and the Extension and Widening of Certain Streets in Connection Therewith.* Supplement to *Current Affairs* 16, no. 32 (December 21, 1925); and Asha Elizabeth Weinstein, "The Congestion Evil: Perceptions of Traffic Congestion in Boston in the 1890s and 1920s" (Ph.D. diss., University of California, Berkeley, 2002), 148–204.

8. "Plans to Ease Jam in Streets," *Boston Daily Globe*, December 12, 1912, 3; "Would Slice the Common," *Boston Daily Globe*, December 9, 1915, 2; "Favors Widening around Common," *Boston Daily Globe*, November 15, 1919, 10; Mona Domosh, *Invented Cities: The Creation of Landscape in Nineteenth Century New York and Boston* (New Haven, CT: Yale University Press, 1996), 138, "Problem of City Traffic," *Boston Daily Globe*, December 21, 1906, 10; "Auto Problems Most Difficult," *Boston Daily Globe*, January 17, 1913, 9; "Auto Parking Problem Grows," *Boston Daily Globe*, July 9, 1923, 5; Boston City Planning Board, *Tenth Annual Report of the City Planning Board for the Year Ending January 31, 1924* (Boston: City of Boston Printing Dept., 1924), 28–30, 67–70; "$25,000,000 Aerial Highway Proposed to Relieve Traffic," *Boston Herald*, August 3, 1929, n.p. "Boston Transportation" clippings file, Boston Globe Library.

9. Arthur A. Shurtleff, "The Metropolitan Plan," in Massachusetts Commission on Metropolitan Improvements, *Public Improvements for the Metropolitan District.* (Boston: Wright and Potter, 1909), 188–200; Massachusetts Joint Board on Metropolitan Improvements, *Final Report of the Joint Board on Metropolitan Improvements*, 30–34; "Will Improve Many Streets," *Boston Daily Globe*, June 24, 1914, 13.

10. Boston City Planning Board, *Eighth Annual Report of the City Planning Board for the Year Ending January 31, 1922* (Boston: City of Boston Printing Dept., 1922): 21.

11. Boston City Planning Board, *Ninth Annual Report of the City Planning Board for the Year Ending January 31, 1923* (Boston: City of Boston Printing Dept., 1923), 3, 55.

12. Boston City Planning Board, *Eighth Annual Report of the City Planning Board for the Year Ending January 31, 1922*, 16–23; Boston City Planning Board, *Ninth Annual Report of the City Planning Board for the Year Ending January 31, 1923*, 3–5, 55–63; Boston City Planning Board, *Zoning for Boston: A Survey and a Comprehensive Plan* (Boston: City of Boston Printing Dept., 1924), 31–34; Kennedy, *Planning the City upon a Hill*, 134–135.

13. Elisabeth M. Herlihy, "Traffic Count Helps Boston Planning," *American City* 35, no. 6 (December 1926): 849–850; Boston City Planning Board, *Thirteenth Annual Report of the City Planning Board for the Year Ending December 31, 1926* (Boston: City of Boston Printing Dept., 1927), 6, 21–24.

14. The City Planning Board had been urging the establishment of a traffic advisory committee since before 1924, though it appears that Nichols's predecessor, infamous Irishman James Michael Curley, did not support the idea. See Weinstein, "The Congestion Evil," 158, 203–204.

15. Weinstein, "The Congestion Evil," 158, 203–204; Albert Russel Erskine Bureau, Harvard University, *A Report on the Street Traffic Control Problem of the City of Boston, Prepared under the Direction of the Mayor's Street Traffic Advisory Board* (Boston: n.p., 1928).

16. Boston City Planning Board, *Thirteenth Annual Report of the City Planning Board for the Year Ending December 31, 1926*, 2; Elisabeth May Herlihy to Mrs. Robert Whitten. May 24, 1924. Elisabeth May Herlihy Papers, Box 9: EMH Correspondence 1923+; Folder: 1924 (1); and Elisabeth May Herlihy to Mrs. Robert Whitten. April 27, 1925. Elisabeth May Herlihy Papers, Box 9: EMH Correspondence 1923+; Folder: 1925. Massachusetts Historical Society.

17. Boston City Planning Board, Robert Whitten, consultant, *Report on a Thoroughfare Plan for Boston* (Boston: Boston City Planning Board, 1930), xiii–xiv, 1–14, 75–101, 80–83; Boston City Planning Board, *Fourteenth Annual Report of the City Planning Board for the Year Ending December 31, 1927* (Boston: City of Boston Printing Dept., 1928), 3–4.

18. Boston City Planning Board, Robert Whitten, *Report on a Thoroughfare Plan for Boston*, 9–12, 80–82.

19. Boston City Planning Board, Robert Whitten, *Report on a Thoroughfare Plan for Boston*, 86–87.

20. Boston City Planning Board, Robert Whitten, *Report on a Thoroughfare Plan for Boston*, 82.

21. Boston City Planning Board, Robert Whitten, *Report on a Thoroughfare Plan for Boston*, 82.

22. Boston City Planning Board, Robert Whitten, *Report on a Thoroughfare Plan for Boston*, 83, 86–87.

23. For more on James Michael Curley see Jack Beatty, *The Rascal King: The Life and Times of James Michael Curley, 1874–1958*. (Reading, MA: Addison-Wesley, 1992).

24. Boston City Planning Board, *Seventeenth Annual Report of the City Planning Board for the Year Ending December 31, 1930* (Boston: City of Boston Printing Dept., 1931), 3–5; Boston City Planning Board, *Eighteenth Annual Report of the City Planning Board for the Year Ending December 31, 1931* (Boston: City of Boston Printing Dept., 1932), 3–4, 10; Kennedy, *Planning the City upon a Hill*, 135; Weinstein, "The Congestion Evil," 182.

25. Charles H. Trout, *Boston, the Great Depression, and the New Deal*, Urban Life in America Series (New York: Oxford University Press, 1977), 51–54.

26. Boston City Planning Board, *Twenty-Third Annual Report of the City Planning Board for the Year Ending December 31, 1936* (Boston: City of Boston Printing Dept., 1937), 15–16, 18–21; Boston City Planning Board, *Twenty-Fourth Annual Report of the City Planning Board for the Year Ending December 31, 1937* (Boston: City of Boston Printing Dept., 1938), 22–23; Boston City Planning Board, *Twenty-Fifth Annual Report of the City Planning Board for the Year Ending December 31, 1938* (Boston: City of Boston Printing Dept., 1939), 20, 42; Thomas H. O'Connor, *Building a New Boston: Politics and Urban Renewal 1950–1970* (Boston: Northeastern University Press, 1993), 83.

27. Commonwealth of Massachusetts, *First Report of the State Planning Board for September 18, 1935, to November 30, 1935*. Public Document No. 156 (n.p.), 1. Massachusetts State Archives; Commonwealth of Massachusetts, *Annual Report of the State Planning Board, November 30, 1937*. Public Document No. 156 (n.p.), 14. Massachusetts State Archives.

28. As quoted in "High-Speed Highway Urged to Relieve Boston Traffic," *Boston Globe*, November 8, 1936, n.p. "Boston Transportation" clippings file, Boston Globe Library.

29. C. Joseph Harvey, "Double-Deck Highway Proposed for Boston," *Boston Globe*, January 10, 1937, n.p. "Boston Transportation" clippings file, Boston Globe Library.

30. "Report to the Legislature of Special Legislative Commission," as quoted in the Mayor's Conference on Traffic, *The Motorists' Case for a Central Traffic Artery* (Boston: City of Boston, 1941), 7.

31. The Mayor's Conference on Traffic, *The Motorists' Case for a Central Traffic Artery*, 12–13.

32. Boston City Planning Board, *Twenty-Ninth Annual Report of the City Planning Board for the Year Ending December 31, 1942* (Boston: City of Boston Printing Dept., 1944), 11–12

33. Massachusetts Postwar Highway Commission, *Report of the Postwar Highway Commission*, Part 1: *HR 1850* (Boston: Postwar Highway Commission, 1945), 49.

34. Massachusetts Postwar Highway Commission, *Report of the Postwar Highway Commission,* Part 2: *Highway Problems.* (Boston: Postwar Highway Commission, 1945).

35. "$50 Million Boston Highway Plan Backed by Gov. Tobin," *Boston Globe*, December 6, 1945, 1, 11. "Central Artery" clippings file, Boston Globe Library; John O'Connor, "State Approval Again Asked for 50-Million City Artery," *Boston Herald*, December 6, 1945, n.p. "Central Artery" clippings file, Boston Globe Library; "Curley Says Boston Can't Afford $50,000,000 Artery," *Boston Globe*, March 28, 1946, n.p. "Central Artery"

clippings file, Boston Globe Library; "Boston Central Artery Plan and New Tunnel Get Set-back," *Christian Science Monitor*, May 2, 1946, 2; "Plan Eight Boston Speed Highways," *Boston Globe*, February 15, 1948, 1, 26. "Central Artery" clippings file, Boston Globe Library.

36. Joint Board for the Metropolitan Master Highway Plan, *Preliminary Report on a Master Highway Plan for the Boston Metropolitan Area* (Boston: Joint Board for the Metropolitan Master Highway Plan, 1947), 17, exhibit 3; Charles A. Maguire and Associates, consulting engineers, with J. E. Greiner Company and De Leuw, Cather and Company, *The Master Highway Plan for the Boston Metropolitan Area* (Boston: Joint Board for the Metropolitan Master Highway Plan: 1948), 60, 72, exhibit 25.

37. Boston City Planning Board, *Thirty-Sixth Annual Report of the City Planning Board for the Year Ending December 31, 1949* (Boston: City of Boston Printing Dept., 1953), 4–5.

38. Robert C. Bergenheim, "Citizens Hit Highway Site in North End," *Christian Science Monitor* May 1, 1950, 2.

39. "North End Protests against Skyway through District," *Boston Globe*, March 29, 1950, n.p. "Central Artery" clippings file, Boston Globe Library; "New Business Group Fights No. End Route of Skyway," *Boston Globe*, April 13, 1950, n.p. "Central Artery" clippings file, Boston Globe Library; "North Enders Protest Highway—Would Mean 'Death of District,'" *Boston Globe*, A.M. edition, May 3, 1950, 2; "At the State House . . . Central Artery Shift Beaten," *Boston Globe*, A.M. edition, June 1, 1950, 2.

40. Arthur Stratton, "State Says Central Artery Superior, Less Destructive," *Boston Herald*, July 17, 1950, n.p. "Central Artery" clippings file, Boston Globe Library.

41. Boston City Planning Board, "Report of the City Planning Board Concerning the Proposed Use of Atlantic Avenue as a Right of Way for the Central Artery," April 21, 1950. Appendix III in Boston City Planning Board, *Thirty-Seventh Annual Report of the City Planning Board for the Year Ending December 31, 1950* (Boston: City of Boston Printing Dept., 1953), 32.

42. Stratton, "State Says Central Artery Superior, Less Destructive."

43. Boston City Planning Board, *Twenty-Fourth Annual Report of the City Planning Board*, 22.

44. As quoted in "Taking of Property for Boston's Skyway to Cost $10,100,000," *Daily Boston Globe*, February 2, 1950, 1.

45. Jane Jacobs, *The Death and Life of Great American Cities* (New York: Vintage-Random House, 1992), 8.

46. Stratton, "State Says Central Artery Superior, Less Destructive"; Robert C. Bergenheim, "Tentative Approval Given Contract for Hub Artery Bridge," *Christian Science Monitor*, September 27, 1950, 1; "State Allocates $30,000,000 for 2-Mile Artery Section," *Boston Globe*, November 11, 1950, 1; "Construction to Start Today on New Artery Bridge over Charles," *Daily Boston Globe*, January 16, 1951, 7.

47. Joseph A. Keblinsky, "Artery Threatens Leather District and Chinatown," *Boston Globe*, A.M. edition, March 25, 1953, n.p. Boston Globe Library.

48. Boston City Planning Board, *Fortieth Annual Report of the City Planning Board for the Year Ending December 31, 1953*. (Boston: City of Boston Printing Dept., 1954), 6–7; Boston City Planning Board, *Forty-First Annual Report of the City Planning Board for the Year Ending December 31, 1954* (Boston: City of Boston Printing Dept., 1955), 6–7; Boston City Planning Board, *Report on Review of Parsons, Brinckerhoff, Hall and MacDonald Plan for Central Artery* (Boston: n.p., October 22, 1953), 3, 14–15.

49. Boston City Planning Board, *Forty-First Annual Report of the City Planning Board*, 7; "City Offers New Artery Route," *Boston Globe*, January 22, 1954, n.p. "Central Artery" clippings file, Boston Globe Library.

50. "By-Passing City Not Object of Artery, Volpe Says," *Boston Globe*, January 27, 1954, n.p. "Central Artery" clippings file, Boston Globe Library.

51. "See Agreement on Artery Plan: Compromise May Save Chinese Merchants Building," *Boston Globe*, February 6, 1954, n.p. "Central Artery" clippings file, Boston Globe Library; William J. Lewis, "Central Artery Plan Changed," *Boston Globe,* A.M. edition, February 10, 1954, n.p. "Central Artery" clippings file, Boston Globe Library; "State Spurns City Artery Plan," *Boston Globe*, A.M. edition, February 11, 1954, n.p. "Central Artery" clippings file, Boston Globe Library; "State's Artery Route Probably Best: Hyland." *Boston Globe*, February 13, 1954, n.p. "Central Artery" clippings file, Boston Globe Library; William J. Lewis, "State's Artery Route Adopted," *Boston Globe*, March 13, 1954, n.p. "Central Artery" clippings file, Boston Globe Library.

52. As quoted in "Plan Too Costly to Industries, Objectors Say," *Boston Daily Globe*, A.M. edition, February 12, 1954, 19. "Central Artery" clippings file, Boston Globe Library.

53. "Artery Shift Spares Chinatown Area: Plan Trims Merchants Building," *Boston Globe*, A.M. edition, May 28, 1954, 1. "Central Artery" clippings file, Boston Globe Library.

54. Boston City Planning Board, Robert Whitten, *Report on a Thoroughfare Plan for Boston*, 82.

55. Telegram from Elisabeth Herlihy to Robert H. Whitten, November 15, 1930. Robert Harvey Whitten Papers, Frances Loeb Library, Harvard Graduate School of Design; and Robert H. Whitten to Elisabeth M. Herlihy, November 15, 1930. Robert Harvey Whitten Papers, Special Collection, Frances Loeb Library, Harvard University Graduate School of Design.

56. Boston City Planning Board, *Thirty-Seventh Annual Report of the City Planning Board*, 6–7.

57. Fay, Spofford, and Thorndike, Inc., *Bulletin* (Spring 1957): 1–4; Cranston R. Rogers, "Planning the First Central Artery in Boston," *Civil Engineering Practice* (Fall/Winter 1998): 57–58; Cranston R. Rogers, telephone conversation with author, April 26, 2005; Cranston R. Rogers, interview with author, tape recording, Medway, Massachusetts, May 16, 2005; and Bruce Campbell, interview with author, tape recording, Newton, Massachusetts, August 16, 2005.

58. Charles A. Maguire and Associates et al., *The Master Highway Plan*, 43–46.

59. Cranston R. Rogers, interview with author, tape recording, Medway, Massachusetts, July 5, 2005.

60. Professional Experience inventory and biographical reflections; "Harold C. Knight Associates" brochure, Harold C. Knight papers. Courtesy Knight/Turek family.

61. Cranston R. Rogers, interview with author, tape recording, Medway, Massachusetts, July 5, 2005.

62. "Harold C. Knight Associates" brochure, Harold C. Knight papers. Courtesy Knight/Turek family; "Knight, Bagge & Anderson Architects" brochure, circa early 1960s. Courtesy Knight, Bagge & Anderson Architects.

CHAPTER 6

1. "Unroof Building over Heads of S. Water Firms," *Chicago Daily Tribune*, October 3, 1924, 3.

2. As quoted in "Unroof Building over Heads of S. Water Firms," 3.

3. "Apparent Destruction Is Really an Improvement," *Chicago Daily Tribune*, December 1, 1924, 36.

4. Oscar Hewitt, "'Wacker Drive' Suggested for Water Street," *Chicago Daily Tribune*, May 18, 1924, 6; "South Water Street," *Chicago Daily Tribune*, August 9, 1924, 4.

5. "South Water Street," *Chicago Daily Tribune*, August 9, 1924, 4.

6. "South Water Street," *Chicago Daily Tribune*, December 29, 1924, 8; "South Water Street," *Chicago Daily Tribune*, December 31, 1924, 6; Mrs. H. Thormalen, "Give Mr. Wacker Some Other Honor," *Chicago Daily Tribune*, December 31, 1924, 6; E. O. Bond, "A Double Deck Name for a Double Deck Boulevard," *Chicago Daily Tribune*, January 5, 1925, 8; Harry R. Sternheim, a Chicagoan, "Honor Burnham and Wacker Otherwise," *Chicago Daily Tribune*, January 5, 1925, 8; "Another for South Water," *Chicago Daily Tribune*, January 5, 1905, 8; "May Duplicate Wacker Drive on North Bank of River," *Chicago Daily Tribune*, June 21, 1925, F24.

7. "South Water St. Project Pushed at Rapid Rate," *Chicago Daily Tribune*, February 27, 1925, 15.

8. "Going Up and Coming Down—Wacker Drive in the Making," *Chicago Daily Tribune*, October 25, 1925, B1.

9. "Wacker Drive Sets Concrete Pouring Record," *Chicago Daily Tribune*, August 11, 1925, 15, 36; Chicago Plan Commission, *Souvenir of Wacker Drive* (Chicago: Chicago Plan Commission, 1926), 14. Municipal Reference Collection, Chicago Public Library.

10. James O'Donnell Bennett, "Autos Swarm on Section of New S. Water," *Chicago Daily Tribune*, September 1, 1925, 4, 38.

11. As quoted in "75,000 Watch Opening of Wacker Drive, First Link in River Boulevard System," *Chicago Daily Tribune*, October 21, 1926, 3.

12. "75,000 Watch Opening of Wacker Drive"; T. A. Evans, *Wacker Drive* (n.p.: October 7, 1926): 1. Box 1, Folder 6, William Emmett Dever Collection, Chicago History Museum; Bennett, "Autos Swarm on Section of New S. Water," 4; "New Sector of Wacker Drive to Be Opened," *Chicago Daily Tribune*, July 29, 1926, 23; "Wacker Drive Opens Today; Parade, Too, Let it Rain or Shine," *Chicago Daily Tribune*, October 20, 1926, 1.

13. R. Stephen Sennott, "'Forever Inadequate to the Rising Stream': Dream Cities, Automobiles, and Urban Street Mobility in Central Chicago," in *Chicago Architecture and Design, 1923–1993: Reconfiguration of an American Metropolis*, ed. John Zukowsky (Munich: Prestel-Verlag [in association with The Art Institute of Chicago], 1993), 58.

14. "Visualize New Downtown Area North of River," *Chicago Daily Tribune*, July 22, 1925, 3; Al Chase, "Wacker Drive and Franklin Corner is Sold," *Chicago Daily Tribune*, September 1, 1925, 16.

15. Al Chase, "Jewelers' New $10,000,000 Bldg. Partly Garage," *Chicago Daily Tribune*, April 16, 1924, 1; "35 East Wacker Drive Building Designated a Chicago Historical Landmark," *Inland Architect* 38 (Spring 1994): 8.

16. "Playhouse and Shops for New River Parkway," *Chicago Daily Tribune*, January 18, 1925, G22; Al Chase, "Porter Gets 107 Feet Frontage on Wacker Drive," *Chicago Daily Tribune*, July 30, 1925, 27; Al Chase, "Pays $500,000 Cash for Wacker Drive Frontage," *Chicago Daily Tribune*, September 19, 1925, 12; "Two More Huge Skyscrapers Considered for Wacker Drive," *Chicago Daily Tribune*, May 9, 1926, B1; Al Chase, "World's Tallest Twin Towers for Boul Mich and Wacker Drive," *Chicago Daily Tribune*, July 18, 1926, B1; "Ask New Public Buildings along Chicago River," *Chicago Daily Tribune*, February 9, 1927, 13; "Way Cleared for U. of C. to Erect Loop Skyscraper," *Chicago Daily Tribune*, February 9, 1927, 6; Al Chase, "$15,000,000 Field Project Puts North Wacker Drive on Map," *Chicago Daily Tribune*, March 13, 1927, B1.

17. "Will the New Wacker Drive Skyline Be A–," *Chicago Daily Tribune*, August 27, 1926, 1.

18. "Build Beauty on New River Drive, Architect Urges," *Chicago Daily Tribune*, March 5, 1926, 10.

19. As quoted in "Dever Acts to Unify Building on Wacker Drive," *Chicago Daily Tribune*, August 12, 1926, 5.

20. "Uniformity on Wacker Drive," *Chicago Daily Tribune*, August 25, 1926, 8.

21. "Wacker Drive Skyline Plait Put under Way," *Chicago Daily Tribune*, August 21,

1926, 9; "Action Begun to Control Wacker Drive Skyline," *Chicago Daily Tribune*, October 27, 1926, 4.

22. As quoted in "Visions Wacker Drive Buildings of the Future," *Chicago Daily Tribune*, December 29, 1926, 13.

23. Edward H. Bennett, "Wacker Drive Plans: Building Projects May Mar or Make General Impression," *Skylines: A Magazine of Real Estate*, April 10, 1927, 8. Series VII, Box 62, Folder 6–Wacker Drive 1917–27. Edward H. Bennett Collection, Ryerson and Burnham Libraries, Art Institute of Chicago.

24. Bennett's stance against repetitive development along Wacker Drive ironically contradicted the imagery that he and the Chicago Plan Commission had crafted to promote the South Water Street improvement. However, it is important to recognize the project renderings as promotional materials that needed to display a unified vision in order to garner public confidence in its plan. The role of private enterprise in shaping the Wacker Drive skyline became increasingly apparent as the road neared completion. Bennett, then, ultimately operated as a mediator between the ideal vision of the *Plan of Chicago* and the whims of the businesses who would actually build the structures along Wacker Drive.

25. "A Suggestion concerning Wacker Drive," *Chicago Daily Tribune*, August 27, 1927, 6.

26. "Architectural Advice to Guide Loop Beauty," *Chicago Daily Tribune*, August 28, 1927, 5; "Architectural Standards in the Loop," *Chicago Daily Tribune*, September 15, 1927, 8; "Rely on Public Opinion to Give Streets Beauty," *Chicago Daily Tribune*, September 17, 1927, 8.

27. Kathleen Nagle, "Building the Profession: 125 Years of AIA Chicago," *Architecture Chicago: Contemporary Architecture and Interiors* 12 (Chicago: AIA Chicago, 1994), 15.

28. "May Duplicate Wacker Drive on North Bank of River," *Chicago Daily Tribune*, June 21, 1925, F24.

29. The exact financing for the project is unclear, as it received little press coverage. However, the Chicago Plan Commission and the Department of Public Works announced in April 1929 that they were about to start construction of a portion of the north riverside drive, and that they expected to eventually connect this section eastward toward the new Wabash Avenue Bridge and Michigan Avenue. There was no mention of necessary land acquisitions or approvals for the project, suggesting that it was indeed occupying the land donated by Marshall Field and Company. See Chase, "$15,000,000 Field Project Puts North Wacker Drive on Map;" Oscar Hewitt, "Ready to Build Drive on North Bank of River," *Chicago Daily Tribune*, April 29, 1929, 1.

30. Carl W. Condit, *Chicago, 1910–1929: Building, Planning, and Urban Technology* (Chicago: University of Chicago Press, 1973), 250–252.

31. Anne Lee, "Chicago's Traffic Problem Solved by Burnham Plan," *Architectural Record* 62 (October 1927): 263.

32. Condit, *Chicago, 1910–1929*, 250.

33. "Hudson Highway Officially Started to Cheers of 5,000," *New York Times*, May 25, 1929, 1; "Express Road Unit Opened by Miller," *New York Times*, November 14, 1930, 3.

34. "Pushes West Side Drive," *New York Times*, May 19, 1931, 27; "West Side Highway to 72d St. Speeded," *New York Times*, June 29, 1931, 19; "New Link is Opened in Express Highway," *New York Times*, March 10, 1932, 23.

35. "Says Pier Plans Bar Elevated Highway," *New York Times*, November 28, 1928, 54; "New Plan Is Drafted for 1,000-Foot Piers," *New York Times*, June 7, 1929, 20; "Hurley to Reopen Pier and Span Pleas," *New York Times*, April 1, 1930, 27; "City to Act at Once on 1,100-Foot Piers," *New York Times*, January 15, 1931, 25; "New Highway Work Is Started by Levy," *New York Times*, August 20, 1931, 17; "To Speed Express Road," *New York Times*, September 25, 1931, 33; "Begins 2d Link Today on West Side Drive," *New York Times*, June 20, 1932, 17; "New Highway Link Opened by O'Brien," *New York Times*, January 6, 1933, 21.

36. "New Links Speeded for City Viaduct," *New York Times*, October 30, 1933, 35; "Third Link Started on West Side Highway," *New York Times*, March 6, 1934, 25; "New Link Opened in West Side Road," *New York Times*, August 31, 1934, 19.

37. "Begins 2d Link Today on West Side Drive"; "Express Highway to Add New Link," *New York Times*, January 21, 1936, 25; "Work on City Piers Begins Tomorrow," *New York Times*, November 2, 1934, 25; "Last Link Started on West Side Drive," *New York Times*, February 14, 1936, 21.

38. "West Side Highway Completed; Traffic Test to Feature Opening," *New York Times*, February 5, 1937, 23; "Motor Speedway Proving a Success," *New York Times*, February 7, 1937, 49; "Mayor Wins 'Auto Race' with Levy as Elevated Highway Link Opens," *New York Times*, February 10, 1937, 25.

39. "West Side Highway to Reach Battery," *New York Times*, August 18, 1934, 11; "Governor Signs Elevated Highway Bill for Link from Canal Street to Battery," *New York Times*, August 24, 1934, 1.

40. "Art Board Approves Canal Street Bridge," *New York Times*, July 14, 1937, 19; "$2,000,000 in Bonds Issued for Bridge," *New York Times*, July 15, 1937, 21; "New Bridge to Rise over Canal Street," *New York Times*, November 12, 1937, 10; "Canal St. Bridge Formally Opened," *New York Times*, February 5, 1939, 2.

41. "Highway Section Opens Tomorrow," *New York Times*, November 28, 1948, 74; Joseph C. Ingraham, "Brooklyn Tunnel Costing $80,000,000 Opened by Mayor," *New York Times*, May 26, 1950, 1.

42. The extension south of Duane Street did not adhere to the Sloan and Robertson design that defined the rest of the highway's length but used bare steel panels to create a more plain abstraction of this pattern. This was likely because of budget concerns and the late date of completion of this segment of the road. Since this portion was not included in the original plans for the highway, this artistic analysis will focus on the majority of the highway (between Duane and Seventy-Second Streets) that was built according to Sloan and Robertson's specifications.

43. D. Zetlan, *West Side Highway Seals*. N.p. (March 1977): 1–2. Vertical files: New York City Highways—West Side Highway (1977), City Hall Library, City of New York; Daniel B. Schneider, "F.Y.I.—The Long Seal Sale," *New York Times*, October 11, 1998, CY2.

44. "West Side Highway Advancing Rapidly," *New York Times*, March 30, 1930, N1; "New Link Is Opened in Express Highway," *New York Times*, March 10, 1932, 23; "West Side Changes Aiding Industry," *New York Times*, July 8, 1934, RE2; Robert M. Fogelson, *Downtown: Its Rise and Fall, 1880–1950* (New Haven, CT: Yale University Press, 2001), 279.

45. "Extending West Side Highway to the North," *New York Times*, January 5, 1935, XX6.

46. Victor H. Bernstein, "West Side Highway to Open," *New York Times*, October 10, 1937, 137.

47. "La Guardia Opens Riverside Project as 'Reply' to Foes," *New York Times*, October 13, 1937, 1; "West Side Highway Completed; Traffic Test to Feature Opening," *New York Times*, February 5, 1937, 23.

48. "New York's West Side Improvement," *American City* 52, no. 11 (November 1937): cover, 52; "West Side Improvement, New York City, Department of Parks," *Architectural Forum* 67, no. 6 (December 1937): 475–477; Robert Moses, "New York's West Side Development at Night," *American City* 53, no. 2 (February 1938): 115–116; "Pictures and Paragraphs from Near and Far: East Side, West Side—With the Replanning of New York," *American City* 42, no. 6 (June 1930): 136.

49. The most recent recapitulation of Moses's career and myriad projects is Hilary Ballon and Kenneth T. Jackson, eds. *Robert Moses and the Modern City: The Transformation*

of New York (New York: W. W. Norton, 2007). This provides a revisionary history of Moses's life and achievements, which previously had been defined by Robert Caro's unflattering biography, *The Power Broker: Robert Moses and the Fall of New York* (New York: Vintage, 1975). See in particular Owen D. Gutfreund, "Rebuilding New York in the Auto Age: Robert Moses and His Highways," in *Robert Moses and the Modern City*, 86–93.

50. "Traffic Rush Jams West Side Highway," *New York Times*, November 24, 1930, 22; "Traffic Tie-Up Eased on Express Highway," *New York Times*, December 1, 1930, 21.

51. "New Plan Drafted for 34th St. Ramp," *New York Times*, November 1, 1935, 23; "2,000 Sign for Ramp to West Side Road," *New York Times*, April 3, 1936, 25; "Merchants Seek Ramp at 34th St.," *New York Times*, March 6, 1938, 36.

52. "Motor Speedway Proving Success," *New York Times*, February 7, 1937, 49.

53. "West Side Highway Speed Travel 25%," *New York Times*, November 5, 1937, 25.

54. S. Earl Honig, as quoted in "West Side Changes Aiding Industry," *New York Times*, July 8, 1934, RE2.

55. "Topics of the Times: Fast and Fair," *New York Times*, February 11, 1937, 22.

56. See "Chinatown," *Boston 200 Neighborhood History Series* (Boston: Boston 200 Corporation, 1976): 1–4; and Walter Muir Whitehill and Lawrence W. Kennedy, *Boston: A Topographical History*, 3rd ed. (Cambridge, MA: Belknap Press of Harvard University Press, 2000), 223–224.

57. "State Allocates $30,000,000 for 2-Mile Artery Section," *Boston Globe*, November 11, 1950, 1; "Construction to Start Today on New Artery Bridge over Charles," *Boston Globe*, A.M. edition, January 16, 1951, n.p. Central Artery clippings file, Boston Globe Library; Plotkin, "Biggest Wrecking Job in Bay State History."

58. Lawrence W. Kennedy, *Planning the City upon a Hill: Boston since 1630* (Amherst: University of Massachusetts Press, 1992), 70.

59. John H. Fenton, "Old Boston Bows to Superhighway," *New York Times*, February 28, 1954, 74.

60. Nat L. Kline, "Huge Rams Plant Legs for Highway," *Boston Globe*, August 23, 1952, 1–2. Central Artery clippings file, Boston Globe Library.

61. The Sumner Tunnel, which was completed in 1934, connected to Logan Airport in East Boston. The entrance to the Sumner Tunnel is at North Street in the North End.

62. William J. Lewis, "New Artery Span Saves 23 Minutes," *Boston Daily Globe* A.M edition, October 30, 1954, 1–2.

63. Fort Hill was one of Boston's original topographical features, rising eighty feet tall and providing a strategic view of the harbor. An upper-class neighborhood had developed on the site by the early nineteenth century, though its proximity to the growing business district tempered its popularity later in the century. By the middle of the nineteenth century it was considered one of the city's most congested and undesirable neighborhoods, leading the city to decide to level and redevelop the area—an eerie precursor to twentieth-century urban renewal approaches. Part of the excavated land was used to create Atlantic Avenue in the 1860s. Fort Hill Square corresponds today to the site of Philip Johnson's One International Place. See Kennedy, *Planning the City upon a Hill*, 57–59; and Jane Holtz Kay, *Lost Boston*, rev. ed. (Boston: University of Massachusetts Press, 2006), 30.

64. "Traffic Pattern Fixed for Artery," *Boston Globe*, P.M. edition, October 31, 1955, n.p. Boston Globe Library.

65. The Dewey Square tunnel and the surface artery to the Southeast Expressway benefited from federal funding thanks to President Dwight D. Eisenhower's 1956 Federal-Aid Highway Act. The Central Artery's connection to the Southeast and Northeast Expressways made it an integral piece of the country's burgeoning Interstate Highway System, which is why it qualified for federal support. The earlier portions of the Central Artery were funded exclusively by city and state coffers.

66. Michael Passanisi, "Development of the Boston Area Highway System," *Historical*

Journal of Massachusetts 23, no.2 (Summer 1995): 175, 180; A. S. Plotkin, "Hub Artery, Expressway Join Today," *Boston Daily Globe*, A.M. edition, June 25, 1959, 1, 6.

67. As quoted in Robert A. McLean, "New Expressway Hailed as Rush Hour Tieups End," *Boston Daily Globe*, A.M. edition, June 26, 1959, 22.

68. McLean, "New Expressway Hailed," 22.

69. Nye Rosa, "Sudbury Nearer by 10 Minutes," *Boston Daily Globe*, A.M. edition, June 26, 1959, 22; Leonard Lerner, "Holbrook-Hub in 32 Minutes," *Boston Daily Globe*, A.M. edition, June 26, 1959, 22.

70. Ronald Wysocki, "32 Minutes to Peabody," *Boston Daily Globe*, A.M. edition, June 26, 1959, 22.

71. "Newsboys Miss Traffic Jams as Old Customers Speed By," *Boston Daily Globe*, A.M. edition, June 26, 1959, 22.

72. "Getting to Boston's Heart," *American City* 73 (July 1958): 131.

73. "Hub Autoists Warned about Artery Shifts," *Christian Science Monitor*, October 21, 1958, 2.

74. "New Roads: The U.S. Tackles Its Traffic," *Time*, January 24, 1955, 15.

75. "Getting to Boston's Heart," 131.

76. Passanisi, "Development of the Boston Area Highway System," 181.

77. Uncle Dudley, "The Squeeze on the Cities," *Boston Daily Globe*, October 14, 1959, 22.

78. *Boston Herald* (July 2, 1959), as quoted in Passanisi, "Development of the Boston Area Highway System," 181.

79. Richard A. Miller, "Expressway Blight," *Architectural Forum* 111, no. 4 (October 1959): 163.

80. Don Fichter, letter to the editor, *Architectural Forum* 3, no. 6 (December 1959): 206.

81. Ada Louise Huxtable, "Renewal in Boston: Good and Bad," *New York Times*, April 19, 1964, X24.

82. Miller, "Expressway Blight," 161.

83. Miller, "Expressway Blight," 161.

84. "Tax Accord Reached on Back Bay Center," *New York Times*, March 20, 1958, 50; Thomas H. O'Connor, *The Hub: Boston Past and Present*. (Boston: Northeastern University Press, 2001), 216. For more on the Prudential Center evolution see Elihu Rubin, *Insuring the City: The Prudential Center and the Postwar Urban Landscape*. (New Haven, CT: Yale University Press, 2012).

85. David Kruh, *Always Something Doing: Boston's Infamous Scollay Square*, rev. ed. (Boston: Northeastern University Press, 1999), 126–129; Thomas H. O'Connor, *Building a New Boston: Politics and Urban Renewal 1950–1970* (Boston: Northeastern University Press, 1993), 141–142.

86. Alan Lupo, Frank Colcord, and Edmund P. Fowler, *Rites of Way: The Politics of Transportation in Boston and the U.S. City* (Boston: Little Brown, 1971), 14–28, 85; Kennedy, *Planning the City upon a Hill*, 198–199.

CHAPTER 7

1. Carl W. Condit, *Chicago 1910–29: Building, Planning, and Urban Technology* (Chicago: University of Chicago Press, 1973), 320.

2. "Autos Adrift Tie Up Traffic in Lower Drive," *Chicago Daily Tribune*, January 25, 1931, 18.

3. "Mayor Assured of 27 Million PWA Grants," *Chicago Daily Tribune*, June 24, 1938, 1; "Mayor Has Hope to Save Wacker Extension Plan," *Chicago Daily Tribune*, September 2, 1938, 18; Hal Foust, "Start Today on Wacker Dr. Second Level," *Chicago Daily Tribune*, June 6, 1949, 5.

4. "142 Eyesores Razed in 1953, 117 by Owners," *Chicago Daily Tribune*, April 16, 1953; Hal Foust, "Congress St. Progress Gives Mayor Boost," *Chicago Daily Tribune*, December 2, 1953, A11, 4; "1¼ Million Use New Sector of Congress St. in 28 Days," *Chicago Daily Tribune*, January 12, 1956, 3.

5. "Initial Phase Set to Extend Wacker," *Chicago Daily Tribune*, February 9, 1969, 10; "Michigan Avenue Link to Outer Drive Opened," *Chicago Daily Tribune*, December 9, 1975, A1.

6. "Congress Snubs Wacker Drive Rehab Plan," 14; Charles Lockwood, "Chicago's Public Works Boom," *Urban Land* 57, no. 10 (October 1998): 99.

7. Margy Sweeney, "Reworking Wacker," *Grid* 3, no. 7 (September 2001): 32; Jon Hilkevitch, "Chicago's Historic Wacker Drive Again to Go with Flow," *Chicago Tribune*, November 19, 2002, Newspaper Source Plus, http://web.ebscohost.com.

8. Bill Ruthhart, "$10M Plan Aims to Upgrade Riverwalk," *Chicago Tribune*, August 5, 2018, 1; Blair Kamin, "Riverwalk Stretches East to Repair the Design Divide," *Chicago Tribune*, May 19, 2019, 1.

9. Owen Gutfreund, "Rebuilding New York in the Auto Age: Robert Moses and His Highways," in *Robert Moses and the Modern City: The Transformation of New York*, eds. Hilary Ballon and Kenneth T. Jackson (New York: W. W. Norton, 2007), 90–91.

10. Mark H. Rose, *Interstate: Express Highway Politics, 1939–1989*, rev. ed. (Knoxville: University of Tennessee Press, 1990), 8–10, 17.

11. John D. Morris, "Eisenhower Signs Road Bill; Weeks Allocates 1.1 Billion," *New York Times*, June 30, 1956, 1; Walter Trohan, "Huge Highway Spending Bill Signed by Ike," *Chicago Tribune*, June 30, 1956, 16; Gutfreund, "Rebuilding New York in the Auto Age," 90–93. For more in-depth documentation of the Interstate Highway System's financial and planning approaches, including discussion of the use of highway projects to disrupt poor and minority neighborhoods in countless cities, see Mark H. Rose and Raymond A. Mohl, *Interstate: Highway Politics and Policy since 1939*, 3rd ed. (Knoxville: University of Tennessee Press, 2012), especially chaps. 7–8; Eric Avila, *The Folklore of the Freeway: Race and Revolt in the Modernist City* (Minneapolis: University of Minnesota Press, 2014).

12. Gutfreund, "Rebuilding New York in the Auto Age," 91–92.

13. Ray Bromley, "Cross-Bronx Expressway," in *Robert Moses and the Modern City: The Transformation of New York*, eds. Hilary Ballon and Kenneth T. Jackson (New York: W. W. Norton, 2007), 217–218.

14. Bromley, "Cross-Bronx Expressway," 212–215.

15. "90° Curve Again Fatal," *New York Times*, October 14, 1941, 44.

16. This service continued until 1953 when it was claimed by budget cuts. "'Jeep Tow' Patrol Starts Tomorrow," *New York Times*, June 8, 1947, 48; Charles G. Bennett, "Free Tow Service to End on Highway," *New York Times*, May 8, 1953, 21.

17. Regina Herzlinger, "Costs, Benefits and the West Side Highway," *Public Interest* 55 (Spring 1979): 77–78.

18. Charles G. Bennett, "West Side Highway Corroded by Salt," *New York Times*, October 13, 1949, 29; "Night Repairs Set on West Side Road," *New York Times*, June 27, 1954, 55.

19. "Truck and Car Fall as West Side Highway Collapses," *New York Times*, December 16, 1973, 76.

20. This viaduct offers concrete supports, a roadbed clad in green steel, and no architectural ornamentation.

21. Dennis J. O'Brien, "The West Side Highway Reconstruction Story," *Public Works* 128, no. 1 (January 1997): 29. Herzlinger, "Costs, Benefits and the West Side Highway," 78–80; Adam Nagourney, "A Ghost of Westway Rises along the Hudson," *New York Times*, March 3, 2002, 33–34.

22. Dan McNichol, *The Big Dig* (New York: Silver Lining, 2000), 28.

23. Boston Redevelopment Authority, *Central Artery Depression: Preliminary Feasibility Study, Draft Report.* (May 22, 1975): xvi.

24. Robert Campbell, FAIA, "The Big Dig: What's Up under Boston?" *Architectural Record* 190, no.3 (March 2002): 85.

25. This is not to say that the Big Dig is without controversy. Some contend that the Big Dig repeated the mistakes of its predecessor by creating an alternate subterranean landscape geared entirely toward speeding movement *to* and *through* downtown. Others argue that the new parks maintain the urban fracture created by the elevated highway instead of extending surrounding street and building patterns to heal the urban wound.

26. U.S. Bureau of the Census, *Historical Statistics of the United States, Colonial Times to 1970, Bicentennial Edition,* Part 2 (Washington, DC: U.S. Government Printing Office, 1975), 716.

BIBLIOGRAPHY

PRIMARY SOURCES

ARCHIVES

Avery Architectural and Fine Arts Library, Columbia University
Corbett, Harvey Wiley, papers
Ferriss, Hugh, papers
Guastavino Collection
New York, Borough President of Manhattan, *Elevated Public Highway . . . from Canal Street to W. 79th Street*, Architectural drawings. (2004.009. A92BB16)
Sloan and Robertson, Wadsworth Building, Architectural drawings

Boston Globe Library
Boston Globe clippings files:
- Boston: Highways: Central Artery
- Boston: Highways: Central Artery—1959
- Boston: Transportation
- Herlihy, Elisabeth M.
- Parker, William Stanley
- Shurcliff, Arthur A. (aka Arthur A. Shurtleff)
- Wilbur, John B.

Microfiche files:
- Inner Belt
- Moses, Robert

Boston Public Library
Government Documents Department

Bostonian Society
Newspaper Scrapbook Collection

Chicago History Museum (formerly Chicago Historical Society)
Dever, William E., Series 2, Mayoralty papers, 1923–April 1927.
Streets—South Water Street—Master Vertical File

Chicago Public Library, Municipal Reference Collection

Chicago (Ill.). Board of Local Improvements. *Advocacy of the Proposal to Construct Two Level Streets or Subways under the Existing Local Improvement Laws*. Chicago: Board of Local Improvements, 1918.

———. Annual Reports, 1901–1910.

———. *Quadrennial Report of the Board of Local Improvements of the City of Chicago, 1915–18*. Chicago: Board of Local Improvements, 1919.

Clippings files:

Burnham, Daniel Hudson

South Water Street Market

Wacker Drive

Ickes, John. *The Traffic Problem and Its Solution*. Chicago: n.p., 1933.

Rex, Frederick. *The South Water Street Market*. Chicago: n.p., 1938.

Wacker Drive Extension, Architectural drawings, 1946.

Whitehead, Helen. *Outline of the History of Wacker Drive*. Chicago: n.p., 1952.

City of Boston Archives

City Council Proceedings, 1927–1929

Fay, Spofford & Thorndike, Engineers, Project Files

John F. Fitzgerald Expressway, architectural and engineering drawings

Frances Loeb Library, Harvard University Graduate School of Design

Vertical files:

Brinckerhoff, Henry M. *The Problem of Street Traffic in a Modern City*. Cleveland: n.p., [192?].

McClintock, Miller. "Street Traffic Segregation Urged." *Michigan Manufacturer and Financial Record* 39, no. 12 (March 19, 1927): n.p.

Moody, Walter D. "War and the Chicago Plan." *Fine Arts Journal* (November 1917): n.p.

Parker, William Stanley. "City Planning in Boston." *Boston Herald*, August 28, 1950; September 4, 1950.

"A Sunken Boulevard for Automobiles." *Scientific American*, October 23, 1923.

Thomson, T. Kennard. "Drastic Changes in Traffic Facilities Will Alone Meet Manhattan's Needs." n.p., 1927.

Harvard University Archives

Green, David Anthony. "Planning the Central Artery: Constraints on Planners and the Limits of Planning in Boston 1909–1979." BA thesis, History, Harvard University, 1979.

Knight, Bagge & Andersen, Architects

Firm Archives

Massachusetts Historical Society

Herlihy, Elisabeth May, papers

Massachusetts State Archives

Central Artery Construction Contract Photograph Collection

General Court of Massachusetts. *Massachusetts Acts and Resolves*. 1925–1960.

Massachusetts Department of Public Works, Annual Reports

Massachusetts Department of Public Works, Public Hearings Files

Massachusetts State Planning Board Annual Reports

Massachusetts State House Library

Massachusetts Department of Public Works and U.S. Dept. of Commerce, Bureau of Public Roads. *Modern Highways: A Safeguard for Living . . . a Guardian for Progress*. Boston:

Massachusetts Department of Public Works and U.S. Dept. of Commerce, Bureau of Public Roads, 1960.
Massachusetts Post-War Highway Commission. *Highway Problems Report*, parts 1 and 2. Boston: Massachusetts Post-War Highway Commission, 1945.

Massachusetts State Transportation Library
1930s Newspaper Scrapbook Collection:
"Elevated Road through Boston Wins Approval." *Boston Traveler*, October 30, 1930.
Marden, Charles F. "Five Routes Radiating from Boston Approved for Through Street Rule." *Boston Evening Transcript*, December 29, 1928.
"Opposed to High Speed on Highway." *Boston Post*, September 26, 1930.
Ryan, Morgan T. "Highway Safety and Auto Sales Are Closely Related." *Boston Transcript*, January 21, 1948.
"The Timid Soul." *Worcester Telegram*, September 13, 1931.
"Where Traffic Crawls." *Boston Traveler*, October 1, 1929.
Massachusetts Department of Public Works. *Facts on the Central Artery*. March 12, 1954.
"The Passing of the Atlantic Avenue 'El.'" *Boston Elevated Railway Co-operation* 21, no. 2 (April 1942): 30.

New York City Hall Library
Vertical files: New York City Highways—West Side Highway

New York City Municipal Archives
Borough President of Manhattan Photograph Collection
Hylan, John F. Departmental Correspondence, Borough President—Manhattan, 1918–25
Walker, James J. Departmental Correspondence, Borough President—Manhattan, 1926–32

New York Historical Society
Ground Breaking Ceremonial Marking the Beginning of the West Side Express Highway, Twelve O'Clock Noon at the Canal Street Plaza on the Island of Manhattan. Friday, May 24, 1929. City of New York.
Majority and Minority Reports of the Mayor's West Side Improvement Architects' Committee. 1929.
New York City Department of Parks. *Opening of the West Side Improvement, October 12, 1937.*
Smith, R.A.C. *The West Side Improvement, and its Relation to All of the Commerce of the Port of New York.* New York: M. B. Brown, 1916.

New York Public Library
Clippings files: Transportation—Elevated
Artists' clippings files: Sloan and Robertson

Ryerson and Burnham Libraries, Art Institute of Chicago
Edward H. Bennett Collection, Series 5, 7, 9–11
Daniel H. Burnham Collection, Archives

Special Collections, Harvard University Graduate School of Design
Whitten, Robert Harvey, papers

INDIVIDUALS

Campbell, Bruce, Former Commissioner, Massachusetts Department of Public Works.
Rogers, Cranston, Civil Engineer, Fay, Spofford & Thorndike, 1950s.
Turek, Barbara, Daughter of Harold C. Knight
Turek, David, Grandson of Harold C. Knight.

PRIMARY SOURCE REPORTS

Albert Russel Erskine Bureau, Harvard University, *A Report on the Street Traffic Control Problem of the City of Boston, Prepared under the Direction of the Mayor's Street Traffic Advisory Board.* Boston: n.p., 1928.

American Institute of Steel Construction. *A National Competition for the Most Suitable Structural and Architectural Design of an Elevated Highway.* New York: American Institute of Steel Construction, 1937.

———. *A Report on Elevated Highways.* New York: American Institute of Steel Construction, 1938.

American Road Builders' Association. *Report of Committee on Elevated Highways.* Bulletin no. 74. Washington: American Road Builders' Association, 1941.

Berry, Charles W. *The Financing of Local Improvements by Local Borough or City-Wide Assessments.* New York: Board of Estimate and Apportionment, 1930.

Borough President of Manhattan. *1932–1933 Annual Reports, President Borough of Manhattan, City of New York. Hon. Samuel Levy, President.* New York: n.p., 1934.

Borough President of Manhattan, and Triborough Bridge and Tunnel Authority. *Miller Highway West Side Elevated Improvement.* New York: n.p., February 4, 1957.

Boston Chamber of Commerce. *Metropolitan Planning and Development in Boston and Its Environs. 1922.* Boston: Boston Chamber of Commerce, 1922.

Boston City Planning Board. *A Compendium of Reports and Studies Relating to the Commerce and Industries of Boston, Compiled by William A. Leahy under the Direction of the City Planning Board, Boston, Mass.* Boston: City of Boston Printing Department, 1924.

———. *Eighth Annual Report of the City Planning Board for the Year Ending January 31, 1922.* Boston: City of Boston Printing Department, 1922.

———. *Eleventh Annual Report of the City Planning Board for the Year Ending January 31, 1925.* Boston: City of Boston Printing Department, 1925.

———. *Fifteenth Annual Report of the City Planning Board for the Year Ending December 31, 1928.* Boston: City of Boston Printing Department, 1929.

———. *First Annual Report of the City Planning Board for the Year Ending January 31, 1915.* Boston: City of Boston Printing Department, 1915.

———. *Fourteenth Annual Report of the City Planning Board for the Year Ending December 31, 1927.* Boston: City of Boston Printing Department, 1928.

———. *General Plan for Boston: Preliminary Report—1950.* Boston: Boston City Planning Board, 1950.

———. *Larger Aspects of Passenger Transportation in Metropolitan Boston. Report of the Boston City Planning Board to the Massachusetts Public Service Commission.* Boston: City of Boston Printing Department, 1914.

———. *Ninth Annual Report of the City Planning Board for the Year Ending January 31, 1923.* Boston: City of Boston Printing Department, 1923.

———. *The North End, a Survey and a Comprehensive Plan. Report of the City Planning Board, Boston, Mass.* Boston: City of Boston Printing Department, 1919.

———. *Progress Report on Proposed Intermediate Thoroughfare.* Boston: Boston City Planning Board, 1925.

———. *Second Annual Report of the City Planning Board for the Year Ending January 31, 1916.* Boston: City of Boston Printing Department, 1916.

———. *Seventeenth Annual Report of the City Planning Board for the Year Ending December 31, 1930.* Boston: City of Boston Printing Department, 1931.

———. *Seventh Annual Report of the City Planning Board for the Year Ending January 31, 1921.* Boston: City of Boston Printing Department, 1921.

———. *Sixteenth Annual Report of the City Planning Board for the Year Ending December 31, 1929.* Boston: City of Boston Printing Department, 1930.

———. *Sixth Annual Report of the City Planning Board for the Year Ending January 31, 1920*. Boston: City of Boston Printing Department, 1920.

———. *Tenth Annual Report of the City Planning Board for the Year Ending January 31, 1924*. Boston: City of Boston Printing Department, 1924.

———. *Thirteenth Annual Report of the City Planning Board for the Year Ending December 31, 1926*. Boston: City of Boston Printing Department, 1927.

———. *Twelfth Annual Report of the City Planning Board for the Year Ending December 31, 1925*. Boston: City of Boston Printing Department, 1926.

———. *Zoning for Boston: A Survey and a Comprehensive Plan. Report of the City Planning Board, Boston, Mass.* Boston: City of Boston Printing Department, 1924.

Boston City Planning Board and Robert Whitten, consultant. *Report on a Thoroughfare Plan for Boston*. Boston: Boston City Planning Board, 1930.

Boston Redevelopment Authority. *1965/1975 General Plan for the City of Boston and the Regional Core*. Boston: BRA, 1965.

———. *Central Artery Depression: A Preliminary Feasibility Study, Draft*. Boston: BRA, May 1975.

Boston Society of Architects Committee on Municipal Improvement. *Report Made to the Boston Society of Architects by Its Committee on Municipal Improvement*. Boston: Alfred Mudge and Son, 1907.

Boston Special Commission on Intermediate Thoroughfare. "Final Report of Special Commission on Laying Out and Constructing New Thoroughfare and the Extension and Widening of Certain Streets in Connection Therewith." *Supplement to Current Affairs* 16, no. 32 (December 21, 1925): 1–19.

Burnham, Daniel H., and Edward H. Bennett. *Plan of Chicago*. Edited by Charles Moore. Chicago: The Commercial Club, 1909.

Charles A. Maguire and Associates, Engineers, with J. E. Greiner Company and De Leuw, Cather and Company. *The Master Highway Plan for the Boston Metropolitan Area*. Boston: Joint Board for the Metropolitan Master Highway Plan: 1948.

Chicago Board of Local Improvements. *Chicago Plan*. Chicago: Chicago Board of Local Improvements, 1922.

———. "Recommendation and Estimate for Improvements from East Randolph Street Northward to East Chicago Avenue." Public hearing at Council Chamber, City Hall. May 13, 1913.

———. *A Report to the Hon. William Hale Thompson by the Board of Local Improvements for the Past Six Years*. Chicago: Chicago Board of Local Improvements, 1921.

———. *A Sixteen Year Record of Achievement, 1915–31*. Chicago: Buckley, Dement, 1931.

Chicago City Council, Committee on Traffic and Public Safety. *Limited Ways: A Plan for the Greater Chicago Traffic Area*. Chicago: Chicago City Council, Committee on Traffic and Public Safety, 1933.

Chicago Plan Commission. *Annual Report of the Chairman for 1911, Chicago Plan Commission*. Chicago: Drovers Journal Press, 1912.

———. *Annual Report of the Chairman for 1912, Chicago Plan Commission*. Chicago: Chicago Plan Commission, 1913.

———. *Chicago's Greatest Issue: An Official Plan*. Chicago: Chicago Plan Commission, 1911.

———. *The Chicago Plan: Souvenir of the Pageant of Progress Exhibit Made Jointly by the City of Chicago, Board of Local Improvements, Chicago Plan Commission*. Chicago: Chicago Plan Commission, 1921.

———. *Eighteenth Annual Report of the Chicago Plan Commission for the Year 1927*. Chicago: Chicago Plan Commission, 1927.

———. *Fifteenth Annual Report of the Chicago Plan Commission*. Chicago: Chicago Plan Commission, 1925.

———. *Fifth Annual Report of the Chairman—for the Year 1914, Chicago Plan Commission*. Chicago: Chicago Plan Commission, 1915.
———. *A List of Suggested New Projects and of Improvements in the Making*. Chicago: Chicago Plan Commission, 1921.
———. *Proposed Expressway Development Program (Initial Stage) for the City of Chicago, December 1943*. Chicago: Chicago Plan Commission, 1943.
———. *Seventeenth Annual Report of the Chicago Plan Commission for the Year 1926*. Chicago: Chicago Plan Commission, 1926.
———. *Sixteenth Annual Report of the Chicago Plan Commission for the Year 1925*. Chicago: Chicago Plan Commission, 1926.
———. *South Water Street Plan*. Chicago: Chicago Plan Commission, 1917.
———. *Souvenir of Wacker Drive, Chicago*. Chicago: Chicago Plan Commission, 1926.
———. *Ten Years Work of the Chicago Plan Commission, 1909–1919*. Chicago: Chicago Plan Commission, 1920.
———. *Thirteenth Annual Report of the Chicago Plan Commission*. Chicago: Chicago Plan Commission, 1923.
———. *Twelfth Annual Report of the Chicago Plan Commission*. Chicago: Chicago Plan Commission, 1922.
City Committee on Plan and Survey. *Report of the City Committee on Plan and Survey*. New York: City Committee on Plan and Survey, 1928.
Cleveland City Plan Commission. *The Cleveland Thorofare Plan*. Cleveland: Cleveland City Plan Commission, 1921.
Committee on Control of Street Traffic, Merchants' Association of New York. *Control of Street Traffic*. New York: n.p., 1924.
Department of Public Works, Borough of Manhattan, City of New York. *Annual Report for the Year 1934*. New York: Herald-Nathan Press, [1935?].
———. *Annual Report for the Year 1935*. New York: F. Hubner, [1936?].
Executive Committee, Chicago Plan Commission. *Proceedings of the 52nd Meeting of the Executive Committee of the Chicago Plan Commission, Held in Room F, Hotel Sherman, Tuesday, February 1, 1921*. Chicago: Chicago Plan Commission, 1921.
Fine Arts Federation of New York. *Report of the Committee on City Development: City Planning, Re-Zoning New York, Specific Developments, Conclusions, and Recommendations*. New York: Fine Arts Federation of New York, 1935.
Hayden, Harding and Buchanan, Inc., and Charles A. Maguire and Associates. *Excerpts from Inner Belt and Expressway System, Boston Metropolitan Area*. Boston: Commonwealth of Massachusetts, 1962.
Isaacs, Stanley M. *Borough of Manhattan, A Report: January 1, 1938–June 30, 1939*. New York: n.p., 1939.
———. *Borough of Manhattan, A Report: July 1, 1939–June 30, 1940*. New York: n.p., 1940.
———. *Borough of Manhattan, A Report: July 1, 1940–June 30, 1941*. New York: Empire State Craftsmen, 1941.
Massachusetts Commission on Metropolitan Improvements. *Public Improvements for the Metropolitan District*. Boston: Wright and Potter Printing, 1909.
Massachusetts Joint Board on Metropolitan Improvements. *Final Report of the Joint Board on Metropolitan Improvements, Pursuant to Chapter 113 of the Resolves of 1909, and Chapters 112 and 134 of the Resolves of 1910*. Boston: Wright and Potter Printing, 1911.
Miller, Julius. *Public Improvements in Manhattan*. New York: Borough of Manhattan, 1928.
New York Board of Estimate and Apportionment. *Report of the Chief Engineer of the Board of Estimate and Apportionment of the City of New York for the Year 1922*. New York: S. L. Parsons, 1922.

———. *Report of the Chief Engineer of the Board of Estimate and Apportionment of the City of New York for the Year 1923*. New York: Stillman Appellate Printing, 1923.

———. *Report of the Chief Engineer of the Board of Estimate and Apportionment of the City of New York for the Year 1925*. New York: Stillman Appellate Printing, 1925.

———. *Report of the Chief Engineer of the Board of Estimate and Apportionment of the City of New York for the Year 1926*. New York: Hickey and Kischel, 1926.

———. *Report of the Chief Engineer of the Board of Estimate and Apportionment of the City of New York for the Year 1927*. New York: I. Smigel, 1927.

———. *Report of the Chief Engineer of the Board of Estimate and Apportionment of the City of New York for the Year 1928*. New York: Hickey and Kischel, 1928.

———. *Report of the Chief Engineer of the Board of Estimate and Apportionment of the City of New York for the Year 1929*. New York: M. B. Brown, 1929.

———. *Report of the Chief Engineer of the Board of Estimate and Apportionment of the City of New York for the Year 1930*. New York: Burland Printing, 1932.

New York Board of Estimate and Apportionment, Committee on the City Plan. *Development and Present Status of City Planning in New York City, Being the Report of the Committee on the City Plan, December 31, 1914, Together with Papers Presented at a Meeting of the Advisory Commission on City Plan, December 17, 1914*. New York: Board of Estimate and Apportionment, Committee on the City Plan, 1914.

New York City Improvement Commission. *The Report of the New York City Improvement Commission to George B. McClellan, and to the Board of Aldermen of the City of New York*. New York: New York City Improvement Commission, 1904.

———. *The Report of the New York City Improvement Commission to the Honorable George B. McClellan, Mayor of the City of New York and to the Honorable Board of Aldermen of the City of New York*. New York: Kalkhoff, 1907.

New York Public Service Commission for First District. *Dual System of Rapid Transit for New York City*. New York: n.p., 1912.

Origin and Destination of New York City's Vehicular Traffic: Staff Report to the Committee on a Regional Plan of New York and Its Environs, May 10, 1926. New York: Committee on Regional Plan of New York and Its Environs, 1926.

Plan to Increase the Capacity of the Miller Highway and Henry Hudson Parkway. [New York?]: Triborough Bridge and Tunnel Authority, [1965?].

Prior, J. H., consulting engineer. *Report to the Board of Local Improvements: The Work of M. J. Faherty, Associates and Staff, 1915–23*. [Chicago?]: n.p., 1923.

Regional Plan Association. *Metropolis in the Making: The Next Twenty-Five Years in the New York Metropolitan Region*. New York: Regional Plan Association, 1955.

Report of a Meeting Held at Chickering Hall, June 21, 1877, to Protest Against the Destruction of Property by Elevated Railroads without Compensation to Owners. New York: Thomas and Hagar, 1877.

Report of the Business and Transactions of the President of the Borough of Manhattan, City of New York. For the Year Ending December 31, 1931. New York: n.p., 1932.

Report of the Business and Transactions of the President of the Borough of Manhattan, City of New York. Julius Miller, President. For the Year Ending December 31, 1928. New York: n.p., 1929.

Report of the Business and Transactions of the President of the Borough of Manhattan, City of New York. Julius Miller, President. For the Year Ending December 31, 1929. New York: n.p., 1930.

Report of the Business and Transactions of the President of the Borough of Manhattan, City of New York. Julius Miller, President. For the Year Ending December 31, 1930. New York: n.p., 1931.

Seven Years of Progress: Important Public Improvements and Achievements by the Municipal and Borough Governments of the City of New York, 1918–1925. John F. Hylan,

Mayor. Report Submitted to the Board of Aldermen, March, 1925. New York, M. B. Brown, 1925.
Stoeckel, Robbins B. *City Motor Vehicle Traffic.* Bulletin no. 39, Hartford, CT: Department of Motor Vehicles, 1927.
Tippetts-Abbett-McCarthy-Stratton. *Report on the Boston Central Artery 1977 Origin-Destination Study.* Boston: Commonwealth of Massachusetts Department of Public Works, November 1978.
United States Federal Highway Administration. *West Side Highway Project Final Environmental Impact Statement.* N.p. 1976.
U.S. Bureau of the Census. *Historical Statistics of the United States, Colonial Times to 1970.* Bicentennial ed, part 2. Washington, DC: U.S. Government Printing Office, 1975.
———. *Statistical Abstract of the United States: 1970.* 91st ed. Washington, DC: U.S. Government Printing Office, 1970.
U.S. Department of Commerce. *Statistical Abstract of the United States: 1920.* 43rd ed. Washington, DC: U.S. Government Printing Office, 1921.
———. *Statistical Abstract of the United States: 1960.* 81st ed. Washington, DC: U.S. Government Printing Office, 1960.
Wacker, Charles H. *Annual Report for 1917 to the Chicago Plan Commission.* Chicago: Chicago Plan Commission, 1918.
———. *Chicago's Financial Needs.* Chicago: Chicago Plan Commission, 1919.
———. *An S-O-S to the Public Spirited Citizens of Chicago.* Chicago: n.p., 1924.

PRIMARY SOURCE BOOKS

Abbott, Berenice, and Elizabeth McCausland. *Changing New York.* New York: E. P. Dutton, 1939.
Adams, Thomas. *Planning the New York Region: An Outline of the Organization, Scope and Progress of the Regional Plan.* New York: Regional Plan of New York and Its Environs, 1927.
Addams, Jane. *Twenty Years at Hull House with Autobiographical Notes.* New York: Signet, 1960.
Bassett, Edward M., Frank B. Williams, Alfred Bettman, and Robert Whitten. *Model Laws for Planning Cities, Counties, and States; Including Zoning, Subdivision Regulation, and Protection of Official Map.* Cambridge, MA: Harvard University Press, 1935.
Bel Geddes, Norman. *Magic Motorways.* New York: Random House, 1940.
Bellamy, Edward. *Looking Backward, 2000–1887.* Boston: Houghton-Mifflin, 1915.
Bibbins, J. Rowland. *Relief of City Traffic, Booklet II: Mass-Transportation in Cities.* New York: National Automobile Chamber of Commerce, 1927.
Bradlee, Francis B. C. *The Boston and Lowell Railroad, the Nashua and Lowell Railroad, and the Salem and Lowell Railroad.* Salem, MA: Essex Institute, 1918.
Chambless, Edgar. *Roadtown.* New York: Roadtown Press, 1910.
Chicago Municipal Subway Co. *Rapid Transit Subways for Chicago Now.* [Chicago: Chicago Municipal Subway Co?], [1924?].
Dixon, Winifred Hawkridge. *Westward Hoboes: Ups and Downs of Frontier Motoring.* New York: Charles Scribner's Sons, 1924.
Ferriss, Hugh. *The Metropolis of Tomorrow.* New York: Princeton Architectural Press, 1986.
General Motors. *Announcement of Winners, Better Highways Awards Contest.* Detroit: General Motors, 1953.
Herlihy, Elisabeth M., ed. *Fifty Years of Boston: A Memorial Volume Issued in Commemoration of the Tercentenary of 1930.* Boston: Subcommittee on Memorial History of the Boston Tercentenary Committee, 1932.
Highway Research Board. *Controlled Access Expressways in Urban Areas: A Symposium.* Bulletin no. 25. Washington: Highway Research Board, 1950.

Huxley, Aldous. *Brave New World.* New York: Harper Perennial, 1998.
International City and Regional Planning Conference. *Planning Problems of Town, City and Region: Papers and Discussions at the International City and Regional Planning Conference.* Baltimore: Norman Remington, 1925.
King, Moses, ed. *King's Handbook of New York City: An Outline History and Description of the American Metropolis.* 2nd ed. New York: Benjamin Blom, 1972.
———, ed. *King's Views of New York 1896–1915 & Brooklyn 1905.* Reprint, New York: Arno Press, 1980.
Knowles, Morris. *City Planning as a Permanent Solution of the Traffic Problem.* National Conference on City Planning, Proceedings, 1925.
Lafferty, Robert C. *The Lafferty Plan: Transit, Traffic, Freight: A Comprehensive True Transportation System of Airways and Speedways for Large Cities.* New York: Culture Press, 1929.
Le Corbusier. *The City of Tomorrow and Its Planning.* Translated by Frederick Etchells. 1929. Reprint, Cambridge, MA: MIT Press, 1971.
———. *Towards a New Architecture.* Translated by Frederick Etchells. 1931. Reprint, New York: Dover Publications, 1986.
———. *Urbanisme.* Paris: G. Cres, 1925.
Lewis, Nelson P. *The Planning of the Modern City: A Review of the Principles Governing City Planning.* 2nd ed. New York: John Wiley and Sons, 1923.
Mackaye, Benton. *Highway Approaches to Boston: A Wayside Situation and What to Do about It.* Boston: Trustees of Public Reservations, 1931.
Moody, Walter D. *Wacker's Manual of the Plan of Chicago; Municipal Economy.* 3rd ed. Chicago: Chicago Plan Commission, 1920.
Moses King Corporation. *King's Hand-Book of Boston.* 4th ed. Cambridge, MA: Moses King, 1881.
National Motor Truck Committee, National Automobile Chamber of Commerce. *Place of Train, Trolley, Truck and Bus in New England: Abstracts and Resolutions Adopted at New England Motor Transport Conference, Boston, December 8 and 9, 1924.* New York: National Automobile Chamber of Commerce, 1924.
Proceedings of the Fifth National Conference on City Planning, Chicago, Illinois, May 5–7, 1913. Boston: n.p., 1913.
Saarinen, Eliel. *The City: Its Growth, Its Decay, Its Future.* New York: Reinhold, 1943.
Sitte, Camillo. *City Planning according to Artistic Principles.* Translated by George R. Collins and Christiane Crasemann Collins. New York: Random House, 1965.
Snyder, George Duncan. *City Passenger-Transportation in the United States.* London: Institution of Civil Engineers, 1913.
Sweetser, M. F. *King's Handbook of Boston Harbor.* 3rd ed. Boston: Moses King, 1888.
Wilgus, William J. *Proposed New Railway System for the Transportation and Distribution of Freight by Improved Methods in the City and Port of New York.* New York: Amsterdam, 1908.
Wright, Frank Lloyd. *The Disappearing City.* New York: William Farquhar Payson, 1932.
———. *Modern Architecture: Being the Kahn Lectures for 1930.* Princeton Monographs in Art and Archaeology. Princeton, NJ: Princeton University Press, 1931.

PRIMARY SOURCE NEWSPAPERS

Boston Globe
Chicago Tribune
Christian Science Monitor
Los Angeles Times
New York Times
Washington Post

PRIMARY SOURCE ARTICLES

"$19,000,000 Highway Plan Adopted: Big Civic Program for Improving Metropolitan District Arteries Goes to Governor; Seabury Takes Winans' Place as Chairman." *Chicago Commerce* September 28, 1929: 11, 27.

Ackerman, Frederick L. "Our Stake in Congestion." *The Survey* 54, no. 3 (1 May 1925): 141–142.

"And How About This? The Henckenway—An Urban Microcosm." *American City* 36, no. 6 (June 1927): 802–803.

"And This? Dr. John A. Harriss Proposes Six-Deck Streets." *American City* 36, no. 6 (June 1927): 803–805.

"Architectural Control by Organized Effort for New and Widened Streets." *American City* 41, no. 4 (October 1929): 181.

"Automobile Men See Parking Need." *Electric Railway Journal* 72, no. 24 (December 15, 1928): 1053–1054.

Ball, Charles B. "The Promotion of Zoning in Chicago." *American City* 28, no. 1 (January 1923): 11–14.

———. "'What of the City': Chicago: Vision—Planning—Promotion—Realization." Reprint from *City Planning* (January and July 1926).

Barnett, Joseph. "Expressways in Relieving Urban Traffic Congestion." *Traffic Engineering* 23, no. 5 (February 1953): 167–169, 172.

Bartholomew, Harland. "Reduction of Street Traffic Congestion by Proper Street Design—How St. Louis Is Meeting Its Problem," in "The Automobile: Its Province and Its Problems," special issue, *Annals of the American Academy of Political and Social Science* 116 (November 1924): 244–246.

Bel Geddes, Norman, as told to Maxwell Hamilton. "Traffic and Transit in the World of Tomorrow." *Transit Journal* 83, no. 8 (August 1939): 272–273, 290–291.

Bibbins, J. Rowland. "Traffic-Transportation Planning and Metropolitan Development: The Need of an Adequate Program," in "The Automobile: Its Province and Its Problems," special issue, *Annals of the American Academy of Political and Social Science* 116 (November 1924): 205–214.

"Big Subway Is Open: Boston's First Underground Trolley in Operation." *Chicago Daily Tribune*, September 2, 1897, 7.

"Billion-Dollar Plan for Chicago Transit." *Electric Railway Journal* 69, no. 4 (January 22, 1927): 154–156.

"Bond Issues and Your Greater Chicago." *Chicago Commerce* (April 10, 1926): 7–8.

"The Boston Electric Subway." *Scientific American* 75, no. 10 (September 5, 1896): 197.

"The Boston Subway." *Scientific American* 73, no. 9 (August 31, 1895): 135.

"Boston's Subway Finished: After Many Protests and Complaints Rapid Transit for the Hub Is Assured." *New York Times*, August 15, 1897, 10.

Brainerd, Harry B., A.I.A. "Considering the Street Picture: A Responsibility Too Long Neglected by Architects and Civic Improvement Bodies." *American City* 44, no. 3 (March 1931): 114–115.

Bright, John Irwin. "The Plan of Philadelphia," in "The Automobile: Its Province and Its Problems," special issue, *Annals of the American Academy of Political and Social Science* 116 (November 1924): 231–235.

"Business Men Seek Best Traction Plan." *Chicago Commerce* (April 8, 1922): 5–6, 12.

Buttenheim, Harold S. "Spaciousness in the City Plan—Its Economic and Civic Importance—II." *American City* 41, no. 6 (December 1929): 123–126.

"Cars under the Hub: Boston's Subway Solves Congested Traffic Problem." *Chicago Daily Tribune*, September 5, 1897, 34.

Chapin, Roy D. "The Motor's Part in Transportation," in "The Automobile: Its Province and

Its Problems," special issue, *Annals of the American Academy of Political and Social Science* 116 (November 1924): 1–8.
"Chicago Double Deck Street for Congested District." *Engineering News-Record* 85 (July 1920): 173–175.
"Chicago Plan Involves Ten Big Projects." *Chicago Commerce* (June 14, 1924): 9–10.
"Chicago Plans Air-Right Roads." *Engineering News-Record* 100, no. 21 (May 24, 1928): 827.
"Chicago Street Traffic Survey Finished." *Chicago Commerce* (September 25, 1926): 9–10.
"A Chicago Traffic Problem Solved by a Week-End Job." *American City* 45, no. 6 (December 1931): 75–76.
Child, Stephen. "Restricted Traffic District Proposed: A Suggestion for Solving the Problem of Extreme Traffic Congestion in the Central Portions of Cities, by an Extension of the Zoning Principle." *American City* 36, no. 4 (April 1927): 507–511.
"Completion of Part of the Boston Subway." *Scientific American* 78, no. 12 (September 18, 1897): 177, 184.
Corbett, Harvey Wiley. "Different Levels for Foot, Wheel and Rail." *American City* 31, no. 1 (July 1924): 2–6.
———. "The Problem of Traffic Congestion, and a Solution." *Architectural Forum* 46, no. 3 (March 1927): 201–208.
Cox, William J. "By-Passing Cities in the Vertical Plane." *American City* 60, no. 10 (October 1945): 95.
Crandell, John S. "Shall We Abolish Sleep?" *American City* 38 (February 1928): 82.
Delano, Frederic A. "Skyscrapers." *American City* 34, no. 1 (January 1926): 1–9.
"Designate Skyway No. 2 from Seattle to Boston." *Chicago Daily Tribune*, March 22, 1948, A1.
"Dever Gives His Views on Public Issues." *Chicago Commerce* (March 24, 1923): 13–14, 26.
"Dever Makes Plea for Traction Ordinance." *Chicago Commerce* (February 21, 1925): 7–8, 24–26.
"Disputes of Architects: Question about the Invention of the Skeleton Construction. The Tower Building Tablet—Messrs. Birkmire and Gilbert's Contradictory Claims—Chicago's Fight for Her Own Skyscrapers." *New York Times*, August 19, 1899: 12.
"Double-Deck Streets as a Relief for Traffic Congestion." *Scientific American* (June 22, 1907): 510.
Eaton, Walter Prichard. "The 'Good Roads' Delusion." *New York Herald Tribune Magazine*, March 27, 1932, 4–5, 31.
"Elevated Highways Only Solution to Traffic Congestion." *Architect and Engineer* 137 (April 1939): 50–52.
"Elevated Highways versus Depressed Highways: Excerpts from Report of Committee on Elevated Highways of American Road Builders' Association." *American City* 55, no. 10 (October 1940): 61–62.
"Elevated Railway Noises: A Grievous Nuisance That Comes with Warm Weather." *New York Times*, June 3, 1879, 8.
"Elevated Road for Boston: Free Transfer System of Novelty to Be Introduced." *New York Times*, June 11, 1897, 1.
Eliot, Charles W., II. "The Influence of the Automobile on the Design of Park Roads." *Landscape Architecture* 13, no. 1 (October 1922): 27–39.
"Engineers Grapple with Street Congestion." *Chicago Commerce*, February 9, 1924, 15–16.
"Establishing Rapid Transit." *New York Times*, June 6, 1878, 8.
"Facilitating Traffic and Preventing Blight by Spacious Planning of Express Highways." *American City* 45, no. 2 (August 1931): 80.
"First Autos Travel Express Road Unit." *New York Times*, October 28, 1930, 23.
Flagg, Ernest. "The City of the Future: Proper Design of Highways, Buildings and Sidewalks

Will Reduce City Congestion to a Comfortable Level." *Scientific American* 137 (September 1927): 238–241.

"A Four-Way Sunken Speedway Proposal Is Submitted for New York's Christie-Forsyth Area." *American City* 45, no. 1 (July 1931): 91.

"Freeway Is Now Urged: Protected Border Express Roads Advocated for New York Region." *New York Times*, December 13, 1936, XX16.

"The Future of the Motor Car." *Scientific American* 77, no. 3 (July 17, 1897): 35.

Gernsback, Hugo. "Solving Metropolitan Traffic Congestion." *Science and Invention* 14, no. 11 (March 1927): 1002–1003.

"Getting to Boston's Heart." *American City* 73 (July 1958): 131.

Goodrich, Ernest P. "The Urban Auto Problem." *National Municipal Review*, July 1920, 435–443.

Goodrich, Ernest P., and Harold M. Lewis. "Projects for Relief of Traffic Congestion in New York and Its Environs." *American City* 21 no. 1 (July 1924): 29–31.

"Graybar Building, 420 Lexington Avenue, New York City, Sloan and Robertson, Architects." *The Architect* 9, no. 2 (November 1927): 197–202.

"The Graybar Building, New York City." *Architecture and Building* 59, no.6 (June 1927): 178–192.

"The Greenwich Village Waterfront: Its Place in West Side Development." *Village Views* 3, no. 4 (Fall 1986): 2–31.

Gunlock, V. E. "Chicago Builds $230,000,000 Superhighway System." *Civil Engineering* 21 (February 1951): 38–39.

Hale, Hal H. "Federal Aid for Urban Highways." *Traffic Engineering* (May 1945): 304–308.

Harbeson, John F. "The Automobile and the 'Home' of the Future," in "The Automobile: Its Province and Its Problems," special issue, *Annals of the American Academy of Political and Social Science* 116 (November 1924): 58–60.

Harder, Julius F. "The City's Plan." *Municipal Affairs* 2, no. 1 (March 1898): 25–45.

Hénard, E. "The Cities of the Future." *American City* 4 (January 1911): 27–31.

Herlihy, Elisabeth M. "Planning for Boston—1630–1930." *City Planning* 6, no. 1 (January 1930): 1–13.

Holleran, Leslie G. "Problems in the Separations of Highway Grade Crossings." *American City* 38, no. 3 (March 1928): 75–77.

Hooper, Parker Morse. "Modern Architectural Decoration." *Architectural Forum* 48, no. 2 (February 1928): 153–175.

"How to Analyze an Express Highway." *American City* 60, no. 5 (May 1945): 13.

Hylan, John F. "New York's Silver Jubilee Exposition." *American City* 29, no. 1 (July 1923): 3–7.

Iden, V. G. "Elevated Highway Design for Speed, Safety and Beauty." *American City* 53, no. 5 (May 1938): 46–48.

Ihlder, John. "The Automobile and Community Planning," in "The Automobile: Its Province and Its Problems," special issue, *Annals of the American Academy of Political and Social Science* 116 (November 1924): 199–205.

———. "Rehabilitation of Blighted Areas: The Part of City Planning." *City Planning* 6, no. 2 (April 1930): 106–118.

Ingraham, Joseph C. "Boston to Chicago: New Section of Thruway Completes Express Route between Cities." *New York Times*, May 24, 1959, XX1.

Isaacs, Stanley M. "New Land Acquisition Procedure Benefits City and Landowners." *American City* 54, no. 9 (September 1939): 57–58.

"Is New York to Lose Commercial Supremacy?" *New York Times*, December 8, 1907, SM1.

"Is Super-Congestion Inevitable?" *American City* 36, no. 6 (June 1927): 800.

Jenkins, Chas. E. "A White Enameled Building." *Architectural Record* 4, no. 3 (January–March 1895): 299–306.

Kelcey, George C. "Traffic Problems of the Large City: What They Were and How They Were Met in a Thoroughly Typical Case." *Scientific American* 131 (October 1924): 236–237, 294.

Kellogg, Paul U. "Boston's Level Best: The '1915 Movement' and the Work of Civic Organizing for Which It Stands." *Survey* 22 (June 5, 1909): 382–396.

Kincaid, H. Evert. "Depressed Highways for Fast Traffic That Pay a Toll, Are Coming." *National Real Estate Journal* 44 (December 1943): 12–13, 15.

"'L' Roads and Property Owners." *Chicago Daily Tribune*, January 27, 1890, 6.

Lamb, Charles Rollinson. "Civic Architecture from its Constructive Side." *City Planning* 6, no. 2 (April 1930): 46–72.

"Launch Attack on Street Traffic Problem." *Chicago Commerce*, February 6, 1926, 7–8, 18, 25–27.

Laurence, F. S. "The Pershing Square Building." *American Architect and the Architectural Review* 124 (October 10, 1923): 319–324.

Lavis, F., and S. Johannesson. "New Jersey Extension of Holland Tunnel Highway." *Engineering News-Record* 100, no. 1 (January 5, 1928): 4–8.

Lee, Anne. "Chicago's Traffic Problems Solved by Burnham Plan." *Architectural Record* 62, no. 4 (October 1927): 262–272.

Lenth, George C. D. "Analysis of the Traffic Count in Downtown Chicago." *Journal of the Western Society of Engineers* 23, no. 2 (February 1918): 79–169.

Lewis, Harold M. "The New York City Motor Traffic Problem," in "The Automobile: Its Province and Its Problems," special issue, *Annals of the American Academy of Political and Social Science* 116 (November 1924): 214–223.

Lochner, Harry W. "Traffic Surveys Essential in Planning Urban Expressways." *Concrete Highways and Public Improvements* 25, no. 2 (Winter 1944): 3–10.

Macauley, Alvan. "Adapting the City to the Automobile." *Public Works* 55, no. 9 (September 1924):285–286.

Mackaye, Benton. "Roads vs. Shuttles: The Lesson of the Mohawk Trail on Hoosac Mountain." *American City* 44, no. 3 (March 1931): 125–126.

Mackaye, Benton, and Lewis Mumford. "Townless Highways for the Motorist: A Proposal for the Automobile Age." *Harper's Monthly Magazine*, August 1931, 347–356.

Malcher, Fritz. "A Traffic Planner Imagines a City." *American City* 44, no. 3 (March 1931): 134–135.

Malley, Frank H. "Thoroughfare Plans and Urban Areas." *Civil Engineering* 7, no. 12 (December 1937): 851–854.

Marshall, Edward. "The Scientific City of the Future: An Authorized Interview with Thomas A. Edison." *The Forum*, December 1926, 823–829.

McBride, Paul E. "Already Overloaded." *American City* 75 (September 1960): 121.

McCarthy, Ray. "For More 'Hub' and Less 'Hubbub.'" *Real Estate*, January 11, 1941, 6–7, 11–12.

McClintock, Miller. "Preventive and Palliative Measures for Street Traffic Relief." *City Planning* 6, no. 2 (April 1930): 99–105.

McClintock, Miller, as told to Maxwell Hamilton. "The Place of Transit in the World of Tomorrow." *Transit Journal* 83, no. 6 (June 1939): 188–189, 223.

Miller, Richard A. "Expressway Blight." *Architectural Forum* 111, no. 4 (October 1959): 159–163.

"A Million Dollars' Worth of Ideas on City and Regional Planning." *American City* 41, no. 1 (July 1929): 81–85.

Moller, Irving C. "Guiding the Traffic Flow." *Annals of the American Academy of Political and Social Science* 133 (September 1927): 114–120.

Moses, Robert. "New York's West Side Development at Night." *American City* 53, no. 2 (February 1938): 115–116.

Mumford, Lewis. "The Fourth Migration." *The Survey* 54, no. 3 (May 1, 1925): 130–133.

"Must We Come to This?" *American City* 36, no. 6 (June 1927): 801.

"The New Filene Store Building, Boston, Mass." *The Brickbuilder* 21, no. 9 (September 1912): 247–250.

"New Parking Ordinance in Chicago." *Electric Railway Journal* 72, no. 24 (December 15, 1928): 1054.

"New Roads: The U.S. Tackles Its Traffic." *Time*, January 24, 1955, 75–78.

"New Through-Traffic Parkway in New York City." *American City* 50, no. 7 (July 1935): 79.

"New York's West Side Improvement." *American City* 52, no. 11 (November 1937): 52.

"New York to Have a $13,500,000 Elevated Express Highway." *American City* 35, no. 1 (July 1926): 8–10.

"No Town Too Small for City Planning." *American City* 29, no. 1 (July 1923): 1–2.

"Office-Building Projects: Some Comparisons between Office-Buildings of Chicago and of New York." *Chicago Daily Tribune*, August 9, 1891, 14.

"Opening of a New Elevated Steam Railway in New York City." *Scientific American* 38, no. 20 (May 18, 1878): 315.

Parker, William Stanley, F.A.I.A. "The Work of the Boston City Planning Board." *American Architect*, November 20, 1928, 700–702.

Phillips, T. Glenn. "The Traffic Problems in Detroit and How They Are Met," in "The Automobile: Its Province and Its Problems," special issue, *Annals of the American Academy of Political and Social Science* 116 (November 1924): 241–243.

"Pictures and Paragraphs from Near and Far." *American City* 42, no. 6 (June 1930): 136–139.

"Plan for Using the Chicago River as a Driveway Submitted by Angus Hibbard." *Chicago Commerce*, February 24, 1923, 13.

Plotkin, A. S. "Biggest Wrecking Job in Bay State History." *Boston Globe*, May 26, 1952, n.p. Boston Globe Library.

Price, Matlack. "The Chanin Building, Sloan and Robertson Architects." *Architectural Forum* 1, no. 5 (May 1929): 699–731.

"Projects for Relief of Traffic Congestion in New York and Its Environs." *American City* 31, no. 1 (July 1924): 29–31.

Quigley, John J. "Utilizing Manhattan's Present Traffic Facilities." *National Municipal Review*, September 1929, 558–562.

"Rail Terminals Increase Traffic Jams." *Chicago Commerce*, November 13, 1926, 13.

"Raised Sidewalks and Traffic Separation Urged for Chicago." *American City* 35, no. 3 (September 1926): 334–336.

"Rapid Transit across Chicago: A Scheme for an Elevated Road from Evanston to Blue Island." *Chicago Daily Tribune*, August 21, 1891, 12.

"Rapid Transit and Trade: New Channels for Business." *New York Times*, June 18, 1878, 8.

"Reducing Loop Peak Traffic Loads." *Chicago Commerce*, March 2, 1929, 7–8.

Reeve, Sidney A. "Congestion in Cities." *Geographical Review* 3, no. 4 (April 1917): 278–293.

Richards, A. G. "Creating a World Famous Street." *Fine Arts Journal* 33, no. 3 (September 1915): 373–385.

Ridgway, Robert. "Engineering New York's New Subway." *The Bulletin* 16, no. 12 (December 1925): 188–191.

"Running on the L." *Chicago Daily Tribune*, June 7, 1892, 9.

Schermerhorn, Richard, Jr. "A Practical Program for the Protection and Development of Roadside Beauty." *American City* 42, no. 3 (March 1930): 140.

"Shall We Have Double-Decked Streets?" *Scientific American* 88, no. 17 (April 25, 1903): 310.

Shurtleff, Arthur A. "Boston Metropolitan Planning." *City Planning* 6, no. 1 (January 1930): 14–22.

Simmons, Lewis G. "The Solution of Big Cities' Traffic Problems." *Illustrated World*, October 1917, 266–269.
"Sky-scrapers and Traffic." *Literary Digest*, March 5, 1927, 21–22.
Slosson, Edwin E. "Back to Nature? Never! Forward to the Machine." *The Independent* 101 (January 3, 1920): 5–6, 37.
"South Water Street Improvement as Proposed by Chicago Plan Commission." *Chicago Commerce*, November 22, 1917, 14–15.
"Start Parks and Stop Skyscrapers!" *American City* 35, no. 3 (September 1926): 316–318.
Stein, Clarence S. "Dinosaur Cities." *The Survey* 54, no. 3 (May 1, 1925): 134–138.
Stote, Amos. "The Ideal American City." *McBride's Magazine*, April 9, 1916, 89–99.
"Street Traffic Tangles Being Unravelled [*sic*]." *Chicago Commerce*, March 13, 1926, 7–8.
Streich, William F. "A Plan for Multiplying the Utility of Business Thoroughfares." *American City* 8 (March 1913): 275–276.
"Subways for Chicago: Trunk Lines May Be Connected at an Expense of $10,000,000." *New York Times*, March 30, 1897, 2.
"Super-Streets and Subways: Tentative Details of a Traffic Plan Recommended for New York City." *Scientific American* (September 1924): 149.
Swan, Herbert S. "The Parkway as a Traffic Artery." *American City* 45, no. 5 (November 1931): 73–76.
T.A.J. "Elevated Railways: Objections to Their Introduction into Chicago—Experience of New York." *Chicago Daily Tribune* June 16, 1879: 2.
Taylor, E. S. "The Plan of Chicago in 1924," in "The Automobile: Its Province and Its Problems," special issue, *Annals of the American Academy of Political and Social Science* 116 (November 1924): 224–231.
Taylor, Eugene S. "A Comprehensive System of Elevated Super-Highways." *City Planning* 7, no. 2 (April 1931): 118–120.
"To Have Street in the Air." *Washington Post*, March 22, 1908, M5.
Tompkins, Raymond S. "Are We Solving the Traffic Problem?" *American Mercury*, February 1929, 153–162.
"Traction Plan Approved by Association." *Chicago Commerce*, February 28, 1925, 11–12, 28.
"Traffic and City Streets." *Public Works* 55, no. 2 (February 1924): 44–47.
"Traffic Congestion in Manhattan." *Scientific American* (January 1903): 18–19.
"Trafficking in Humor." *American City* 36, no. 4 (April 1927): 511.
"Traffic Ordinance Goes to Committee." *Chicago Commerce*, January 8, 1927, 15.
"The Traffic Problem." *Engineers and Engineering* 47, no. 9 (September 1930): 235–239.
Turner, Daniel L. "Is There a Vicious Circle of Transit Development and City Congestion?" *American City* 35, no. 3 (September 1926): 314–315.
———. "Rapid Transit Progress in Detroit, Pittsburgh and Northern New Jersey." *The Bulletin* 16, no. 12 (December 1925): 191–195.
Uncle Dudley, "Get Off the Earth," *Boston Globe*, June 6, 1923, 16.
"Under the Elephants." *Architectural Forum* 111, no. 6 (December 1959): 206.
Unwin, Raymond. "America Revisited—A City Planner's Impressions." *American City* 28 (April 1923): 334–336.
"Value of South Water St. Changes Shown." *Chicago Commerce*, May 31, 1924, 11–12.
Vickers, S. J. "Graybar Building." *Architectural Record* 188, no. 3 (September 1927): 177–189.
"Views Differ Regarding the L Loop." *Chicago Daily Tribune*, February 10, 1893, 3.
Waldon, Colonel Sidney D. "Width of Right-of-Way the Foundation of a Rational Highway System." *American City* 37, no. 1 (July 1927): 45–46.
Walsh, George Ethelbert. "Traffic Congestion in New York." *Cassier's Magazine*, June 1908, 151–155.

Weeks, J. Borton. "Philadelphia's Traffic Problems and Their Solution," in "The Automobile: Its Province and Its Problems," special issue, *Annals of the American Academy of Political and Social Science* 116 (November 1924): 235–240.

"West Side Improvement, New York City, Department of Parks." *Architectural Forum* 67, no. 6 (December 1937): 475–477.

Whitten, Robert H. "Unchoking Our Congested Streets." *American City* 23 (October 1920): 351–354.

"Why Not Make Motor Travel as Stimulating to the Eye as It Is to the Speedometer?" *American City* 61, no. 4 (October 1929): 121.

Wilbur, Ray Lyman. "Must Our Fine Highways Be Bordered by Bewildering Signs, Tawdry Buildings, Weeds, Waster Paper and Old Cans?" *American City* 41, no. 1 (July 1929): 85.

Wright, John L. "Boston's Useful Subway: A Minute Description of This Great Enterprise of New England's Busy City." *New York Times*, October 10, 1897, 21.

Young, Hugh E. "Ten-Mile $60,000,000 Motor Express Highway Proposed for Chicago." *American City* 38, no. 3 (March 1928): 91–92.

SECONDARY SOURCES

SECONDARY SOURCE BOOKS

Abramson, Daniel M. *Skyscraper Rivals: The AIG Building and the Architecture of Wall Street.* New York: Princeton Architectural Press, 2001.

Adas, Michael. *Machines as the Measure of Men: Science, Technology, and Ideologies of Western Dominance.* Cornell Studies in Comparative History. Ithaca, NY: Cornell University Press, 1989.

Agrest, Diana, ed. *A Romance with the City: Irwin S. Chanin.* New York: Cooper Union Press, 1982.

American Institute of Architects, and Kathleen Nagle. *Architecture Chicago: Contemporary Architecture and Interiors.* Architecture Chicago 12. Chicago: American Institute of Architects, Chicago Chapter, 1994.

Appleyard, Donald, Kevin Lynch, and John R. Myer. *The View from the Road.* Cambridge, MA: MIT Press, 1966.

Armi, C. Edson. *The Art of American Car Design: The Profession and Personalities.* University Park: Pennsylvania State University Press, 1988.

Avila, Eric. *The Folklore of the Freeway: Race and Revolt in the Modernist City.* Minneapolis: University of Minnesota Press, 2014.

Ballon, Hilary, and Kenneth T. Jackson, eds. *Robert Moses and the Modern City: The Transformation of New York.* New York: W. W. Norton, 2007.

Banham, Reyner. *Megastructure: Urban Futures of the Recent Past.* London: Thames and Hudson, 1976.

Barnett, Jonathan. *The Elusive City: Five Centuries of Design, Ambition and Miscalculation.* New York: Harper and Row, 1986.

Barrett, Paul. *The Automobile and Urban Transit: The Formation of Public Policy in Chicago, 1900–1930.* Technology and Urban Growth Series. Philadelphia: Temple University Press, 1983.

Baumbach, Richard O., Jr., and William E. Borah. *The Second Battle of New Orleans: A History of the Vieux Carré Riverfront-Expressway Controversy.* Tuscaloosa: University of Alabama Press for Preservation Press, National Trust for Historic Preservation, 1981.

Beatty, Jack. *The Rascal King: The Life and Times of James Michael Curley, 1874–1958.* Reading, MA: Addison-Wesley, 1992.

Benton, Charlotte, Tim Benton, and Ghislaine Wood, eds. *Art Deco 1910–1939.* London: V and A Publications, 2003.

Berger, Michael L. *The Devil Wagon in God's Country: The Automobile and Social Change in Rural America, 1893–1929.* Hamden, CT: Archon Books, 1979.

Berman, Marshall. *All That Is Solid Melts into Air: The Experience of Modernity.* New York: Penguin, 1988.

Black, Edwin. *Internal Combustion: How Corporations and Governments Addicted the World to Oil and Derailed the Alternatives.* New York: St. Martin's, 2006.

Blake, Angela M. *How New York Became American, 1890–1924.* Baltimore: Johns Hopkins University Press, 2006.

Blanke, David. *Hell on Wheels: The Promise and Peril of America's Car Culture, 1900–1940.* Lawrence: University Press of Kansas, 2007.

Bluestone, Daniel. *Constructing Chicago.* New Haven, CT: Yale University Press, 1991.

Bogart, Michele H. *The Politics of Urban Beauty: New York and Its Art Commission.* Chicago: University of Chicago Press, 2006.

Boston 200 Neighborhood History Series. Boston: Boston 200 Corporation, 1976.

Boyer, Christine. *Manhattan Manners, Architecture and Style, 1850–1900.* New York: Rizzoli, 1985.

Brooklyn Museum of Art. *The American Renaissance, 1876–1917.* Brooklyn: Brooklyn Museum of Art, 1979.

Buttenwieser, Ann L. *Manhattan Water-Bound: Planning and Developing Manhattan's Waterfront from the Seventeenth Century to the Present.* New York: New York University Press, 1987.

Caro, Robert A. *The Power Broker: Robert Moses and the Fall of New York.* New York: Vintage Books, 1975.

Cheape, Charles W. *Moving the Masses: Urban Public Transit in New York, Boston, and Philadelphia—1880–1912.* Cambridge, MA: Harvard University Press, 1980.

Cherry, Gordon E., ed. *Shaping an Urban World.* New York: St. Martin's Press, 1980.

Chicago and New York: Architectural Interactions. Chicago: The Art Institute of Chicago, 1984.

Choay, Francoise. *The Modern City: Planning in the 19th Century.* Planning and Cities Series. New York: George Braziller, 1969.

City of New York, Landmarks Preservation Commission. *Chanin Building Designation Report.* November 14, 1978.

———. *Fred F. French Building Landmark Designation Report.* March 18, 1986.

———. *Upper East Side Historic District Designation Report.* New York, 1981.

Condit, Carl W. *Chicago, 1910–1929: Building, Planning, and Urban Technology.* Chicago: University of Chicago Press, 1973.

———. *The Chicago School of Architecture: A History of Commercial and Public Building in the Chicago Area, 1875–1925.* Chicago: University of Chicago Press, 1964.

———. *The Port of New York.* Vol. 1, *A History of the Rail and Terminal System from the Beginnings to Pennsylvania Station.* Chicago: University of Chicago Press, 1980.

———. *The Port of New York.* Vol. 2, *A History of the Rail and Terminal System from the Grand Central Electrification to the Present.* Chicago: University of Chicago Press, 1981.

———. *The Rise of the Skyscraper.* Chicago: University of Chicago Press, 1952.

Corn, Joseph J., ed. *Imagining Tomorrow: History, Technology, and the American Future.* Cambridge, MA: MIT Press, 1986.

Corn, Joseph J., and Brian Horrigan. *Yesterday's Tomorrows: Past Visions of the American Future.* Edited by Katherine Chambers. Baltimore: Johns Hopkins University Press, 1996.

Cowan, Ruth Schwartz. *A Social History of American Technology.* New York: Oxford University Press, 1997.

Cronon, William. *Nature's Metropolis: Chicago and the Great West.* New York: W. W. Norton, 1991.

Cudahy, Brian J. *Change at Park Street Under: The Story of Boston's Subways*. Brattleboro, VT: Stephen Greene Press, 1972.

Davidson, Janet F., and Michael S. Sweeney. *On the Move: Transportation and the American Story*. Washington, DC: National Geographic Society, 2003.

De Long, David, ed. *Frank Lloyd Wright: Designs for an American Landscape, 1922–1932*. New York: Harry N. Abrams, 1996.

De Marco, William M. *Ethnics and Enclaves: Boston's Italian North End*. Studies in American History and Culture 31. Ann Arbor, MI: UMI Research, 1981.

DiMento, Joseph F. C., and Cliff Ellis. *Changing Lanes: Visions and Histories of Urban Freeways*. Cambridge, MA: MIT Press, 2012.

Domosh, Mona. *Invented Cities: The Creation of Landscape in Nineteenth-Century New York and Boston*. New Haven, CT: Yale University Press, 1996.

Draper, Joan E. *Edward H. Bennett: Architect and City Planner, 1874–1954*. Chicago: Art Institute of Chicago, 1982.

Duncan, Alastair. *American Art Deco*. London: Thames and Hudson, 1986.

Eaton, Ruth. *Ideal Cities: Utopianism and the (Un)Built Environment*. New York: Thames and Hudson, 2002.

Ellis, Clifford Donald. "Visions of Urban Freeways, 1930–1970." Ph.D. diss., City and Regional Planning. University of California, Berkeley, 1990.

Fein, Michael R. "Public Works: New York Road Building and the American State, 1880–1956." Ph.D. diss., American History, Brandeis University, 2003.

Field, Cynthia R. "The City Planning of Daniel Hudson Burnham." Ph.D. diss., Columbia University, 1974.

Finstein, Amy D. "Harbinger of Change: Boston's Central Artery and the Arrival of the Automobile Age in an Old New England City." M.Arch.Hist. thesis, Architectural History, University of Virginia, 2002.

Fishman, Robert, ed. *The American Planning Tradition: Culture and Policy*. Washington, DC: Woodrow Wilson Center Press; dist. Johns Hopkins University Press, Baltimore, 2000.

———. *Bourgeois Utopias: The Rise and Fall of Suburbia*. New York: Basic Books, 1987.

———. *Urban Utopias in the Twentieth Century: Ebenezer Howard, Frank Lloyd Wright, and Le Corbusier*. New York: Basic Books, 1977.

Flink, James J. *American Adopts the Automobile, 1895–1910*. Cambridge, MA: MIT Press, 1970.

———. *The Car Culture*. Cambridge, MA: MIT Press, 1975.

Fogelson, Robert M. *Downtown: Its Rise and Fall, 1880–1950*. New Haven, CT: Yale University Press, 2001.

Foglesong, Richard E. *Planning the Capitalist City: The Colonial Era to the 1920s*. Princeton, NJ: Princeton University Press, 1986.

Foster, Mark. *From Streetcar to Superhighway: American City Planners and Urban Transportation, 1900–1940*. Technology and Urban Growth Series. Philadelphia: Temple University Press, 1981.

Fotsch, Paul Mason. *Watching the Traffic Go By: Transportation and Isolation in Urban America*. Austin: University of Texas Press, 2007.

Gakenheimer, Ralph. *Transportation Planning as Response to Controversy: The Boston Case*. Cambridge, MA: MIT, 1976.

Gartman, David. *Auto Opium: A Social History of American Automobile Design*. New York: Routledge, 1994.

Gelernter, David. *1939: The Lost World of the Fair*. New York: Free Press, 1995.

Goddard, Stephen B. *Getting There: The Epic Struggle between Road and Rail in the American Century*. New York: Basic–HarperCollins, 1994.

Goldberger, Paul. *The Skyscraper*. New York: Alfred A. Knopf, 1981.

Grant, H. Roger, ed. *We Took the Train*. Dekalb: Northern Illinois University Press, 1990.

Gutfreund, Owen D. *Twentieth-Century Sprawl: Highways and the Reshaping of the American Landscape*. New York: Oxford University Press, 2004.

Hall, Peter. *Cities in Civilization: Culture, Innovation, and Urban Order*. London: Weidenfeld and Nicolson, 1998.

Halprin, Lawrence. *Freeways*. New York: Reinhold, 1966.

Harmon, Robert B. *Raymond M. Hood and the American Skyscraper: A Selected Bibliography*. Architecture Series, Bibliography A206. Monticello, IL: Vance Bibliographies, 1980.

Hart, Steven. *The Last Three Miles: Politics, Murder, and the Construction of America's First Superhighway*. New York: New Press, 2007.

Hayden, Dolores. *Building Suburbia: Green Fields and Urban Growth, 1820–2000*. New York: Pantheon, 2003.

———. *The Power of Place: Urban Landscapes as Public History*. Cambridge, MA: MIT Press, 1997.

Hines, Thomas S. *Burnham of Chicago: Architect and Planner*. New York: Oxford University Press, 1974.

Hirsch, Arnold R., and Raymond A. Mohl, eds. *Urban Policy in Twentieth-Century America*. New Brunswick, NJ: Rutgers University Press, 1993.

Hitchcock, Henry-Russell, Albert Fein, Winston Weisman, and Vincent Scully. *The Rise of an American Architecture*. New York: Metropolitan Museum of Art by Praeger Publishers, 1970.

Hobsbawm, Eric. *The Age of Capital: 1848–1875*. New York: Vintage Books, 1996.

Holleran, Michael. *Boston's "Changeful Times": Origins of Preservation & Planning in America*. Baltimore: Johns Hopkins University Press, 1998.

Hood, Clifton. *722 Miles: The Building of the Subways and How They Transformed New York*. 1995. Baltimore: Johns Hopkins University Press, 2004.

Hood, Raymond Mathewson, and Carol Willis. *Raymond Hood, City of Towers [catalog]: January 7–March 7, 1984*. New York: Whitney Museum of American Art at Philip Morris, 1984.

Hughes, Thomas P. *Rescuing Prometheus: Four Monumental Projects That Changed the Modern World*. New York: Pantheon, 1998.

Huxtable, Ada Louise. *Will They Ever Finish Bruckner Boulevard?* New York: Macmillan, 1970.

Isenberg, Alison. *Downtown America: A History of the Place and the People Who Made It*. Chicago: University of Chicago Press, 2004.

Jackson, Kenneth T. *Crabgrass Frontier: The Suburbanization of the United States*. New York: Oxford University Press, 1985.

Jackson, Kenneth T., and Stanley K. Schultz, eds. *Cities in American History*. New York: Alfred A. Knopf, 1972.

Jacobs, Jane. *The Death and Life of Great American Cities*. Vintage Books ed. New York: Vintage–Random House, 1992.

Jennings, Jan, ed. *Roadside America: The Automobile in Design and Culture*. Ames: Iowa State University Press, 1990.

Jerome, John. *The Death of the Automobile: The Fatal Effect of the Golden Era, 1955–1970*. New York: Norton, 1972.

Johnson, David A. *Planning the Great Metropolis: The 1929 Regional Plan of New York and Its Environs*. Studies in History, Planning and the Environment 18. New York: E&FN Spon–Chapman and Hall, 1996.

Kasson, John F. *Civilizing the Machine: Technology and Republican Values in America, 1776–1900*. New York: Grossman, 1976.

Kay, Jane Holtz. *Asphalt Nation: How the Automobile Took Over America, and How We Can Take It Back*. New York: Crown, 1997.

———. *Lost Boston*. Rev. ed. Boston: Mariner-Houghton Mifflin, 1999.

Kennedy, Lawrence W. *Planning the City upon a Hill: Boston since 1630*. Amherst: University of Massachusetts Press, 1992.

Kilham, Walter H., Jr., F.A.I.A. *Raymond Hood, Architect: Form through Function in the American Skyscraper*. New York: Architectural Book Publishing, 1973.

Kirschner, Don S. *The Paradox of Professionalism: Reform and Public Service in Urban America, 1900–1940*. Contributions in American History no. 19. New York: Greenwood Press, 1986.

Krieg, Joann P., ed. *Robert Moses: Single-Minded Genius*. Long Island Studies. Interlaken, NY: Heart of the Lakes Publishing, 1989.

Krieger, Alex, and David Cobb, eds., with Amy Turner. *Mapping Boston*. Cambridge, MA: MIT Press, 1999.

Krueckeberg, Donald A., ed. *The American Planner: Biographies & Recollections*. 2nd ed. New Brunswick, NJ: Center for Urban Policy Research, Rutgers University, 1994.

———. *Introduction to Planning History in the United States*. New Brunswick, NJ: Center for Urban Policy Research, Rutgers University, 1983.

Kruh, David. *Always Something Doing: Boston's Infamous Scollay Square*. Rev. ed. Boston: Northeastern University Press, 1999.

Labatut, Jean, and Wheaton J. Lane, eds. *Highways in Our National Life: A Symposium*. Princeton, NJ: Princeton University Press, 1950.

Landau, Sarah Bradford, and Carl W. Condit. *Rise of the New York Skyscraper 1865–1913*. New Haven, CT: Yale University Press, 1996.

Lears, T. J. Jackson. *No Place of Grace: Antimodernism and the Transformation of American Culture 1880–1920*. New York: Pantheon, 1981.

Leavitt, Helen. *Superhighway—Superhoax*. Garden City, NJ: Doubleday, 1970.

Levine, Neil. *The Architecture of Frank Lloyd Wright*. Princeton, NJ: Princeton University Press, 1996.

Lewis, David L., and Laurence Goldstein, eds. *The Automobile and American Culture*. Ann Arbor: University of Michigan Press, 1983.

Lewis, Lucinda. *Roadside America: The Automobile and the American Dream*. New York: H. N. Abrams, 2000.

Lewis, Tom. *Divided Highways: Building the Interstate Highways, Transforming American Life*. New York: Viking, 1997.

Lienhard, John H. *Inventing Modern: Growing Up with X-rays, Skyscrapers, and Tailfins*. New York: Oxford University Press, 2003.

Longstreth, Richard. *City Center to Regional Mall: Architecture, the Automobile, and Retailing in Los Angeles, 1920–1950*. Cambridge, MA: MIT Press, 1997.

Luberoff, David, and Alan Altshuler. *Mega-Project: A Political History of Boston's Multibillion Dollar Artery/Tunnel Project*. Rev. ed. Cambridge, MA: A. Alfred Taubman Center for State and Local Government, John F. Kennedy School of Government, Harvard University, April 1996.

Lupo, Alan, Frank Colcord, and Edmund P. Fowler. *Rites of Way: The Politics of Transportation in Boston and the U.S. City*. Boston: Little Brown, 1971.

Lynch, Kevin. *The Image of the City*. Cambridge, MA: MIT Press, 1960.

Marx, Leo. *The Machine in the Garden: Technology and the Pastoral Ideal in America*. New York: Oxford University Press, 2000.

Mayer, Harold M., and Richard C. Wade. *Chicago: Growth of a Metropolis*. Chicago: University of Chicago Press, 1969.

McCarthy, Tom. *Auto Mania: Cars, Consumers, and the Environment*. New Haven, CT: Yale University Press, 2007.

McNichol, Dan. *The Big Dig.* New York: Silver Lining, 2000.

McShane, Clay. *The Automobile: A Chronology of Its Antecedents, Development, and Impact.* Westport, CT: Greenwood Press, 1997.

———. *Down the Asphalt Path: The Automobile and the American City.* Columbia History of Urban Life. New York: Columbia University Press, 1994.

Miller, Ross. *American Apocalypse: The Great Fire and the Myth of Chicago.* Chicago: University of Chicago Press, 1990.

Mohl, Raymond A., and Neil Betten, eds. *Urban America in Historical Perspective.* New York: Weybright and Talley, 1970.

Moudry, Roberta, ed. *The American Skyscraper: Cultural Histories.* New York: Cambridge University Press, 2005.

Mumford, Lewis. *The City in History: Its Origins, Its Transformations, and Its Prospects.* New York: Harcourt, Brace and World, 1961.

———. *The Highway and the City.* New York: Mentor, New American Library, 1964.

———. *Technics and Civilization.* New York: Harcourt, Brace and World, 1963.

Myott, Colonel E. B. *Railway Progress Institute Committee on Passenger Traffic: The Transportation Problem of Boston, Massachusetts.* N.p. February 26, 1964.

Norton, Peter D. *Fighting Traffic: The Dawn of the Motor Age in the American City.* Inside Technology Series. Cambridge, MA: MIT Press, 2008.

Nye, David E. *America as Second Creation: Technology and Narratives of New Beginnings.* Cambridge, MA: MIT Press, 2003.

———. *American Technological Sublime.* Cambridge, MA: MIT Press, 1994.

———. *Narratives and Spaces: Technology and the Construction of American Culture.* New York: Columbia University Press, 1997.

———, ed. *Technologies of Landscape: From Reaping to Recycling.* Amherst: University of Massachusetts Press, 1999.

O'Connor, Thomas H. *The Athens of America: Boston, 1825–1845.* Boston: University of Massachusetts Press, 2006.

———. *Building a New Boston: Politics and Urban Renewal 1950–1970.* Boston: Northeastern University Press, 1993.

———. *Eminent Bostonians.* Cambridge, MA: Harvard University Press, 2002.

———. *The Hub: Boston Past and Present.* Boston: Northeastern University Press, 2001.

Owen, Wilfred. *The Accessible City.* Washington: Brookings, 1972.

———. *Cities in the Motor Age.* New York: Viking, 1959.

Page, Max. *The Creative Destruction of Manhattan, 1900–1940.* Historical Studies of Urban America Series. Chicago: University of Chicago Press, 1999.

Pescatello, Paul Ramon. "Westway: The Road from New Deal to New Politics." Ph.D. diss., American Government, Cornell University, 1986.

Peterson, Jon A. *The Birth of City Planning in the United States, 1840–1917.* Creating the North American Landscape Series. Baltimore: Johns Hopkins University Press, 2003.

Pursell, Carroll. *The Machine in America: A Social History of Technology.* Baltimore: Johns Hopkins University Press, 1995.

Radde, Bruce. *The Merritt Parkway.* New Haven, CT: Yale University Press, 1993.

Rae, John B. *The Road and the Car in American Life.* Cambridge, MA: MIT Press, 1971.

Reed, Robert C. *The New York Elevated.* New York: A. S. Barnes, 1978.

Reps, John William. *The Making of Urban America: A History of City Planning in the United States.* Princeton, NJ: Princeton University Press, 1965.

Revell, Keith D. *Building Gotham: Civic Culture and Public Policy in New York City, 1898–1938.* Baltimore: Johns Hopkins University Press, 2003.

Rose, Mark H. *Interstate: Express Highway Politics, 1939–1989.* Rev. ed. Knoxville: University of Tennessee Press, 1990.

Rose, Mark H., and Raymond A. Mohl. *Interstate: Highway Politics and Policy since 1939.* Knoxville: University of Tennessee Press, 2012.

Rose, Mark H., Bruce E. Seely, and Paul F. Barrett. *The Best Transportation System in the World: Railroads, Trucks, Airlines, and American Public Policy in the Twentieth Century.* Historical Perspectives on Business Enterprise Series. Columbus: Ohio State University Press, 2006.

Rosen, Christine Meisner. *The Limits of Power: Great Fires and the Process of City Growth in America.* New York: Cambridge University Press, 1986.

Rubin, Elihu. *Insuring the City: The Prudential Center and the Postwar Urban Landscape.* New Haven, CT: Yale University Press, 2012)

Ryan, Mary P. *Civic Wars: Democracy and Public Life in the American City during the Nineteenth Century.* Berkeley: University of California Press, 1997.

Sandercock, Leonie, ed. *Making the Invisible Visible: A Multicultural Planning History.* Berkeley: University of California Press, 1998.

Schaffer, Daniel, ed. *Two Centuries of American Planning.* Baltimore: Johns Hopkins University Press, 1988.

Schaffer, Kristen. *Daniel H. Burnham: Visionary Architect and Planner.* Edited by Scott J. Tilden. New York: Rizzoli, 2003.

Schlichting, Kurt C. *Waterfront Manhattan: From Henry Hudson to the High Line.* Baltimore: Johns Hopkins University Press, 2018.

Schultz, Stanley K. *Constructing Urban Culture: American Cities and City Planning, 1800–1920.* Technology and Urban Growth Series. Philadelphia: Temple University Press, 1989.

Schuyler, David. *The New Urban Landscape: The Redefinition of City Form in Nineteenth-Century America.* Baltimore: Johns Hopkins University Press, 1986.

Schwartz, Joel. *The New York Approach: Robert Moses, Urban Liberals, and Redevelopment of the Inner City.* Urban Life and Landscape Series. Columbus: Ohio State University Press, 1993.

Scobey, David M. *Empire City: The Making and Meaning of the New York City Landscape.* Philadelphia: Temple University Press, 2002.

Scott, Mel. *American City Planning since 1890: A History Commemorating the Fiftieth Anniversary of the American Institute of Planners.* Berkeley: University of California Press, 1969.

Seasholes, Nancy S. *Gaining Ground: A History of Landmaking in Boston.* Cambridge, MA: MIT Press, 2003.

Seely, Bruce E. *Building the American Highway System: Engineers as Policy Makers.* Philadelphia: Temple University Press, 1987.

Segal, Howard P. *Technological Utopianism in American Culture.* Chicago: University of Chicago Press, 1985.

Shand-Tucci, Douglass. *Built in Boston: City and Suburb, 1800–2000.* Rev. ed. Amherst: University of Massachusetts, 1999.

Shanor, Rebecca Read. *The City That Never Was: Two Hundred Years of Fantastic and Fascinating Plans That Might Have Changed the Face of New York City.* New York: Viking, 1988.

Sies, Mary Corbin, and Christopher Silver, eds. *Planning the Twentieth-Century American City.* Baltimore: Johns Hopkins University Press, 1996.

Sites, William. *Remaking New York: Primitive Globalization and the Politics of Urban Community.* Globalization and Community Series, vol. 12. Minneapolis: University of Minnesota Press, 2003.

Sloan, Allan K. *Citizen Participation in Transportation Planning: The Boston Experience.* Cambridge, MA: Ballinger, 1974.

Smerk, George M. *Urban Transportation: The Federal Role.* Bloomington: Indiana University Press, 1965.

Smith, Carl. *The Plan of Chicago: Daniel Burnham and the Remaking of the American City.* Chicago Visions and Revisions Series. Chicago: University of Chicago Press, 2006.

Snow, W. Brewster, ed. *The Highway and the Landscape.* New Brunswick, NJ: Rutgers University, 1959.

Solomonson, Katherine. *The Chicago Tribune Tower Competition: Skyscraper Design and Cultural Change in the 1920s.* New York: Cambridge University Press, 2001; Chicago: University of Chicago Press, 2003.

Spain, Daphne. *How Women Saved the City.* Minneapolis: University of Minnesota Press, 2001.

Stamper, John W. *Chicago's North Michigan Avenue: Planning and Development, 1900–1930.* Chicago Architecture and Urbanism Series. Chicago: University of Chicago Press, 1991.

Steinbeck, John. *Travels with Charley in Search of America.* Rev. ed. New York: Penguin Books, 1997.

Stern, Robert A. M. *Raymond Hood.* Institute for Architecture and Urban Studies 15. New York: Rizzoli, 1982.

Stern, Robert A. M., Gregory Gilmartin, and John Montague Massengale. *New York 1900: Metropolitan Architecture and Urbanism 1890–1915.* New York: Rizzoli, 1983.

Stern, Robert A. M., Gregory Gilmartin, and Thomas Mellins. *New York 1930: Architecture and Urbanism between the Two World Wars.* New York: Rizzoli, 1987.

Stern, Robert A. M., Thomas Mellins, and David Fishman. *New York 1880: Architecture and Urbanism in the Gilded Age.* New York: Monacelli Press, 1999.

Stine, Jeffrey K. *Nelson P. Lewis and the City Efficient: The Municipal Engineer in City Planning during the Progressive Era.* Essays in Public Works History 11. Chicago: Public Works Historical Society, 1981.

Stone, Tabor R. *Beyond the Automobile: Reshaping the Transportation Environment.* Englewood Cliffs, NJ: Prentice-Hall, 1971.

Sugrue, Thomas J. *The Origins of the Urban Crisis: Race and Inequality in Postwar Detroit.* Princeton, NJ: Princeton University Press, 1996.

Tarr, Joel A., and Gabriel Dupuy, eds. *Technology and the Rise of the Networked City in Europe and America.* Philadelphia: Temple University Press, 1988.

Thernstrom, Stephan. *Poverty and Progress: Social Mobility in a Nineteenth Century City.* New York: Atheneum, 1969.

Thoms, David, Len Holden, and Tim Claydon, eds. *The Motor Car and Popular Culture in the 20th Century.* Brookfield, VT: Ashgate, 1998.

Trout, Charles H. *Boston, the Great Depression, and the New Deal.* Urban Life in America Series. New York: Oxford University Press, 1977.

Turner, Frederick Jackson. *Rereading Frederick Jackson Turner: "The Significance of the Frontier in American History," and Other Essays.* Commentary by John Mack Faragher. New York: Henry Holt and Co., 1994.

van Leeuwen, Thomas A. P. *The Skyward Trend of Thought: The Metaphysics of the American Skyscraper.* Cambridge, MA: MIT Press, 1986.

Wachs, Martin, and Margaret Crawford, eds. *The Car and the City: The Automobile, the Built Environment, and Daily Urban Life.* Ann Arbor: University of Michigan Press, 1992.

Ward, David, and Olivier Zunz, eds. *The Landscape of Modernity: Essays on New York City, 1900–1940.* New York: Russell Sage Foundation, 1992.

Ward, James. *Architects in Practice, New York City, 1900–1940.* Union, NJ: J&D Associates, 1989.

Warner, Sam Bass, Jr., ed. *Planning for a Nation of Cities*. Cambridge, MA: MIT Press, 1966.

———. *The Private City; Philadelphia in Three Periods of its Growth*. Philadelphia: University of Pennsylvania Press, 1968.

———. *Streetcar Suburbs: The Process of Growth in Boston, 1870–1900*. 2nd ed. Cambridge, MA: Harvard University Press, 1978.

———. *The Urban Wilderness: A History of the American City*. New York: Harper, 1972.

———. *The Way We Really Live: Social Change in Metropolitan Boston since 1920*. Learning Library Program 4. Boston: Boston Public Library, 1977.

Weinstein, Asha Elizabeth. "The Congestion Evil: Perceptions of Traffic Congestion in Boston in the 1890s and 1920s." Ph.D. diss., City and Regional Planning, University of California, Berkeley, 2002.

Weiss, Marc A. *The Rise of the Community Builders: The American Real Estate Industry and Urban Land Planning*. Columbia History of Urban Life Series. New York: Columbia University, 1987.

White, Dana F. *The Urbanists, 1865–1915*. Contributions in American Studies 94. New York: Greenwood Press, 1989.

Whitehill, Walter Muir, and Lawrence W. Kennedy. *Boston: A Topographical History*. 3rd ed. Cambridge, MA: Belknap Press of Harvard University Press, 2000.

Willis, Carol. *Form Follows Finance: Skyscrapers and Skylines in New York and Chicago*. New York: Princeton Architectural Press, 1995.

Wilson, Richard Guy, Dianne H. Pilgrim, and Dickran Tashjian. *The Machine Age in America, 1918–1941*. New York: Brooklyn Museum in association with Abrams, 1986.

Wilson, William H. *The City Beautiful Movement*. Baltimore: Johns Hopkins Press, 1989.

Zukowsky, John, ed. *Chicago Architecture 1872–1922; Birth of a Metropolis*. Munich: Prestel Verlag in association with The Art Institute of Chicago, 1987.

———. *Chicago Architecture and Design, 1923–1993: Reconfiguration of an American Metropolis*. Munich: Prestel-Verlag in association with The Art Institute of Chicago, 1993.

Zunz, Olivier. *Making America Corporate, 1870–1920*. Chicago: University of Chicago Press, 1990.

SECONDARY SOURCE ARTICLES

Axelrod, R. A. "Breaking Ground in Chicago's Downtown." *Urban Land* 57, no. 109 (October 1998): 76–77.

Barrett, Paul. "Public Policy and Private Choice: Mass Transit and the Automobile in Chicago between the Wars." *Business History Review* 49, no. 4 (Winter 1975): 473–497.

Bedarida, Francois, and Anthony Sutcliffe. "The Street in the Structure and Life of the City: Reflections on Nineteenth-Century London and Paris." *Journal of Urban History* 6, no. 4 (August 1980): 379–396.

Bellalta, Maria. "Another Shade of Green." *Land Forum* 14 (2002): 26–27.

Brown, Jeffrey. "A Tale of Two Visions: Harland Bartholomew, Robert Moses, and the Development of the American Freeway." *Journal of Planning History* 4, no. 1 (2005): 3–32.

Brownell, Blaine A. "A Symbol of Modernity: Attitudes toward the Automobile in Southern Cities in the 1920s." *American Quarterly* 24, no. 1 (March 1972): 20–44.

Burnham, John Chynoweth. "The Gasoline Tax and the Automobile Revolution." *Mississippi Valley Historical Review* 48, no. 3 (December 1961): 435–459.

Campanella, Thomas J. "American Curves: Gilmore D. Clark and the Modern Civic Landscape." *Harvard Design Magazine* 1, no. 2 (Summer 1997): 40–43.

Campbell, Robert, F.A.I.A. "The Big Dig: What's Up under Boston?" *Architectural Record* 190, no.3 (March 2002): 84–86, 88.

Comey, Arthur Coleman. "The Plan of Boston, Massachusetts: A Capital City." *American Society of Civil Engineers*, 1929, 777–788.

"Congress Snubs Chicago's Wacker Drive Rehab Plan." *Civil Engineering* 69, no. 3 (March 1999): 14.

Cromley, Elizabeth. "Riverside Park and Issues of Historic Preservation." *Journal of the Society of Architectural Historians* 43, no.3 (October 1984): 238–249.

Davis, Donald F. "The City Remodelled: The Limits of Automotive Industry Leadership in Detroit, 1910–1929." *Histoire Sociale—Social History* 13, no. 26 (November 1980): 451–486.

Dunster, David. "Financing and Building Wacker Drive, Chicago." *Construction History* 16 (2000): 63–76.

Fein, Michael. "Tunnel Vision: 'Invisible' Highways and Boston's 'Big Dig' in the Age of Privatization." *Journal of Planning History* 11, no. 1 (2012): 47–69.

Finstein, Amy D. "Before the Big Dig: Boston's Central Artery as a Construct of Mid-Century Modernity." *ARRIS: Journal of the Southeast Chapter of the Society of Architectural Historians* 16 (Winter 2005): 69–81.

———. "From 'Cesspool' to 'The Greatest Improvement of its Kind': Wacker Drive and the Recasting of the Chicago Riverfront, 1909–1926." *Journal of Planning History* 14, no. 4 (November 2015): 287–308.

Flink, James J. "Three Stages of American Automobile Consciousness." *American Quarterly* 24, no. 4 (October 1972): 451–473.

Foster, Mark. "City Planners and Urban Transportation: The American Response, 1900–1940." *Journal of Urban History* 5, no. 3 (May 1979): 365–396.

Fotsch, Paul Mason. "The Building of a Superhighway Future at the New York World's Fair." *Cultural Critique* 48 (Spring 2001): 65–97.

Gordon, David L. A. "A City Beautiful Plan for Canada's Capital: Edward Bennett and the 1915 Plan for Ottawa and Hull." *Planning Perspectives* 13 (1998): 275–300.

Gutfreund, Owen D. "The Path of Prosperity: New York City's East River Drive, 1922–1990." *Journal of Urban History* 21, no. 2 (January 1995): 147–183.

Herzlinger, Regina. "Costs, Benefits and the West Side Highway." *Public Interest* 55 (Spring 1979): 77–98.

Johnson, Elmer W. "Taming the Car and Its User: Should We Do Both?" *Bulletin of the American Academy of Arts and Sciences* 46, no. 2 (November 1992): 13–29.

Kemp, Louis Ward. "Aesthetes and Engineers: The Occupational Ideology of Highway Design." *Technology and Culture* 27, no. 4 (October 1986): 759–797.

Konvitz, Josef W. "William J. Wilgus and Engineering Projects to Improve the Port of New York, 1900–1930." *Technology and Culture* 30, no. 2 (April 1989): 398–425.

Krauss, Celene. "The Elusive Process of Citizen Activism." *Social Policy* 14, no. 2 (Fall 1983): 50–55.

Krinsky, Carol Herselle. "The Fred F. French Building: Mesopotamia in Manhattan." *Magazine Antiques* 121 (January 1982): 284–291.

Lindsey, Robert. "West Side Highway: 43 Years, All Downhill." *New York Times*, June 23, 1974, 189.

Lockwood, Charles. "Chicago's Public Works Boom." *Urban Land* 57, no. 10 (October 1998): 72–75, 99–100.

Mallach, Stanley. "The Origins of the Decline of Urban Mass Transportation in the United States, 1890–1930." *Urbanism Past and Present*, no. 8 (Summer 1979): 1–17.

McQuaid, Kim. "An American Owenite: Edward A. Filene and the Parameters of Industrial Reform, 1890–1937." *American Journal of Economics and Sociology* 35, no. 1 (January 1976): 77–94.

McShane, Clay. "The Origins and Globalization of Traffic Control Signals." *Journal of Urban History* 25, no. 3 (March 1999): 379–404.

Mestrovic, Marta. "All Quiet on the Western Waterfront?" *Metropolis* 12, no. 2 (September 1992): 15, 18.

Meyers, Andrew A. "Invisible Cities: Lewis Mumford, Thomas Adams, and the Invention of the Regional City, 1923–1929." *Colloqui: A Journal of Planning and Urban Issues* 13 (Spring 1998): 14–32.

Mohl, Raymond A. "Stop the Road: Freeway Revolts in American Cities." *Journal of Urban History* 30, no. 5 (July 2004): 674–706.

Murphey, Rhoads. "Boston's Chinatown." *Economic Geography* 28, no. 3 (July 1952): 244–255.

Newcomb, James. "Depression Auto Styling." *Winterthur Portfolio* 35, no. 1 (Spring 2000): 81–100.

Nobel, Philip. "The Pleasure of the Road: For Intrigue and Dark Wiles, Nothing Rivals the Pulaski Skyway." *Metropolis* 20, no. 10 (June 2001): 86.

Norton, Peter D. "Street Rivals: Jaywalking and the Invention of the Motor Age Street." *Technology and Culture* 48 (April 2007): 331–359.

O'Brien, Dennis J. "The West Side Highway Reconstruction Story." *Public Works* 128, no. 1 (January 1997): 28–30.

Pantzar, Mike. "Domestication of Everyday Life Technology: Dynamic Views on the Social Histories of Artifacts." *Design Issues* 13, no. 3 (Autumn 1997): 52–65.

Passanisi, Michael. "Development of the Boston Area Highway System." *Historical Journal of Massachusetts* 23, no. 2 (Summer 1995): 166–182.

Peatross, C. Ford. "Symbol and Catalyst: The Automobile in Architectural Representation before 1930." In *Frank Lloyd Wright: Designs for an American Landscape, 1922–1932*, edited by David De Long, 170–183. New York: Harry N. Abrams, 1996.

Raitz, Karl. "American Roads, Roadside America." *Geographical Review* 88, no. 3 (July 1998): 363–387.

Rogers, Cranston R. "Planning the First Central Artery in Boston." *Civil Engineering Practice* 13, no. 2 (Fall/Winter 1998): 57–60.

Schultz, Stanley K., and Clay McShane. "To Engineer the Metropolis: Sewers, Sanitation, and City Planning in Late Nineteenth-Century America." *Journal of American History* 65 (1978): 389–411.

Schuyler, Montgomery. "The Works of R. H. Robertson." *Architectural Record* 6, no. 2 (October–December 1896): 184–219.

Schwantes, Carlos A. "The West Adapts the Automobile: Technology, Unemployment, and the Jitney Phenomenon of 1914–1917." *Western Historical Quarterly* 16, no. 3 (July 1985): 307–326.

Seely, Bruce E. "Engineers and Government-Business Cooperation: Highway Standards and the Bureau of Public Roads, 1900–1940." *Business History Review* 58, no. 1 (Spring 1984): 51–77.

———. "Railroads, Good Roads, and Motor Vehicles: Managing Technological Change." *Railroad History*, Bulletin 155 (Autumn 1986): 35–63.

———. "A Republic Bound Together." *Wilson Quarterly* 17, no.1 (Winter 1993): 19–39.

Smith, M.J.P. "So Bigger: After a Number of False Starts and Design Proposals, the Laggard Blocks of Wacker Drive Are Finally Coming to Life." *Inland Architect*, January/February 1987, 62–69.

Sugrue, Thomas. "Miller McClintock." *Scribner's Magazine* 102, no. 6 (December 1937): 9–13, 99.

Sweeney, Margy. "Reworking Wacker." *Grid* 7, no. 3 (September 2001): 32–33.

Tager, Jack. "Urban Renewal in Boston: Municipal Entrepreneurs and Urban Elites." *Historical Journal of Massachusetts*, Winter 1993, 1–32.

Tarr, Joel Arthur. "From City to Suburb: The 'Moral' Influence of Transportation Technology." In *American Urban History: An Interpretive Reader with Commentaries*, 2nd ed., edited by Alexander B. Callow Jr., 202–212. New York: Oxford University Press, 1973.

Tsipis, Yanni. “Central Corridor Planning in Boston, 1900–1950: The Long Road to the Old Central Artery.” *Civil Engineering Practice* 18, no. 2 (Fall–Winter 2003): 33–52.

“Urbane Freeway.” *Architectural Forum* 129, no. 2 (September 1968): 68–73.

Ward, David. “The Industrial Revolution and the Emergence of Boston’s Central Business District.” *Economic Geography* 42, no.2 (April 1966): 153–171.

Weisman, Winston. “New York and the Problem of the First Skyscraper.” *Journal of the Society of Architectural Historians* 12, no. 1 (March 1953): 13–21.

Weiss, Marc A. “Developing and Financing the ‘Garden Metropolis’: Urban Planning and Housing in Twentieth-Century America.” *Planning Perspectives* 5, no. 3 (September 1990): 307–319.

INDEX

Note: Page numbers in italics indicate figures.

Amy D. Finstein is an Assistant Professor in the Department of Visual Arts at College of the Holy Cross in Worcester, MA.